Growing Up with the Country

Children on a Colorado homestead. (Courtesy Colorado Historical Society).

Growing Up with the Country

Childhood on the Far Western Frontier

Elliott West

Histories of the American Frontier
Ray Allen Billington, General Editor

Howard R. Lamar, Coeditor
Martin Ridge, Coeditor
David J. Weber, Coeditor

University of New Mexico Press
Albuquerque

Library of Congress Cataloging-in-Publication Data

West, Elliott, 1945-
Growing up with the country: childhood on the far-western
frontier / Elliott West. — 1st ed.
p. cm. — (Histories of the American frontier)
Bibliography: p.
Includes index.
ISBN 0-8263-1154-7. — ISBN 0-8263-1155-5 (pbk.)
1. Children—West (U.S.)—History—19th century. 2. Children—
West (U.S.)—Social conditions, 3. Frontier and pioneer life—West
(U.S.) 4. West (U.S.)—History—1848–1950. I. Title. II. Series.
HQ792.U5W425   1989
305.23'0978—dc20
89-4938
CIP

10 09 08 07 06   5 6 7 8 9

ISBN-13: 978-0-8263-1155-9
ISBN-10: 0-8263-1155-5

For my parents,
Dick and Betsy West

Contents

Illustrations   ix

Foreword   xi

Preface   xvii

1.   The Frontier   1

Caesar Brock   23

2.   First Perceptions   25

Anne Ellis   47

3.   At Home   51

Grace Fisk   71

4.   Child's Work   73

T. W. Dobbs   99

5.   Child's Play   101

Fiorello La Guardia   119

6.   Growing Up   121

    Charles Gallagher   145

7.   Family And Community   147

    Mari Sandoz   177

8.   A Great School House   179

    Lillian Miller   211

9.   Suffer the Children   213

    Owen McWhorter   243

10.   Children and the Frontier   245

    Notes   265

    Bibliography   303

    Index   335

Illustrations

Children on a Colorado homestead.   *Frontispiece*

A pioneer family in Cripple Creek, Colorado.   9

Children were rare sights in a mining region like
Jefferson County.   16

The Hopkins family settled near Berwyn, Nebraska,
in the late 1880s.   21

Boys and girls headed west entered a new realm of experience.   31

The open sweep of the Great Plains left some children feeling
exposed and terrified.   43

The Sykes family at home in Turkey Tanks, Arizona.   54

An emigrant wagon was arranged into parlor and living room.   59

These Kansans crammed their dugout with necessities and
other furnishings.   62

A Nebraska family and their parlor organ.   64

A plains family and a staked sapling stand before a new soddie.   66

The children of W. A. Hamill grew up in this Georgetown,
Colorado, mansion.   68

Boys in Victor, Colorado, could help with odd jobs
above the mine.   81

Near Clifton, Texas, children stand proudly before a garden
they helped tend.   83

A young Montana hunter and his dog pose with their prey.   85

At work at one of childhood's most familiar chores in
the Middle Loup Valley, Nebraska   87

Providing water was often the job of children.   89

Hauling by turkey power.   107

Pupils at the Pine Creek School near Livingston, Montana, practice one of their games. *111*

Parents gave social messages with toys. *115*

Child cowboys learned an independence that often startled outsiders. *126*

Children playing around mines and smelters in Cripple Creek, Colorado. *129*

Young hunters grew to know the land as well as or better than any adults. *132*

Branding taught children to work in close cooperation with others. *137*

Youngsters spent much of their time close to the West's seediest influences. *151*

A Montana homesteader's infant rests warmly in a coffee-box pram. *159*

Relaxation made up an important part of frontier family life. *163*

Bachelors taught children about frontier life, loaned them books, and entertained them. *167*

Church gathering in Nebraska in 1889. *170*

Children mixed easily with the crowd at frontier dances. *176*

Dugout school during first years of settlement in western Kansas. *187*

Pupils stand with their teacher before their Choteau County, Montana, school. *193*

Idaho schoolchildren have brought outside the basic tools of instruction. *202*

Minnie Bridges gives a lift to John Prude. *205*

The clutter and filth in streets of Butte, Montana. *232*

The Andrews family at the grave of son, Willie, at Cedar Canyon, Nebraska. *238*

The primary force behind westward expansion—the family. *248*

Family portrait hints at a different view of the world. *254*

A girl and young woman on a Montana homestead. *258*

Children of Custer County, Nebraska. *261*

Foreword

In the drama of American frontier history, many actors have been ignored, and none more than the children. From the time of James Fenimore Cooper to the present, the adventures celebrated in folklore, novels, movies, and television have been mostly those of adults—trappers and hunters, cowboys and lawmen, prospectors and outlaws, dance hall queens and "civilized" eastern women. Until quite recently, scholarly works also have been dominated by stalwart cattle barons, intrepid explorers, dashing military officers, mining kings, and other such figures, most of them self-reliant males and all of them past the age of eighteen.

This picture is doubly distorted, because the West was not settled by trappers, traders, and lonesome cowboys. If this element had held sway on the frontier, the prairies would never have been broken to the plow and the raw resources of the region would still be untapped. The true settlers of the West, whether farmers or townsmen, came as families. It was because of his family that the male pioneer was willing to build a town and make a farm or ranch. This commitment, not the exploits of a Wild Bill Hickock or Davy Crockett, spelled lasting change and the final occupation of the West. And these families, in turn, cannot possibly be understood without their children, the young pioneers who played essential roles in the shaping of western history.

Lately students of the frontier and American West have shown an admirable interest in social and family history. They have made almost no attempt, however, to view the past from the point of view of some of society's most important, interesting, and perceptive members—its young girls and boys. This is so despite a rich tradition in other genres of remarkably effective stories told through the eyes of children. From Charles Dickens' *Great Expectations* to Mark Twain's *Huckleberry Finn* and Günter Grass's

Tin Drum, novelists have found in the lives of children compelling ways to comment on adult society. Film makers, too, have either invented children's lives or recalled their own childhoods as in John Boorman's *Hope and Glory*, Louis Malle's *Au Revoir les Enfants*, Neil Simon's *Brighton Beach Memoirs* or Woody Allen's *Radio Days*.

In this latest volume in the Histories of the American Frontier Series, Elliott West restores the perspective of children to frontier history by telling a gripping narrative of their experiences on the overland trails, in the mining camps and towns of the Sierra and Rockies, and on farms and ranches of the Great Plains. He also argues convincingly that this children's history should stand on its own—in part because their view of their world was frequently quite different (psychologically at least) from that of their parents, and in part because the frontier, often the only environment they would know, shaped them in ways unique to their generation.

Growing Up with the Country is all the more remarkable because—given the lack of secondary works that one ordinarily turns to in writing a synthesis—West manages to achieve that synthesis using the raw materials of letters, diaries, government documents, oral histories, and autobiographies. And although readers will take delight in West's deft, humor-laced prose, they will nevertheless realize that whether he is discussing "First Perceptions," "Child's Play," "Growing Up," or "Family and Community," he is solidly grounded in the literature on the psychology of childhood and childhood development. Building on existing works about American childhood, he situates the western experience squarely in a national context.

These are but some of the structural features of *Growing Up with the Country*, however. West's greatest contribution has been to penetrate the world of the children themselves and to let their experiences tell the story. In a brilliant narrative about their development, he traces their responses first to their homes, whether sod house, log cabin, or mining town mansions, then to the larger world of nature and animals, and finally to the frontier's tragedies, including the deaths of their friends, parents, and brothers and sisters. He provides fresh definitions of work and play, analyzes rite-of-passage patterns, and examines child-parent and child-community relations.

In telling this story, West has placed the children's experiences clearly within their proper setting. He has not endeavored to tell the whole story, but he has given the reader an insight into family life as no one to date has. He finds that frontier families were more Victorian than we previously assumed; that companionate marriage was more common than not; and that children, then, as now, were central figures in family life. Further, parents were "modern" in the sense that they recognized and respected the individuality of the child. Travelers' impressions that children had to do hard, backbreaking outdoor work were true, but their belief that girls and boys were cruelly treated and destined to be shaped by the West's corrupting vices and crass materialism was far wide of the mark. On the less positive side, West describes the frustrations both parents and youth felt about the frontier, including its inadequate school systems. He also tells how growing up western could leave young people with deep and troubling contradictions about themselves, their futures, and their place in family and society.

Besides using specific individuals to give the text a warmly personal and intimate quality, Elliott West brings to his book a sureness of language, fact, and organization that will make his work unique. Each chapter has an internal logic, and that logic is strengthened by West's capacity—stemming from his own experience—to include expressions and phrases that will bring home to the reader the flavor of the nineteenth-century settler and his family. Language is the clearest expression of culture, and West's skillful use of language conveys the essence of the nineteenth century and rural America in ingenious ways. To quote him or to paraphrase him in this context would do him a disservice. The reader will savor much that West has to say because of the way that he expresses it.

The original volumes in the Histories of the American Frontier were essentially regional. They represented in a broad way the perspective on the frontier established by Frederick Jackson Turner. These were somewhat broadened in scope in later volumes through the imaginative work of Ray Allen Billington. If Turner and Billington had read this volume, they doubtless would have welcomed it into the series because both had a deep and profound interest in the activities of ordinary people. As their work disclosed, both felt that an understanding of a society in transition in a developing environment is possible only through an appreciation of its commonfolk and popular culture.

Elliot West's *Growing Up with the Country* is a fresh and timely addition to the series. Like its predecessors it tells a fascinating story, and it may be read as part of the overall history of the American people as well as an illustrative segment of a region. It will also provide an insight into the history of childhood and the family, a part of our national past that is only now being explored. This is a pioneering work about a pioneering people. With consummate skill and expertise, Elliott West has provided the general reader and the specialist with a highly informed account of those people who were most influenced by moving and living on the frontier and in the West.

Howard R. Lamar
Yale University

Martin Ridge
The Huntington Library

David J. Weber
Southern Methodist University

Spring 1989

When everything else has gone from my brain—
the President's name, the state capitals, the neighborhoods
where I lived, and then my own name and what it was on earth
I sought, and then at length the faces of my friends, and
finally the faces of my family—when all this has dissolved,
what will be left, I believe, is topology: the dreaming memory
of land as it lay this way and that.
—Annie Dillard.
An American Childhood

Of course one starts with ancestors.
—Anne Ellis
The Life of an Ordinary Woman

Preface

Lee Whipple-Haslam was seven when she crossed the plains from Missouri to California. It was 1852, the year cholera killed many hundreds of the sixty thousand emigrants, but Lee's family made it through and took up the search for gold, first in Shaw's Flat and then near Turnback Creek. Homesick miners doted on her, called her "Little Sister" and "Miss Pike," and the family's luck held until her father was murdered in 1856. Even then, with Lee learning to hunt and helping her mother run a boarding house, they did well enough. Looking back from the 1920s, however, Whipple-Haslam wondered whether the story of children like herself would ever be told. From the distance of seventy years, those times on "the isolated rim" of the world seemed hopelessly out of reach: "How could any writer . . . know the details of our daily life?"[1]

The question is worth asking. In histories of the American frontier, children are rarely seen and almost never heard. Adults seem responsible for all accomplishments and villainies. The emotional traumas, hard-won victories, appalling lapses in moral sense—all are described from men's and women's perspectives. Children are there, of course, but they are oddly passive figures. Their main role seems to be to inspire their parents' protectiveness and determination.

This impression is woefully distorted, although not because the children's story is beyond the modern historian's grasp. The experiences of the pioneer young have rarely been told because very few writers have ever tried.

That is curious, for scholars in other fields have taken children far more seriously. In the study of Europe and of the eastern half of the United States, the history of childhood has had quite a boom. Thirty years ago, the literature in the field was like a child—small, but growing every day.

Today it is more like an adolescent—large and gawky, full of promise, but also a little uncertain about its future.[2] The study of western children, however, cannot even be called infantile; it is at best embryonic. Library shelves groan with volumes on George Custer, gunslingers, and the cattle trails. More recently students have explored the experiences of women and the region's many ethnic groups. Only a handful of items, however, address directly the history of children, though these youngest pioneers made up a substantial part, in some places a majority, of western settlers.[3]

Some might question the wisdom of singling out this one part of western society. No one would think of writing a history of left-handed pioneers or frontier redheads. Why, then, focus on those who had lived only twelve years instead of twenty? Certainly children cannot be abstracted from the larger history of western development. In certain fundamental ways, however, their experiences differed from those of persons even a few years older. For three reasons in particular, the children's history stands on its own. Those reasons have determined my goals in writing this book.

First, children perceive the world differently than adults do. And so, in a sense, the frontier that children knew was not that of their elders. Westward expansion is, among other things, one of the great stories of our history. Its appeal is nearly universal. Most readers have some interest in what happened when ordinary people encountered an extraordinary place, one that presented them with unexpected dangers and challenging opportunities. This story has been told many times and from many points of view, but as seen by the children, it is fresh, sometimes disturbing, and often illuminating. With their help, I have tried to recapture some sense of what the frontier looked and felt like from two or three feet off the ground.

Second, the children's part in settling the West was distinctively their own. They spent much of their time independently of adults; they acted and were treated differently; they played different roles in events of the day. I have tried to tell part of this neglected story of how the children affected frontier society and contributed to the development of their pioneer West.

Finally, the children's story adds something to western history's most familiar theme—the ways in which the frontier changed those who lived there and thus created a new and distinctive part of America. Moving into country previously unsettled by their own kind, pioneers encountered unfamiliar conditions, both physical and social. These forced them to adapt, to change their ways. The result was a seemingly endless variation of new and old, innovation and custom. From this came a new way of life, one which has contributed both to the making of a region, the West, and to our evolving national character. Those who have studied the fascinating interplay of society, environment, and tradition, however, have left out one of the most important components of that change— the complicated process of growing up. Like all children, those in the West were both changing and being changed by what was around them. Of all the pioneers, they felt the frontier's shaping force most of all. As a result of my research, I have suggested a few of the implications of that change, both for the children themselves and for the societies they were helping create.

In a book of this kind, some chronological limits of childhood obviously must be set. I have considered as children all persons under the age of fifteen. That is an arbitrary definition, especially in this subject, since, as will be seen, the lines between childhood and adulthood became vague and imprecise on the frontier. Among children, furthermore, experiences of younger ones differed in some ways from older. When pertinent I have tried to make those distinctions, though, once again, life in the West tended to disrupt clear age categories and an orderly transition from infancy through adolescence.

Rural Americans describe an ideal fence as hog-tight, bull-strong, and horse-high. This book makes a sorry fence, for in trying to contain my subject, I have left out as much as I have kept in. Nothing will be said about the children of the American Indians and Hispanics living in the West at the time of the pioneer invasion. Only rarely have I dealt directly with families of European and Asian immigrants, the many thousands of Scandanavians, Germans, Czechs, French, Russians, Italians, Irish, Chinese, and others drawn by the new country's promise.

Instead, I decided from the start to concentrate almost entirely on white families who came into the West from elsewhere in the United States. I have studied those families in three diverse frontier settings— the great overland migration between 1840 and 1870, the mining towns of the Rocky Mountains and the Sierra Nevada, and early farms and ranches, mostly of the Great Plains and Southwest.

There were several reasons for limiting the scope of my work. Most obvious was the need to keep a research project within reasonable bounds; studying the children and families of all western groups would have increased this book's gestation period several times over. Source materials for the families I studied were widely available and posed no linguistic difficulties. I also chose to reduce the topic's many variables. How families lived on the frontier depended partly on the cultural assumptions they brought with them. The traditions among westering Americans were diverse enough; taking into account the backgrounds of those from other nations would have extended the project considerably. For the same reason I neglected almost entirely the many black Americans who went West with traditions and a history quite different from those of their white neighbors. Finally, I concentrated on white, native-born pioneers precisely because they have been the ones most studied by historians. This, I hoped, would emphasize that if we consult new evidence and imagine western history from new points of view, the most familiar subjects, scholarly fields that we have plowed and replowed dozens of times, can yield a new and surprisingly vigorous harvest.

To study frontier children, I consulted a variety of sources. There are some surviving diaries and letters written by children. Virtually all the authors were eight years or older; most were between twelve and fifteen. Archival collections contain hundreds of other contemporary journals, diaries, letters, and other documents written by adults. These throw light on frontier conditions, family life, and children's experiences. Public documents, particularly published and manuscript censuses and manuscript mortality schedules, are rich lodes of materials on the structure of frontier society, changes in western populations, and the traumas of pioneers.

A casual look at the notes and bibliography will show that I have relied especially on oral testimony, reminiscences and memoirs of those who knew the frontier as children. Anyone acquainted with historical research—or, for that matter, with human nature—knows that such evidence poses significant problems. Memory plays tricks. People never recall everything exactly as it was, and often their accounts are wildly inaccurate. Memories of the distant past, especially of youthful years, can be the most distorted of all. Nonetheless, these reminiscences represent a huge body of evidence from those who are the subject of the book. The only thing more foolish than accepting all this at face value would be to ignore it.

To try to correct for this material's bias, I have used three standards. First, specificity. The more particular and exact a memory, the more likely it is to be accurate. So, for instance, we should question a man's general statement that his youth on a Texas ranch was uniformly happy, but if he recounted in precise detail the species of grasses, methods of herding, kinds of cattle, names of games, how they were played, and which he preferred, we can have somewhat greater faith that those memories were grounded in reality. Second, repetition. The appearance of the same or similar remarks time after time from many different persons means something. Of course, it might mean that individuals distorted their pasts in similar ways, but that, in turn, is significant, for it suggests that their upbringing compelled these people to define their identities by rearranging past reality along particular lines. Third, congruence. When reminiscent evidence corresponds to what is learned from other sources, such as contemporary documents written by adults, we can give those statements greater credence.

In interpreting children's experiences, I have occasionally drawn upon recent work in other disciplines, such as sociology, folklore, and particularly developmental psychology. This borrowing should raise questions among careful readers. Can research into modern child behavior, some of it done under closely controlled conditions, be applied to fragmentary evidence about young people who lived in quite different circumstances a century ago? In general I have used such research only when it seemed to apply in a general, commonsensical way to phenomena that, according to most authorities, have changed little during the past several generations. Though children's play today differs in its specifics from that in Kansas of 1860 or Idaho of 1880, for instance, many of the reasons and purposes behind that play apparently have not changed. Many fundamental childhood fears, arising from biological and evolutionary causes, are basically no different today than a century ago. In cases like these, I have taken what help I could from the literature of other disciplines.

Between the chapters are short vignettes on frontier children. I offer these as tastes of sherbet among the main courses, as testimony to frontier childhood's diversity, and as reminders that grand themes are meaningless apart from the unique experiences of individual children.

The story of these pioneer children, however elusive, should be pursued. This book is meant to suggest what seem to me some major themes and implications of children's experiences in the developing West. I hope it will encourage others to test and challenge those suggestions and to pursue the study of children among the many groups ignored in the pages that follow.

Tradition has it that about 1850 Horace Greeley gave perhaps the best-known advice in American history: "Go West, young man, and grow up with the country." The famous editor's thought, though muddled, was still revealing. His "young man," about to strike out for the frontier, presumably *was* grown up, or at least was twenty years or so into the process. Behind this discrepancy was the assumption that the very young counted for little in the enterprise at hand. Like most politicians and reformers of his day, Greeley considered western conquest the job of vigorous, ambitious, dedicated men in their prime of life. Women and children were part of pioneering, but they seemed peripheral to the main action, vulnerable transplants dependent on strong and courageous males. Greeley believed, in fact, that it was "palpable homicide" for a man to take his wife and children west. Other outsiders, like James Meline, agreed. Traveling along the Platte River in 1866, he saw a woman watering an evergreen by her door as her son sat nearby: "Poor child! Poor evergreen! Poor mother!"[4]

He should have saved his sympathy. Young boys and girls did have their troubles, yet the huge majority did not think they lived blighted lives. As much as the stalwart pioneer men, they were making places for themselves in the new country. And these children, who truly *were* growing up with the West, in some ways could explain what was happening better than anyone else. They deserve our attention.

Like most historians, I am a chronic debtor. My future favors are hopelessly mortgaged to those who have helped in innumerable ways in the research and writing of this book. In searching out the children's history, I was aided by grants from the Fulbright College of the University of Arkansas, Fayetteville, and by fellowships from the Henry E. Huntington Library in San Marino, California and Chicago's Newberry Library. I am most grateful to those institutions.

Gathering the scattered evidence demanded visits to two dozen research libraries—quite a pleasant chore, as it turned out, largely because of the courtesy, helpfulness, and expertise of librarians and archivists who cheerfully hauled out folders and document boxes, steered me to the proper finding aids, and above all gave me good advice and countless leads. I owe particular thanks to Bob Knecht and Patricia Michaelis of the Kansas State Historical Society, George Miles of the Beinecke Library at Yale University, David Murrah and Rebecca Herring of the Southwest Collection at Texas Tech University, Lori Davisson of the Arizona Historical Society, Paul Geyl of the Newberry Library, David Walters of the Montana Historical Society, Judith Austin of the Idaho Historical Society, Michael Dabrishus of the Special Collections of the University of Arkansas Library, as well as the entire staffs of those institutions. I thank also the staffs of the Henry E. Huntington Library; Bancroft Library of the University of California, Berkeley; Barker History Center at the University of Texas at

Austin; Special Collections of the Montana State University Library; the Western History Collections of the Denver Public Library; the Special Collections of the University of New Mexico Library; the California Historical Society; the Western History Collection of the University of Oklahoma Library; the Oklahoma State Historical Society; the Panhandle-Plains Historical Museum of Canyon, Texas; the State Historical Society of Colorado; the Oral History Collection of the University of Nevada Library; the Western History Collection of the University of Colorado Library; Special Collections of the University of North Carolina Library; and Special Collections of the Duke University Library.

Several friends helped in the revision and refining of the manuscript: Timothy Donovan, Thomas Kennedy, Herb Luthin, Wendy Taylor, Kate Torrey, Peter Olch, and Thomas Smith. Bill Lang and Marianne Keddington of *Montana: The Magazine of Western History* improved and polished an article that became the book's fifth chapter. Four industrious graduate students, Christopher Huggard, Fon Gordon, Kim Scott, and Susan Parks, generously shared discoveries and insights from their research on frontier families. Elizabeth Jameson, Brian Shovers, Fred Quivik, and Susan Armitage shared of their own research and expertise. Professor Emmy E. Werner of the University of California, Davis, gave me the benefit of her fascinating research on children's responses to stress. Mrs. R. H. Merrill kindly allowed me to read her sister's lengthy memoir of her childhood on the Kansas plains. Teresa Garrity cheerfully typed much of the manuscript and did brave battle with the gremlins in the departmental word processor. To all these, I give my thanks.

Early in this project, David Weber encouraged me to make this book part of the Histories of the American Frontier series; his continuing confidence kept my spirits up as the work progressed. He and Martin Ridge, also an editor of this series, gave invaluable advice on the evolving manuscript. Howard Lamar, general editor of the series, is well known within our profession for the wide range of his knowledge, his shrewd advice, and his genial and enthusiastic support. As one who now has benefited from all these, I can testify that his reputation is well deserved. I also thank David Holtby and the staff of the University of New Mexico Press for the book's final editing and production.

My colleague Robert Finlay applied his superb editorial skills to the entire book. His suggestions, even when painful, were always pertinent, and the final product is much better for his efforts. He has my thanks, as does Elizabeth Payne for her comments and encouragement and Conwill Payne Finlay for general inspiration.

My second family, Daniel, Linda and Kairos Marquardt, gave me bed and board and splendid conversation while I worked in the wilds of Chicago. I offer special appreciation and apologies to my children, Elizabeth, Bill, Richard, Garth, and Anne. My walking footnotes, they helped me understand, even as they put up with father's preoccupation. Suzanne Stoner, good wife and dear friend, has given generously of her intelligence and perception and has kept me going through the doldrums. For that, and for her patience and humor, I am deeply thankful.

I began my research expecting to learn a lot about children. I did, but I learned just as much about parents and the overburdened, underthanked job of rearing daughters and sons. More than ever, I now understand that what I value most—some sense of what is important and the ability to give my own children all I should—I owe to my mother and father. This book is for them.

1

The Frontier

Standing on a hill several miles west of the Missouri River, East S. Owen looked back toward the Big Muddy and felt that he was ready. He had come with friends to cross the plains to the gold fields, there to knock about and gather his fortune. Now, on this cold May morning in 1852, "all hands faced about to take a farewell look at the United States & give the parting kick until we get to California." Owen told his journal that he felt like the Irish lad whose father asked if he had said his prayers: "Yes, he answered—I have said my prayers—and I have crossed myself— and have blessed myself, and the Devil may kiss my a—till morning."[1]

Samuel Frances's mood was more restrained. By mid-April of that year, he had sold his Illinois farm for cash to buy another—as yet unseen, but surely better—two thousand miles away, within a hound's howl of the Pacific. He had sifted through his family's belongings and jammed his wagon with pieces of their jigsawed life. The final barrier was soon removed:

> April 19. In the morning we were presented with the second son.
> April 20. Myself, wife and five children in company with Mr. Whipple and wife & one child with five men, started 2 o'clock P.M. in the rain for Oregon.[2]

Frontier children grew up in a world created when tens of thousands of parties like these moved into that half of the young republic lying beyond the Missouri River. This world was more than the background of the children's story; it also was an active force that helped shape their values and attitudes, their views of the future, and their understanding of themselves.

Of the many elements that made this world, three were particularly

1

important. The land itself, the geographically diverse country that drew the pioneers westward, presented them with physical and psychological challenges. The second element, the motives and resources that settlers brought into the land, also varied considerably. East Owen, the cocky bachelor, and the Frances family, setting off for Oregon in the rain with an exhausted mother and suckling son—these pioneers apparently moved with a similar restlessness, but they set out with quite different goals, circumstances, feelings, and responsibilities. Together the land's lure and the settlers' purposes made for the third consideration—the human mix that constituted western society.

Each of these elements was different when compared to the rest of America. Yet within each were equally striking variations. The frontier West was a place apart and a place of many parts.

"The eastern half of America offers no suggestion of its western half," the journalist Samuel Bowles wrote after a tour beyond the Missouri.[3] Like Bowles, most emigrants were suddenly confronted with environments jarringly different from any they had known.

The West included several subregions, each quite different from one another.[4] Leaving the Missouri valley, a newcomer first would encounter the Great Plains, a windswept, rolling grassland that stretched from deep into Canada to west Texas. Larger than western Europe, the plains rose gradually from about two thousand feet above sea level on their eastern fringes to more than five thousand on the other side. Adult travelers found this country monotonous, some oppressively so, though many children like Frank Hughes were impressed. "It seemed the whole world had opened up, . . . no horizons, no limits," he recalled of the Montana plains.[5] In fact, the plains were not all the same. In time farmers discovered crucial, if sometimes subtle, distinctions in terrain and soil composition. The northern plains were punctuated by the Black Hills and the Judith and Bear's Paw mountains. If a man had been able to soar above it all, he could have seen thousands of creekbeds and countless depressions that spring rains filled with water.

Several eastward-flowing rivers drained the plains, among them the Missouri, Yellowstone, Platte, Smoky Hill, and Arkansas. These were shallower than eastern streams and their flow was erratic, but they served well as avenues of migration and later as vital connections between settlers and the outside world. "God bless river," was the first prayer composed by May Flanagan's sister, who grew up at Fort Benton, Montana, high on the Missouri, which "brought us everything and took everything away."[6]

On the far side of the plains, the land tilted suddenly upward into the Rocky Mountains. In the next fifty miles the land rose more than three times what it had in the previous five hundred. This made the view from the plains one of the continent's most inspiring. Spanish explorers, seeing the red dawn light on the snowy peaks, imagined the blood of the martyred Christ—thus, the Sangre de Cristo range. The English romantic Fitz Hugh Ludlow, a veteran world traveler with a fondness for hashish, thought the first glimpse of the Front Range was "a sudden revelation of the truth."[7] Lonely French trappers in Wyoming thought of great, beautiful breasts when they sighted the Tetons.

But westering settlers worried mostly about how to get through this vast cordillera that covered 180,000 square miles. As it happened, the way was relatively easy. The northern and middle branches of the Rocky Mountains were separated from the southern by the Wyoming Basin, a broad break in that imposing barrier just beyond the headwaters of the North Platte River. Through this gate would march tens of thousands of Pacific-bound pioneers.

The Rockies' three branches were composed of ranges with names exotic to eastern ears—the Wasatch, Big Horn, Sawatch, Uinta, Bitterroots, and San Juans. Their scores of rugged peaks, many over fourteen thousand feet, were thickly forested in fir and spruce. Newcomers at first felt shut in. Emma Hill's younger brother cried every day, saying he wanted "to see out." In time, however, most children felt the mountains' special appeal. Estelline Bennett loved to climb to a divide "and look down on all the world."[8] But farmers found the going tough. The soil was thin and stony and the growing season hopelessly short in most places, though nestling within the high country were grassy valleys that fed and sheltered herds of bison and other large game. In time cattle would graze there.

Beyond the Rockies waited the huge intermontane region. In its middle was the Great Basin, a desert lowland ridged like a washboard with several barren ranges running north and south. The Humboldt and Carson rivers flowed into this country, but finding no way out, they sank finally into the thirsty soil. North and southeast of the basin were two large plateaus named for a pair of the West's greatest rivers. The Columbia Plateau was a gigantic sheet of lava, covered with sagebrush and gouged by deep canyons cut through the soft rock by the Columbia, Snake and other streams. The Colorado Plateau was rugged and lofty, averaging nearly a mile in altitude, and crisscrossed by dozens of deep gorges that made travel tortuous at best. Much of the water in this arid country was beyond reach, for the Colorado and Green rivers, rushing through the deep canyons they had created, were almost inaccessible to anyone stubborn enough to try to settle there. The southernmost parts of California, Arizona, and New Mexico were extensions of the Sonoran Desert, one of the world's largest and most hostile. Most adults found the intermontane West—parched, rocky, spectacularly eroded—a forbidding landscape. "A horrid place," a mother wrote of a village along the Humboldt: "Wind and dust and pigs." For a few, including some of the youngest emigrants, it held a strange appeal. It was "like traveling over the great domains of a lost world," a young girl wrote.[9]

Having crossed prairies and plains, mountains and deserts, a traveler next would have confronted another stone wall a thousand miles long—the Sierra Nevada and Cascades. He could pass through the latter by floating the Columbia River, but the Sierra demanded more, a hard pull up narrow, boulder-choked gullies and over wind-scoured passes. But then, whichever route he took, the traveler would find a more inviting country. A string of valleys stretched from Canada southward nearly to Mexico—the fertile, well watered Puget Trough and Willamette River valley in Washington and Oregon and in California a more arid floodplain, four hundred miles long, drained by the Sacramento and San Joaquin rivers. A final barrier then stood ahead. The Coastal Ranges rose out of the interior valleys and sloped steeply into the Pacific, ending in some places in black, craggy cliffs and in others in hills covered with dun-colored grass. Along the western edge of the continent, there were few harbors and no broad tidal plains like those that had welcomed the earliest arrivals on the Atlantic frontier.

Samuel Bowles was correct. From its eastern fringe to the sea, the West had little that would remind anyone of the rest of America. This was a land of extremes. Those who entered it would find the world's deepest canyon, largest gorge, and oldest and tallest trees; there, too, were the nation's highest and lowest spots, its hottest and coldest, and its wettest and driest. Its denizens included the country's longest and deadliest snakes and its fastest and largest mammals (and the only ones that ate people). New arrivals may be forgiven for exaggerating when they wrote home of mountains reaching to the pearly gates, mosquitoes with snouts like boat oars, and bears that dined on spans of oxen, then picked their teeth with the doubletrees.

Settlers naturally were particularly concerned with the West's climatic extremes. Much of the newly settled country was of relatively high altitude and far from the ocean's moderating influence. This made for an astounding range of conditions. The weather of the northern plains was some of the most erratic in the world. Temperatures could span 150°F during a single year. A cold front could roll out of the arctic in early autumn and send thermometers plunging 100°F in a day; warm and blustery chinook winds could sweep out of the Rockies in deep winter and raise temperatures 40°F in two minutes. In the mountains, twenty feet or more of snow often accumulated in a winter, and even in late spring, a storm could dump enough to cover a standing man. The Colorado Plateau and much of the far Southwest were exposed to scorching southern winds in the summer and in winter brutal storms out of the Northwest.

Yet for all the region's variations, one supremely important consideration applied to much of it. In most of the region it rained very little—and in some places, less than that. The Pacific coast was watered well by the fronts that moved off the ocean; western Washington, in fact, received more precipitation than any other part of the nation. But as these fronts passed inland over the mountains, the water carried from the sea was left as rain and snow in the high country. The Sierra Nevada and Cascades cast a giant "rain shadow" over the land to the east. Like sponges wrung dry, these fronts now sopped up moisture from the soil. When not swept by these evaporating winds, the western interior usually felt the influence of weather systems out of northern Mexico and the arctic—deserts, both of them.

The western half of the United States consequently was much more arid than the rest. The "line of semi-aridity" ran roughly along the ninety-eighth meridian; west of it, the annual rainfall was less than twenty inches, a figure that dropped steadily as one moved toward the Rockies. Most of the region between those mountains and the Sierra received less than ten inches per year, and some got less than two.

Vegetation was a handy guide to the amount of rain an area could expect. Newcomers to the plains were typically struck first by the absence of timber. "What a fine counthry for patathers," an Irishman remarked: "The hills are all ready made up & cleared of trees."[10] But before they were transformed into vast checkerboards of wheat and other staples, the eastern plains were a profusion of native grasses and flowers—compass plant and skullcap, horsenettle and fog fruit, spiderwort, goldenrod, and snow-on-the-mountain, needlegrass, cordgrass, switchgrass, and bluestem. These grew tall, some up to a horse's withers, and when the wind rolled down, outlanders thought of the ocean on a rough day. On the western plains, plants were progressively shorter and more sparse. Eventually the tough, shallow-rooted grama grass dominated. In the deserts of the Great Basin, west Texas, and southern New Mexico and Arizona, the relatively wetter areas supported sagebrush and mesquite, while the driest country had cacti and creosote bushes, the "greasewood" that put out oily, foul-smelling smoke when desperate immigrants burned it as a last resort.

This one climatic factor—the annual rate of precipitation—shaped the lives of pioneers more than any other. Most obviously, it determined whether they could farm and, if so, what they could grow. The drier the country, the more acres a farmer needed to make a go of it. Much of the region of short grass and sagebrush allowed only ranching, but here, too, the extent of ground cover determined how much land was needed to feed each cow or sheep. In parts of the Southwest and Great Basin, ranchers required fifty acres or more for every animal. The density of a place's population thus depended somewhat on how much water fell on it.

Rainfall determined in part how quickly an area was settled, how many towns would appear, what people would do after they came, and how closely they would live to one another. For frontier children, the relative scarcity of water helped decide their work and responsibilities, their concepts of community, the influence of their neighbors upon them, the number of their friends, and even the games they played.

Parched and arid as it was, however, the West was in fact America's storehouse. Waiting for the pioneers were virtually all of the nation's precious metals and most of its copper, lead, zinc, and mercury. There were vast stands of timber and deep, rich soil that in time would be the world's most productive. If a man wanted to raise cattle, he could have stood in the middle of Kansas in 1870 and looked out onto a pasture bigger than New England, with plenty more beyond that.

These resources were exploited simultaneously. Families could always choose among several dreams to chase. Farmers drawn to the eastern Dakota land boom of the early 1870s might flirt with prospecting for gold in the Black Hills in 1877, mining silver in Leadville and Tombstone in 1878 and 1879, or raising cattle in parts of west Texas and Arizona opened to ranching late in the decade. The value of all this was especially great because of the voracious demand for the West's bounty. This last and most rapid advance of the frontier happened as the United States was racing through its industrial revolution. This was no coincidence, for the two enterprises fed each other. The technological marvels of the new age helped westerners grapple with the challenges of the new country, while the need for raw materials encouraged people to go west and exploit its resources. Out there was the essential stuff of industrialization—corn, wheat, and beef for hungry workers, coal for fuel, lumber for buildings and railroad ties, copper for electrical wiring, and gold and silver to help pay for it all.

This did not mean, of course, that fortune-seekers necessarily profited. Many would fail miserably, and there was a yawning gap from the beginning between the poorer and the more well-heeled pioneers on many parts of the frontier. Still, most families saw opportunity in the land. "You just tickle the earth with a hoe, and it laughs into harvest," as one man predicted.[11] In this sense, the western environment, so different from the East's and so varied within itself, was the most important force shaping the frontier family. It demanded that newcomers adjust to its diversity, deficiencies, and erratic temper, but it had its greatest effect before that process began. With its image of splendid possibilities, it drew outsiders to it, thereby creating frontier society in the first place.

Moving west, pioneers brought with them certain attitudes and resources. These made up the second element that created the world of pioneer children. Before the land had affected a single person in the slightest way, frontier society already was different, shaped by decisions of those who emigrated. Millions of people throughout the world had the choice of going into the West. Many thousands actually did so, and that set them apart. For all their variety, those who came west had that in common—they had imagined something compelling out there and had been willing to seek it out. Emigration was a sifting. It made for a society heavily weighted with persons of a particular bent.

Naturally, specific motives varied. Some claimed moral reasons. "This country needs much Christian exertion," wrote a woman who felt it her duty to come and stay in Oregon. Religious concern could bleed into politics, as it did for Charles Athearn, who came to Kansas in 1855 "not merely to get possession of this rich country—but to stay the tide of slavery."[12] These were updated expressions of the old impulse to use the new land in saving the best of the past while avoiding its sins.

Others trusted the West to cure their ills and keep their families healthy. Wounded Civil War veterans hoped their aches would be eased, and "the one-lung army," sufferers of pulmonary ailments, thought the dry climate and champagne air would restore their strength. A Wisconsin schoolmaster fell down a well during a blizzard and escaped only by hacking steps out of the frozen mud with a pen knife. The experience left him soured and consumptive. Soon he was off for California.[13]

The most common drive was economic. Like all immigration, that to the frontier was a process of push and pull. "High rents . . . hog cholera, and floods drove us west," recalled a mother who left Missouri for Montana.[14] Families like hers were pressured by a variety of troubles. Some could not afford land at a time of rising prices; many groused about taxes going up and soil playing out.

Westward was the fresh start. In the early 1840s, it was Oregon with its "free land . . . , the very best soil in the world, the wonderful timber, water, and a balmy, mild climate that could not be surpassed"—or so one girl's father was assured. "There has been a strange fever raging here. . . , the Oregon fever," an Iowa farm wife wrote dryly in 1847. "Nothing seems to stop it but to tear up and take a six-months trip across the plains with ox teams to the Pacific Ocean."[15]

The disease flared up often, but like influenza, its various strains took the names of different places. In 1849 the "California fever" conjured up visions of fortunes in gold as well as in farming and ranching. The contagion was transmitted by mail. "Sell your farm, buy cows, horses and come to this valley," a father wrote his son and grandchildren. The limitless promise was worth the surrender of security: "I would rather eat off a tin plate and live in a tent than have the best house and farm in Illinois."[16] A decade later, Colorado was the attraction. "The effect was electrical," Thomas Sanders said about his father in Missouri hearing about gold near fabled Pike's Peak. The man was revived, transformed, and soon the family was on its way up the Platte. The malady took the names of Montana and Idaho in the 1860s, the Dakota homestead country and the Black Hills in the 1870s and 1880s, the southwestern drylands and the far northern plains in the 1880s and 1890s. The particulars changed; the symptoms did not. "Uncle went out to Navarro County [Texas] and sent word back," a woman wrote of her Arkansas girlhood in 1892: "They soon had my Father in a High Texas Fever."[17]

Children often heard that they were an important part of this momentous decision. "It was for our Sakes he broke up [their Mississippi farm] and moved to Texas," Melissa Everett and her siblings were told. Parents who owned land still worried that their grown children might not be able to afford any of their own. Beyond that, the West, just starting to be exploited, seemed to promise all sorts of opportunities for at least the next few generations. Many a father like William Rudd justified his actions on dual grounds—"to get a new start and let [my] children grow up with the country."[18]

Many of these families moved as part of a long tradition. Their parents and grandparents might have come with the edge of settlement through

A pioneer family, one of tens of thousands that invaded the West, pauses with their well-equipped wagon in downtown Cripple Creek, Colorado. (Courtesy Amon Carter Museum, Fort Worth, Texas.)

the Ohio Valley and Gulf coastal plains, and they themselves might have moved as often as half a dozen times before launching westward. This tendency could become an ingrained itchiness, a life rooted in rootlessness. "It was more instinct than anything else," a young wife remembered of leaving west Texas for New Mexico. The children knew this trait well. One called it "a natural disposition to remove to new country," another "being in love with the idea of movement." Their parents seemed always to be looking for a reason to move on. It did not take much. Benjamin Franklin Bonney's father, an impassioned fisherman, packed his family off for Oregon in 1845 after he tired of pike and dreamed of trout and salmon. Twelve hundred miles up the road, when a booster told him that California fish were bigger and hungrier, the Bonneys veered toward the Sierra Nevada. As a boy F. M. McCarty already had moved from Indiana to Illinois to Iowa when word arrived of gold in Colorado. Soon afterwards his family saw a meteor to the west. That settled it. A month later the farm was sold and they were gone.[19]

These families were like those common on past frontiers. Practiced at confronting new conditions, they typically left for the Far West from the nearest jumping-off place, in this case that most recently settled region just past the Mississippi. They were joined, however, by others who had come much farther and were far more ignorant of the challenges awaiting them. Earlier frontiers had always attracted some who had been willing to make a difficult transition from a distant life. Now, however, the transportation revolution was making the new land increasingly accessible. By 1860 railroads and steamboats could carry immigrants to the eastern plains. Thirty years later several rail lines reached to the Pacific; with smaller "feeder lines" and thousands of miles of stage roads, they opened much of the West to anyone with the inclination and a ticket. Paradoxically, much of this last, most remote frontier was also easiest to reach.

The intrusion of technology helped make the far western frontier society fundamentally different from earlier ones. It was peopled by some unlikely pioneers. Seasoned farmers from Missouri and Iowa settled near sallow New York clerks, Norwegian clockmakers, and Tennessee dentists. Alabama farmers tried their hands at mining; Pennsylvania coal miners filed on homesteads in South Dakota. These new westerners were jumping gaps of experience as well as space, and often ignorance was their unwitting ally in daring the unknown. Chester Dutton, a Yale graduate, recounted how he moved his wife and four sons from upstate New York in 1868 to farm near the Republican River in Kansas: "There is an old proverb which says *'Them that knows nothing fears nothing.' We feared nothing.*"[20]

There were also significant differences in the resources these settlers brought with them. The greatest range was in the more promising mining towns, where a relatively affluent class of investors, engineers, and other professionals lived amid financially humbler prospectors, muckers, and day laborers. But even in the farmlands some arrived with the latest equipment and funds to buy good land, housing materials, and draft animals, with some money left as a cushion against disaster. A section away a family's assets might amount to five or ten dollars, an outdated plow, and a spring wagon pulled by tired oxen. Thus immigrants came with similar expectations, but they varied considerably in the experience and wherewithal needed to achieve them. As the children would learn, these differences left some families with greater difficulties than others.

In a sense, however, it is misleading to speak as if all immigrants were equally enthusiastic. Some came west much more reluctantly than others, and the most obvious distinction was that of sex. Women who moved to the frontier were giving up more than men. Their prime duties—caring for and educating children and wrestling with the extraordinary range of homemaking tasks—were easiest in a familiar setting and a well established home, especially when supported by nearby female friends and relatives. The move west often took away those advantages.[21] Some women pioneers, to be sure, were sacrificing less than others. Newly married, childless wives and middle-aged mothers with older sons and daughters usually looked forward to the move in good spirits; mothers caring for a gaggle of young children were less eager for the ordeals ahead. Many women brought with them the help of mothers, sisters, aunts, grandmothers, cousins, and neighbors, while others broke almost wholly with the past.

Understandably, the most anguished departures often were of mothers in their twenties, some of them pregnant, with toddlers clinging to their skirts as they tearfully gave their goodbyes to weeping kin and companions. They had an idea of what was before them. Not all these women bore their burden gladly. Several hundred miles down the overland trail, one mother refused to take another step toward Oregon, and when her husband insisted, she set fire to their wagon.[22]

Yet some wives, far from holding back, refused to stay behind even when urged to. "A rolling stone gathers no moss," Eleanor Knowlton's sister warned her as she left: "A setting hen never gains any feathers," Eleanor replied. Some children remembered mothers prodding their husbands to take the leap and boasting of their gypsy spirit and love of the westering adventure. Moreover, a surprising number of single mothers took the trip West. One was Elizabeth O'Neil's, who headed for the Montana gold fields in 1863 with a trunk of clothes, a cow, and her two young daughters. When Albert Neighbors's father died on their New Mexico farm, the boy's mother did not return east to her family but instead packed her ten children into a small wagon, then drove westward to a spot near Warner's Mill, deep in Arizona's Apache country. A few days later, she delivered her eleventh child, then started building a temporary house.[23]

Such extraordinary women to the contrary, the general pattern is undeniable. The vast majority of those who resisted going west were women, and in all the record, there are virtually no cases of wives overruling their husbands' objections, selling farms and businesses, and stuffing families into wagons and railcars for the new country.

The children knew this—they were, in fact, especially aware of this conflict, given that women with young daughters and sons were most apt to speak out against moving—and they often expressed their sympathy. One wrote that "mother's mind and heart, I know, resisted the change, though with no perceptible effect." Tom Sanders recalled his mother vainly begging his father not to leave "the known, the trusted, the tried" to chase a mirage. Wallace Wood's mother had endured plenty of pioneering as an Iowa girl, she told her husband and family, but they still went to Kansas. Effie Conwell watched her mother weep bitterly much of the way from Kentucky to their new land along the Arkansas River.[24]

Clearly girls and boys understood that pioneering could have different implications for their mothers and fathers—and perhaps for themselves when they grew into women and men. This darker message was clear, but it was not dominant. The new western society was created through many thousands of individual decisions to emigrate, hence its prevailing mood was necessarily optimistic. It assumed that the main business at hand was to develop the new country's bounty. Emigrants generally trusted in their luck and their ability to better their condition by making the land pay, and with this came a willingness to move on in search of the opportunity presumed to be there.

Along with the environment and the pioneers' motivations, the West was distinctive because of the makeup of its society. The essentials were summarized nicely in that crowd of humanity that filled the overland trails. More than a quarter of a million people made their way to the Pacific coast between 1840 and 1860. At its peak the migration filled the overland highway twelve wagons abreast. Besides these, there were buggies, wheelbarrows, horses, oxen, mules, cattle, sheep, dogs, and throngs of people afoot. Some travelers wore goggles to shield their eyes from the dust and debris kicked up by the immigrant army.

This great column can be pictured as a long, winding city—one that could change dramatically from year to year. The trickle of overlanders in 1841 grew by 1847 to more than four thousand. These were mostly farming families, with the midwestern majority joined by others from the South. Most were headed for Oregon and its promise of rich, free land. The news of gold in California suddenly transformed this overland city. Its numbers leaped—nearly 150,000 made the crossing between 1849 and 1852—and now the great portion were adult males. Fort Laramie's official register of June 3, 1850, for example, told that the year's migration thus far had included 99 children, 119 women, and 17,443 men. They were a promiscuous mixing from all over the nation and the world. Nowhere else in nineteenth-century America would so many persons of such varied origins be thrown so closely together. Then, from 1853 until the Civil War, the city changed again. Again, more families were coming along, though men still dominated the ranks. Children still accounted for only about 20 percent of the crowd, about half the proportion found elsewhere in the country. The same pattern of change could be seen among the overlanders headed to Colorado after 1858 and to Montana and Idaho after 1863. An early bearded surge of bachelors and "baching" husbands gradually gave way to a mix of single men and families, though at no point were women and the young as common a sight as in the places the pioneers had put behind them.[25]

The changing overland city was a mirror of the frontier's various social settings. Like the population of the trails, that of the West at large was unlike the rest of the nation, yet it differed also within itself.

During these years, for instance, the West was the most cosmopolitan part of the nation, with between a fourth and a third of its people born outside the United States. As late as 1900, the percentage of foreign-born in Montana was twice that of Pennsylvania, and nearly eight out of ten North Dakotans had either been born abroad or born of immigrant parents.[26]

Most polyglot of all were the mining camps. "This is emphatically the world's convention," a Californian wrote in 1850, and an Idaho journalist found "Saxon, Celt, Teuton, Gaul, Greaser, Celestial, and Indian."[27] He might have added Italian, Belgian, Russian, Scandanavian, Portuguese, Greek, Turk, West Indian, Australian, and Hawaiian. Four out of ten persons in Yuba County, California in 1880 had been born beyond American shores, and half of those in Deer Lodge County, Montana, and Storey County, Nevada. Aliens made up 70 percent of the population in some Idaho camps; in Shoshone County the figure was an astounding 87 percent. Many mining towns had far greater proportions of foreigners than any precinct of turn-of-the-century Chicago or New York.[28]

The farming frontier, especially that of the Great Plains, also was peopled by immigrants from throughout much of Europe. Scandanavians and German-Russians were more common on the northern plains and Czechs and Germans to the south, but in any given county a child might know, as young Frank Waugh did,

> a motley array of neighbors. On one side a German who could scarce speak English married to a Bohemian who could speak little English and no German; on another side a family of Swedes fresh from the old country; on an adjoining farm a Scotsman with a Missouri wife; nearby a family from Iowa; another family from Illinois; some old, some young; some illiterate, some well educated; yet all engaged in the same enterprise. . . .[29]

As Waugh mentioned, native-born pioneers also were a mix. In a pair of California mining camps in 1850, about half the residents had come from the northern states, another third from the south, and the rest from the Mississippi Valley frontier.[30] On the farmlands Alabamans and Missourians were stirred together with midwesterners and New England yankees, and all of them with Finns and Czechs. Frontier children typically grew up used to a variety of accents and customs.

Westerners were also among the most transient citizens of a footloose nation. That they were there in the first place indicated that they were willing to move, and the West's expanding economy, its booms and busts, and its rapidly developing transportation system kept many families on the road for years. Studies of farming regions, market towns, lumber centers, and mining districts show their populations were turning over at a rapid, sometimes dizzying pace, with rates of mobility—that is, the percentages of persons in a particular place who moved on within ten years—typically greater than the most migratory easterners.[31] Mining camps in their first bloomings were the most unstable societies in American history. Some lost 95 percent of their populations within a decade. Frontier farmers were less transient, but they still were less likely than their eastern cousins to stay in place. A study of one rural Iowa county showed that seven out of ten persons in the work force moved on between 1850 and 1860. Nor did these agricultural settlements necessarily become more stable as time passed. Farmers in central Kansas, for instance, were about as likely to pack up and leave in 1925 as others had been in 1875.[32]

Individual stories flesh out these broad, anonymous patterns of restlessness. Some families, like the Van Courts, bounced about initially in search of secure income. This couple added four children to their number as they moved around California between 1855 and 1862—ranching in the Santa Clara valley, running a hotel, taking in boarders, managing a dairy farm, mining, farming, raising cattle on shares, and at last removing to San Francisco. Other children, like Dora Miller and her eleven siblings, were almost constantly on the road throughout their early years. Their father, a trapper and squatter, moved his brood dozens of times, living sometimes in dugouts, sometimes in shanties and tents, but in none of them for more than a couple of months. For some this became a tradition passed on through the generations. In the 1850s, Melissa Everett's family left Mississippi, tried farming in east Texas, then settled for a few years near Gainsville. There Melissa married and moved west to Whitesboro. Widowed and remarried, she was off again in 1879 for Montague County, only to come down with the "western fever" again six years later, leaving for Albany, then San Angelo, Sterling City, Big Spring, Glasscock County, and finally Garden City. Only when she reached her sixties, her own children now scattering throughout the region, did Everett light again on a piece of land for more than a few years.[33]

Frontier societies differed in yet another way—one particularly important in the children's story. The balance among the generations and the sexes almost always was unlike that found in the East. This peculiarity affected popular attitudes toward the young, the work and responsibilities that boys and girls would face, and the ways they perceived their places in society.

The new country's widely publicized blend of risk and opportunity attracted an inordinate number of single adult males, full of dreams and high spirits. The West's rowdy reputation convinced many husbands to leave their families at home while they chased after fortune. This meant the frontier had a heavy concentration of men and fewer women and children.

The published census points up the contrast between the West and the rest of the country. Imagine a man traveling through the settled parts of the United States sending people off to the frontier. Wherever he stopped—North or South, countryside or town, Pike County, Missouri, or Philadelphia, or Knox County, Illinois—he would have found that the numbers of males and females were about equal, while children outnumbered men, sometimes by as much as two-to-one [Table I].

But if this inquisitive traveler had left those places for the western mining camps, he would have found a very different situation. In Summit County, Colorado, there were five males for every female and eight men for each child. Had he kept going, over the Rockies and across the Great Basin to White Pine County, Nevada, the figures would have been even more disproportionate, and by the time he turned northward to Shoshone County, Idaho, the imbalance would have become more startling. Males outnumbered females nearly three-hundred-to-one, and there were more than two hundred men for every child.

The reasons are suggested in the "Sucker Bar Song," recorded by a California diarist:

Our friends all so kind we have left far behind,
Our wives and our little ones too,
And those who have not any little [ones] got
Have sweethearts
or wives, most true.

Children were rare—and usually much appreciated—sights in a mining region like Jefferson County, Montana. Here a boy and girl are surrounded by the crew of the Bluebird Mine. (Courtesy Montana Historical Society.)

> We see the gold shine in the damp, cold mine;
> It cheers and rejoices our eyes,
> For with it we mean at home to be seen
> 'Neath our own native sun and skies.[34]

A man singing these verses planned a short but profitable stay on the frontier, and there seemed little that women and children could do to help. Besides, families living in the camps would be exposed to some of the continent's harshest weather and sleaziest citizens.

Farmers, by contrast, had better reasons than miners to bring their families along. Cultivators usually planned to stay indefinitely, and women and children could help greatly with the labors at hand. It was assumed that schools, churches and other elements of "good society" soon would appear. But be careful, some argued. By some reports the rural West had its own dangers, the beasts and savage Indians that had haunted popular perceptions from the beginning. At its best, furthermore, the farming frontier had plenty of discomforts and an especially heavy load of work. Much of it was isolated, some of it remote.

With emigrants pulled between optimism and caution, one part of the farming frontier could differ dramatically from another. Kansas in 1870 nicely illustrated the point. The far eastern counties, settled during the free soil fight fifteen years earlier, appeared much like Indiana or Tennessee [Table 1]. The balance between the sexes was about even, and there were more young folk than men. About 150 miles to the west, along the 98th meridian, there were more foreigners and fewer women among the more scattered population. Men in their prime working years slightly outnumbered the young. Nevertheless, the change thus far was gradual. But 100 miles farther was the frontier's cutting edge—a drier, open grassland around the 100th meridian where homesteaders' soddies had just started to sprout. There males outnumbered the opposite sex by eight-to-one, and for every youngster of school age, there were twenty men.

The full range of the rural frontier's social settings was telescoped in three hundred miles of this one state. In places settled several years—Polk County, Oregon, for example—families often predominated and children found plenty of company their own ages. Elsewhere family units were the exception and men living alone were the rule. Like central Kansas, some areas passed quickly from the second condition to the first, but there were many exceptions and variations. Even in eastern Nebraska, where farmland was easily available to families, the percentage of single males had actually increased substantially a generation after the first settlement.[35] In many places, the transition to a well settled, family rural community happened over a decade; in others it required a generation or two, or even longer.

Such was the case in much of Wyoming and Nevada, western Texas and the panhandle, parts of the Colorado plateau and southern Arizona, and a large portion of North Dakota and eastern Montana. These areas had in common a relative isolation and scarcity of rainfall, and some of them suffered until late from Indian troubles. Settlers lived by a mix of herding and cultivating, raising cattle and sheep and farming a bit, especially if some irrigation was possible. The environment could support only a thinly spread population, and families nervous about long distances to towns and between neighbors were understandably reluctant about venturing there. Whatever the reasons, those social characteristics of early settlement continued in a good part of the rural interior West for many years after the first pioneers' arrival.

Clearly the frontier's social settings varied considerably from time to time and place to place. Mining communities had a different human mix from that of the farm country, while the ranchlands could differ from

Table I
Sex and Age Ratios, 1870.

	Number of Males per 100 Females	Number of Men per 100 Children[a]
East:		
Philadelphia, Pa:	91	76
Tolland Co., Conn:	95	73
Nashville, Tenn:	97	69
Limestone Co., Ala:	97	53
Knox Co., Ill:	103	65
Pike Co., Mo:	105	56
West:		
Mining:		
Summit Co., Colo:	529	880
White Pine Co., Nev:	646	1,061
Shoshone Co., Ida:	2,788	2,100
Farm/Ranch:		
Kansas:		
Eastern	121	85
Central	146	122
Western	718	1,962
Polk Co., Ore:	123	49
Bexar Dist., Tx:	492	654
Laramie Co., Wyo:	312	622
Western Dakota:	647	1,160

[a]In these calculations, numbers of school-age children (five- to eighteen-years-old) are compared with numbers of men of military age (eighteen to forty-five).

Data from *Ninth Census, Volume 1. The Statistics of the Population of the United States* (Washington, D.C.: Government Printing Office, 1870), 623–38.

them both, and all these changed with the years, though not necessarily in the same ways or at the same pace. The scene might shift within a few miles. Oregon's towns and cities in 1850 teemed with young, unmarried men from the Northeast and Europe; the surrounding countryside was the home of midwestern and southern families, a place crawling with children and with nearly as many women as men. In 1865 Virginia City, Montana was a raucous gold camp full of bachelors, but a farmer along the nearby Gallatin River wrote of families flocking in. He expected a couple of dozen youngsters before the snow flew.[36]

This diversity itself was an important fact of life. Wherever a family landed in the West, they would likely find themselves in a society different from the one they had left—one with people who were unusually transient, gathered from all over the country and the world, and of a different social mix. When that family continued to move about, it would find different variations of that mixed and mobile society.

At the same time, many families carried with them an element of stability—relatives and friends who would help through the uncertainties and trials sure to come. Emigrants knew the value of cooperative networks, and whenever possible they relied on them. Overland archives abound with accounts of extended families traveling the Arkansas, Platte, Bozeman, and other trails. The names in a party did not always suggest the full story. When William Gray led a group to Oregon in 1853, the roster of thirteen included the Dix, Godley, Schuyler, and Van Renssalaer families. It might have been a collection of strangers, but the crowd included Gray's widowed mother-in-law, his two sisters-in-law, the husband of one of these and their three children, his wife's sister's son and that man's cousin and her husband.[37] This was a family reunion on wheels, and children on such a trip probably were in more frequent and intimate contact with relatives than ever before. Young travelers at least had plenty of playmates. An Englishwoman in the California diggings met four mothers, all sisters or sisters-in-law, who had crossed the plains together with thirty-six of their children: "They could, of themselves, form quite a respectable village," she wrote.[38]

Despite appearances, the western migration was never an atomized scattering. Even on the Oklahoma land rushes, symbols of the frontier's individualistic scramble, related boomers devised strategies to seize adjoining sections. The flow of emigrants often worked like a siphon. Once established, settlers tried to persuade others from back home to join them, and before long there could be quite a pool of related pioneers. Some related groups came not sequentially but *en masse*. The Black clan, five families strong, took up nearly three thousand acres near Breckenridge, Texas, in 1877, and the Pughs, who filled sixteen wagons when they rolled out of Daisy, Arkansas, stayed together until they found a spot they liked in western Oklahoma. They unloaded, filed on the land, then named the place Pughtown.[39]

Within a generation a latticework of family connections could span whole counties and more. The intricate linkages of the Reynolds-Matthews family reached over much of the Brazos River valley around Ft. Concho, Texas. A couple of hundred miles farther west, Lena Martin would grow up within a day's drive of seventeen households of relatives. It was difficult for such a child *not* to run into in-laws or blood kin, as Zella Hunter of Kansas learned, when on her first day as a schoolmistress, she found fourteen of her cousins in her class.[40]

These were unusual cases, however. The majority of pioneers had no relatives at all living near them, at least during their early years of settlement. A student of Oregon's rural frontier estimated that 40 percent of its families were linked to at least one other in the area.[41] The figure is quite high, but turned around, it still tells us that six out of ten families were apparently on their own. Even those who did settle as groups often broke apart as the disappointed turned back and the hopeful took off for other opportunities. This clustering, furthermore, was far less common on parts of the frontier, such as the mining towns and the thinly settled ranch country, than on others.

Nonetheless, perhaps a third to a half of those living in regions heavily settled with families had at least some relatives nearby. These connections were valuable to both children and adults, providing emotional support, care for the sick, and help in the frontier's physical tasks. The bonds of blood, marriage, and friendships pulled hard against pioneering's natural fragmentation.

This was the setting of the frontier children's story. As a geographical and social environment, the West was distinctive within the nation and varied within itself. This had some obvious implications for everyone, young and old. There was a heavy premium placed on adaptability. Families would need to adjust to varied landscapes with many economic possibilities; they would have to live and work with the frontier's shifting mix of people of different origins. The demands of adjustment drew family members together as they looked to one another to deal with the challenges at hand.

Yet in another way the new environment was pulling the family apart,

The Hopkins family, an extended clan with seventeen children, settled near Berwyn, Nebraska in the late 1880s. (Solomon D. Butcher Collection, Nebraska State Historical Society.)

for the westering experience meant one thing to older pioneers and quite another to the younger. The youngest emigrants had little of the East to remember, and those born in the new country had none whatsoever. For the young, in a sense, this was not a frontier at all—not, that is, a line between the familiar and the new. Rather, it was the original measure for the rest of their lives, and that measure was not the one their parents had known.

Children and adults were drawn together in their common need; with their different responses to the country, they grew apart. Out of this pull and tug, a distinctive generation was born.

It began when they looked at the land.

Caesar Brock

The horseman came around midnight and stole him from his bed. Was it his father? Caesar never knew for sure, but by the time they had left the piney woods of east Texas and crossed the cottonlands into the broken, cedar-studded Brazos valley, his life had plenty more uncertainties.

Caesar Brock had been born in 1862 on Henry Miller's plantation. He had been happy there. Miller's grown daughter, Lucy, played with him, took him riding, and cuddled him in her bed. But when Caesar was seven, Lucy was thrown from her horse and killed, and "then Hell tightened." His next memory was of waking to a bad dream—a hand clapped over his mouth as he was dragged out, quickly dressed, and carried off. "I had little boots on," he remembered.

He moved westward with a California-bound party, among them a young black-haired woman he did not recognize. She claimed she was his mother, but Caesar never believed it: "For her, I was something to beat on." Bob Wilkes, the swarthy southerner who had grabbed him, treated him better. Caesar suspected that Wilkes and Lucy Miller were his parents. Just who Wilkes was, however, was hard to say. He had a wife and three children with him, though he passed time with the black-haired woman, too. There were whispers around camp—that he was John Wilkes Booth, Lincoln's murderer and villain to a nation, that he had escaped from a burning barn and run to Mexico before slipping back into Texas. That made some sense to Caesar. Wilkes had Confederate sympathies and a limp, and he was mean enough to kill a good man.

After an attack by Apaches, the party decided to settle near Silver City in southwestern New Mexico. Caesar's "mother" married a German machinist, but Wilkes shot that man dead and headed west. Caesar never saw him again. The widow took up with the Fort Selden sutler, a man named Yamens. "I guess she done the best she could," Brock allowed. So did Caesar, though it was not easy herding all day and washing dishes for soldiers at night. "I would work until I didn't know what I was doing," he remembered, and when he crossed her, the black-haired woman would vow to "just whip the blood out of you," then do her best to keep her word.

Caesar did not run away: He worked his way out. He made extra cash by selling meat he hunted in the Burro Mountains, north of Lordsburg, where Yamens had a roadhouse. Soon he was on his own most of the time. At fifteen he was supplying venison and antelope to boarding houses and cutting hay in the flats to sell to the cavalry. Within a couple of years, after Yamens drank himself to death, Caesar had taken charge. He tried ranching but soon turned to mining, living in a cave for weeks at a stretch, alone, high in the *barrancas*. He wore moccasins, cinched his overalls with a piece of flour sack, and let his hair grow loose to his shoulders. Locals were not sure what to make of him.

At forty Brock came out the cave and married. He turned back to ranching and piped water from his mine tunnel into homemade cattle tanks he also used to irrigate his pear and peach orchards. Others were welcome to share the bounty—at a dime a swallow. He had learned to keep accounts, big and small, to pay and be paid by a rough equity.

For the next fifty years Caesar ranched successfully. His two daughters were his best hands; from the age of nine until they married and helped run their own ranches, they mended fence, branded his stock, and broke wild horses. Women were better than men at handling cattle, Brock said. He died in 1952.

Years before, he had settled his debt with the black-haired woman. He always took care of her, even during his hermit days. He built her a house on his land, fed and watched over her. Long ago he had stopped asking from whom he had come. When she died, Caesar buried her in the hills. He did not mark the grave, and he told no one where it was.

2

First Perceptions

On July 7, 1853, Harriet Ward, her husband, and their children paused on their way west to visit one of the overland trail's best known landmarks. More than twenty million years before they arrived in what is today southwest Wyoming, the restless earth had begun to hoist up a great granite formation. By luck this ridge of rock emerged under a river flowing across a plain of volcanic dust, and it moved against this rushing water as a piece of pine does against a table saw. For twenty thousand millennia the stream cut cleanly through the rising stone. The result was spectacular—a narrow canyon with sheer walls looming four hundred feet above a tumbling river. As always, people gave these ancient things names from their own fears and hopes. The surrounding hills they called the Rattlesnakes; the stream, the Sweetwater. They called the canyon the Devil's Gate.

As her family gazed up from the gloom of the canyon floor, Harriet noticed "the curious . . . effect of the same object upon different constituted minds." Her daughter Frances, eighteen, wished her relatives back home were there to see it, and she gathered a wildflower bouquet in their memory. Harriet's eleven-year-old son responded differently: "When Willie first beheld it, his words expressed astonishment and awe mingled with fear," his mother told her journal that night, "but after looking awhile he became perfectly enraptured. He laughed and sang and appeared as if he hardly knew how to express his delight."[1]

This vignette touches upon an important aspect of the frontier experience, for the history of westward expansion is partly one of perceptions. The frontier story begins with what happened when hundreds of thousands of human minds met an old, indifferent landscape. Perceptions were especially significant in the story of frontier children. The outlines

25

of the children's characters—their sense of who they were and of what was to be expected of life—were still being shaped, and part of that shaping came from how they responded to what was around them.

For, as Harriet Ward realized, perceptions could vary tremendously, depending upon who was doing the looking. Harriet herself had likely been taught that a woman's social role and character traits were different from those of men, and so her expectations of life in the West probably were unlike her husband's. A man and a woman might look at the same landscape but see separate places.

Differences of age, however, were even greater than those of sex. Children do not see the world as their elders do. There is a rough schedule to human mental development, and a pioneer of five or ten was still in the early stages of this growth. He viewed what was happening in a way his parents would have found strange indeed.[2] In this difference is an important clue to the uniqueness of the children's frontier.

The great overland migration, that rigorous and rushed introduction to life in the West, demonstrated the youngsters' distinctive way of looking at things. This youthful point-of-view is best understood when set beside that of adults. In the hundreds of diaries and journals kept by older pioneers on the trip, one impression stands out. Though these men and women were taking part in what surely was some of the most unusual times of their lives, their writing was dominated by the trivial—miles covered, quality of grass, weather, chores performed, tedious problems overcome. The entries click along like a metronome. These diaries provide a feel for the daily rhythms of travel, and they reveal their authors as responsible persons coping with pressing personal duties. But they tell little about the extraordinary world through which the pilgrims moved. "There are multitudes who will, after having passed here, have about as intelligent a notion of the valley of the Platte as their oxen," a diarist noted. "Such are the masses."[3]

When they rose above these concerns, adults often wrote of homesickness and feelings of loss. Women in particular felt keenly the separation from relatives and from the security of past lives. They sat staring at daguerreotypes, carried on conversations with absent loved ones, and burst into tears at the sight of a house or even a chair that reminded them of home. Men, especially those traveling without their families, also kept looking over their shoulders. When not worrying about their wives' welfare and sending back instructions on business and their children's schooling, many moralized on the foolishness of leaving the hearthside to chase material wealth. Sleep brought no relief. "In my dreams last night I was at home six days—and nothing ever seemed more real," Addison Crane told his diary. "Which are the realities, the dreaming or waking moments?"[4]

Which, indeed? In a way the places the adults had left were more real to them than the ones through which they were passing. They kept their spiritual base in the farmlands, small towns, and cities to the east. As if trying to domesticate the strange sights along the road, they described them in terms of the familiar world behind them. The few hardwoods along the Platte were called old and beloved friends; the rare glades in the sheltered canyons became "Fairy Springs" that inspired thoughts of sinless childhood—back East, of course.[5]

When at last they confronted the most spectacular landscapes and weather, many adults re-created what they saw in terms of the artistic cliches and cultural imperatives of their mother society. They found in the land a variety of ominous religious lessons. One mother saw in a hot spring a reminder of Hell and torments of the damned. Who could gaze upon those jumbles of boulders, another wondered, and not fear the God who could "cause the earth to tremble . . . while its bowels melt with fervent heat?" Scenes of "Aufull Grandure" were pictured in romantic passages. A plains thunderstorm became a "natural meteorick exhibition" of "electrik fluid," or a hellish blast that severed pole from pole. Besides these, diaries featured another romantic familiar—the isolated individual standing against God's handiwork. "Oh solitude solitude how I love it," wrote one young woman. "If [only] I had about a dozen of my acquaintances to enjoy it with me."[6]

Most revealing were the images these travelers saw in the bluffs, cliffs, and canyons along the road. Four of the most famous landmarks—Independence Rock, Courthouse Rock, Steeple Rock, and Chimney Rock—suggested the emigrants' most hallowed institutions: republican government, law, religion, and home or industry. Here were symbols of what the overlanders had lost but hoped to find again. Besides these, there were the ancient cities of Thebes and Babylon, towers and fortifications, tombs and spires, thatched cottages, railroad cars, steamboats, and figures on horseback. Some men saw romantic companions in the rock formations. One found "a female in an artistic posish." Another discovered a woman in a black satin dress and green-fringed silk cape, her raven hair done up and her right hand laid upon her left arm barely above the elbow. The next day he saw another lovely, this one in pink. Many visions were astonishingly precise. Two Kentuckians, traveling to the Pacific two years apart, recorded what they saw in the rocks along the same stretch of trail in Utah. One found Henry Clay, while the other saw the First Presbyterian Church of Louisville.[7]

These descriptions told more about the observers than about the things observed. Emigrants saw reflected in the land what was in their own minds—what they missed, believed, and hoped for. They were interpreting an unfamiliar landscape through the lens of tradition and personal concerns. More than anything else, this distinguished the adults' first perceptions of the West.

And it throws into relief their children's distinctive way of looking at the world they were entering. Children did not respond to the land as their parents did for the good reason that they could not. Their minds were not ready to let them. The earliest first-hand observations of the trail are from emigrants four or five years old. A child at that age was naturally egocentric. To him, all the world was what he could see, and the only way of viewing it was his own. He could not understand that an object looked different to someone several feet away, for instance. By seven or so, he could imagine better how things looked to others and could begin to grasp natural processes and classify what he observed. But he still could not think in formal abstract terms or imagine clearly events and places beyond what he could see and feel. He was largely "an unknowing prisoner of his own point of view" and "bound up in the world as it is." Even at eleven or twelve, he could not think of the future nearly so specifically as his elders could. Neither was his capacity for long-term memory as developed as it would be a few years later. Only in early adolescence could this young pioneer have abstracted and imagined possibilities beyond the concrete realities around him. He could hypothesize and reason his way to broad principles and create a detailed vision of the life he might know as an adult.

From the outset the children's emotional responses to the trip differed from those of their parents. As families set out on the long journey, the usual scene was one of grief and anguish. Relatives and friends crowded around, weeping and embracing the loved ones they believed they were touching for the last time. The older children were somewhat infected by this mood, but even they seemed puzzled by the intensity of feeling. An astute thirteen-year-old, on the cusp between childhood and adolescence, caught the difference between the generations:

> I slipped around where I could watch the older folks. They seemed to be trying to make the best of something they wished would not happen. . . . The younger kids know something unusual is

going on but don't understand it like the older folks do. . . . The older folks seem to understand some things we younger ones don't grasp. Some of the older ones seem to welcome the solitude away from the fire. They have said their good-byes and are just waiting.[8]

Children's alarm came from the immediate physical experience of leaving, not from its long-term implications. Catherine Pringle remembered older companions crying out for those left behind as the ferry carrying their wagons finally started across the Missouri, while she and her friends wept in fear of the river's swell "that came rushing down and seemed as though it would swallow [us] up."[9]

Most children shed few tears at all. Their greatest concern was for their immediate family, and as long as they were close at hand, these young pilgrims enjoyed the excitement. Besides, "we did not have sense enough to realize our danger," one of them wrote later. This was a recurring comment. Parents typically had promised a good time over the next several months, and "we looked upon [the trip] . . . as a great picnic excursion," recalled a fourteen-year-old.[10]

Although they often found the outing a rough one, the youngest pioneers took it all in day by day and mile by mile. Jesse Applegate, eight when he headed West with his father, a prominent Oregon booster, later recorded a particularly revealing memory. The trip was nearly half done, and as the family wagon crept along the Sweetwater River, a question suddenly dawned on the boy:

> I remember one afternoon, when the teams were tired and some of the oxen limping with sore feet, I was looking far away in the direction we were traveling across a dreary sage plain, to all appearances extending to the end of the earth, and I got to wondering where we were trying to get to, and asked the question, when someone said, "To Oregon." I did not know any more but was satisfied. I think I made up my mind then and there not to ask that question any more. . . . To me, Oregon was a word without meaning.[11]

Since Jesse was ignorant of where he was and what lay ahead, he had virtually no sense of continuity. Years later, when he tried to recall great stretches of the trip, he could summon up only an image of traveling, one afternoon after another, toward the sun. When he tried to place his memories in order, he sometimes was three hundred miles off in his backward reckoning.[12] The stark landscape might as well have extended "to the end of the earth," for in a way his world at each moment did stop at the horizon. As a guide to precise routes and a chronology of travel, Jesse's memories, and those of most children, are hopelessly jumbled.

Paradoxically, however, these limitations made such impressions especially valuable and appealing. Unable to imagine much beyond what they could see, children's minds were uncluttered by thoughts of past and future, unencumbered by cultural traditions. They looked on the passing scene for what it was. Despite its muddled chronology, for instance, young Applegate's narrative is full of extraordinarily vivid images of a perilous crossing of the North Platte, an Indian encampment, and a newly killed bison.

These youngsters had a close look at the land. Busy and tired, adults could not keep close watch over their restless broods, and children quickly learned to slip from the cramped wagons, hopping from the brake block to the ground to walk or jog along, sometimes drifting behind or wandering off the trail and then rushing to catch up. Many ranged several miles from their companies. When draft animals or wagons were lost, children walked whether they wanted to or not. There was nothing sheltered about these children's experiences.[13]

In their view of the trip, the young pioneers were above all literalists. They expected the land to be as previously advertised, and when it was not, they were confused. One boy had his first doubts when he neither saw any ashes nor heard anyone yell at "Ash Holler." Later he found the Black Hills full of color, the Blue and Green rivers faded out, the Sweetwater River brackish, Chimney Rock only a pointed stone column, and the Devil's Backbone merely a rocky ridge: "What a string of disappointments for a small boy, who had his mind made up to see all these marvelous sights." Even when they wrote of these experiences decades later, they rarely used metaphors, and when they did, they typically chose for comparison some simple object from their immediate environment. Years after he saw a herd of bison, a man described the animals stretching "so far away that a buffalo seemed no larger than a man's hat." Another recalled a young Cheyenne woman with "eyes as soft and bright as [those of the] antelopes."[14]

They were sensualists as well. Their initial physical sensations, compared to nothing else and unrefracted by the lens of a larger culture, retained their freshness. "To this day, the scent of mountain sage or the odor of dry burning manure brings to mind the campfires of the plains," Mary Boatman remembered more than half a century after crossing. Sixty-

Like these children in camp in Arizona, boys and girls heading west entered not only a new country but a new realm of experience. (Museum of New Mexico, Neg. # 3083.)

two years after he watched an enormous herd of bison plunge into Arkansas River, Thomas Sanders wrote of the air filled with a cataract roar and the ground quivering from thousands of hooves. Parents saw railroad cars and Egyptian ruins in the bluffs, while their children saw towering rocks of different colors. Often it is the youngsters' words that are better at pulling the reader back into the experience, as when Barsina Rogers told her diary of camping by a rock "so high that when you look up to the top & see the clouds moving over it, it looks as if you had better get out of the way."[15]

Viewing this landscape from the perspective of physical sensation, the young naturally focused upon the most distinctive aspects of the overland trek. When Jesse Applegate described his first plains thunderstorm, he captured its frightening power without mentioning blasts from Hades or "electrik fluid:"

> Some time during the night, I suddenly awoke. The rain was pouring down into my face, my eyes were blinded with the glare of lightning, the wind was roaring like a furnace, and the crash

of thunder was terrible and almost continuous. I could see nothing but what looked like sheets of fire, and hear nothing but the wind, the pouring rain, and the bellowing thunder. For a minute I was dazed and could not realize the situation, and before I had fairly recovered my senses, Uncle Mack picked me up and put me into the hind end of a covered wagon. . . . In the morning the little river had overflowed its banks and the encampment was flooded.[16]

One never knew at dawn what might be seen by dusk—a wounded buffalo bull tossing a wagon around like a bag of straw or a dust devil sweeping through camp at dinner and carrying all the food and dishes into a river.[17]

Animals particularly fascinated the children. Besides the herds of bison that blackened the earth for miles, they told of antelopes that sped from sight before the dust they raised had even begun to settle. Underfoot were "the snakes [that] dig their houses in the deep sand," and streams teemed with colorful fish. At night there were "singing wolves," and during the day squirrels that lived in towns and yipped like dogs.[18]

Food, another important part of the sensual history of the journey, was often remarked upon. The new cuisine of the plains, such as antelope and bison calves, generally received high marks, as did sourdock and other weeds gathered along the way. The quality of the water often was dismal, however. "Burnt sage brush & drank red mud for coffee," a young girl wrote. The supplies so carefully packed sometimes contained surprises, as when one twelve-year-old found the family flour "plentifully seasoned with mouse pills." The bitterest complaints were directed at the relentless regimen of bacon and salt pork, flapjacks, bread and dried fruit their parents had packed for the months on the road. Elisha Brooks, eleven when he went to California, could recommend the last item for its economy: "You need but one meal a day; you can eat dried apples for breakfast, drink water for dinner and swell for supper."[19]

Dried apples, prairie dogs, and whirlwinds—these, not distance traveled daily or scenes from the past, were the focus of attention in the child's-eye view of the overland journey.

There was a darker side to the story. Boys and girls carried a burden of their own. Adults went west with memories and learned responsibilities; children brought along anxieties peculiar to the young. Those fears have changed remarkably little over time.[20] Many arise from such fundamental physical needs as feeding and protection, from universal experiences like birth trauma and weaning, and from lingering adaptations to primitive dangers. Because these fear-producing forces are much the same today as they were a century—or a hundred centuries—in the past, modern psychological research can be applied generally to experiences of frontier boys and girls. When this is done, one observation stands forth: The overland crossing seems designed to terrify children.

During children's first two years, they gradually understand that they are separate from their surroundings. They also perceive that part of what is around them will protect them, but part is indifferent or threatening. With that is born a fear, which persists for several years, of powerful forces they sense are beyond anyone's control. Moving overland, children seem to have perceived such a threat in the openness and immensity of the plains. In the course of a day or even a few miles, they emerged into a rolling sweep of grassland with virtually no points of reference. Unlike their parents, they did not wish for houses, leafy glades, and other particulars missing in this environment; rather, they felt caught in the enormity of something that dwarfed all they had ever known.

Some children had a vague idea of their family's purpose, but because they were not sensitive to sequences of changes and unable to imagine the land ahead, the sudden sameness of the plains left them disoriented. A young man wrote in his diary of comforting his sister early in their trip:

> I came to the wagon [and] found little sister Jane who had just waked from a sound sleep crying like her heart would break: why Jane what's the matter? Oh we will never get to Oregon if we come back and camp in the same place every night. But we assured her that we were at a new camp and she was soon satisfied and lively as ever.[21]

Others recalled their initial impressions of the plains in ominous terms—"boundless," "endless," "a shoreless sea." The spaces appeared illimitable, a man remembered thinking as a four-year-old, and the entire world seemed a circle of sky with its edge mysteriously receding where it touched the earth.[22] Their words suggested a dislocation and isolation in a place with too much room to move.

If the immensity of the Great Plains left children fearful, another of its famous characteristics—its spectacular thunderstorms—filled them with terror. The worst were those that struck during the night. Oxen bawled and bellowed, men screamed their orders and called for missing family, tents were lifted and tossed and canvas sheeting ripped off the wagons. Everywhere was the thunder, a physical presence that struck them time after time, "as if it would tear up the earth," and the rain that stung and threatened to choke them. The lightning brought the brightness of noon, then "black as the depth of the pit." At the peak of one storm, a girl saw a neighboring wagon struck by a bolt, its brilliant charge racing and crackling around the iron wheel rim for several seconds.[23]

These were scenes of a world unhinged. It would be difficult to imagine a more impressive demonstration of a force that overwhelmed all else. Making it worse was the knowledge that out in the blackness was that sea of land without shore or shelter. The two phenomena, though quite different, conspired to the same disturbing end.

No doubt contributing to these feelings was the unfamiliar soundscape of the night. There were the cries of night hawks and occasionally the screams of a panther. Most disturbing were the wolves and coyotes. "Ferocious animals [are] howling around our camp by night, and flying before us by day," an overlander wrote in 1853. Adults usually made light of the eerie wailing, though one admitted it "made me rather sick & fearful." The children, however, found nothing amusing about it.[24] The howls and calls gave substance to the perennial childhood fear that "something is out there."

The most deeply disturbing of children's fears, however, could be grouped under the broad category of "separation anxiety." The term refers to the forbidding anticipation of being taken by circumstance or by some ungovernable power from the essential source of support and comfort— parents, usually the mother, but also others who give protection and love. These, the most intensely felt fears that children know, are strongest among infants from six months to two years. But they continue into adolescence and even beyond, and they are brought closer to the surface during times of dislocation, stress, and uncertainty, such as the journey west.[25]

The crossing to the Pacific became for many travelers an accumulation of partings. Pilgrims might move along together for weeks, then abruptly go their own ways, as one boy remembered: "It was simply 'There is your California road,' or 'There is your road to Oregon. Good-bye,' and each party was off to its chosen land of promise." Emigrants quarreled over the pace of travel, politics, and whether to rest on Sunday. The basic abrasive was that of different personalities rubbing against one another, as Charles Parke suggested when he blamed his party's dissolution on a friend's wife: "The D——l got into her as large as an ox." Many groups could not stand the strain. A diarist described the result: "Our company is split all to smash."[26] Children felt the pain of departure less acutely than did adults, but as they learned the trip could be unsettling and unpredictable, these breaks with familiar faces added to their uneasiness. The instability of overland groups was the emotional backdrop against which youngsters confronted fears of far more disturbing separations.

There was the possibility of becoming lost. This threat, the subject of some of the most enduring fairy tales of children's culture, suddenly seemed more real when facing that vast sameness of the Great Plains. There even adults could become disoriented and wander aimlessly for days. The anxiety of mothers, some of whom kept their young on leashes while in camp, surely was communicated to the girls and boys. In fact there were enough cases of youngsters losing their way to give this fear substance. A twelve-year-old, lost while gathering firewood, stumbled into a distant camp after walking for hours. Others disappeared while playing or looking for lost toys. A three-year-old boy walked away unnoticed as his parents made supper. Everyone searched all night, as a terrible storm raged, then all the next day, but to no avail; finally a stranger rode up with the boy, whom he had found, nearly dead, whimpering under some sagebrush.[27]

But this anxiety paled beside another. "A dreadful fear of the Indians was born and grown into me," remembered Anne Ellis. Years after crossing to Colorado, she still dreamed "of running from them til my feet rose from the ground and I ran in the air." Like most children, she had listened from infancy to stories of slaughter and captivity, of hot-eyed savages snatching babies from their cradles. These tales were "the folklore . . . [of] my childhood," Adrietta Hixon wrote. Some mothers made special preparations for the worst. One sheared most of her daughter's hair to make her less attractive to scalpers. Another carried cyanide capsules in a locket for herself and her youngsters in case of capture. Children surely absorbed their parents' foreboding. "Stranger, you are taking your family into the jaws of death!" a girl heard a man tell her father.[28]

No wonder children often flew into a panic at their first sight of an Osage or a Pawnee, hitherto only a frightening abstraction. Suddenly, a nightmare walked out of the wilds and looked at them. In fact, there was little to worry about. Between 1840 and 1860, the number of emigrants who fell before the natives was statistically miniscule; more Indians were killed by whites than vice versa.[29] But the children did not know this. They scuttled for their mothers' skirts or cowered behind flour barrels. Indians' behavior often seemed to justify these fears. They crowded around, peeked under wagon covers, grabbed at the reins and begged for clothes and "beeskit, beeskit!" An Oregon-bound family with ten children pressed through a crowd that chanted perhaps the only English the natives knew: *"Who Haw God Dam."* Robert Thoroughman saw a scalp hanging from the belt of a dancing man, a sight that made him instantly homesick.[30]

Interestingly, some children still sought out and observed the objects of their dread. Many beyond the age of ten or so were determined not to pass through without some artifact. They swapped for clothing, beadwork, and weapons. Perry Kline got up his nerve to look inside a tipi, then backed out quickly at the sight of a woman eating animal entrails. These children admired Indian skills and had their eyes opened by exotic encounters, as when Ada Millington told her diary of braves who "amused us by eating grasshoppers."[31]

The education of some went farther. Elisha Brooks, eleven, set out in 1852 with his mother and five siblings to join his father in California. When a hired teamster deserted them, they were left to muddle through as best they could. They had some troubles in Indian country, but when his desperate mother approached some Sioux for help, their fears began to give way. After some trading with the Indians, Elisha decided they were "not so bad as they were painted." Later, along the Sweetwater, a band of Crows helped the family along for more than a week. For Elisha, powerful and shadowy fears were banished by reality. He painted the scene vividly:

> Red men in rich robes of bear and panther skins decked out with fringe and feathers; red men without robes or feathers, and unwashed; favorite and actually handsome squaws in elegant mantles of bird skins, tattooed and adorned with beads; unlovely squaws in scanty rags and no beads, and unwashed; papooses rolled in highly ornamental blankets; papooses without a rag, and unwashed; ponies hidden under monumental burdens; packs of dogs creeping under wonderful loads; and, bringing up the rear, an old ox team with six wild, ragged children and a woman once called white, and sometimes unwashed. We were a Wild West Show.[32]

Most children, however, kept their distance and never came to grips with their dread. Indeed, some parents actually cultivated this anxiety as a tool of discipline. Anne Ellis was told to behave or face the infamous

Ute chief Colorow, whom she believed had special designs on her yellow hair. He crept into her dreams: "[I] have felt him lift [my scalp] from my head and [have] seen it dangling from his belt." An emigrant father told his misbehaving three-year-old that no one wanted her and she had to leave:

> She started away and kept going on and on till we all became very anxious [wrote a fellow traveler], for the Indians were bad there. Finally her mother . . . told her husband he would have to go after her for she would never come back. We all felt relieved when he came with her on his shoulder.[33]

The circle of firelight held the last few familiar things these children knew. Beyond were menacing shapes Emma Shepard and her sister imagined in the moonlit brush as they lay, unable to sleep, beneath the wagon. They passed many nights "full of terror," besieged by their anxieties.[34]

These feelings were deepened by fears of a far more terrible separation—death. The mortality rate among overlanders—4 to 6 percent—was not especially high,[35] but conditions of travel made it likely that girls and boys would come face-to-face with death in some of its most disturbing forms. Children are aware of death as early as their second year; their understanding of it grows until, about the age of eight or nine, they grasp that dying is an irreversible and unbridgeable separation, one that eventually will happen to them and to all living things. First impressions of death often come from pets and smaller wild beasts. From these, children learn that dying is associated with alarming physical changes.[36] This lesson was intensified along the road. Children could not have missed some of the thousands of draft animals left to rot where they dropped, especially in the last desert stretches. One man wrote of 130 dead oxen and horses in a morning, another of 40 on a quarter acre, yet another of 82 in 500 feet. Youngsters, sensually attuned to their surroundings, surely were impressed. "Nothing but ravens and crawling worms are here from choice," a man wrote of one place: "I taste it. I feel it. I smell it."[37]

As for evidence of human mortality, children found Indian burial platforms close to the road. Tribes along the route were ravaged by diseases brought by travelers, and children often saw the grisly results. As a mother spread a cloth on the ground for lunch, a child saw the foot of a dead Indian sticking from the sand.[38] Another girl in the same party found a stack of bloated corpses in an abandoned tipi, then stumbled over another body as she fled in horror.

Deaths among their own parties were even more disturbing. Though many companies made it through without a loss, others were devastated, especially during the years before 1855. A survivor among some Arkansans in 1852 wrote home:

> Huffmaster and wife and Manerad are dead. Uncle Enos is dead. James Hanen and wife and child are dead. Craig and wife and child are dead. James Crawfords babe is dead. David's child is dead, and Samuel Hanen has been at the point of death but was on the mend. . . . Nelson's crippled girl got shot by pulling or moving a gun as she went to get in the wagon. She lived about an hour. L———B———lost another girl. Even Hanen's child died. Stephen C———'s child died. Nancy Graham and William Ingram's children are both dead. Elvy Hanen is delirious and is an object to look at. Jacob Rushe's widow and little girl are dead.[39]

Such calamities became part of the folklore of the trail, told around campfires as wide-eyed youngsters listened. If they needed reminding, there were the graves. Most of the ten thousand or so emigrants who died were buried within easy sight of the trail. A young boy counted thirty-two graves in fourteen miles; a girl saw twenty-five in a day, lying in clusters of twelve, five, and eight. John Clark, crossing in 1852, counted 327 graves before South Pass—an average of about five a day, or one every three miles for nearly a thousand miles. By the Humboldt Sinks, the total had risen to 478 graves, as well as 2,980 dead draft animals.[40]

Many graves were no more than shallow trenches scooped out by hurried travelers. This made for some gruesome sights. The worst for him and his five children, Enos Ellmaker recalled, were "the skulls, and bones, and grave clothes laying by the road side . . ., dug up by the wolves." Strolling away from camp, overlanders saw parts of skeletons still strung together by sinews and legs protruding from the ground with the flesh eaten from hips to ankles. Travelers with a macabre sense of humor occasionally set human skulls on stakes along the road and wrote messages on them to friends on the way. Two girls found the head of a woman, a comb still in her hair, pulled from its grave. A week later they and their younger sister reburied parts of a body, "not liking to see the lifeless clay thrown about." When another family came across similar desecrations, a daughter took a strand of amber beads as a souvenir from the skull of "a Lady with long auburn hair."[41]

Faced with these things, children could not ignore the terrifying thought of their own parents' deaths—a possibility that usually dawns on young-sters at about the age of six or seven. Diaries and reminiscences contain enough cases to suggest numbers of children either witnessed or heard about such tragedies. Parents died quickly of mountain fever and chol-era, lingered with pneumonia and dysentery, dropped from strokes and heart attacks, and drowned in rivers.[42] And worse: "Yesterday passed grave of a woman, today saw husband buried, with children left to go on with strangers," a diarist wrote. The seven Sager children, who lost both parents in 1844 and were taken in by the missionaries Marcus and Narcissa Whitman, were the best known orphans of the trail, but they were not unique. A boy who crossed at fifteen watched his consumptive parents die within five minutes of each other. Most orphans were taken in immediately by sympathetic fellow travelers. But not all. A forty-niner found a girl and boy, ten and twelve, standing by a wagon which held the bodies of their parents, dead two days from cholera. Outraged, he buried the corpses and hurried on to catch those who had abandoned the sick couple. This party took in the children, though reluctantly.[43]

A few children later wrote of how they felt at times like these. Three weeks after her mother's death from cholera, Mary Ackley's father became lost while hunting his oxen. As the hours passed, Mary's spirits sank. "I never felt so miserable in my life," she remembered. "I sat on the ground with my face buried in my hands, speechless. . . . What would become of us children?"[44] Her father returned, but others had their worst fears confirmed. An argonaut wrote in his diary:

> I was one day traveling alone and in advance of our Teams when I over took a little girl, who had lingered far behind her Com-pany. She was crying, and as I took her into my arms [I] discov-ered that her little feet were bleeding by coming in contact with the sharp flint stone upon the road. I says why do you cry, does your feet hurt you, see how they bleed. No (says she) nothing hurts me now. They buried my father and mother yesterday, and I dont want to live any longer. They took me away from my sweet mother and put her in the ground. . . .[45]

Ordinarily in close touch with the sights and sounds around them, these children found their senses extraordinarily acute in times of terrible stress. The scenes remained, seared into their memories. "Sickness, deaths and burials I seem to see just as they occurred," wrote one man sixty-six years after he was orphaned on the plains. He described the willows near his father's resting place, the split cottonwood logs lining the grave and the inscription on his headpost. Catherine Sager Pringle recalled the tiniest specifics of her mother's last hours, down to her final words ("Oh, Henry, if you only knew how we have suffered"), while another woman's mind crowded with details of her mother's burial, seventy-five years in the past, whenever she saw or smelled a wild rose.[46]

Finally, children of the trail confronted the fear of the ultimate separation—their own death. Most boys and girls can conceive of their mortality by the age of eight. By then many could have read the simple messages on the markers they passed:

> Two Children Killed by a Stampede
> June 23, 1864
>
> Our Only Child
> Little Mary

Diarists recorded four children's graves in a day, two infants buried side-by-side, and brother and sister cholera victims laid to rest together. There was more direct, and gruesome, evidence. An Oregon-bound physician wrote, after a day's float through the Columbia's rapids: "Came down about 15 miles & Landed for night & buried a child which we found upon the Bank of the river drowned."[47]

Furthermore, children knew that in death they would be left behind, alone in a strange land. The final parting often was hasty. "I have seen a man stop and dig a grave for his own child, put the little creature into it and drive on, the whole business performed in less than half an hour," an appalled traveler remembered. Many "little creatures" had seen enough to know the implications. When one girl realized she was about to die of mountain fever, she worried about what might follow. "She told her mother she wanted her to dig her grave six feet deep for she did not want the wolves to dig her up and eat her . . . ," her sister recalled. Her companions were "to Pile a lot of rocks on her Grave after they had covered it up right," the girl added. She soon died, and her mother fulfilled the wish.[48]

The great majority of children neither died nor lost a parent on the journey west. But they were forced to confront the most dreadful fears within them. For all its wonders, there was something nightmarish about the passage as a child perceived it, a quality usually found only in the most frightening fairy tales. With no warning, these youngest pioneers were plunged into a space without the security of limits, a land of baby-stealers, slavering animals, and storms that tore at the earth, a place where mothers were taken away and children were abandoned forever, put alone into the ground as a portion for wolves.

Most children who went west did so by easier routes than the over-land trails. But their perceptions, too, were woven through with the theme of fear and uneasiness. A girl who settled in early Kansas entitled her childhood memoir *"I'm Scairt."* Effie Wood was another who confessed she was "a veritable little 'fraid cat'—afraid of everything—of snakes, of wolves, of storms, but most of all, of Indians." They drew upon the same folk tradition, stories of the natives' butcheries and child-stealing. Long after any threat of depredations had passed, the appearance of Indians— any Indians—left many children trembling. Years after the actual events, Frances Moore listened to tales of Indians tossing captured babies into steaming wash boilers. For all her life, washday kept a special meaning for her.[49]

The intensity of fear often seemed greatest where the danger was the least. In the Southwest, where the Indian threat was genuine until late in the century, children were alarmed at attacks by Apaches, but there was a matter-of-factness, not terror or hysteria, in their words. "It was ever the Indians, ever on guard, ever a revolver around the waist," wrote a woman who as a child had seen bodies, bristling with arrows, laid on her schoolroom benches. Mary Gardner was frightened when Apaches besieged her family's cabin in Arizona, but the peril had long been part of her life, and she felt enough at home with it to badger her mother, busy molding bullets, to let her out for a closer look.[50] The deepest panic, by contrast, was usually felt by those less exposed to the actual embodi-ment of their fears. Those newly arrived on the frontier especially stood on a hazy, uneasy middle ground. Something in their new environment made their instinctual but abstract fears suddenly seem imminently possible—not exactly there, facing the children in flesh and blood, but not altogether absent either.

Many were most fearful of the nocturnal hunters, the coyotes, pan-thers, and wolves that kept just out of sight. Perhaps these creatures gave voice to the land's disturbing unfamiliarity. Newly arrived on a west Texas farm, Andrew Davis and his sister never spoke above a whisper at night. Neither did their friends: "Like little scared partridges, they hover down as if trying to fill the least possible space." Maggie Holden described her earliest nights in west Texas: "The silence throbbed ominously, so every noise outside would sound like the beating of drums and clarion blasts." Her heart hammered even when skunks made the chickens squawk. Was it "altogether fear," she wondered, "or partly stark loneliness I felt in that vast emptiness of sight and sound?"[51] The young overlanders passing through that "vast emptiness" had felt its power, but those who settled the plains and deserts realized this would be their home. Some were emotionally numbed. An eleven-year-old sat mute and unmoving when he first saw the homestead his father had picked. "There was not a thing to be seen but the bare, burned prairie," he wrote later. "There was not a stick of timber or anything."[52]

This barrenness was most threatening to those, like Grace Snyder, who had come from wooded or mountainous country. Her clearest memories of coming to Custer County, Nebraska, at the age of seven were of what frightened her—the drab town of Cozad, but even worse the place her father had waiting. "I can still see the homestead as it looked when we pulled into it that day—just two naked little soddies squatting on a bare, windswept ridge above a narrow winding canyon." The feel of isolation was nearly overpowering: "Not another building in sight, not a tree, not an animal, nothing but grassy flats, hills, and more canyons." Augusta Dodge, making the less dramatic move from Iowa to central Kansas in her fourth year, found the combination of the openness and the gentle swell of the hills "a mystery and a terror." From a distance the hills appeared as mountains, then they would melt away as she watched, with others appearing beyond. For years she lived with a nightmare: as the family wagon struggled up a hill, the straining horses suddenly pitched and began to fall back into the wagon, and "I would wake with terror of it, feeling that it would really have happened but for my waking."[53] Whatever the variations, the disturbing first impressions had in common a sense of exposure and drift, a separation from what had been protective, and a foreboding of imminent disaster.[54]

Other themes, however, always ran beside those of fear and anxiety. Their intense awareness of the land could bring other, pleasing responses. The open space that seemed filled with awful possibilities also invited anyone to fly across it. Children's early memories are filled with images of easy and willful movement. "Every traveler chose his own way," galloped or drove as he pleased, Oello Martin recalled. She enjoyed sitting on a hill near her home in western Kansas, gazing over the grassland, country wind-stroked and unlined even by wheel ruts. Louise Kreipie's

The open sweep of the Great Plains unnerved some children and left them feeling exposed, vulnerable, and sometimes terrified. (Courtesy United States Geological Survey.)

first words in her youthful reminiscence were of "one vast prairie all unfenced." A road was whatever was under your wagon.

Some impressions are more dramatic and suggestive. Soon after settling in the Texas panhandle in his eighth year, Walter Posey was riding with his father when a herd of wild horses suddenly came upon them:

> There was two bunches of mustangs run in front of us. . . . And when they'd get by us, the stallion would drop back and hold his head up just as proud and haughty. And I declare, I can remember to this day how pretty they looked to me. . . . Some of them had flowing manes, tails nearly drug the ground. It was wide open.[55]

Also remembered were impressions of the beauty of a unique environment. Children were struck by the climate's great annual swings. By August, spring's greenness had turned dusty and sun-colored, and the confident burst of wildflowers had given way to the hardiest grasses and thorny plants. There was much to enchant them. For Ralla Banta of north

Texas, it was the grass so tall it hid the cattle and showed only a man's head when he rode through it on horseback. To others it was the wind, often a source of irritation and loneliness to adults. A Montana mother was filled with sadness and despair by the "incessant screeching, whining and screaming," but young Augusta Dodge was surprised at how the wind picked up sounds and carried them cross-country with no trees and crops to stand in the way; she often heard a neighbor curse his mules three miles distant. Just arrived from Sweden, Alma Carlson loved the wind from the start, its soothing murmur as it blew through the grass and pines in a nearby canyon. In time she was comforted by all the sounds of the Nebraska plains, even the cries of coyotes.[56] The beautiful and the fearful seemed always to touch and blend.

This ambivalence was summed up well in an experience of George Hockderffer. Not long after George came to Clay Centre, Kansas, just east of where the plains began their roll toward the Rockies, an older man took him to visit friends, a two-day hike to the west. George's first hours in the buffalo grass country left him wide-eyed. There were curlews and prairie chickens and what seemed like thousands of jackrabbits. He saw his first antelope, then his first bison, and that night, like small coals of fire in the blackness, the eyes of coyotes. "Never before," he recalled, "had I seen so much open rolling prairies and so much blue sky . . . We were constantly in sight of running animals and flying birds. . . . To me this was all so new and beautiful." Then, while the two were visiting at their destination, a prairie fire moved over a broad swath of tall grass through which they had passed. The trip back through the blackened land unnerved George: "[Before], we saw no living thing here, [and] neither did we now, except we could see that there *had* been life here. Everywhere we saw the burned carcasses of animals: coyotes, rabbits, and antelope. Neither of us were sorry when it became so dark that we could not see them." He had felt both the land's promises to the young—its freedom and excitement and fullness of life and its awesome power of annihilation.[57]

From this mix of intense impressions came an intuitive belief for children that their relationship with the country was their own, fundamentally different from that of their elders. Their particular way of looking at this place, and the feelings that flowed when they did, gave the children a special claim of possession. Owen McWhorter remembered of the Texas high plains:

The horizon, as far as I was concerned, circumscribed the world. I mean that was the world we lived in. I had little conception of anything except what I could see. . . . In those days the grass, especially in wet years, was knee high to a horse—beautiful, actually, a beautiful, beautiful scene. There was nothing to break it. . . . There was something about it a kid loved, the country, I mean. It was good earth.[58]

Owen McWhorter would have understood Willie Ward's feelings at Devil's Gate. First awed and fearful, then laughing with delight, Willie was acting out a drama that took place within the many thousands who went west as children.

The young did not look at the frontier as their elders did. They acknowledged far fewer responsibilities and felt less powerfully the tug of the society behind them; they could not think as far into the future or recall the past as elaborately. A child's horizon formed his compass box, the farthest landmarks his points of bearing. In that sense, children were prisoners of the here-and-now, but precisely because they were trapped in the present, they were freed to view their immediate world with a special clarity.

Their perceptions helped forge a bond to the country that was stronger and more fundamental than that of their parents. This environment, after all, helped shape and define reality itself—those ideas of what was possible and expected in life—among children taking their first steps toward mental maturity. When youngsters wondered how they fit into the world, this was the setting in which they pictured themselves; looking around, they found the peculiar nature of the challenges they would have to master. This was the starting point of the children's story. As Mary Ronan wrote of her first exposure to the plains at the age of ten:

I remember walking just ahead of that halted wagon, venturing out alone to gaze across that expanse of country. I recall so vividly the feeling of wonderment and perplexity at the bigness of the world and how I so eagerly struggled to stretch my childhood experience and imagination to comprehend some of its meaning and its promise. . . .[59]

Anne Ellis

Anne Ellis's family never escaped poverty, but they tried to outrun it. She was born in Missouri in 1875, and by her fourth birthday her parents had taken her from there to Colorado, returned, then recrossed the plains in a typical frontier dreamchase. There was rarely much to eat. Once her mother, humiliated, sold a precious pieced quilt to passing strangers to buy some food. Anne's earliest, deepest fears were of ghosts, Indians, and starvation.

As a girl, and later as a wife and mother, Ellis would continue to move among western mining towns for thirty years—to Silver Cliff, Querida, and Bonanza, Cripple Creek, White Pine, Denver, and Gunnison, White Horn, Bingham, and Goldfield. It was not the love of movement that kept her on the road but the search, sometimes desperate, for the means of living.

Her father was a lazy charmer, a self-styled free thinker full of schemes rarely attempted and never realized. "I believe his talents lay in getting ready to do a thing," Anne wrote of him. Soon after their second trip to Colorado, he abandoned the family.

Anne's mother, Rachel, soon remarried, this time a hard-working miner without serious vices but also "utterly without feeling." From this union Anne got several brothers and sisters. To help support them, the illiterate Rachel—tall, small-boned but strong—washed for bachelor miners and made them clothes, including buckskin shirts. She found time to make suits for her sons, underwear from flour sacks, and a new dress for each daughter every Christmas and Fourth of July. Anne's first nightgown was of canvas torn from an abandoned cabin wall. Later she sported a bustle made from a tomato can. Always, Rachel provided. At her housework she would sing:

> When I can read my ti-tul clear to man-shuns in the skies,
> I'll bid farewell to every fear, and wipe my weepin' eyes.

Anne began her schooling in her sixth year. It was often an agony. She was poor even by working class standards, and her classmates taunted her. She had no close girl friends: "I could not be a leader and they would not have me for a follower." Arithmetic bewildered her, and her passage through the school's five readers was a grim march.

But outside classes, her considerable curiosity found much to feed upon. Delivering laundry for her mother, she once snuck inside a bawdy house;

two men, "seemingly in their right minds," lounged and laughed with several pretty women in loose, lacy gowns. She was photographed with a crowd of regulars in front of the House of Lords Saloon, and she acquired a repertoire of street songs, "Don't Go To That City, They Call it Cheyenne," and

> Chippie get your hair cut, hair cut, hair cut,
> Chippie get your hair cut, short like mine.

With locals like Slippery Joe she talked of women's rights and the latest rumors of grandly named mines—the Cornucopia, Exchequer, Empress Josephine.

She found her friends among this crowd. Lil, who reportedly had nearly been sent to a "home for *encourageable* girls," was her confidante. She knew both Lil's devoted husband and her principal lover, Billy, with his flowing red mustache and his boast of fifteen years without a bath: "My skin is as white as a baby's." There was Charley Eat and the alcoholic Picnic Jim, who could play any song and imitate any animal, and J. Frazier Buck, whose Vesuvian temper inspired a certain eloquence. "Female, Hell's death traps are yawning to receive you," he told Anne's sister when she kicked rocks on him in his prospect hole. Anne's more formal education flourished here. She struggled with spelling in school, then at night devoured literary masterpieces loaned by freighters and remittance men.

School did give Anne her first and deepest love—the flat-nosed, thick-lipped, stubby-fingered Jim Chipman. Her sexual awakening was suitably Victorian, painful and sweet, progressing by gestures and sentiments fitting the era: the lock of hair, long walks, veiled affections. At dances they twirled to the calls of Butcher Knife Bill and the rhythms of the polka, schottische, Newport, waltz, minuet, varsovienne, and rockaway. Then they quarreled, and he left to look for adventure in Mexico.

Shortly afterward, on Christmas Day of Anne's sixteenth year, her mother died. Rachel had been generous and sheltering, Anne wrote later; she was, in fact, "the root, stem, and branches of my family tree." Over the next ten years Anne would marry twice and, like her mother, support her family by washing, sewing, and cooking. One husband died in a mine explosion, the other of a ruptured appendix. Diphtheria took one of her three children.

On a dare, Ellis turned to politics, but after winning three elections as treasurer of Saguache County, Colorado, she developed a severe asthma that left her an invalid for years. So she wrote. *The Life of an Ordinary*

Woman (1929), telling of her early years, was called by one reviewer "the most veracious and beautiful portrait of the American pioneer woman I have read." Two later books continued her story, but none brought in much income.

Anne was broke once again—she had to borrow train fare for the trip—when the University of Colorado invited her to receive an honorary master of letters degree in 1938. The honor did not go to her head, she said, "But, Lord! How it does go to my heart." A few months later she died in a Denver hospital. She was taken to Bonanza and buried beside her mother.

"You have brought us courage, fortitude, and determination never to lie down," the university's president had told her in conferring the degree. She appreciated that, but she was uneasy and a little shocked when some readers said they felt sorry for her. "I wish they wouldn't be," she wrote: "I'm really the happiest person I've ever met."

3

At Home

At the end of the westward journey came the next stage of pioneering—settling in. The first step, before fields were prepared or creekbeds panned for gold, was the search for shelter. The making of houses, however, involved much more than finding protection from the West's formidable weather.

For a house is a performance. Like a play, it can be observed—vicariously lived in—to learn something of its creator's values and purposes. Those who build and fill a house are telling a little about the life they hope to. live there, of the relationships among those who will occupy it and how they should behave. These messages are continually rehearsed, reminding and reinforcing.[1]

Frontier houses were especially revealing precisely because their builders were working with so little. Pioneers had to choose carefully the few items they could bring with them, and upon arrival they labored within severe limits of space and material. They had to think about what they believed, then keep it brief. The messages in their houses were reduced to basics.

But these were the statements of parents, not of children. To boys and girls, frontier houses had a different meaning. To them, a dwelling was not an expression of values already formed; rather, it was a force acting upon them as they made up their own minds about what they believed. At home children found food and rest and the other sorts of sustenance that were part of family life. The furnishings and decorations, the hundreds of details within those walls, were full of persuasive lessons the young would absorb. What came before his sod house hardly mattered, one man remembered of his Kansas boyhood. His home was "the datum from which everything else was reckoned."[2]

Most settlers' first houses could have been grouped into three categories. On the eastern edges of the plains, in much of the Pacific region,
and wherever else ample timber was found, new arrivals built log dwellings that were variations of the sort pioneers had used for generations.[3]
On many parts of the frontier, others lived in frame houses made of lumber produced by "an . . . unsung member of the pioneer vanguard," the
sawmill operator.[4] These operations were most prominent in the mining
camps, where sawmills supplied timber for mines and planks for a domestic market, but they appeared surprisingly early in rural regions, some
quite remote. Locals in the Texas panhandle gathered timber from the
Washita River and waited for occasional visits from a portable sawmill.
A traveler consequently would have grown used to "single-wall" and
"balloon frame" houses, particularly in the mountain regions but to some
degree throughout the far West.[5]

The third type of housing, sod houses and dugouts, was confined mostly
to the Great Plains, Southwest, and part of the intermontane deserts.
The classic soddie was made from large bricks cut from the soil with a
plow. These bricks, held together by a thick weaving of roots, were placed
grass-side down in overlapping layers to make walls up to eight feet tall.
A ridge pole, supported by upright beams, held up the rafters, upon which
was laid a roof of sod and, if available, tar paper. The dugout, first cousin
to the soddie, was suited to areas, like the south plains, where the soil
consistency and lack of grass did not make for durable bricks. The home
builder dug a cave into the side of a hill or burrowed several feet into a
gentle rise. Then he raised wood or stone walls a few feet more from the
excavation's edge to make a house partly underground, partly above. A
soddie or dugout could be built in a few days at a cost ranging from a
dollar and a quarter to fifty dollars.[6]

There were many variations on these basic patterns. One could see in
the subtleties of construction and decoration the ethnic and geographic
origins of the builders.[7] The pioneers, always marvelously inventive, also
fashioned houses that fit none of these categories. A family might dig
straight into the earth and cover the hole with their wagon bed, while
their neighbor might take his wagon bed off its wheels, raise a canvas
roof, and move in, perhaps for as long as a year. Some new arrivals in
North Dakota spent their first winter in an abandoned boxcar, "worse
than a coyote hole." An Oregon wife convinced her husband to hollow
out two enormous tree stumps to shelter their family of eight.

The greatest diversity was seen in those confused swarmings called
mining camps—Albert Richardson termed Austin, Nevada "a city lying

around loose"—where thousands of persons might crowd into a narrow gulch, scrambling to find protection from the elements.[8] J. Ross Browne described the result in Virginia City, Nevada:

> Frame shanties, pitched together as if by accident; tents of canvas, of blankets, of brush, of potato sacks and old shirts, with empty whisky-barrels for chimneys; smoky hovels of mud and stone; coyote holes in the mountain side forcibly seized and held by men; pits and shafts with smoke issuing from every crevice; piles of goods and rubbish on craggy points, in the hollows, on the rocks, in the mud, in the snow, everywhere, scattered broadcast in pell-mell confusion, as if the clouds had suddenly burst overhead and rained down the dregs of all the flimsy, rickety, filthy little hovels and rubbish of merchandise that had ever undergone the process of evaporation from the earth since the days of Noah.[9]

For all their eccentricities and differences, however, most frontier houses shared certain similarities.[10] They usually were rectangular or square, with each wall between ten and twenty feet long; most measured twelve to fifteen feet on a side. Families had few materials and little cash, and they had to build quickly. They had neither the time nor the resources to worry about elaborate design. Size was a compromise between an absolute minimum of living area and the simplest structural support. Given this, the square was the most efficient shape. A father who built a cabin twenty-by-twenty feet, rather than taking five feet off one wall and adding it to another, gained twenty-five square feet—nothing to sniff at under the circumstances. Thus was established a remarkably pervasive fact of life among frontier children. From the plains to the northwest forests to the badlands to the Sierra, the vast majority of pioneer families cooked, ate, slept, made love, visited, argued, and played within rectangular spaces of roughly three hundred square feet.

Inside, there were limited possibilities of arrangements.[11] Some early houses had interior walls making up to three rooms, though most consisted of one room with bunks or beds at one end, a kitchen at the other, and perhaps a table and a few chairs between. Furniture could be improvised from local materials, but not so the kitchen utensils. A goodly portion of all objects brought west to put indoors had to do with the preparation of food. A visitor to a California shack or a Dakota soddie would have seen the same items—a large bean pot, a dutch oven, flour barrel,

The Sykes family at home in Turkey Tanks, Arizona. (Courtesy Arizona Historical Society.)

and a chest for coffee and sugar. On the wall were simple shelves for eating utensils, baking powder, and a few precious condiments, and near them a skillet and coffee pot hanging by nails or pegs. For heating and cooking, most houses had traditional fireplaces. Cook stoves eventually could be carried in, though high freight rates and limited floor space demanded they be small. "I could almost put it in my pocket," a Nevadan wrote of one he bought.[12]

Not surprisingly, children and parents living in these places had many of the same complaints. Topping the list was overcrowding. The problem was worst among those new arrivals who had to stuff themselves—two, four, even six families at a time—into tiny dugouts and shacks. Elizabeth Geer's husband was dying and her children were sick when she begged space in a leaky shed at the end of the Oregon trail. Hers was the fourth family to take shelter there. Were they crowded? "You could have stirred us with a stick." Immigrants soon found their own quarters, but with only slight improvement. " 'Snug' is the only word I can think of that properly described our condition," a west Texas boy said of his first house. A Montana mother could lie on her bed as she flipped flapjacks in her kitchen. It is all the more remarkable, then, that these settlers still welcomed company into their cramped spaces. A Kansas father did, though he had to sleep on his stove when visitors spent the night. Families discovered that whatever else they could bring westward, one thing was almost always left behind—privacy. One boy described his mother and sister dressing each morning in bed, then springing from their blankets so their dresses would quickly cover them.[13]

Some hastily built houses soon came apart. A Dakota family's roof began to lift from its walls during their first windstorm; at the height of the blast, they were all hanging from the ceiling to keep it with them. Planking and logs warped and shifted. Gaps appeared in the walls and floors, then all sorts of creatures crawled and slithered through. Mice, centipedes, and spiders seemed everywhere; snakes came out of the walls, dropped from ceilings into beds. A Colorado girl learned to check under her pillow every night after finding a bullsnake curled there. Walter Posey's least pleasant memories of his dugout youth were of sleeping with salamanders, or "water dogs," that were "just about as cold as a dog's nose when he smells of you."[14]

Sod houses were by definition dirty. Inhabitants whitewashed walls and ceilings and covered them with ducking, but still a continuous sifting covered everything. Frame and log houses avoided that problem, yet because they were rarely tight—young Lucy Fosdick could lie on her bed and reach through the wall to pet her favorite cow—dirt still blew in. The problem was especially bad in mountain towns with their unpaved streets and on plains and deserts swept by terrible dust storms. "Dirt and manure and everything moveable goes in clouds," a Kansan wrote. Worst were the vicious, frigid winds of early spring. Though Susan Newcomb's house in Ft. Davis, Texas was closed securely, the howling "dry northers" sent dirt into her most tightly sealed trunks and boxes and "filled my eyes so full of dust that I could scarcely open them."[15]

Charles Oliver and his five siblings lived in a "little box house" that was "just a good windbreak, that's all." Some were not even that: "The snow falls upon my book while I write by the stove," a Kansas mother noted in her diary. Settlers flapped their arms and blew into their hands even when fires were roaring. Luna Smyer and her thirteen brothers and sisters learned basic principles of business negotiation during winters spent in their west Texas frame shanty. With the stove at full blast, they would trade toys and promises of future favors for each other's extra clothes to wear over their own. Mountain dwellers found the going tougher. A young Montanan awakened each morning to find the bedclothes frozen with her moist breathing. During winter storms, a mother in Pioneer, Arizona herded her youngsters close to the stove, and as the wind moaned outside, she would hover over them for hours to see that they did not fall against it. She propped her youngest backward in a chair, his feet through the slats, inches from the glowing iron. It was necessary. Diapers hung to dry a few feet away often froze solid.[16]

Another problem was virtually universal. Sue Summers, fresh to Arizona from California, was puzzled when new acquaintances all asked the same question: "How's your roof?" Dugouts, soddies, cabins, and shacks—they all leaked. "I never saw a finer shower inside a house before," a Nebraska traveler wrote. Grass roots opened fissures in dirt ceilings, which then dripped mud for days after a soaking. "There was running water in our sod house," as a Nebraska girl put it: "It ran in through the roof." In dugouts water also came through the walls; some far-seeing settlers dug drainage trenches across the floors. Drenched families summoned up the best spirits they could. One father lay on his bed and made "dry jokes" while holding a milk pan on his face to catch the drips. But when an evening downpour put several inches of cold water on their floor, some new Dakotans were not so chipper. Several children crowded into bed with their parents, others perched shivering on a table. One of them recalled: "Everybody was . . . in a stand-offish mood."[17]

In their discomforts and shortcomings, these early houses were lessons on the rigors of frontier life. Almost immediately, however, settlers began to reshape domestic spaces, and as they did, they revealed something of their goals in the new country. Houses grew organically, toward a purpose. A first step typically was to add sleeping space, sometimes a small side room but more often a loft or half story for the children. When confined indoors, youngsters could play there out of the parents' way, and during cold stretches the rising heat would keep them warmer. The family thus achieved a bit more privacy and breathing room.

Most changes were devoted to making the house a more efficient workplace. To increase the working area of the kitchen and keep the house cooler, a lean-to often was built off an outside wall, or perhaps an adobe or dugout a few steps from the door. Nearby would be a woodpile or shed in wooded areas and a "chip house" on the plains, perhaps a well and, for the luckiest, a spring house, with its water-beaded damp to keep butter and other perishables fresh for the table.

As for animals, those crucial sources of food and power, settlers were almost as concerned with their shelter as with their own. "I dug a mansion, a stable, and a hen house on the south bank of the Solomon River," a Kansas homesteader wrote.[18] Some European immigrants followed the old world practice of living in connecting rooms, cheek-and-bristle, with their pigs, cattle, and sheep. Even the most squeamish settlers gave their beasts harbor from the harshest storms. (There were drawbacks: one man awoke during a cold snap to find a calf had eaten his only pair of pants.) But most built some sort of sod or log barn close enough to reach in the fiercest blizzard. A hen house and an outbuilding or cellar for storage were equally useful.

The houses of the mining towns grew in similar ways. A typical home soon had a sleeping loft and, outside, a garden and work yard. Probably nearby was a shed that was at once a collecting place for ashes and fat for soap, a work shop, a kitchen and laundry, and a storehouse for ore samples, boots, snowshoes. There were adjustments to the setting. One father put his house on jackscrews so it could be raised above debris washed down from hydraulic mining.[19] A front fence might be built to keep infants from wandering off, though nothing else cut families off from the life of the streets. Survival depended on an economic intimacy with the town. Fathers worked the diggings; mothers cooked and washed for men without women; children ran errands and scoured the hills for food.

In a mining camp or on a frontier farm, the domestic setting spoke to children of the primacy of work and of the intricate ways a family was bound to the world outside the doors. Inside were domestic utensils, rifles for hunting, and smaller tools used in the fields and mines a short walk away. From the window could be seen a garden and perhaps a cow, which would feed the family and produce income to help buy field seed or work boots or more land. These evolving houses were more than shelter. They showed how settlers were reaching out to establish a hold, and their details were reminders of the labor, interwoven and unavoidable, that all family members faced.

The most noticeable changes spoke of another purpose, one equally important to adult pioneers. As they made these houses into better workplaces, parents, especially mothers, were also trying to transplant cultural traditions and preserve ties with the past. The home was the main arena of that struggle.

Since children had little or no knowledge of the past their parents hoped to save, they did not feel this urge. True, they recognized some shortcomings of their surroundings. "The total effect can best be summed up by the word *crude*," Nebraska's Charley O'Kieffe thought of the spare furnishings of plains houses. A young girl like Anne Ellis felt oppressed by the rawness of her cabin home, in which mountain rats quickly moved in behind the ducking tacked to the ceiling to hold in the dirt. Anne's exasperated mother once stuck a fork through the canvas. "The blood dripped through, and I cried," Anne remembered, "not because I was sorry for the rat, but just at the sordidness of it all." She fled to a hillside and stared at the sky, relieved, "knowing that nothing dirty will drop into my eyes."[20]

Compared to their children, adults defined their houses' limitations out of a broader context. Interiors were not just simple or sordid; they lacked particular refinements that stood for a proper ordering of their families' lives. Some despaired at their first sight of their new homes. Albert Reed's mother burst into tears when she saw her dugout, declaring she would not live like a prairie dog. Other children told of their mothers' depression and pathetic attempts to add touches of refinement. Most women, however, were troubled yet determined. Carrie Robbins at first found her Kansas soddie "low, dark, gloomy," but she took heart: "I think I can make [it] home-like."[21]

"Home-like"—the phrase was full of meaning. It summed up the Victorian woman's obligation to make of her family's dwelling place a proper setting for fulfilling her moral responsibilities. During the last half of the nineteenth century, wives and mothers were increasingly expected to bear the burden of upholding and teaching ethical standards. The home was perceived as a haven from a corrupt world and as a school for lessons in refined living. The size and arrangement of a house's rooms, the objects set on its tables and hung from its walls, the face it presented to friends and strangers—all these declared a family's values.[22]

Many parents pictured themselves as moving into something like a cultural void, and they were especially sensitive to this dimension of housemaking. Of course they worked under severe restraints, for compared to what they had left, most would be living in smaller spaces with few furnishings. Just when the challenge was the greatest, they were denied most of what they needed. The Eckles family of Silver City, New Mexico, learned this lesson when the father went ahead and secured a one-room adobe house; when the rest of the family arrived, they had with them all that had filled the fourteen-room house they had left behind.[23]

Usually mothers began by partitioning the space under their command to replicate something like the home's traditional arrangement. Sarah

An emigrant wagon, heading overland to the Pacific coast, was arranged into parlor and living room. (Courtesy of National Archives.)

Royce saw the impulse even in the emigrant camps along the Missouri River, where travelers hauled out furniture and set it "in a home-like way" among trees, logs, and bushes that suggested the contours of a kitchen or sitting room. A teenager on the road to California was surprised when she stepped into the tent of a fellow traveler: It "had to be fixed just so. It was just like stepping into a parlor." In the first cramped family quarters at the end of the road, blankets and canvas were hung from the ceilings to simulate walls, the "first gesture toward the home-making which she was desperately resolved to achieve," a daughter remembered of her mother.[24] A basic order was thus established.

Pioneers then worked with these spaces, beginning at the bottom. "Mother disliked sweeping her floor with a hoe," one boy wrote. Others also found dirt floors uncomfortable and humiliating. Some brought carpet with them, but most scrambled for replacements. An Oregon woman made a loom from a trundle bed and hoop skirt and wove a bright rag carpet from linen twine and cloth scraps. Lacking cloth, some settlers covered their floors with animal hides or even large pieces of green peeled bark.[25] The subdued colors of the landscapes oppressed some newcomers, who decorated their interiors with any scraps of color available to offset the tans and ochres outside. A mother in the Texas panhandle set up a jar of beet-stained vinegar, "the prettiest thing I ever saw," to brighten her dugout.[26]

New nineteenth-century architectural styles featured banks of windows that flooded interiors with light. Pioneers who had known such places naturally found their new houses, with one or two windows or none at all, close and gloomy. As soon as possible they punched holes in their walls and hung shades or curtains. One mother made curtains by bleaching flour sacks and embroidering them with tiny cardinals. These mothers were hoping that their children would see at least a shred of the way things ought to be. A visitor to a low, windowless Montana cabin reported a poignant case in point. On the floor was a wagon cover and a small piece of Brussels carpet, and on the log walls, where windows should have been, hung printed shades.[27]

The walls of soddies and dugouts were covered with canvas or ducking that held in the dirt; drafty frame houses were lined with cheap cloth, calico if it was available. These practical measures were also gestures of gentility, a veneer over a new life's rawness. Some added another layer of newspapers and pages from periodicals. These too were excellent insulators and even more explicit links to places left behind. English immigrants to Kansas put up illustrated papers from the home country; many homesteaders favored hometown newspapers and *Godey's Ladies' Book*. Houses thus could offer a remarkable selection. On the walls of a Kansas dugout were copies of the *New York Ledger*, the same city's *Tribune*, the *Fire-side Companion*, and weeklies from several states. A tourist high in the Rockies slept in an isolated cabin papered with the *Phrenological Journal*.[28] Links with an earlier time had been established, however tenuously, and these places now were called "neat and . . . quite warm" and compared to modest houses of New England suburbs. It happened quickly. After an arduous plains crossing, Lucy Cooke, her husband, and young daughter moved into their new house in White Rock, California, only a week after construction began. With walls lined with calico and the ceiling muslin-covered, "so cozy we felt, and happy."[29]

Looking into these houses, one could instantly distinguish between bachelor quarters and those of families. Men on their own often could fit all their belongings into a chest or knapsack. All other things were "useless extravagances," one thought. Yet when such men told their wives what to bring west, they listed a variety of furniture, utensils, creature comforts, and many items of little practical value. Emigrant guides similarly told a solitary man to pack only what he needed to scrape by, then advised a family to take much more—not only cooking paraphernalia but also a chamber set and mirror, clock, shoe brushes, a portfolio, and a collection of "interesting books."[30] The distinction was clear. A man on his own needed only the means of physical sustenance, while a family was the basis of a social order whose survival demanded artifacts of civilized life. Working under restraints of space and expense, pioneers carefully chose what meant most to them in this transplanting of tradition.

Consider a typical list. Almost always there were some small items linking settlers with a specific past—framed photographs of parents and relatives and painted scenes from the home country. Nearby was a mirror, another piece of family heritage laden with personal memories. Usually it was hung among pictures of distant loved ones, so those who saw themselves reflected would be reminded of their parent stock and of the need to "keep up appearances."

There was also a clock. Timepieces, rarely seen in American houses before 1820, were commonplace when pioneers began moving into the Far West. Although town dwellers and market-oriented farmers needed clocks to coordinate their lives with the world around them, frontier families were concerned mostly with the coming and going of the sun and the seasons. It would seem a clock was hardly worth the effort spent to bring it. Yet there it sat, perched prominently on the wall. By these years, a clock had become a cherished part of familial tradition, passed from parents to children who had grown up winding it, studying its details, playing and sleeping with its reassuring tick and chime at the edge of their consciousness. It was a link of both sound and sight. Handed down through the generations, it proved that though individuals died and dispersed, the family as a bond of blood and love was intact. The ticking of a clock was a family's pulse.

These items were deeply personal. They encouraged private thoughts among those who looked and listened to them. Other articles connected the family as a group to a common past. At mealtime parents and children ate food from dishes given by grandparents and packed carefully in flour barrels for the trip west. Covering the table might be a meticulously embroidered cloth, a daily reminder of the care of the one who had made and given it. Rising from the table, adults and youngsters could move, usually in only a few steps, to an area of lounging and relaxation. Here was a house's cultural inner sanctum, consecrated to the family

These Kansans crammed their well-built dugout with necessities and an assortment of Victorian house stuffings, including china, mirrors, and a birdcage. (Courtesy Kansas State Historical Society.)

bond and filled with objects of special resonance. Sarah Royce arranged her one-room cabin's furnishings to outline a kitchen, bedroom, and dining room:

> But the parlor—that was my pride. There was against the wall a small table, covered with a cloth and holding a knick-knack or two, and a few choice books, and some papers. There were two or three plush-covered seats, which Mary [her daughter] and I called "ottomans." Their frames were rough boxes, which I had stuffed and covered myself. The rocking chair, when not required near the stove for baby, was always set in the parlor beside the table, suggesting leisure and ease. . . .[31]

Here fathers and mothers, daughters and sons would pass time together, reading, talking, and playing games, all in a setting ostensibly little different from one in Vermont or Ohio.

Included in many of these scenes were musical instruments. A guitar, violin, or banjo could be brought west without much trouble. Almost as common were others—pianos, melodeons, and parlor organs—that demanded a substantial investment of money and energy. A Colorado-bound family packed their piano beneath the tents and supplies in their farm wagon, and though they later cast off much of their furniture, the piano stayed. Others sent for these instruments as soon as they could, like the mother who had her Steinway freighted to her remote New Mexican ranch and the Kansas homesteaders who hauled a new organ the last hundred miles from the nearest railhead. The plink and wheeze of such music was heard in most unlikely places. Elinore Stewart was entertained on an isolated Wyoming ranch by a young girl playing a battered organ. Some of its keys had fallen mute, others keened and moaned "entirely outside the tune," but the small audience beamed and sang along.[32]

Bulky, expensive pieces of musical furniture were of no apparent help in surviving and prospering. To the contrary, they consumed a good bit of two precious resources—space and money. Anne Ellis's parents could barely pay for her shoes, yet they still sold a cow to buy a sixty-dollar organ that none of the family ever learned to play. The children loved to pull at the plugs, making thunderous rumblings that sent shivers up their backs and soft, low sounds that reminded Anne of roses and of cows chewing their cuds at twilight. The organ "gave such an air to the Front Room."[33] As she hinted, the open splurge of funds and space was part

A Nebraska ranch family has hauled out the family pride, a parlor organ, to be photographed among signs of economic accomplishments. (Solomon D. Butcher Collection, Nebraska State Historical Society.)

of the point, an announcement that a family had risen to some economic and social respectability. Parlor organs—impossible to miss and widely advertised at a fourth of a piano's price—were especially favored. Moreover, music has always been one of the most effective means of preserving tradition. Families sang songs celebrating prevailing values and sentiments; familiar melodies and lyrics triggered memories and reinforced emotional links with distant places. Music as literature and singing as ritual—together they drew the family together and connected them all with so much so far away.[34] No wonder, then, that a wife in western Kansas cherished her piano as her "one link with luxury and life Back East," and a plains tourist found in a dugout's parlor organ irrefutable proof that "frontier settlers . . . [are] capable of extending a desirable civilization into the wilderness."[35]

That wilderness had other limitations. James Price found the Kansas plains magnificent, "but one thing was lacking—there was not one vestige of a green leaf anywhere," while another newcomer admitted the promised land had its drawbacks: "The worst is the want of society and fruit." But it was possible, a mountain child wrote, to tell from a distance which houses had families in them, "for about these homes were attempts at lawn and garden . . . that would make the rough little shanties remember the Eastern homes which had been so bravely left behind." Some plants had more cultural weight than others. Parents scorned such native growth as cactus—"the infernal machine of the vegetable kingdom," one mother called it—and instead tried valiantly to cultivate fruit trees, partly to provide vital nutrition but also to be sure their children would know the wonders of a fresh peach or apple. In one mountain town the local pool hall housed seedlings during the winter's worst weather. Vines were also sorely missed. One mother thought that the flora of the western country were as fiercely independent as the people: "Every plant stands on its own ground." Parents planted and pampered ivy, and beside it they set brightly colored flowers from their past lives. Shade trees were most desired. Some immigrants brought seeds and small plantings with them; others begged relatives to send seedlings of maples, elms, walnuts, ashes, and oaks. Precious time was taken from long workdays to water and care for them. The daughter of Henry Moore Teller recalled the future U.S. Senator digging a well by their house in Central City and promoting a public water system mainly to keep alive the eastern trees in their yard. These various plantings, nurtured and coddled, spoke to pioneer men and women of the way the world ought to look. Lillian Miller's mother edged her garden with candituft and mignonette, which, Lillian thought, "makes you think of old English gardens you read about in books." To a California mother, the balm-of-gilead tree her husband planted outside her window was "the first step in the way of refined cultivation," and she "watched it constantly during the day as I would a child."[36]

It was an apt comparison. Women were trying to shape the development of their houses toward an ideal, just as they hoped to mold their sons and daughters. In the rearing of their children, they believed, the domestic setting of the home was especially important. The two responsibilities, making their houses "home-like" and directing their young along the proper path, were intertwined. So homes underwent a swift evolution. It proceeded by a progressive layering—cloth and carpet upon logs and dirt, paper upon cloth, shelves and pictures and mirrors upon paper, a few pieces of carefully chosen furniture set about, books and bits of porcelain atop the furniture, and surrounding it all a garnish of imported flowers and trees.

Some were better equipped than others to make these changes. As usual, money and good transportation could make a substantial differ-

As if in similar resolve, a plains couple, their daughter, and a staked sapling, a symbol of civilized living, stand before a new soddie. (Solomon D. Butcher Collection, Nebraska State Historical Society.)

ence. Coming to their Nebraska homestead by railroad, the Roosa family carried with them a dining table and a dozen chairs, a large chest of drawers, a mirror, clock, and organ.[37] Thus rails and improved roads were more than links to the national economy; they were also umbilicals feeding settlers from their mother cultures. With enough funds, even isolated pioneers could bring much of their past with them. The prospering homesteader Elam Bartholomew retained his soddie's original construction, but he furnished it with rugs, walnut tables, deep and comfortable reading chairs, and a large library, all shipped from the East at considerable expense.[38]

Differences among homes were greatest and most visible in the richer mining towns, where the earth's wealth paid for early rail connections. At first, the newly appointed chief justice of Idaho Territory could find only a log house with one large room and kitchen for his family, though its wooden floor and partitions still put them a cut above their Bannack neighbors.[39] As towns matured, however, distinctions grew more glaring. Within a few minutes' walk of the cabins and shacks of miners and day laborers were the larger houses of modestly successful merchants and mine managers. In Empire, Colorado, one of the latter installed his family in a four-room cottage with upholstered furniture, a large bookcase, and mahogany piano.[40] Beyond them were the dwellings of the wealthiest local businessmen, engineers, professionals, and speculators. Some were Victorian showplaces quite properly the pride of town boosters. In Georgetown, Colorado, the five children of the English investor William A. Hamill, Jr. lived in a gothic mansion that included an extensive library and a solarium with a two-ton fountain. Visitors marveled at the gilded door knobs, diamond dust mirrors, camelhair wall paper, floors of polished maple and walnut, central heating system, and Italian marble fireplaces. Behind the main house were servants' quarters, stables, and offices built of native granite. Between the house and stable stood a gingerbread-trimmed, neo-gothic outhouse with a servants' entrance and six seats, walnut for the family, pine for the hired help, proof that civilization had arrived in the Rockies.[41]

These economic elites were buying more than elegant furnishings. Their money also let them construct the styles of family living that suited them. Often they distanced themselves from the moral dangers of the towns. Poorer families had to be intimately involved with the hurly-burly of the streets, while among the more well-to-do, whose wives and children typically did not have to work, husbands set the houses symbolically apart, above the mud and swirl of the business district. Two prosperous saloonmen, who "knew that our *wives* were of a *romantic disposition*," built high on a hill above White Pine, Nevada.[42] The author and illustrator Mary Hallock Foote spent her days sketching and reading in a cabin a steep walk up Leadville's Capitol Hill. She recognized neither social nor philanthropic duties to the teeming silver camp. Her only visitors were brought home by her engineer husband, and she descended into town only briefly to dine "with the mob" at the Clarendon Hotel. Once, while watching a sunset, the pair ignored a crowd threatening to lynch a thief. There was no reason to question what happened down there, "in that life which twilight covered."[43]

The daughter of a Deadwood judge later would write that her time inside such a house was "as sheltered as the courtyard of a convent."[44] Mothers had the space and time to pursue domestic obligations. The youngest Hamill children were kept in their house's nursery, the older ones privately tutored in a third-floor schoolroom. Elizabeth Fisk of Helena, Montana, entertained guests in a large parlor and a dining room adjacent to a roomy, well-equipped kitchen. Three bedrooms upstairs and one down permitted privacy and plenty of room for lengthy stays by

The children of W. A. Hamill grew up in this Georgetown, Colorado mansion with manicured lawns, plush furniture, camel's hair wallpaper, and fountains inside and out. (Courtesy Colorado Historical Society.)

friends and relatives. There were carpets, New England furniture, a large family clock, curtains, chromos, and lithographs brought in by steamboat and wagon. In the parlor and on the bright, airy porch, Fisk spent hours every day playing with her children and seeing to their lessons.[45] Evenings were filled with sheltered family companionship, much like that pictured in the diary of a Nevada businessman's wife:

> How comfortable and cozy the sitting room did look this evening by twilight. The shelves laden with books, specimens, minerals, shells. The Piano, the Sewing Machine, comfortable sofa and easy chair, with healthy, happy prattling, chipper, little children. . . . I with Guitar in hand and Mr. Chapin looking at pictures in "Home Scenes."[46]

The scene could have been in the home of a successful journalist or prominent merchant in Cincinnati or Buffalo.

These family enclaves were striking evidence of the economic stratification found on all frontiers, especially that of the mining camps. Money bought time and a degree of isolation. Parents could monitor their children closely and instruct them without much distraction. In a more general sense, however, these wealthier families were perfectly in step with the rest. All were trying to create within their walls a domestic setting dictated by tradition and conventional values. Whether outfitting houses with mahogany pianos or with newspapers on the walls, parents acted on a common impulse. Home interiors took on weighty meanings, both for those who lived there and for observers testing the cultural waters. A tourist like C. Aubrey Angelo could wax eloquent over the few books and pieces of simple eastern furniture he saw in the rough log cabins of Red Warrior City, Idaho: "Ah! what tales of past, present, and future do these mementoes bring to mind!" Especially when these spaces were graced by the sweet smile of woman and the "noisy, innocent prattle of tender pledges," he felt assured that barbarism and low habits were on the way out in the frontier's fledgling communities.[47]

A house was the one part of the frontier environment where the newcomers' control was nearly absolute. It was there that pioneers expressed themselves most clearly. A typical house told of the twin goals of adult pioneers—their desire to profit from the West's resources, and their need to bring along those parts of the past that meant the most to them. A house was a workplace that made efficient use of minimal space, and it was the frontier's densest concentration of tradition. Most children regarded their homes with affection, and they drew from them a sense of security and place. Much of the contact between generations happened within those walls, and girls and boys grew up listening to the messages built into their dwellings. Nonetheless, children did not make and transform these places. For a child, a house was a starting point, not part of a striving toward something else.

In the end, therefore, houses tell more about parents than about their sons and daughters. That is precisely why they are important in the story of frontier children. A house epitomized the intentions of adults, including what they hoped to pass on to their young. Against those intentions can be set what the children actually would do, learn, and become.

Grace Fisk

Grace Fisk was born in Helena, Montana, on May 21, 1869, the daughter of Elizabeth Chester Fisk of Vernon, Connecticut, and Robert Emmett Fisk of upstate New York. Begat of the gold frontier, she was once-removed from the certainties of the well-educated upper middle class of the Northeast.

Her father, part of a clan destined to play prominently in territorial politics, had come west to edit the *Helena Herald*, a Republican paper recently bought by his brothers. He returned east in 1867 to marry Elizabeth and bring her back to the bustling mining and commercial center that was Montana's capital. Elizabeth was a model of the genteel Yankee—schooled in Congregationalist piety, good works, abolitionism, and feminine decorum. Her values were whole and firm. But once in Montana, she found herself making subtle compromises. She set a few ideals briefly aside; she shaved others around the edges.

What, then, of her children, who would know only "this wild, wicked country," where the grossest vices were flaunted and the most basic conventions shrugged away? "Only as the ground is filled with good seed and pure thoughts can the evil be kept out," she wrote her mother. Elizabeth worried about Helena's harvest.

As a result Grace spent her first years in loving confinement, first in her uncle's house and then in the home her parents built on Rodney Street when she was two. There she was "happy as a little bird," playing in the bedrooms, parlor, sun porch, dining room, and a kitchen as large as some neighbors' houses. She sat beside her mother at the piano and sewing machine, trailed her through her housekeeping rounds. She was pampered and bright. Elizabeth called her "cunning."

Grace was also familiar with her father's world of journalism and high politics. She listened to the nightly speculations. At three, looking through *Harper's* and *Leslie's Illustrated*, she could recognize caricatures of all leading figures in the spirited 1872 campaign. "She says 'Dreeley has gone west!' " her mother reported, "and swings her hat and hurras for Grant."

As if to assure anyone wondering about Fisk standards, Elizabeth made sure that Grace kept up appearances. As an infant she wore flannel gowns with white aprons over bronze kid shoes. Her wardrobe soon expanded—white pique smocks and braided, ruffled, and lace-trimmed dresses. At four, Grace sported high-necked and long-sleeved calico aprons, cashmere wrappers, a plaid poplin, a flannel-lined blue empress jacket, and turquoise silk bonnet.

Not all of Grace's life was so easily controlled. A neighbor read to her Mother Goose stories spiced with western slang. "Must my little girl soil her sweet mouth with such words and expressions?" Elizabeth lamented. "I sometimes think I will bring her home to grandma and let her grow up in the peace and quiet of New England." By her sixth year, Grace was writing her grandmother about sledding on the streets, where she likely encountered the "oaths and other disgusting language" a journalist had heard from five-year-old boys sliding down Helena's thoroughfares. Elizabeth told of Grace finding comfort and companionship in reading at home; Grace wrote excitedly of excursions into town, especially to the Chinese quarter, where on holidays she was given firecrackers, candy, dried fruit, and small cakes. When her mother gave birth to twins in 1882, Grace assumed greater responsibilities. Her sense of independence, already well rooted, blossomed and spread.

She grew toward friends, other neighborhoods, and all the while widening her experiences. Leaving Rodney Street was natural but hardly complete. If Grace was no longer in her family's bosom, she remained in their close embrace. But Helena was her home in a way it would never be for her parents. Elizabeth negotiated with western life; Grace absorbed it. Inevitably, the daughter took up ways pernicious in her elders' eyes.

By the end of her teens, Grace was headstrong and, worse, heartstrong. She turned to painting and listed herself as "artist" in the city directory. She considered homesteading with friends instead of attending college as Robert and Elizabeth wished. Then, over Elizabeth's bitter opposition, she married Hardy Bryan, a local bookkeeper, in 1890. When Grace was four, her mother had written of the typical Helena girls whose "thoughts are [always] wandering away to the . . . present flirtation." Her words must have haunted her now.

For several years mother and daughter were unreconciled. When at last the wounds seemed to be healing, Grace surprised everyone again by divorcing Bryan. For four years she helped support herself and her son, Stanley, by working as telegraph editor and reporter for the *Herald*. In 1902, with Stanley in tow, she moved with a mass Fisk exodus to Berkeley, California, where she remarried and worked as secretary in the English Department at the University of California. She died in 1935.

4

Child's Work

She seemed a little tired just remembering. Sixty years after her childhood on a Texas frontier farm, Edna Matthews Clifton was setting down her thoughts on that time, filling more than a hundred pages with an even, precise script. She recalled happy family celebrations and the good times of play and school, but crowding these memories aside were images of a different sort—washing, mopping, soapmaking, and gardening, cutting wood, weeding, harvesting, gathering, and hunting. It would be difficult, in fact, to name any part of the family's labor that this young girl had not done. Some memories were painful. She had especially dreaded picking time. Early on August mornings, the sun already hot, the cotton and corn fields stood "like a monster" before her: "Sometimes I would lie down on my sack and want to die," she wrote. "Sometimes they would pour water over my head to relieve me." Still, Edna understood why she was there: "It was instilled in us that *work was necessary*. Everybody worked; it was a part of life, for there was no life without it."[1]

Tens of thousands of children like Edna spent countless hours doing much of the essential work of western settlement. Although their fathers' labors have long been celebrated, and their mothers' more recently recognized, the part played by these boys and girls has been virtually ignored. As long as that is the case, we cannot hope to give a fair account of how ordinary people struggled, succeeded, or merely endured on the frontier.

The work of the developing West was done in many economic settings. Consider the variety among the three examined here. The overland migration was a dash for cover. Travelers were not concerned with making money or producing at all. Their goal was essentially defensive—to survive, with the help of only a few resources, the crossing of a wild and

73

unfamiliar country. The trip above all tested their endurance and their ability to cope with the unexpected. By contrast, frontier farmers embarked on a much longer quest inspired by a more complex vision. They set out to make over the land, usually to work it in ways no one had before, and to profit by that change. This they would do by a mixture of traditional techniques and the new tools and methods of a revolution then transforming American agriculture. Their struggle went on for many years. It rewarded those who could perform a variety of tasks and adjust to changing needs—from region to region, season to season, and good times to bad. A mining camp represented yet another economic environment. In a sense it was a bit of the new America tucked away in the far western high country. The main business at hand, especially in its more complex forms, was industrial, and its workers included both independents and wage laborers. Unlike the first two, this was an urban frontier. Even the smaller, struggling camps supported cash-fueled market and service economies with an occupational diversity much greater than in the rural West.

Yet in all these settings children were essential to their families' well-being. In this, the pioneers were increasingly out-of-step with the rest of the nation. Boys and girls were working in all parts of the country, of course, but as the far western frontier was being settled, children elsewhere were beginning to be withdrawn from workplaces. In some tasks, at which the young had always labored, a new technology had made their help inefficient or even dangerous. Besides, a new view of childhood, sentimental and idealized, insisted that boys and girls be segregated as much as possible from adults. The pace of change varied according to economic circumstances, but in time the result was what one writer has called the "economically useless child," a hallmark of modern family life in both rural and urban America of this century.[2]

On the frontier, however, the child's working sphere was expanding, not contracting. The reason was simple. The needs of the developing fringe of American settlement were different from those in most of the rest of the nation, and so were the resources with which pioneers tried to meet those needs. Most families could not afford idle children.

By definition, the frontier was a place with much work to be done and few people to do it. Many settlers had left behind relatives, friends, and other sources of help outside the family. As a result, fathers, mothers, sons, and daughters all had to shoulder heavier burdens of labor. Pioneer children not only worked more; they also took on a far wider range of tasks. Back East, heavier labor and more complex responsibilities usually were given to young people only after they reached their early or middle teens. Chores were also divided by sex; girls did mostly the work of women, boys that of men.[3]

That was impractical in the new country. When only a boy or girl was available to do a necessary job, that child did it, or tried to. Sons did women's work, and, far more often, young girls moved into the realm of men—herding, harvesting, and hunting. Arduous and complicated responsibilities, from plowing to clerking, were turned over to children of seven or eight. Younger ones did jobs only slightly less demanding. "Little Baz can run all over, fetch up cows out of the stock fields, or oxen, carry in stove wood and climb in the corn crib and feed the hogs and go on errands down to his grand ma's," a Kansas farmer wrote of his son.[4] At the time "Little Baz" was two years, three months old. Among the young, the demands of the frontier ate away at distinctions of age and gender.

At the time of the frontier and ever since, most who have written about the pioneers' work have concentrated upon the tasks of "production." This term—rather misleading, as it turns out—refers to what had to be done to accomplish those goals that ostensibly had brought people westward in the first place. In the cases here, this included the creation of farms and the extraction of gold and silver. Children played a crucial part in one of these, but they barely dabbled in the other.

The making of a farm consisted of two stages, one linear and the other cyclical. The first, that of the frontier's earliest settlement, was meant to change the country fundamentally. None of the West was virgin land, for humans had been working the country and enjoying its fruits for thousands of years. The pioneers, however, planned to develop the region in their own way. Their preparation of the land usually began hard upon arrival. In forested regions, trees were girdled, the brush burned away, and a few acres cleared for a garden. Dead trees were felled over the next few years, and later the decaying stumps pulled like rotted teeth from the soil. Farmers on the plains were freed from clearing the land, but enormous human and animal energy was needed to break the sod woven thick and deep with the roots of grasses. Frequent plowing and harrowing had to follow before the soil was ready for traditional methods of planting. A farmer also had to fence his gardens and fields to protect them from foragers. In the meantime there was a house to build, as well as out-buildings for animals and storage. Economists call these first years of prodigious effort a labor-intensive period of capital formation through construction and land preparation. The settlers thought of it in simpler terms. It was grunt work, backbreaking and relentless.

Gradually, as the initial jobs got underway, families moved into the second stage. They began the many annual tasks of planting, cultivating, harvesting, and herding, looking toward that day when they could farm as their cousins did in Indiana or Alabama—though with more land and richer yields, of course. The pioneer wished the first stage done as quickly as possible, while he hoped the second would go on forever, year upon year, as the seasons unrolled and the good earth gave up its bounty.

In that early stage of rigorous labor, settlers with money often paid others to clear and prepare the land for planting. Many "traded out," helping others, who in turn helped them—good reason to settle among clusters of relatives or established friends. Many others, strapped for money or living without associates in more isolated regions, could neither hire nor swap for labor. They had to rely wholly upon the family as a working unit, and then sons and daughters toiled alongside their parents at the most physically demanding jobs of frontier farming.

Such families often arrived with only the simplest equipment. Their children's muscle power thus became essential. The father of Linnaeus Rauck had to borrow an old plow from a neighbor for the first assault on his homestead in western Oklahoma. This was tough sod. The grass had had thousands of years to grab hold of the soil. As always that first plowing left large clods and a matting of roots that somehow had to be broken up. The parents each took up an axe and gave each child a knife, then all set upon the land, hacking and chewing their way through several acres to make a seed bed for a garden and the first crop of kaffir corn. As an Arizona mother remembered, this kind of work went slowly: "It had taken 14 years of Such hard toil for Merrill [her husband] and the little boys to make that farm with its dam fences Alfalfa fields Orchard and pasture."[5]

Boys too young to cut trees and grub out brush trimmed the felled timber and piled and burned the bushes. As for the next step, girls of ten might be seen breaking sod on the large homesteads of west Texas. At eleven, Fannie Eisele and her brother plowed their family's quarter section in the Oklahoma panhandle in six weeks, and even in the Red River Valley of North Dakota, where exchange of labor was common, R. D. Crawford claimed to have begun his farming career at eleven by breaking three full sections. Crawford guessed that over the next dozen years he walked nearly thirty thousand miles behind a plow.[6]

Crawford was probably telling it with too much mustard, but his brag points up an important fact. While new equipment and techniques eventually would reduce drastically the need for working children on western farms, during the late nineteenth century technology was doing just the opposite. Even giant, steam-driven plowing rigs depended on young boys scuttling before them, pulling rocks from their path—"the hardest work I have ever done," one youth remembered. More common were steel plows of improved design that could be handled with relative ease by girls and boys, particularly once the tough plains grass had been turned under. Percy Ebbutt, who emigrated from England to Kansas at ten, compared the old and new ways of preparing the land. In his homeland, a sturdy plowman did most of the work, perhaps with a small lad to whip along horses; in the new country, "a boy can run the whole thing." With the reins around his neck and a whip in hand, Ebbutt wrote proudly, he had walked in confident command of a light plow as it sliced through the soil: "I have ploughed acre after acre . . . from when I was twelve years old."[7]

Next the fields were planted, and here children also played useful, occasionally essential, roles. Corn, still one of the most important staples of the frontier family, was planted by a system tested for generations. Children and adults—and sometimes children alone—moved across newly broken fields, gashing the clumpy soil with axes or punching it with sharpened sticks and dropping in kernels of corn with a practiced aim. Just behind came another to cover the seed with a hoe or short sweep of a foot. After a few crops the soil lost its lumps, and then even a gouge of the toe was enough to make a hole. The new tools and techniques that speeded up this process in no way excluded children. They could easily use the simple "hand dropper" that combined digging, seeding, and covering. The more sophisticated riding corn planter usually was driven by an adult, while a child often operated the lever to drop the kernels at just the right moment so the plants would line up as straight as parading soldiers for easy care.[8]

In fact there was no crop a child could not help plant. Before enough land was broken to justify an expensive seed drill, wheat and other grains were sown by broadcasting. This was a grown-up's work—achieving the right distribution of seed took years of practice—but close behind a boy or girl came with a simple harrow, perhaps only a log drawn crosswise by a horse, to cover the seed before the birds took it. Potatoes and beans were planted along rows of earth thrown up by a plow. Girls on a Texas frontier farm carried short sticks and armfuls of yam seedlings, or slips, and "with an inward curve we stuck a slip into the soft earth ever so far apart, a long step for a child, then we raked up a little dirt and stamped it down. And there!"[9]

It was in caring for the growing crops, however, that children made their greatest contributions. Fathers often drifted away to look for work during the early weeks of summer or used that time for repairs and construction. Sons and daughters then held the line against weedy invaders. Of all stages of farm production, this was the least affected by mechanization, and those who did it needed stamina and perseverance more than strength or experience. A young boy could drive a simple cultivator, or "go-devil," between the rows of a cornfield, its disks uprooting weeds and throwing a fresh layer of dirt against the young plants, but much of this work still was done by hand. Day after day in June, 1888, a Kansas farmwife left much the same entry in her diary: "The children was working in the corn field," or "The children pull the weeds." When not doing that, they served as human scarecrows. Frontier fields were defended by an army of youthful arm-flailers who did battle against the hungry cattle and the quail and prairie chickens that trampled and swarmed over the ripening crops.[10] The long hot growing season, critical for the fortunes of the coming year, demanded one of the greatest outlays of time in the annual work cycle. In many families, the children's work was indispensable.

Soon it was harvest time. Families brought in some crops by methods that had changed little for centuries. When the time came to cut and shuck corn, an Oklahoman's children took to the fields with borrowed knives. The work was "a little tough for a youngster six to eight," one remembered, and produced many cuts on his arms and legs. Still, a child could cut several shocks a day. Their cousins on the eastern fringes of the plains hand-picked cotton, and even when potatoes, sugar beets, and beans were grown commercially in large fields, they still often were harvested by children. Even in the frontier's grain belt, crops were often harvested in traditional ways, particularly on more modest farms in newly settled areas. Once cut by hand, the grain stalks were scattered on a round area that had been cleared, wetted, and packed down, then a horse or ox was marched or ridden around it to pound out the grain. Sometimes the wheat was tossed into a wagon bed and beaten out with flails. In either case the grain and chaff then were separated with the help of the wind and winnowing basket or sheet. Nothing in all this was beyond the abilities of an eight-year old, and to many frontier children, threshing became a routine part of the agricultural cycle.[11]

Many farmers, however, were eager to mechanize this kind of work more than any other, for it was physically demanding labor that had to be done quickly before storm or frost destroyed a year's efforts. Out of this came a familiar autumn ritual. Expensive harvesting and threshing machines, equipment either owned by one family or hired by them all, moved through the prairie to bring in the crops. This did not end the need for child labor. With the wheat cut, bound and ready to be stacked for the thresher, a young boy "turned bundles," placing the sheaves butt-first beside the man who would fit them together, layer-on-layer, into egg-shaped stacks. When the thresher arrived, the youngest boys drove the plodding horses around their circle if the machine was animal pow-ered, while their older brothers stood at the start and finish of the pro-cess, one cutting the bands of the sheaves while another, choking on dust and smut, cleared straw from the machine to prevent its clogging.[12]

Hay making also was drastically altered by a new technology, although here, too, the role of children was changed, not eliminated. On smaller farms boys and girls learned the haymaker's old juggling dance, cutting the wild hay with a scythe or hay knife, then collecting it under one arm and tying it with straw into a bundle. Hay grown on a larger scale was left to dry after cutting. A child then gathered it into windrows with a riding hay rake, while younger brothers and sisters "raked after," step-ping gingerly through the sharp stubble as they gathered the scatterings. These windrows in turn were heaped up by large hickory-toothed rakes pulled at each end by a horse ridden bareback by a child ("a hard seat . . . when a boy sits on it all day long!" one recalled). Even in the most sophisticated and elaborate team operations, "pull back boys" and "derrick boys" still were used in the final, crucial steps. Youngsters grew up through these changes. Andrew Crofut of Nevada's Diamond Valley had his first taste of haying at ten, and by sixteen he had learned enough to travel with professional crews for much of the summer.[13] As in all aspects of the farmer's frontier, children worked at every stage and at every task of production, from the first assaults on the land to bringing in the crops.

In another part of the opening West, however, the story was dramati-cally different. The main business of the mining frontier was looting the land of its gold and silver, and in this children were largely irrelevant.

The mining of precious metals fell into two broad categories. Placer miners searched out the dust and occasional nuggets of gold eroded from their original deposits into streams and ancient gravel beds. This was the simplest and cheapest way to get gold, and so it was most within reach of the ambitious hardware clerk out on his own. It was also the least productive, for placer miners, after all, were gathering crumbs from the table. Most of the richest camps depended instead upon lode min-ing, in which ore was taken from its "mother" deposits, the veins of gold and silver lacing the mountains. Although lode mining promised far greater profits, it also demanded a staggering investment to locate, extract, and process the bonanza. A typical miner in such a camp was a wage laborer in an industrial enterprise not so different from a worker in a Maine glass factory or a Carolina textile mill. These two ways of finding and extracting wealth were quite different. In neither, however, did children play much of a part.

The simpler forms of placer mining, it is true, were within the abilities of even young children. Five-year-old Emma Jane Davison and her brothers, two and seven, amused themselves by working the creeks around Placerville, Idaho, in 1863. Their mother had made them a rocker, a common mining tool, and Emma would move it back and forth as one brother shoveled in the gravel and the baby poured in water from a tomato can. While the best claims were grabbed early, the children's special status permitted them to get close to the booty. The young Montanan Mary Ronan and a friend arrived each evening as the men were leaving their claims. With their hair brushes they teased out the fine gold that had sifted into the cracks of the sluices. It was a rare privilege: "A man would have entered another's sluice box at the risk of being shot on sight, but it amused the miners to have us little girls clean up after them." Slightly older boys occasionally worked as day laborers. F. M. McCarty was shoveling gravel in a placer operation at eleven. Some children followed the golden trail one step farther. The precious dust, washed out of its home in the mountains and picked up by sourdoughs, often was taken directly to stores and saloons, where, inevitably, some was dropped during transactions. Boys and girls would wash the refuse under sidewalks and the dirt swept out of emporiums, groggeries, and whorehouses. There, they discovered, were the real bonanzas.[14]

In one sense these children stood for something remarkable. Barely past infancy, they were independent operators in a semi-industrial enterprise. But it is easy to make too much of this. The dust they mined represented an infinitesimal part of that taken from the diggings, and it could not have made much difference to the family economy. Though some pitched in for family expenses, most spent their dust in other ways—for rock candy, a pet goat, and some raisins as a Christmas gift. Only foolish parents counted on that income.[15]

As for lode mining, its physical demands and grave risks kept the children almost entirely out of it. Some did work along the fringes. They hauled water and cared for the horses and mules that pulled the ore carts

Though they did not take part in the main labors of mining, boys like this one in Victor, Colorado, could help with odd jobs up top. (Courtesy Amon Carter Museum, Fort Worth, Texas.)

and wagons; they picked up tools, hung up brass for the time keepers, and helped freight the machinery and supplies that fed the elaborate operations. In the mining itself, however, boys stepped in only on the verge of manhood, and even then they usually were taken in by older men who showed them the ropes. For Frank Crampton, it was John T. and Sully, two veterans he met on the road after running away from home, who led him into the dark stopes of Cripple Creek at sixteen. They introduced him to shoveling ore, or "mucking," and to single- and double-jacking, the pounding of steel drills to make holes for blasting. "Neither were jobs for softball players," he noted. The letters of Walter Smith, thirteen, give us a rare look at this initiation as it was happening. When Walter took a job as an assistant mine cook in Tellurium, Colorado, the workers took a liking to him, and within two weeks he was below ground. He handled the sledges, carried rocks, and learned some of the blacksmith's skills, all the while becoming fast friends with the miners. Soon he was describing his life with the spirit of a seasoned working stiff.[16]

These boys needed the men around them much more than they themselves were needed, however. Smith weighed only ninety-five pounds; he could not have been much help when he hefted and swung hammers weighing a tenth of that. The miners who taught boys their trade acted out of an amused admiration for the youngsters' independence and grit. It was a familiar impulse—affectionate, paternalistic, pedagogical—found in societies with many older persons and few younger ones. The stories tell something of the attitudes of the mining frontier, but they have little to do with the labor needs of the business. From its simplest to its most highly technical forms, the production of mineral wealth could have proceeded perfectly well without anyone under the age of fifteen.

In farming and mining, then, the value of working children varied enormously. It would be a grave mistake to stop here, however. There was much more to the family's economic life than the work considered so far. Throughout the frontier, even in the mining towns and the most commercialized farming regions, families had to provide much of their own food and other necessities. The so-called work of "production" in fact depended upon a wide variety of other labor, much of it highly productive in its own way. This was the "subsistence" side of the family economy. Its burdens rested heavily upon shoulders of women and children, the latter in particular.

Most obviously, sons and daughters spent long hours helping to plant, chop weeds, and gather produce in family gardens. A typical farmer had barely unpacked his wagon when he began clearing and plowing a few acres, and except in the frostiest mountain country, where locals claimed the two seasons were winter and the Fourth of July, mining families also set out several rows behind their cabins. Once the ground was broken, the men usually turned the work over to wives and children, who spent an hour or two each day cultivating corn, tomatoes, cabbages, squash, beans, turnips, melons, and other vegetables.[17] Having weeded and battled crows in the fields, children turned their skills to these gardens as well. It was important business. Everyone knew that failure could leave dinner tables bare indeed.

This was only one way the family fed itself, however. Modern accounts of frontier farm life ignore almost completely another important source of food—the gathering of wild plants. An extraordinary bounty was waiting to be picked up, greenstuff and fruits that added a healthy diversity to the diet. This was particularly welcome among overlanders who soon tired of the bland starches and preserved foods packed in their wagons. At day's end children fanned out to search for wild onions, currants, and lamb's quarters in the ravines and along the streams. Properly cooked, the result was "a symphony in eating," a boy recalled.

Near Clifton, Texas, children stand proudly before a huge vegetable garden they helped tend. (Courtesy Amon Carter Museum, Fort Worth, Texas.)

This wild harvesting was especially important in the earliest stages of farming and mining. When the fields and gardens were being prepared and the search for gold and silver just beginning—at the point, in other words, when other food and income were least reliable—these wild plants were the most abundant. Families drew upon them even later. Children learned to roam the woods and meadows as soon as productive plants began to ripen. Along the watercourses they looked for black and red haws, fox and winter grapes, "creek plums," dewberries, elderberries, chokecherries, and many others. In open areas there were tasty and nutritious weeds, purslane and pigweed the most popular. Some Oklahoma boys and girls bypassed the middle step of cooking, standing on boxes to graze from the sheep sorrel that grew along the edges of their soddie's roof. Children grew up calling such things "vegetables out of place," and they lived by the motto of the O'Kieffe family: "If you can't beat 'em, eat 'em."[18]

Hunting, too, was relatively more important early on, when game was plentiful and the land less developed. According to the popular image of western life, it was the intrepid father who would use his rifle to bring home meat for his family, but in fact adult men usually were too busy at other things. Hunting became the business of older children. Just as squirrels had saved many earlier forest pioneers, the lowly rabbit fed the newcomers waiting for their first crops and the veterans who saw their fields withered by drought. Settlers in part of west Texas ate so many cottontails that outsiders called them "rabbit twisters." Antelope, deer, turkeys, geese, ducks, prairie chickens, bison, bear, and wild hogs also fell under the pioneers' guns. From Dakota homesteads to silver camps of southern New Mexico, boys did much of the stalking and shooting for their families. Girls, too, took up the hunt. Fresh to Kansas in 1871, Luna Warner soon was boasting to her diary of bringing home rabbits, ducks, turkeys, and even a stray steer she found mired beside a river.[19] Ironically, the pioneers, who believed they were civilizing the frontier, survived at first by adopting a hunting-and-gathering economy similar to that of local Indians. And children often did more than their parents to fill the family larder.

To cook this food and heat their homes, settlers used a variety of fuels. In mountain forests and along the creeks and rivers of the plains, there was wood to be hauled by wagons or worried out by horses and oxen, and in the arid Southwest there were the toughened roots of mesquite trees. This was dirty, difficult work usually taken on by men. In expanses of the treeless West, where settlers had to be more inventive, the job could be handled easily by the young. Some used twists of hay, sunflowers and corn stalks, even bison and cattle bones. One girl was sent daily to strip the bark off fence posts. The most common fuel was the dried dung of bison and cattle, which many learned to gather on the road west. The forty-niner John Clark described boys and girls filing into his camp with great stacks of chips balanced on their heads. Just arrived at her Kansas homestead, a mother wrote that "George [her son, seven] has found his calling (picking up buffalo chips or B.S. coal.)" For many children this chore began and ended each day's work, though some, in a youthful version of a cattle roundup, would set out over the plains a few times a year, the younger ones finding and stacking the bovine "calling cards" and the older tossing them into a wagon to be hauled home and piled in enormous heaps or stored in "chip houses." The young pioneers grew intimate with their quarry. Charley O'Kieffe remarked on the aesthetics of those straw-colored cakes, comparing them to matzo and Swedish health bread.[20]

Another element was essential for a family's daily survival—water. Like fuel, it was plentiful in much of the mountain West and on the Pacific

A young Montana hunter and his dog pose with their prey. (Courtesy Montana Historical Society.)

coast but all too rare in the arid heartland of the plains and Southwest. Settlers unable to locate near streams faced bleak alternatives. They could travel overland, often for miles, to the nearest creek or spring, or they could burrow as much as two hundred feet down. The latter route, shorter but more difficult and dangerous, was left to fathers and professional well-diggers. The former job was usually given to children if any were around. With barrels or lard buckets they set out, walking or riding wagons or leading horses that dragged sleds or the forked branches of trees—anything that would bring the burden home. Meat, vegetables, or fuel might be lost for a while without much damage, but there was no substitute for this cargo.[21]

The children's contribution was just as clear in their care and handling of the animals so necessary for many families' well being. These beasts—horses, sheep, chickens, pigs, and especially cattle—provided food, transportation, power to work the land, and precious cash income. Although most children heading west knew something of caring for farm animals, their experience certainly expanded during the trip. Most families took along extra oxen or mules for fresh teams, as well as cattle and horses as seed herds for their new homes. Harried and overworked, parents turned these over to the children's care. It was a solemn responsibility. A crucial part of the pioneers' hopes for a better life, these animals might stampede during a storm, fall prey to Indians, or simply wander away at night or during the day's travel. Nevertheless, W. A. Hockett was only nine when he was assigned to ride all night to urge along straggling cattle during the arduous desert crossing between the Big Sandy and Green rivers. Girls, too, learned to drive stock when adults were sick or exhausted. Watching over the stock at night was somewhat riskier. Still, when times demanded it, children were drafted even for this. At eleven, Elisha Brooks regularly took his turn with his company's men, though once as he dozed Indians stole his last two oxen. The next day he and ten others retrieved the animals.[22]

The lesson of the trails—that children could take on virtually the full care of animals—was taught again and again on the frontier. In the ranchlands, of course, raising cattle and horses was the family's main enterprise. The land, however, put a terrible strain on available manpower. When every cow needed thirty or fifty acres each year to graze, even a hardscrabble rancher with fifty head had to cover a lot of ground to watch his investment. In many parts of the West, moreover, the ranching and farming frontiers bled into one another. Settlers of the Texas panhandle, for instance, found that cultivation alone could not support them in that

At work at one of childhood's most familiar chores, this girl in the Middle Loup Valley of Nebraska probably was contributing both nourishment and cash to her family. (Solomon D. Butcher Collection, Nebraska State Historical Society.)

arid country, so they hedged their bets, raising cattle in fair numbers and becoming "stock farmers."[23] In these dry and open spaces, a son or a daughter was of great help, for though it took years to develop into a top hand or experienced rancher, the basic skills of handling cattle were learned by children still shy of their tenth year.

In fact, so many cowboys and ranchers claimed to have started their saddle education when barely out of diapers that the modern reader is tempted to suspect exaggeration; but evidence for the claim is remarkably consistent. "I was raised on horse's back; never did learn to walk good," one recalled. Bill Dobbs was riding when he was too small to reach the stirrups as he stood beside his horse; by five he was riding herd, by twelve working roundups. David Hilger trained as a herdsman on the trail to Montana at nine and began herding professionally a couple of years later. At eleven Richard Murphy left home to ride fence for the T-Diamond ranch. W. H. Childers was thirteen when his father headed farther west to ranch and left him and his brother, nine, in charge of a stock farm. Troy Cowan was barely six when his father took him on a cattle drive from east Texas to the panhandle, and H. C. Cook just ten when he went up the trail to Dodge City.[24]

Girls worked beside the boys. "It has been a novel sight to watch a little girl about ten years old herding sheep near town, handling her pony with a masterly hand, galloping around the herd if they begin to scatter out, and driving them into a corral," a visitor to Nebraska wrote. The young Dowdy sisters and their younger brother handled all the cattle on their Texas hill-country ranch. At ten, Helen Brock was riding the range, and by fifteen she was branding calves and building fences. She and her sister were nine when they broke their first horses. These jobs demanded a surprising range of knowledge. Agnes Cleaveland wrote of a neighbor, Claude, at the age of six a veteran of bovine deliveries, who was sent by his father regularly to check on the progress and condition of pregnant cows. With such an early start, skills seemed to come naturally. "They just grew up to be cowboys," a ranch mother of eastern New Mexico recalled of her sons, a little bewildered: "They didn't know any better."[25]

Yet these cow-country children were not so different from their cousins on the farms. Hamlin Garland recalled boyhood friends who could "ride like Comanches," not amid the cactus and greasewood of Arizona but the hazelbrush and bluestem of Iowa's agrarian heartland.[26] They learned to ride during thousands of hours of herding, for even in regions devoted mainly to raising crops, a family often kept a dozen or more cattle, which generally became almost wholly the responsibility of boys and girls, some as young as eight.

Early in an area's settlement, animals were grazed on the open range—that is, on land as yet unclaimed. They were kept close to the house for protection during the winter's worst, though even then there were problems. During an especially brutal Montana winter, Bertha Andersen and her three young daughters had to care for freezing sheep close to their house while the men searched for others farther away. As the thermometer fell to forty degrees below zero, "the animals would lie right down in the snow. The girls had to carry them!" When the spring grass was up, cattle and sheep were turned out upon it, there to wander more or less at will. Each day youngsters checked on them and brought in cows for milking. Then, as the land was taken up and foraging animals became a nuisance to fields and gardens, new laws forbid cattle and horses from roaming unattended. With this, the children's work grew in importance. Often they would stay with the grazing animals all day, moving them sometimes along the primitive roads between fenced fields when no other pasture was available. Well before dawn a child would bring in a horse from its picket and help milk several cows. After breakfast a child might spend twelve hours in the saddle, usually working alone, before returning at dusk for more milking, dinner, and bed.[27]

Providing the West's most precious commodity, water, often was the job of children, many of whom had to drive miles to find it. (Courtesy Montana Historical Society.)

This work also supplemented family finances. Most settlers had animals to be tended, though not all had children to take charge. To take up the slack, some hired youngsters from nearby farms, either boarding the children or turning the herds over to them for the grazing season. Thus parents with children to spare had a special advantage. At eight, Edward Teachman was herding six days a week for two neighbors, for which he got a dollar a week plus dinners—quite a help for his family, just getting started in Oklahoma's Cherokee Outlet. Between their herding and bone gathering, the Norton boys brought in most of their family's cash during their first few years in western Kansas.[28] In fact, herding was the most common form of children "hiring out" on the agricultural frontier. Many families doubtless would have been sorely strapped without the money it brought in.

The most self-reliant families needed at least some cash income to buy what they themselves could not provide—sugar, salt, coffee, and a few manufactured items, such as needles. While these goods generally cost less than a hundred dollars a year, cash was hard to come by, particularly during the early years before the family enterprise began to pay. Income from fields, a placer operation, or mining camp business, furthermore, often went to expand operations or to buy new equipment. In short, making money for daily household needs became one more responsibility of a wife and children who were doing the other jobs of subsistence.

Like farm families all over the nation, those in the West often looked to extra produce from the barnyard to fill this need. Between September 1882 and May 1883, Anne Davies marketed fifty-five pounds of butter and forty dozen eggs. Her husband also found some work off their Kansas farm, but her sales of twenty dollars still made up about 60 percent of their cash income.[29] Such work was done mainly by mothers, though children did help by gathering eggs and churning.

There were many other possibilities, distinctive to the frontier, that girls and boys pursued largely on their own. Many became "bone pilgrims." During the dozen years after 1871, millions of plains bison were slaughtered for hides that helped feed American factories then gobbling up leather for machine belts and gaskets. This left the land from North Dakota to Texas littered with bleaching bones. Shipped east, these in turn were ground up for fertilizer and made into corset stays and buttons. Children roamed the countryside, picking up animal remains to sell at the closest railhead. During their family's first years in western Kansas, the four Norton boys provided a good part of their income by combing the land for bones to sell in nearby Larned. For the Crockets of the Cherokee Outlet, spending money came from animals trapped and skinned by the six girls and six boys. Another set of sons gave some of the meat they hunted to their family and traded the rest to Indians for hides, which they then sold for necessities.[30]

While these youngsters were learning to wring money from the rural West, others were doing the same in the mining towns. Here, in fact, this money-making aspect of subsistence was even more important. Compared to their rural cousins, urban families were less able to produce food and other necessities for themselves, so they needed the wherewithal to buy them. To make matters worse, miners' incomes were notoriously erratic. At the same time, however, market and service communities offered a far wider range of opportunities to make money than the farm and ranch country. Thus it happened that those children virtually excluded from any significant roles in mining moved instead into a variety of jobs to bring in desperately needed income.

Walking the rutted, crowded streets of Grass Valley or Silverton, one would have seen youngsters handling many tasks. Bennett Seymour, in time a prominent Colorado merchant, began his career at twelve clerking for a grocer in California Gulch (later Leadville). Within a few months his boss was leaving him in charge, and the next year Bennett was traveling by wagon all the way to South Park on supply expeditions. Many like him did similar service in mercantile establishments, while others, like Anne Ellis, helped in their mothers' enterprises, in her case by delivering wash around town and to a nearby camp. Some helped clean hotels and cook for boarders. Appealing, no doubt, to his customer's homesickness as well as to his sweet tooth, Milton Barnhart peddled pies baked by his mother for a dollar apiece.[31]

Most striking was the way these children sniffed out businesses on their own. They saw quickly that food, especially the fresher sort, brought a high price from hungry men on the streets. Mary Ronan and her friends sold lamb's quarters and edible weeds gathered from gullies and benchlands around Virginia City, Montana, for a dollar and a half a bucketfull; later they diversified into wildflower bouquets for hotel dining rooms. Martha Collins and her brother cleared eight hundred dollars from a summer's sale of butter and bacon, and others hunted wild game with the same lucrative results. Jack Stockbridge walked up to thirty miles a day selling vegetables he raised. Still others worked as free-lance woodchoppers and dishwashers; some, like Martin Wenger of Telluride, left town to find work but sent their pay home. By fourteen or fifteen, boys were given jobs of surprising responsibilities and risks—such as driving a stage through Arizona Indian country and running a ferry on a Montana river.[32]

A few, particularly those from more prosperous families, moved into white-collar occupations. When no adult would take the job, thirteen-year-old Willie Hedges took charge of Helena, Montana's library society for forty dollars a month. Lee Travis and James Sanders, fourteen and fifteen, founded a weekly newspaper, the *News Letter*, in 1875, setting out in a buckboard over three sprawling Montana counties, soliciting subscriptions and hobnobbing with local editors. Most youngsters flitted among a remarkable array of commercial and manual labors. Between their sixth and sixteenth years, three mining-camp boys tried their hands at freighting, feeding mules, hunting and selling meat, hawking newspapers, peddling bills, shoveling snow from the streets, delivering milk, waiting tables, dishwashing, working in a sawmill and in a printer's shop.[33]

Young people like these were making a double contribution. They were helping relieve a labor shortage chronic in most mining towns. Though many services had to be provided, men often scorned any work except prospecting and mining or refused to work for the low pay of a bill peddler. Children helped make up the difference. Young workers also helped support their families, though exactly how much they did is not always clear. At one extreme, the young of prominent professionals and the most successful businessmen surely did not have much impact. Willie Hedges pitched in money for clothes and washing expenses, but in the light of the income of his father, a well-connected attorney and politician, the man's boast that Willie was "indispensable" seems only a bit of fatherly chest-puffing.[34] Among poorer families, on the other hand, the cash youngsters brought in probably made a significant difference. Given the high cost of living and the unpredictable income of their parents, the wide-ranging work of children no doubt provided some security in an unstable world.

A family's economic survival also depended upon a cluster of jobs done mainly in the household. Those who plowed and mined needed clothes and a place to sleep; food gathered and hunted had to be cooked and preserved. "As I look back it doesn't seem possible that I ever did the work that I know I did," recalled a mother who settled in western Kansas in the 1870s.[35] Usually this work was done mainly by adult women, for husbands did little and children usually spent more of their working hours outside the home than in it. Still, sons and daughters played their parts.

The load was far lighter for some families than others. Especially in the mining towns, the economic elite usually hired help for household chores. The Chinese servant of an Idaho family got forty dollars a month to wash, iron, cook, clean, can, and care for the yard and a horse. A Montana railroad official not only hired night and day nurses for his two young children but also paid to have all washing and ironing done. His wife wrote to assure her mother: "I don't think there is any need of anybody wasting pity for me living on the 'outskirts of civilization.'"[36] Children of the well-to-do in mining towns might chop a bit of wood, deliver messages around town, and handle a few other chores, but their contribution was minimal. In her diary, the eleven-year-old Edna Hedges, an attorney's daughter, told of babysitting, dusting, and wiping dishes, all for twenty-five cents a week and the privilege of hosting tea parties.[37] Fortunate parents like hers were apparently more concerned with apprenticing their offspring to social roles than with getting chores done.

Several rungs down the economic ladder were pioneers who lived quite differently. Whether miners, farmers, or ranchers, these families had no money for servants, and mothers were more likely to take in washing than to send it out. The frontier left them with more work to do and less help in doing it:

Tell Alice I have not forgotten her [wrote a Nebraska woman of her sister]. She must remember that she has no one but herself, husband and baby to look after, while I have the same, and two or three men some of the time, and one all the time, washing and everything to do for him. I have butter and milk to look after, am my own dressmaker and milliner. So it makes me pretty busy.[38]

Sons and daughters played their part—sometimes a substantial one—in carrying this burden.

On the trail and after arrival, the work of the household was organized by an ascending scale of difficulty. By about the age of five, some children were given virtually full responsibility for the easiest tasks. Interestingly, this included the care of infants, at least those past nursing. "Anna raised all the children with Agnes helping her along," a Montana mother wrote of two of her ten youngsters born within thirteen years. Slightly older siblings bathed and amused the babies and kept them out of mischief. When oxen failed on the trek west, they did more: "We all walked over the worse places," remembered one youngster, eleven when she crossed the Cascades, "Mother and Louvina [her sister] leading Cynthia and I carry little Elijah." The Kansan Augusta Dodge was five when she began watching her newborn sister, and soon she took over the job almost completely. Children at her age could fetch kindling and other fuel, dust, tend the bedding, and help with minor chores that added up to an appreciable amount of work.[39]

In the middle range, boys and especially girls helped at work demanding more strength and experience. While her parents chased wild New Mexican cattle for milk each morning, Meda Perry began her domestic career by cooking, though she had to stand on a chair to see over the table's edge. Edna Matthews and her sisters scrubbed their wooden floors with white creek sand and a mop made from corn shucks. Bedsteads had to be treated with kerosene to ward off vermin, windows washed, and brass utensils scoured with salt, vinegar, and ashes. The young also shared in the hundreds of hours a year spent churning, canning, and drying and smoking meat.[40]

Of all household work, the care and production of clothes probably took the most time. Two full days typically were needed for washing and ironing for a large family. It was one of the least favorite tasks of youngsters, for usually water had to be hauled to the house or the washing paraphernalia taken to a nearby creek, then fires built and the water heated. The dirtiest items were soaped and soaked and beaten on a bench with a "battling stick," the white goods boiled in a separate tub, then all of it rubbed on a hardwood washboard before a vigorous rinsing. It was a job equal in rigor to many kinds of field work, and all its veterans testified of sore backs and chapped hands.[41]

Finally, topping the scale of household labor was the making of clothes, for this required skill, experience, and time. Daughters were introduced early to this work and trained as they grew; only in their mid-teens did they take on much of their mothers' burden.[42] But as in all the frontier family's working life, children made their contributions very early. Just as they weeded so their fathers could leave in search of work, they also hunted chips and scrubbed clothes to give their mothers time for carding and sewing. The roles of younger and older meshed in an intricate, complementary system.

Simply to follow, piece by piece, the family's economic life distorts the picture. It implies that parents arriving in Nebraska or Nevada could plot their course confidently through the seasons to come, assigning this job to one person, that to another. Pioneering was never so predictable. Its veterans learned to expect the unexpected; their hopes rested in responding effectively to whatever calamities and opportunities confronted them. This placed a premium upon flexibility above all else, and in that regard, children were among the greatest resources a family possessed.

The most striking examples came on the overland migration, when the buffer between success and disaster was often as thin as onion skin. Should a family suddenly face a crisis as their resources dwindled and adults were pushed to their limits, the young were called upon to do the difficult and demanding because there was no alternative. Such a moment usually came during the last grueling weeks, as when Joseph and Esther Lyman found themselves stranded in southern Oregon after losing the way on an untested shortcut. When Joseph set out for help, his son, Luther, took charge of the sick Esther and her baby daughter, at one point nearly dying of thirst before leading them to safety. The testing of D. B. Ward, fourteen, came at The Dalles, when women and younger children took boats down the Columbia and the men hauled the wagons down the last tortuous stretch of trail. Driving the horses and cattle over the Cascades by a separate route, and in command of two others, young Ward led the way over a rugged, poorly marked trail. Although for the last thirty-six hours he was without food, he arrived with no losses.[43]

The story of Octavius Pringle, also fourteen, was more dramatic. By early November 1846, his family and their weary company had run perilously short of food while still a mountain range away from the Willamette Valley. The scenario was ominously similar to that of the Donner party, at that moment beginning to freeze and starve a few hundred miles to the south. Octavius was given the only surviving horse and sent for help. The rainy season had begun, and for three days he slogged his way through mountains to the nearest settlement, then after a night's rest he started back, leading a mare loaded with wheat flour and a bushel of peas. His despairing family, having gotten by on some tripe and a cow's head, gave Octavius a warm reception. His father noted in his diary that it was "the happiest day to us for many."[44]

On the fringes of the farming frontier, crises came less dramatically, but the pressures were almost as great. The drought of 1893 hit the Dyer family as it edged onto the south plains of Texas. That year they produced a bushel and a half of corn. "There's where we liked to starve to death," one son remembered. With his brothers and sisters he stripped the river grass of its seeds for two dollars a bushel while his father cut and sold wood. They made it through the winter and headed farther west the next year to try again. The same drought caught the Poseys to the north in the panhandle, and twelve-year-old Walter supplemented the family income by gathering buffalo bones to sell in Amarillo, though he was so small he could not take the bridles and collars off the horses without happening on an adult during his solitary wanderings.[45]

The loss of a parent most commonly thrust a youth into new responsibilities. It was not only death that took away a father or mother. Some abandoned their families, others were gone for months or even years searching for work or wandering about. Accident or sickness could leave a parent giving nothing except moral support to meet the needs at hand, and in a situation where there were no relatives or friends to help them through the hard times sure to follow. On farms and ranches the unavoidable, brutal round of labor had to be faced. In the mining towns the situation was even worse because so much had to be bought at inflated prices. Single mothers found the going especially tough, for only the least remunerative jobs were open to most of them. The divorcee Louisa Walters had a better income than most, $125 a month for teaching school, but she paid $40.00 of it for a room, and with eggs at $5.00 a dozen and butter at $1.25 a pound, she barely supported herself and her seven-year-old daughter. "This is a good place to make money," she wrote home, "and it is a capital place to spend it." Poorer mothers were not so lighthearted. A Nevada wife, left on her own for weeks by her drifter husband, spoke for many others: "I wonder what will be the end of my miserable life—only for my little children have I any hope or courage."[46]

Hard times. But in them, children like hers had more to give than just inspiration. Some were called upon to meet the immediate needs of survival, as when pressed by the ruthless timetable of the overland trail. In Oregon's rugged Cow Creek Canyon, Samuel Smith collapsed and died while exhorting others in his company to push ahead beyond the rocks and fallen trees blocking the way. His widow took charge, abandoning the wagon, parcelling out essentials among her nine children, and herding them before her. When Blanche McCullough's father died, he left a wife and twelve children crowded into a west Texas dugout with no money, almost no food, and no way to leave. Luckily a passing circuit rider taught the widow to make a cabbage-like dish by soaking the blooms and leaves of bear grass and simmering them with a little bacon. By sending her brood out over the plains to gather weeds and wild plums, she fed the family for weeks.[47]

The McCulloughs survived and stayed on. One might expect the loss of a mother or father would send most families back East to the shelter of relatives. Many did retreat, yet many others remained, adjusting, shifting roles, with the young moving to fill in where needed. This meant a rapid education. At ten, Mary Olive Gray of Silverton, Colorado, had to write her grandmother in Kansas to learn how to make biscuits, but soon she was handling all the cooking and housekeeping for herself and her father. There were even some unexpected monetary possibilities in work like hers. A bachelor, tired of housekeeping and lonesome for a woman's presence, offered to pay a widower and his two daughters one hundred dollars a month to live with him; except for cleaning the place occasionally, he promised, "they could do just as they pleased." (The suspicious father declined the proposal.) Most who took on a mother's work, however, shouldered a terribly heavy load. When her mother was blinded by lye while scrubbing floors, Mamie Rose of Silver City, New Mexico, found herself doing all cooking and housework for a family of fifteen. She was eight. Her story, at least, ended on a victorious note. With ten years of this life behind her, she launched a successful career in an obvious field—catering.[48]

In filling a father's role, boys would have gladdened the heart of the most ardent frontier go-getter. R. T. Alexander's widowed mother homesteaded a ranch on the Washita River high in the Texas panhandle, but until the venture began to pay, R. T., thirteen, had to support her and four younger siblings. The first season he cut wild hay in the river bottom and carried it thirty-five miles to sell in Mobeetie. Come winter, he and his siblings scoured the land for bones, which brought eight dollars a ton when hauled far across country to the town of Canadian. Two years of this cleaned the land of the woolies' skeletons, and R. T. turned to a career in freighting. Throughout these years he had provided all the family's meat by hunting rabbits, prairie chickens, and deer and had made extra cash by selling wild turkeys shot during forays into Oklahoma.[49]

Young people found seemingly limitless possibilities to meet these staggering responsibilities. They ranged across the full spectrum of work common among frontier children while they made the chancy decisions that were part of the adult world. After breaking, planting, and harvesting an Oregon wheat farm for their mother and three siblings, the eleven-year-old Martha Collins and her younger brother took a speculative plunge by buying two dozen wild Mexican cattle. They broke them for milking—a risky undertaking—and peddled the milk and butter for a tidy profit. The market economy of the towns held out all sorts of opportunities. For Mose Drachman, eight when he quit school to help support his fatherless family of eleven, it was advertising auctions on Tucson's streets ("Remate! Zapatos muy barrato!"), an apprenticeship for his career as a prosperous Arizona merchant. Fifteen-year-old Joseph McDonald hawked newspapers and fought in boxing exhibitions to feed himself and his mother during Goldfield, Nevada's boomtime. When news arrived of a strike at Rawhide, he joined the rush and soon made enough to send for his mother.[50]

A letter written by a newly widowed mother suggests how children like these—inventive, savvy, assertive—could form a web around a parent, supporting and protecting her or him in a time of troubles. "Kate thiss has bene a very harde winter on us . . . ," Mary Brophy wrote a married daughter from Oregon. "You dont know what a lonsome time I have." But she had help:

> henry sold the sorel Colte for to yearlen heifers and astear and six hed of hogs I have three hefers one I louve henry had eleven hed of hogs Ellen has eleven hens setting she has fifteene little chickens I have a very good garden in the crops looke very well here. . . . Andrew has worked as hard as enny on coulde the children are agoin to school. . . . Andrew started this morning of to work he will be a way two or thre weaks . . . the children are at school Andrew is away I have every thing to look after there is no on hom with me to day but Charls Jef and little Nicholas[51]

There is a complex family story in this stream of consciousness. Andrew, apparently the oldest, who had been home working "as hard as enny on coulde," had gone away looking for extra income, much as a father would. Henry and Ellen, presumably the ones at school, had taken charge of the animals, and the former had done a bit of horse trading. That left Mary with much to do, including the care of her three youngest, but with the three older ones taking on both work and responsibilities, the family was surviving. Near the letter's end, Mary managed a note of classic frontier optimism: "If we can get a long till harvest I think our hard struggle is over."

The families that invaded the Far West faced an extraordinary range of work in an unfamiliar, often threatening land. Survival and success, if they came at all, were won by all family members working together. Husbands and wives depended on one another, and both relied heavily on their sons and daughters.

Children, in fact, were the frontier's most versatile workers. They helped in the celebrated labors that transformed the land, they did even more in subsistence and household work—unheralded tasks upon which all else rested.

The children's greatest contribution was the gift of adaptability. Families moved from one place and occupation to another; their needs varied greatly from season to season and from drought to storm. Time, even in small increments, could bring dramatic changes to the developing West. Rewards usually came to those who could adjust most easily to the widest array of challenges—and that was precisely what the children allowed. The twelve McCullough children gathering bear grass to stew, R. T. Alexander hauling hay and searching for bison bones, Joseph McDonald brawling to pay the bills, the Dowdy sisters herding cattle—these stories are among the most heroic of westward expansion, homely epics that deserve to be remembered.

As they played an indispensable part in western settlement, they helped create a modern region and boost the nation toward power and affluence. Until their accomplishments are recognized, we cannot begin to understand the economic and human dimensions of western history.

T. W. Dobbs

T. W. Dobbs spent three months of his life's first year on the road, howling with the colic as he rolled in his parents' wagon from Texas to Arizona. He later believed that this determined his life's course. Boy and man, he would be prone to strong opinions and to moving as much as staying put.

His father, Elijah, a Kentucky unionist, had come after the war to Marshall, Texas, where T. W. was born in 1877. A farmer and freighter, Elijah was drawn to the modest boom Arizona enjoyed on the eve of the big bonanza at Tombstone. T. W. spent his earliest years in Tucson. There his clearest memories were of food his mother cooked in the fireplace of their adobe house. She wrapped potatoes in cloth, covered them with clay, and set them on the hearth close to the fire. Cracked open later, they were delicious. He loved as well the cactus fruit his mother stewed and made into preserves. T. W. was emphatic, however, that his finest eating was a cow's head, also rolled in clay, that had been thrown, with the hide and hair still on, into a pit to bake.

Though T. W.'s father put little stock in education, his mother was determined that her children would have at least some learning. She used her rare spare hours to teach them a few fundamentals, and when T. W. was six she sent him to school. On his first day he lost, badly, a schoolyard brawl. Then, when the teacher whipped him for fighting, he "talked to [her] as I had heard the drivers talk to the mules." She in turn sent him home with a note for his mother, who read the news and beat him for cursing. "I think the reason I never did better in school was due to the bad start I got," he later reflected.

Nonetheless his mother would enroll her children in classes whenever they paused long enough in one place. That, as it turned out, was infrequently. The elder Dobbs led the family out of Tucson in 1886, hoping to freight his way to fortune among the Colorado mines. He tried Durango a while, then Ouray. He worked in St. Elmo and Aspen briefly before moving on to South Park, Colorado Springs, Walsenburg, Rouse, Trinidad, Rico, and finally back to Durango. Only in Colorado Springs was T. W. in the same classroom for more than a few months. Finally, still in the fifth grade at fifteen, Dobbs was allowed to end his formal education. Precipitating the decision, he recalled, was a fire that destroyed the Durango school, *"but I did not do it."*

In the meantime, he learned to handle animals, repair wagons and harness, and cut timbers for railroads and coal mines. When the silver crash of 1893 triggered a depression that devastated the mountain West, he learned lessons in basic economics and human nature. "Hungry people will do strange things," he wrote, recalled his enlisting at sixteen in Coxey's Reserves. He could not understand how the government could turn away from men like his father who had risked everything for the union. Vowing to support Coxey's Army as it marched on the national capital, T. W. and his friends tore limbs off trees to practice the manual of arms under the command of a Civil War veteran. They marched to an anthem of defiance:

> Are you tired? Yes, we're tired
> Of the yoke that we wear.
> We are fainting, we are falling,
> For the yoke it is galling.
> Yes, we're tired of the yoke that we wear.

A few years later, Dobbs and many of his fellow rebels were lining up in full patriotic blush to volunteer for the crusade against Spain.

T. W. would be a working man all his life, traveling around the West and laboring through good times and tough ones. After another, more withering economic calamity in the 1930s, he concluded that "the big interests can cause a panic or depression any time they think that the people in general are getting too rich." Nonetheless, his memories, except of school, were happy. In later years he was fond of pointing out that of his parents' six children, he had been the skinniest, most sickly, and the last to walk, yet he had survived them all.

5

Child's Play

Somewhere along the Platte River in the summer of 1841, there occurred the West's first recorded ox-bouncing competition. Boys from one of the earliest parties along the Oregon trail came across a dead ox, its paunch swollen tight with gasses of decay, and somehow they discovered that if they jumped against the animal's bloat, it would fling them vigorously back. Champions rose and fell as boys ran faster, jumped harder, and bounced farther. Finally, Andy, a long-necked redhead, backed off a great distance, lowered his head, sprinted, leaped—and plunged deep into the rotting carcass. His friends pulled him out, though with some difficulty, and the contestants went on their way, the observers with a good story, Andy with a deeply entrenched memory.[1]

Frontier children at play were worth watching. Indeed, no part of their lives was more revealing than the ways they amused themselves. Like Andy and his friends, youngsters found fun and diversion in a variety of forms and under the unlikeliest circumstances. Their games and romping were not simply an escape, however, for play was part of their most practical concerns. They found in it an encouragement in their difficulties, a help in understanding, and a flexible tool in adapting to the special demands of the western frontier.

The many kinds of children's play could have been grouped roughly into four categories. The first was the play of exploration, a prominent part of life from infancy through adolescence. During a baby's first few years, in fact, play and discovery of the immediate environment are virtually one and the same. An infant grabs anything within reach and gawks at it, tastes it, thereby practicing physical coordination and learning to discriminate among objects. As he instinctively tests his surroundings, he has his first try at forming concepts and remembering. Exploring play continues for years in more sophisticated and adventuresome forms. Through it, the young mold their mentalities and come to identify with the place in which they find themselves.[2]

This play was especially significant on the frontier. Just as children's work shaped them in distinctive ways, so their amusements naturally drew them apart from their parents. The young were establishing a frame of reference for the rest of their lives, but the setting was the developing West, not the world their elders had known. Thus play helped separate and define the generations.

The process began immediately. Adults on the overland trails wrote, with some irritation, of the seemingly limitless energy of the young. Inside the wagons boys and girls squirmed and picked up everything around them, and, as soon as they could, they jumped out to explore the scenes they had been watching for hours. Tired and harried parents noted only that "all [is] well, and young ones in high glee" and that "the children is grumbling and crying and laughing and hollowing and playing all around." Along California's Feather River, at the end of the long passage, J. Goldsborough Bruff saw them "laying and playing on the green sward, happily unconscious of the troubles of others."[3]

They were doing more, however. Theirs seems to have been a passionate investigation. The very young examined the tiny details within their grasp—colored pebbles, hailstones, everything. One mother panicked when she could not see her two-year-old after setting him in the dirt to play. Soon she found him where he had burrowed himself out of sight in the deep dust of the road. Slightly older children took off to pick wildflowers and chase prairie dogs; they searched for animal bones and tasted the gum that oozed from trees. Lucy Fosdick noticed that older travelers soon tired of the trip, while she and her friends never did. There was so much to see, so many new experiences. These times were "a never ending pleasure," one wrote later.[4]

This irrepressible urge continued after families reached their destinations. While some of what the young found frightened them, much excited their curiosity. "A happier set of children I think I never saw," a mother, newly arrived in Kansas, wrote her relatives: "Johnny [two] goes 'yout' [out] to his hearts content." They were everywhere—gathering fossils, pottery shards, snakeskins, beetles, and animal dung. They caught (and usually executed) snakes, centipedes, and tarantulas. Older children soon were manipulating what they found with seemingly endless invention. Allie Wallace made hats from cottonwood leaves and balloons from pig bladders. A party of young Nebraskans turned some muskmelon rinds inside out, strapped them to their feet, and skated around their cabin floor.[5] As children will, some found more than they bargained for. While an Arizona mother was hanging out her clothes, her daughter, three, was investigating some mesquite roots nearby. The girl's scream and the whirring of a rattlesnake came simultaneously. The horrified mother kicked away the rattler and snatched up her daughter, asking in terror if the snake had bitten her. "No," the girl sobbed, "but it said it would."[6]

As the older youngsters roamed outward in expanding circles, gathering knowledge with growing confidence, they developed a deepening affection for their surroundings. The memories of a woman growing up in Montana's Deer Lodge Valley were dominated by

> fields of wild hay . . . , or gathering, with my brother, bright colored stones in the dry gulches for playthings. . . . From early March, when the snow was disappearing and the first flowers beginning to bloom, until October, when the hardiest fall flowers and the autumn leaves covered the mountain sides with treasures, I with my brothers and sisters roamed the mountains and hills and explored the streams for miles in every direction.[7]

Mining town children could choose between the urban wilderness and the countryside beyond. "We spent our leisure playing in the back streets or learning the haunts and names of the wild flowers," Mary Ronan said of Alder Gulch. Boys prowled around mines and back streets and then headed for the hills to sight a bear or puma. To Carolyn Palmer, "our real books were the sagebrush plains" around Boise. Yet she and her friends also loved the streets where they were scared by free-roaming bulls and charmed by Indians, miners, and soldiers: "What a picturesque tableau it all made."[8]

These descriptions often are richly sensual. This was predictable, since the children's feelings were based on an intimate physical contact that occurred as their perceptions were still evolving. A girl of the California camps, for instance, would slip outside in deep winter to sit under a fir and scrape away the snow so she could feel and look at the earth, smell it and hold it to her skin. An Arizona boy would write later that he loved "the familiar damp, the blasted rock smell" in the mine tunnels where he played.[9]

As with all the children's especially pleasant memories, those of play must be taken cautiously. No doubt the passage of years lightened the facts. Still, the abundance of happy recollections of exploring play suggests that they were based in a measure on genuine pleasures.

That the children chose to emphasize this part of their lives hints at something more. Their parents had set them down in the environment at that stage when sensations of things immediately at hand meant more to the young than they ever would again. Exploring their surroundings, they were also mentally arranging the world and deciding their place in it. Many would look back on this as "some virgin chance conquered," as Erik Erikson has defined play at its best.[10] The result was a claim of emotional possession, a unique bond with the country.

A second category—the making of work into play—was close kin to the first. Children were exploring their surroundings as they performed their chores, and they found some of this work enjoyable. It was thus a small step to transform their labor into recreation. Such play helped them develop skills they would need in the years ahead, and like their explorations, it contributed to independence and a sense of identity.

Young workers raced one another to enliven the tedious jobs of picking hops and sweet potatoes or weeding rows of corn. To break the monotony of herding and of keeping the stock and birds out of the fields, they invented riddles and conundrums and organized various contests. Martha Collins of Oregon learned to make even threshing fun:

> When the wheat was harvested we put the shocks in a corral and turned the calves and young stock in on it to tramp it out. I greatly enjoyed the process of threshing out the grain. I would go in and catch a young heifer by the tail and hang on like grim death while she would fairly sail around the corral trying to get away. I would take steps about ten feet long as she ran around the corral. This would start all the calves running and the grain got well tramped.[11]

Some work became an amusement in itself, such as hunting. Boys and girls new to the frontier found in stalking the abundant small game an excitement they had never known. During his first year in western Kansas, the fourteen-year-old John Norton peppered his diary with accounts of killing jackrabbits, ducks, and various varmints, some of them eaten but many not. Soon he was ready for larger prey, and his friends' tales of a foray to the Canadian River inspired wonder tinged with jealousy: "Game! Buffalo! 2 antelope and a deer!"[12] Sunday rabbit hunting was "about the only good time that we ever had," Dora Bryant remembered of her Oklahoma girlhood. For others, it was snake chasing, as with a young girl who bagged a dozen victims early in the 1872 summer season. Game birds on the ponds and wallows of the plains, raccoons to the south, deer and bears in the mountains, squirrels in the woodlands, rabbits and coyotes everywhere—children found enjoyment in bringing them all down. "Hunting seemed to me the greatest sport in all creation," one remembered: "Compared with [it] everything else was as dust in the cyclone."[13]

The gathering of wild greens and berries, another important children's chore, also was turned to their enjoyment. Hunting raspberries was the one job she never had to be driven to, a Colorado girl recalled, for it was a chance to search out secret spots in the meadows and hills, to fantasize about future adventures. Children had much the same response to all sorts of tasks that took them out into the country. For a plains daughter, the burning of a fire-break around her farm was "one of the joys of our childhood." In mountain towns boys and girls loved to search the streams for "float," particles of ore hinting of a vein nearby, and traces of gold dust overlooked by prospectors.[14]

In all this, they were aided by one of their most essential companions—the horse. Parents recognized that riding was an invaluable skill, and they usually put their youngsters into the saddle at an early age. A Montana rancher conducted a weekly "Sunday school" for his stepson by saddling all available yearlings and making the boy ride them all. Even when the introduction was painful, however, girls and boys took to riding enthusiastically. Many were herding and delivering messages by their fourth or fifth years. In the more arid and sparsely populated regions they rarely left the saddle. As a general rule, Agnes Cleaveland wrote, "one must never be seen afoot except in the business of looking for a horse." An acquaintance claimed never to have been off his animal for more than two weeks while growing up—and then he had the measles. A mother fresh to Utah wrote home that her young son's love for riding came instantly: "He says you could not hire him to go back."[15]

Children on horseback had a freedom of movement and sense of power they could find no other way. Their familiarity with the animals and their seasoned skills gave them a special pride. "I was a fearless rider, and nothing pleased me more than to be mounted on a swift horse," wrote a girl among the forty-niners. Consequently, their work atop their ponies is most difficult to separate from their play. While watching over cattle and sheep, they raced, practiced stunts, and chased (but rarely caught) coyotes and antelopes. In their spare time they still galloped after that swift prey; a west Texas girl claimed to have covered fifty-five miles one Thanksgiving day in a futile run after coyotes.[16] "Wasn't it fun, though!" Luna Warner crowed to her diary after a similar race across the Kansas grasslands. That, however, paled beside the time she and her father went hunting bison:

> Pa fired and then the buffalo came right for me. My horse sprang and snorted and whirled around me but I kept fast hold and talked to her and she arched her neck. Patty [a friend] had just come up and she went for him and worried him until Pa had shot four times. Then he [the bison, not Pa] fell dead in the ravine.[17]

Luna's words capture that blend of adventure and blossoming self-confidence that was the horse's gift to the child. No wonder Hamlin Garland could write of his youthful friends on the Iowa frontier: "They lived in the saddle when no other duties called them, . . . and the world seemed a very good place for a boy."[18]

Horses were only one part of a menagerie in the children's world of play. A woman newly arrived in Arizona wrinkled her nose at the "chickens, children, and dogs . . . promiscuously mixed together." The most isolated girls and boys had few human playmates. Marquis James was so unused to company his age that he was terrified at the sight of other children on the rare occasions when his father took him to town. Animals were the natural companions of these youngsters. One mother rounded up a puppy, two lambs, a fawn, two kittens, and a calf to entertain her baby on their remote Arizona claim. Children romped and ran with bear cubs and coyote pups. A young Kansan found baby badgers particularly intelligent; others tamed infant antelopes. Children sat for hours talking and playing with ground squirrels, prairie dogs, owls, and pigeons. When Bayard Taylor, the traveller and essayist, found a girl frolicking with prairie dogs in the corner of a stage station, he speculated that she was learning to cope with the loneliness she would likely know as an adult. When she told him she actually preferred animals as companions, he was vastly impressed: "What a western woman she will make!"[19]

The children's affection for animals was more than an adjustment to isolation, however. Horses expanded their opportunities to push out into the land; wild and tame creatures were part of the landscape that excited their curiosity. Significantly, girls and boys were far less likely to make play of their labor in the houses and fields. At most, they might pass

Hauling by turkey power. The lowliest animals were drafted for fun and, occasionally, locomotion. (Courtesy Kansas State Historical Society.)

those hours fantasizing where they would rather be, as the future historian Edward E. Dale and his brother did, swapping fantastic tales of Alaska and Antarctica while they picked corn on their Texas farm. The wandering work of herding, hunting, and gathering was another matter, for they turned those chores into camping expeditions, excursions that were also practical tests of their knowledge of the country. Children as young as eight lived for days in wild desert and mountain country, miles from their parents, a display of self reliance that was considered part economic necessity, part a natural weaning.[20] Play as exploration and play as work—the two meshed as the children grew. Through them, the young developed useful skills, learned of their surroundings, and developed a remarkable self-confidence.

A third category included the more formal games that have been so much a part of childhood culture throughout history. These amusements usually became an important part of frontier children's lives at about the age of five. Then and now, those are the years when the young begin to assume new roles and responsibilities that take them beyond their families into a widening circle of peers and adults. The play of children adjusts accordingly. Among other things, games are social exercises. Through them, a youngster grapples with complex questions such as the nature of social cooperation and getting along and surviving in society.[21]

At first glance, the range of games played by frontier children seems enormous. There were ones played in circles and in lines, with sticks and cans and balls and bones, some pitting girls and boys against each other and others not, chanting, singing, and dancing. Just as striking, most games were played in all the West's many settings. Children passed time with Anti-I-Over in emigrant camps on the Truckee River and on the Llano Estacado; they played blackman from southern Arizona to the Montana mountains and told the same riddles in Silver City, New Mexico and Silver City, Idaho. Of all institutions brought westward by persons of all ages, children's games were among the most pervasive and consistent.[22]

That was partly because recreations had certain practical advantages to commend them. They usually were highly physical and thus fit a vigorous life spent mostly out-of-doors. Most could be played without special equipment and were easily organized even among strangers. Anti-I-Over (or Anthony-I-Over), one of the most popular frontier games, is a case in point. Two teams stood on either side of a barrier large enough to hide one from the other (on the trails, a wagon was used); a member of the "it" team had a ball—or, if none was available, a rock or perhaps a sock tied into a knot—and play began when this child called out "Anti" and threw the ball over the barrier. If the opposition failed to catch the missile, they became "it" and repeated the procedure, but if they caught the ball, they raced around to the other side and tried to hit one of their fleeing opponents. Anyone struck joined the other side, and when one team was wiped out, the game was over.

The widespread appeal of that contest went beyond its simplicity and excitement. Certain elements in many games, as well as in songs, chants and riddles, have a nearly universal appeal. The particulars of Anti-I-Over, for instance, may have allowed children to act out fears, common to all young people, of being hunted down by people or animals determined to steal them or do them harm. The need to face that fear was felt by boys and girls in France and Borneo as well as in Wyoming and Oregon. The emotions expressed in these amusements change slowly over the generations. Not surprisingly, then, similar games appear among children in widely varied cultures, and in a given society a game often persists over long periods, sometimes for centuries.[23]

When pioneer children brought these games westward, they were car-

rying into the new country useful traditions expressing the child's peculiar view of life. Girls and boys of the cross timbers of Texas amused
themselves with "How Many Miles to Miley Bright," a game with rules
and rhymes originating in medieval English pilgrimages.[24] Children like
these were implanting a rich inheritance they in turn would pass on to
younger siblings and friends. Parents brought books, teacups, sermons,
and much more that told of their values and concerns; their sons and
daughters contributed blindman's bluff, rhymes, rounds, and riddles.
Like all youngsters, these were "tradition's warmest friends, . . . respect-
ers, even venerators, of custom."[25] Their determination to carry this bag-
gage with them was an important facet of the pioneers' conservative
impulse.

Precisely because they did not change, furthermore, games were of
great help in dealing with some of pioneer childhood's thorniest problems. In particular, games aided the young in coping with a potentially
difficult fact of frontier life—the extraordinary mobility of western settlers. Pioneer families were forever arriving in unfamiliar places, starting
over among people who likely had arrived recently themselves. Out of
their longing for some sense of community, they developed the West's
legendary hospitality toward strangers and the tradition of frequent, unan-
nounced visits. They quickly established public institutions that provided
a sense of belonging. Churches, saloons, fraternal lodges—all had structures, symbols, and rituals that a lonely newcomer recognized immediately. Stepping inside, a person was on familiar ground, at home among
strangers. Children also longed for community, but they had no Masonic
halls or grog shops. They did, however, have games.

Picture how it worked. It is lunchtime, first day of the term, at a schoolyard in the Niobrara sand hill country, or in Hangtown, or in the Cherokee Strip. The children gather, as usual with some unfamiliar faces among
them. When a call goes up for a game, sides form for wolf-over-the-river.
The splay-footed girl in the gingham dress, recently arrived from Caribou, knows the rules, of course. She takes her place in one of the two
lines that face one another, holding the hands of her teammates and taunt-
ing the other side with the usual jibes. With feelings running properly
high, the two lines run full-tilt at each other, each child yelling and squeal-
ing, fighting to cross the field of battle, grabbing at the enemy while trying
to avoid their clutches, for anyone taken captive thereby joins the opposition. The melee is fairly rough. In the second charge the new girl grabs
a tow-headed boy and wrestles him into submission, but the tide is against
her side and at the next round she is carried away. Soon the few surviv-

ing stalwarts are subdued. It is over. Thoughts turn to pop-the-whip and shinny-in-the-hole.

The play looked simple, but the newcomer had taken part in both a group experience and a competition. In the first process, the established patterns of play allowed children to merge quickly and easily into a group. The specifics might fit some universal need of girls and boys—the expression of hostility or the desire for otherwise taboo physical contact—but the particulars here were less important than the fact that all players knew what to do and were ready to participate. A game was a ritual, like Holy Communion or "treating" in a barroom, and in a ritual there are no strangers. Yet within this shared experience every child competed as an individual, put himself on display. A player began to establish a public identity. In outdoor games there was a chance for a bit of bravado and a show of strength, speed, agility, and strategy; word games stressed quick thinking and experience. In all of them a youngster could introduce himself, physically and mentally, and learn something about the other children.

Considered in this way, games were among the most impressive of those institutions the pioneers relied on to help balance the fragmenting, centrifugal force of the settlement process. They were crucial to the children's search for their own community. Certainly no tools, cultural or mechanical, were easier to carry westward. Wherever children came together, the games were in place and ready to do their work.

From another perspective, however, it is the differences between frontier play and that elsewhere, not the continuities, that are significant. Games can be studied as tools with which children acquaint themselves with the values, goals, and tensions of adult societies they will soon enter as full members. Such amusements are a form of training, one that children use in their own ways and on their own terms. It follows that as societies change over time, so does this kind of play. Thus games can be a reflection of the special attitudes and moods of their time and place.[26]

If that is the case, then play on the frontier should have differed from that to the east. In fact, children seem to have been choosy in the games they brought westward. Pioneers of all ages were continually rummaging through their institutions and customs, tossing some aside and keeping those that best fit their needs. The young took part in this cultural sifting, and the result was a catalogue of games suited to the frontier setting.

This adaptation was part of a larger change in the play of American children. As the Far West was being settled, an "achievement game cul-

Along the slopes of the Rockies, pupils at the Pine Creek School near Livingston, Montana practice one of the many games that helped hold together the community of children. (Courtesy Montana Historical Society.)

ture" was emerging in the United States. In earlier games, those of the colonial era and the early republic, children often imitated their elders acting in situations with lines of deference precisely drawn. The action was choreographed, not spontaneous; in this play children learned to accept traditional roles and to respect authority. The new "achievement" games emphasized aggression, competition, and imagination. They reflected a rapidly changing society that celebrated individualism and social mobility.[27]

Frontier children apparently turned to this kind of play even more enthusiastically than youngsters elsewhere. Polls taken among eastern boys and girls showed that they preferred particular types of competition, such as highly organized sports, especially baseball, and board and "parlor" games.[28] By far the most popular games on the frontier were others—prisoner's base (or darebase), blackman (or black Tom or wolf-over-the-river), flying Dutchman, pom-pom-pullaway, shinny, anti-I-over, and old two cat.

So while youngsters West and East were all playing more competitive and aggressive games, their favorites apparently differed considerably.

Perhaps these children were choosing the play that best fit the needs they saw ahead of them. A sport like baseball was played by rigorous rules and complex strategies, and it rewarded players who knew each other well, worked together smoothly, and sometimes sacrificed individual glory for the good of the group. It embodied a cooperative individualism that mirrored the increasingly urban, interdependent, industrialized culture of the East. The most popular frontier games also began with contestants on two teams, but the play quickly turned into individual displays of strength, skill, and spontaneous maneuvering. Compared to eastern favorites, these seemed a democratic scramble. A player was much more on his own, and he would shine or fail in the full glare of the group's attention. Games favored in the West trained children for a society that applauded individual aggressiveness kept within broad rules that were loosely enforced. In short, pioneer America was an achievement culture writ large, and so were the games of its children.

Often, the young amused themselves by imitating adults in much more specific ways. Some of this they did in miniature, as if reducing the baffling to a manageable scale. In mimic of those awesome figures, the freighters, youngsters were fond of crafting tiny wagon outfits from pill boxes, bottles, spools, buttons, and twine. A Kansas brother and sister harnessed large locusts to their rigs and drove them mercilessly. Had they carried their goods north to Nebraska, they could have sold them in two entire toy counties laid out to scale by a pair of sisters, who created a pair of families of corn cob dolls which led a fantasy life amid dugouts, roads, fences, ditches, and fields. A South Dakota daughter constructed a tiny farmhouse and barn with a well made from a three-quart can, a spool for a pully, and shotgun shell for a bucket. A Texas boy's toy ranch had popcorn sheep and pecan cattle. The larger the children, the bigger the mockups: a reporter in Virginia City, Nevada, ran across a company of "juvenile firemen" pulling around a ten-foot outfit, complete with diminutive hooks and ladders. "A large crowd of boys were running 'wid de machine,' and we didn't see but that they made as much noise and enjoyed the fun quite as much as firemen of more mature age," he wrote: "They were a gallus lot."[29]

Theorists call this "rehearsal." Some was vicarious adventuring—those imitated were often heroic types, like firemen and bullwhackers—but the children also were using these games to think through the various roles they hoped to live as adults, now in this situation, now in that. Their play was a kind of exploration, this time not of the land but of social relationships.[30]

Most revealing were those spontaneously invented games that captured some fundamental aspect of the adult world the children had observed. Those same boys who developed the sport of ox-bouncing provided an excellent illustration. Along the trail they made a competition out of their evening chore of gathering fuel: at day's end they formed teams, each with its own district, and raced to pile up buffalo chips. Soon each side was raiding one another's dung stacks, hurling chips at claim jumpers and even shedding a little blood in their battle. The boys were acting out and nurturing those impulses that had driven their parents westward—the passion for property, an impetus toward competition, and the fight for the main chance. As they did, they learned also that those desires could have violent implications.[31]

In a similar way, the young create games reflecting their tensions and fears, not universal anxieties in this case but others arising from their specific surroundings. As they play, they live through these fears, act them out, and thereby begin to gain mastery over them. Children in an isolated camp in Arizona's Huachuca Mountains invented one they called All the Tigers Are Gone. This game was always played at night. One child, the Tiger, would slip away among trees and boulders. The rest remained at home base for a time, then dispersed in to the dark, calling occasionally, "All the tigers are gone." Guided by these shouts, the Tiger would stalk and pounce, and anyone caught became in turn a tiger who began prowling for victims.[32] There was a delicious tension here, for no one wanted to be among the first caught, yet to be the last, creeping among the deep shadows, enemies all around, was even less enviable.

This was a variation of chase and tag—though one with a twist suggestive of the frontier. Traditionally the "it" player waited and counted while the others ran and hid, but now the "it" instead went out to hide. Children, especially those relatively new to the West, harbored fears about what might be waiting in the unfamiliar landscape; hence, home base became like the frontier cabin or soddie, a sanctuary surrounded by dangers never quite articulated. Still, the players had to leave their place of safety, calling out their reassuring lie ("all the tigers . . .") as they ventured forth to meet the accumulating dread. It was a child's nightmare of the new country in microcosm.

Some of the children's fears arose from the distinctive frontier institutions of the older generation. The West's volatile style of religion, with its stress on the imminent agonies of damnation and its tumultuous meetings full of shouting and wailing, provided a release of tension among adults struggling with a precarious way of life. The literal-minded children, however, frequently found the fearsome messages of itinerant preachers terrifying. What was a comfort and catharsis to their parents only deepened their anxiety. Some children responded by taking the adults' search for release one step farther. They made religion into play.

Kansas youngsters in the 1870s invented the game of Heaven and Hell. Two boys, chosen as God and Gabriel, climbed atop a haystack in a barn, while Satan descended into the lower regions—a cellar dug beneath the floor to store broom corn. The divine drama then began:

> People were married and were given in marriage, stole horses, murdered and jumped claims. To be realistic, because "straight is the gate and narrow is the way and few there be that find it," and since each was anxious to experience what hell was like, there were more fit subjects for Hell than Heaven. When the earth was full enough of violence, Gabriel blew his trumpet, a buffalo horn, and the dead came to life (all who had been buried in the hay) —there had been many violent deaths and sad funerals. . . .
>
> God pronounced judgment by telling each sinner of his evil deeds and with "Depart from me, ye workers of iniquity," or "No liar or drunkard shall inherit the kingdom," chucked the offending children of men through a hole where they slid down into the shed (Hell) and were burned by Guy, the Devil, who threw broom corn chaff all over them, as the substance nearest to fire. If it wasn't eternal, it at least lasted until we changed our clothes.[33]

All the play considered so far was the children's own creations, arrived at instinctively or learned from others. The fourth category was fundamentally different. It included amusements that adults encouraged among their children. Through this play, too, the young learned about frontier life and their place in it, but it occurred partly as an exchange between older and younger. As such, it involved an element of manipulation. Parents and children realize early that play can be used to influence one another.[34]

During the late nineteenth century, play was increasingly recognized by parents and reformers as useful in molding the young—and, through them, the future. Child rearing manuals recommended certain games and warned against improper amusements, and social reformers preached the need for urban playgrounds and wholesome amusements to elevate the character of street children.[35]

Parents gave messages with toys. A young Texan rides a hobby horse and his younger sister tends her dolls—rehearsal for later responsibilities their sister already has assumed. (Courtesy Amon Carter Museum, Fort Worth, Texas.)

Frontier parents also knew the manipulative power of play. Many, in fact, felt a special need to use this influence, for in that early stage of the West's development, their vision of a proper future hinged partly on their sons and daughters learning and accepting cultural norms. Yet their crowded lives left parents with little time to direct their children's leisure hours. In the end, most mothers and fathers did what they could, selecting and pressing on their children amusements that encouraged those values that adults considered most important.

Like parents in all parts of the country, those in the West tried to define and reinforce the boundary between the sexes. Most believed their children should learn that men and women should live by different roles and perform different tasks. Two instances from the overland journey suggest how adults tried to teach these lessons. Adrietta Applegate, heading for Oregon with her family in 1851, was given a reticule, a small bag filled with scraps of quilting, thread, and a thimble; she was to amuse herself along the way by learning to sew. A three-year-old boy heading for the same country a few years earlier, however, got a toy with a different message: His mother converted her sewing basket into an imaginary emigrant wagon, harnessed wooden blocks as oxen and fashioned whips out of small sticks and string, so as the father drove the family's wagon westward, the son sat inside driving his own.[36]

The lessons were repeated everywhere on the frontier. Parents gave boys wooden horses, guns, tiny wagons, and lassos to fling at posts, dogs, chickens, and sisters.[37] Otherwise, boys were encouraged to find their amusement mostly in the hills, fields, and streets—in short, in the wider world of men. Their sisters, by contrast, received toys that suggested an indoor future of domestic tasks. Affluent children received delicate, hand-painted porcelain dolls with large wardrobes, sewing sets, cradles, miniature pewter dishes, and china cups. Poorer girls made do with dolls of wood, rag, socks, and cornshucks and dressed them in clothes of grass, old rope fiber, and castoff garments. When a young Californian was given her first doll, her mother thought she was enchanted with her maternal role: "She danced about and her tongue went like a millrace. 'It looks at me! It's glad to see me!' "[38] The earliest and most pleasant memories of many daughters were of receiving and playing with favorite dolls, and their first tragedies came when these playthings were lost or broken.

Yet, girls enjoyed taking these domestic portents outdoors, setting up their imaginary households with the bits and pieces of the world they knew so well through their other play. A gold camp girl used chunks of wood for extra children and called formally at bushes she named after neighboring houses. A young west Texan furnished her improvised doll house with fragments of broken pottery and imagined a cow chip into a piano. A daughter of the Kansas flint hills gathered her dolls into a dwelling she had constructed of buffalo bones.[39] These girls were trying to fit and adapt their parents' lessons within their own experience and fondnesses, despite intrinsic difficulties:

> I was an only child [wrote a daughter of northern California], so there were no children to play with at home, only myself and cows and the dogs and the chickens. Mother brought me dolls, tried to get me to play with them. "Pretend you're keeping house," mother said. So I took the dolls out to the shed and sat them down in chairs and tried to talk to them, but they didn't talk back. The chickens were lots more fun.[40]

This play overlapped, often in the same evening, with recreations that introduced children to the society of adults. These activities included lyceums, literary societies, debating clubs, group readings, dances and musical entertainments, and informal visits and tale telling. In all these, adults were enjoying the company of their friends and children. They also were trying to teach the young certain traditions and values and to demonstrate proper behavior. Affection, pleasure, and cultural education were assumed to be in harmony. As a Kansas mother told her diary after relaxing hours with her husband, sons, and daughters: "We have been spelling and laughing this evening. It is a good thing to do both."[41]

Of all parts of children's lives, play was the one they controlled the most and adults understood the least. Even when girls and boys acted instinctively, they were using their amusement creatively. At play, as at some of their work, they were learning about what was around them and exploring their own abilities, and through both of these they were forming a sense of who they were. Their organized games were exercises in understanding society's mysteries. With them, children were easing into adult roles and practicing the skills of living around others. Their games also provided a common ground among children of a transient culture and helped these youngsters face their fears and manage the special tensions of frontier life. New and traditional, spontaneous and ritualized, play was an adaptation that was innovative and complex even for a society long studied for its many adjustments to a demanding environment.

To adults, however, this was mostly background noise, "laughing and hollowing and playing all around." Parents were most aware of the play they themselves encouraged, the toys and amusements meant as affectionate lessons to the younger generation. These had a part in shaping the youngsters' lives, but for every hour at these pastimes, children spent many more at their own. In doing so, they were not rejecting wholesale their parents' values. Rather, they were making their own accommodations with the country, and having fun doing it.

Fiorello La Guardia

In 1882, two years after his parents emigrated from Italy, Fiorello La Guardia was born in Greenwich Village. Three years later, his family left New York City, and Fiorello did not return for twenty-one years. The Little Flower would grow up in the soils of other places.

His father, Achille, enlisted in the U.S. Army as chief musician of the Eleventh Infantry. After a posting at Fort Sully in North Dakota—Fiorello later could recall only a prairie fire—the La Guardias lived briefly at Madison Barracks in New York, then headed west again, this time to Fort Huachuca in far southern Arizona, twenty-five miles from Mexico.

It was now 1890. The eight-year-old Fiorello doubtless heard stories of Geronimo, who had surrendered just four years earlier at Skeleton Canyon, and of the Earp brothers blazing away at the Clantons in nearby Tombstone. There was plenty to keep him amused. He learned to ride burros and to shoot, visited with Indians and prospectors. Many adults found living in that country an unpleasant desert exile, but to Fiorello and his friends it was "paradise," a playground "not measured in acres, or city blocks, but in miles and miles." What other boys dreamed of, he could do.

In 1892 Achille was transferred to Whipple Barracks, near Prescott, a market town catering to the miners and cattlemen of central Arizona. By the end of Fiorello's six-year stay, Prescott had become the closest thing he had to a hometown. New York and Paris had their advocates, but he recalled this mountain town of two thousand as "the greatest, the most comfortable, and the most wonderful city in the whole world."

He learned a lot about taking care of himself there—lessons, he later told the Bronx *Home News,* that helped him survive as an adult. Other influences would surface in time. Fiorello first heard the word "politician" tagged to "loudly dressed, slick and sly" Indian agents who stole government funds from Indians, some of whose children would stare at the young La Guardias eating apples and cookies. Professional pols were licensed thieves, he decided.

Professional gamblers, "tinhorns," also received the full weight of this ten-year-old's contempt. Monte and faro dealers were leeches; worst were those who ran "the policy," or what others called "the numbers." Each week his mother, Irene, bought a slip for a dime, sometimes for a quarter if her dreams were right, until Fiorello used his first serious mathematics exercise to measure her chances. Gamblers, he concluded, were "economic vermin."

There was other unpleasantness. Railroads, so important for western life, were built by workers who were helpless before management's power.

If they were hurt, they lost their jobs; if killed, no one was compensated or necessarily even notified. Then, in 1894, Fiorello saw his father's regiment called out to help break the Pullman strike. Surely both sides had their rights, but should government stand with the strong against the weak? He thought not.

He first heard "dago" when an Italian organ-grinder came to Prescott. His friends turned from the man to him: "Hey, Fiorello, you're a dago, too. Where's your monkey?" It was painful and puzzling, suddenly being an outsider, since he knew that some of the taunters had been in America no longer than his family.

Still, he remembered the people of Prescott as open and kind. At civic events and private parties, Fiorello would play the cornet and his sister, Gemma, the violin. "The second Sousa," the handsome, bearded Achille predicted of his son. The boy shone also in the local literary society, The Crescents, and at thirteen he was elected secretary. Soon he was jumping on tables at home, jabbing holes in the air with his finger, declaiming on children's rights.

By then La Guardia knew that other places had their problems. Every week he pored over the Sunday *New York World* when it was displayed by a local merchant. He loved the comics. Forty years later he would take to the radio during a newsmen's strike ("Here's Dick Tracy!") to keep his youngest constituents abreast of the latest strips. In the *World* he also discovered Tammany Hall and read of the corruptions exposed by the Lexow investigations. It struck him "like a shock." He could not grasp why people put up with such things, and he resented it. So it was that the toppling of the Tammany dynasty in a sense began at Ross's Drugstore in Prescott, Arizona.

War with Spain in 1898 took the family away from Prescott for good, but Fiorello La Guardia would trace many of his strongest leanings to his territorial days. Locals may already have suspected what was ahead. A couple of months before he left, the sixteen-year-old addressed proud parents at his grammar school graduation. His topic: "The Office Seeker's Platform."

By 1906 he was back in New York City, which would remain his home until his death in 1947. As U.S. Congressman (1917, 1923–33), La Guardia fought for labor reforms and with the Nebraskan George Norris cosponsored the Anti-Injunction Act of 1932. As president of the city's board of aldermen (1920–21) and as mayor (1933–45), he turned Tammany Hall out of power and engineered a new city charter. He led the city through its hardest times, all the while railing at ethnic prejudice, trying to keep relief funds out of politicians' pockets, and harassing bookies and "numbers monarchs."

6

Growing Up

A frontier child matured in an environment that itself was evolving with remarkable speed. Neither change can be understood independent of the other. Children's sense of themselves grew out of thousands of exchanges with their surroundings. That setting was shaped in part by children's acts of self-definition. So, in a way, children and the country were growing up together.

Their kinship with the land had begun with their first glimpses of it. Living in the new country strengthened that bond. At play, children adapted to the special requirements of the developing West and learned something of what awaited them as adults. Work was even more a creative force.[1] Though they carried a heavy load of labor, children were not entirely its prisoners. Andy Crofut practiced valuable skills as he tended cattle and stacked hay in Nevada's Diamond Valley, and as Mary Ronan gathered and sold wild greens from the Montana hills, she learned about the land and about dealing with others. When their maturing minds allowed them to conceive of life several years ahead, children were creating, through their actions, images of how to fill that future.

Work and play, then, helped the young answer two of the most important questions anyone ever asks: "Who am I?" and "Who can I be?" Growing up in the West's several peculiar environments, children were discovering and reshaping themselves, a task done partly through things produced, failures endured, services performed, and problems mastered.

At first glance, it might seem that children's experiences confirmed and deepened the doubts and fears that many felt upon their introduction to the frontier. They learned first-hand that the land was a tough adversary and that pioneering was full of disappointments and grim surprises. A mining town could wither and die in a few weeks if placers or veins gave out. Boys and girls grew up atuned to the gossip and news that was in the air, in snatches of conversation in homes and on the streets. In more developed towns, they followed closely the ups and downs of distant corporations. John Waldorf of Virginia City, Nevada, fed the curiosity of a blind neighbor by reading her the latest stock quotations as well as news of the dips, spurs, angles, winzes, upraises, and cross-cuts of local mines. He and his friends were especially aware of how bad news affected family relations. Once John saw a pal running from his house, fleeing his father. "Gee," his friend lamented, "I wish the Kentuck would declare a dividend."[2]

Farm children, like those in the camps, learned that defeat sometimes was inevitable, despite everyone's best efforts. The periodic swarmings of locusts made the point dramatically. Katherine Williams thought the voracious creatures sounded "like a train of cars on a railroad" as they devoured her family's corn, stalks and all. Other plains youngsters recalled the pathetic efforts to save something from the scourge. Frances Moore saw her mother run frantically to bring in a few roasting ears as the whirring clouds descended, though the insects ate the corn out of her arms before she reached the house. Augusta Dodge remembered that the cow went dry for lack of pasture and the flesh of chickens was tainted from the birds' gorging on the pests.[3] Another boy described the first assault's aftermath, when locust eggs hatched just as the new crops were coming up:

> I can remember . . . when the nights were cool and the wheat would green up during the night, then . . . the sun warmed up the hoppers in the morning, [and] they ate up the growth of the night. A field that looked fresh and green at ten o'clock in the morning would look as bare and brown as though it was un-planted by noon.[4]

Like the "hoppers," drought was beyond the power of settlers of any age to stop; parents and children could only watch its awful results and feel the same desperation. "Rain! Rain! Will it never come?" John Norton, thirteen, asked his diary, while children of another Kansas homestead unwittingly answered: "It never rains! It never will rain!" An Oklahoma girl knew what worrying about hunger sounded like: when the July wind turned the corn a sickly yellow and sucked moisture from the leaves, the fields' soft whisper became a rasping, like chapped hands rubbed together.[5] Edna Matthews was eight when drought destroyed her family's crops, yet more than a half a century later it was still vivid to her:

The roasting ears turned to nubbins, the tomatoes cooked on the vines. We could not preserve them for lack of sugar. For lack of rain the grass dried up and so did the cows. . . . To see the things you gave your life to parched and twisted and baked beyond hope of harvesting was very discouraging.[6]

"Whenever it undertook to do anything, " a girl wrote of the Colorado plains, "it acted in the most wholehearted way."[7] Children like her could calculate the odds against economic survival in country baked and blown by drought and sandstorms, pounded by hail, eroded by flood, and eaten by locusts. Those who grew up on the frontier, however, disagreed about the prevalence of suffering. Many claimed the land's fertility and the abundance of small game and edible plants kept plenty of food on the table even in tough times.

Others said hunger was common enough. One farm produced 3,800 bushels of wheat in a good year, 76 during drought. When William Holden's family suffered such a loss, they "had to do everything on earth to keep alive" and subsisted mainly on rabbits and milkless gravy. C. F. Patton knew of no one who starved to death during the Kansas dry years of 1885–87, though survivors had precious little to eat. So it was for Dollie Jones in Oklahoma, whose parents told her to fill her belly with water if her few kaffir corn cakes were not enough. She worried most about losing the family's only piece of salt pork—it was all they had to grease the griddle. This left children with troubled memories. The Matthews family made it through one dry stretch on bluish milk, cornbread, and bacon so rancid it made eight-year-old Edna cough and gag when she smelled it frying thirty yards away. Soon after, at a wedding of a more prosperous neighbor, she was invited to eat from a table covered with food. She was paralyzed. First bursting into tears, she finally asked for bread and some clabber with sugar. "It wasn't funny," she remembered: "Everybody understood."[8]

Pride helps explain these contradictions. One father told his children never to reveal the many times they had gone hungry, though if pressed they could say they had "postponed" some meals.[9] Some families arrived better equipped to meet the crisis, however. Settlers schooled in hunting and trapping, especially if they had older children to help, had an advantage over those with infants and limited experience. Many brought help with them. Frank Waugh's father, a skilled and innovative farmer, arrived in Kansas with tools, money, and his parents, and he settled near his sister and brother-in-law. By lending his new neighbors equipment and services, he soon had a backlog of favors owed to him. With a certain lack of perspective, Frank considered talk of hungry pioneers vastly overdone.[10]

At the other extreme were the poor and inexperienced who had few resources and little support. The Martin and Neher families, Germans from Russia who homesteaded in the Knife River region of North Dakota, had virtually no knowledge of the country—in fact, they had thought they were headed for South Dakota—and they survived their first winter largely by their young boys begging the locals for food. With little to eat the first two years, the pair of infants under two years wailed almost continuously, and the older children pulled up stalks of new grain and washed down handfuls of grass and weeds with puddled water. But gradually they learned, and with the aid of neighbors and the loan of animals, they planted a reasonably successful farm.[11]

Most families fell somewhere between these two cases. Seasoned at farm making and usually able to find some help nearby, they nonetheless found that life on the frontier was always a gamble. So it was for young Osseon and Augusta Dodge and their parents. Experienced, well provisioned farmers, they settled in 1874 near one set of the children's grandparents in western Kansas. The first few years went well; Augusta remembered good times and full tables. Then came drought, and after it the locust plague of 1878. Eventually the Dodges retreated for a year to the other grandparents back in Iowa, though not before watching their resources dwindle as they tried to fight hoppers and hot winds. Only eight, Augusta did not fully grasp the mounting specifics of defeat, but she never forgot the desperate mood in their home, nor the dinners of cornbread and water, and the time her father broke down and sobbed during the prayer of thanksgiving: "I never thought I would bring my family to this!"[12]

Even as they learned about the worst of the frontier's disasters, however, children were testing themselves against the new country and discovering something of their own capabilities. The demands of the day required them to confront, often alone, the same conditions that at first had inspired some of their gravest fears. When they did, they began to gain some mastery over the land around them—and over themselves.

Children developed an independence and self-reliance through the daily practicalities of coping with new situations. Among those who moved to the frontier, the process often began right away. One of Wallace Wood's earliest memories of his new Kansas home was of the "long and solitary journey" across unfamiliar plains to take food to his father, who was breaking sod and building a house miles from their home camp. Another Kansas father devised a rite of passage. On his or her fifth birthday, each son and daughter would be sent on a long errand alone on horseback. He understood that children probably would have to move often through the country by themselves, so they had best get used to it. Agnes Morley and her younger brother, thirteen and eleven, once covered 130 miles of rugged New Mexico countryside in a few days while arranging for the sale of steers.[13]

"We didn't think nothing about it," Cliff Newland recalled of similar episodes from his west Texas youth. After his mother died in his ninth year, a local rancher paid Cliff fifty cents a day to haul supplies to drovers seventy-five miles away. From this Cliff turned to wrangling. To teach him to break horses, his father tied the boy's hat to his head, then tied him to a horse—an unconventional method that worked so well that by thirteen, having already gone on three cattle drives, Cliff earned a job breaking yearling horses. He took on five at a time, taming one to saddle quickly so he could ride it to school, his first brush with more traditional education.[14]

Herding especially forced children of both sexes to fend for themselves. Much of this work was dreadfully monotonous. "[The romance] wears off if one has six months of it at a stretch in all weathers, rain, blow, or shine, Sunday or weekdays," a young veteran noted. Difficulties varied with the seasons. Cattle were little trouble during the spring weeks of plentiful grass, but as the withering ground cover was eaten away, the scattered animals kept the herders on the move continuously. Autumn brought more rain, as well as cold and discomfort. "Water filled my boots when I happened to be wearing such luxuries, and ran over the tops as I sat in the saddle," a boy recalled. Another described how the slightest move pressed cold and clammy clothing against some part of him that was just getting warm. The Norton brothers found it a miserable business, and they were happy to see it end. "The cattle went away on the 5th of December," John exulted in his diary: "Curt and I leaped with joy."[15]

Nonetheless, herding was a superb education in the land, what lived on it, and what dangers it posed. Children reveled in the fun of exploration. "Some of us would go in one direction, some in another," Ralla Banta recalled of her sheepherding days in west Texas: "When we returned home in the evening we enjoyed telling where we had been, to what creek, up what branch and what we had seen." In time, many acquired an extraordinary self assurance. At nine, Marvin Powe knew enough of handling horses to be sent after those that had wandered from their usual

Child cowboys, like these in Cherry County, Nebraska, learned an independence that often startled and alarmed outsiders. (Solomon D. Butcher Collection, Nebraska State Historical Society.)

range. Once the animals strayed much farther than expected, but Marvin's father had told him not to return without them, so he kept on their trail, living off the land and bedding for a while with some cowboys. Marvin was gone for a week, yet his father was just setting out to look for him when the son appeared with the errant horses.[16]

Those who grew up to write about their herding and hunting often included episodes that, while different in their details, still have a strikingly similar feel to them. In these stories the narrators typically are off tending to their work in the open country, alone or with others their age, when they face a sudden, unexpected threat, something to do with the land's wildness. They meet the challenge, not through confrontation or conflict, but rather by calling upon something within—nerve and savvy— to meet the danger.

In his memoir of growing up in Arizona, Joe Pearce wrote of sitting with his brother around the evening fire of a sheep camp when an ominous, smooth-faced Apache man and his woman companion appeared out of the darkness to ask for food and a spot to sleep. Though uneasy, the boys obliged and later played cards and swapped stories with the visitors. As the strangers were preparing to leave the next morning, the woman whispered to Pearce what he had half-suspected: the Indian was a ruthless murderer, infamous in that region. Another child herder, Ralla Banta, was watching over her animals in west Texas when a wolf suddenly showed itself on the top of a nearby rise, sitting on its haunches and staring at her and the sheep. Ralla stared back for several minutes, "just a bit afraid, I guess, of what I do not know," until the wolf turned and trotted away.[17]

There is more than a little of the dime novel and the folk tale in these anecdotes. But the theatrical, even ritualized, quality of these stories, as well as the narrators' putting them so prominently before the reader, suggest that they speak of feelings the writers were at pains to emphasize. Significantly, children were faced with what newcomers of their ages usually found most terrifying in the western country—an Indian and a wolf in these two cases. The reader understands that a show of fear might have spelled disaster, but the boy and girl make their way past the threats with an ease born of working and learning by their own devices. There is almost an affinity between the children and the wild things—Joe playing high-five casino with the renegade, Ralla and the wolf locked eye-to-eye. Strictly factual or not, the accounts are small literary performances, the storytellers boasting of earning the self-respect that came with being intimate with the alien and fearsome.

In the mining camps, too, children were drawn into the world beyond their homes. They became acquainted with the life of the streets, a kind of wilderness in its way. A typical camp was squeezed into a valley or narrow gulch. Life here was jumbled together, and no child, not even those of wealthier families, could easily avoid its many parts.

"I tell you a person learns a good many things by coming out to this country," a precocious eight-year-old wrote his grandparents from Virginia City, Montana. Children seemed to absorb impressions and information, including much about the frontier's seamier side. Though her affluent parents tried to segregate her from much of the town's life, an eight-year-old in Deadwood sometimes saw more than intended. Returning from an errand at dusk along the "dead line" that isolated the town's bordellos and gambling halls, she saw a sleeping prostitute through the open door of a crib, the woman's pink negligee, dark lashes, and wavy hair illuminated by a lamp with a red shade. Hurrying home, the girl said nothing, but she wondered whether the woman could have had a mother like hers.[18]

Working-class children panned for gold under sidewalks and in gutters in front of saloons and brothels, and as they neared their teens, boys were often invited in. Peddling bills and delivering goods, there was little they missed. Some, like Earl Lewis of Creede, the envy of his friends, ran errands for the girls of the line; others picked up occasional pay by carrying notes from men to their favorites in the red-light districts. Newsboys had the run of the camps, and they learned quickly that sales were surest where life was wildest. When the worst of winter set in, Joseph McDonald took his fifty newspapers into the house of a madam who would persuade an expansive customer, usually a young engineer with a heavy wallet, to buy him out. Later she would give Joseph a cup of coffee and return all the papers, which the young businessman would take home and roll into logs to warm himself and the mother he was supporting.[19]

Children came to understand the working life remarkably well. In particular, freighting drew their fascinated attention, perhaps because of the sight of one man in command of so many snorting, stamping beasts, and certainly because of the bullwhackers' legendary profanity. "I was always amazed how a small man could handle a long string of animals with a little rope and a mouth full of cuss words," a boy of the Idaho camps remembered, and though they were sometimes appalled by the cruelty of the spectacle, most mountain children dwelt on the freighters in their memoirs, sometimes with a wealth of detail about the men and their work. So it was with other parts of the economy, including mining. Though boys could not handle the heaviest work until their teens, youngsters, girls included, still absorbed a working knowledge of mining as they played around the shafts and diggings and took part in the lighter labor above ground.[20]

A few documents, mostly from girls and boys near the end of their childhoods, tell of their changing feelings as they came to know the frontier. Luna Warner, fifteen, at first was homesick when she arrived in western Kansas in 1871, but less than two weeks later, she reported to her diary:

> Gena [a friend] took Henry's revolver and I took Louie's [her younger brother's] and we waded across the river . . . I shot at a turkey but did not hit it. We waded back and went home. It was dark when we got there and the folks were hunting for us. I shot at a large animal in the dark [her father?] but did not hit it.

Soon she and Louie were ambushing buffalo, missing again but "How they did run!" Over the next few months Luna ventured out more and

Prowling and playing around mines and smelters, children naturally absorbed much about working life and lore in a camp like Cripple Creek, Colorado. (Courtesy Amon Carter Museum, Fort Worth, Texas.)

more, exploring, gathering food and stone for building, and shouldering home turkeys killed by her uncle. By January she and Louie were becoming accomplished hunters, and her descriptions of the land had turned lyrical:

> After breakfast Louie and I started up the river with gun and revolver . . . The weeds and grass were bent with frost. It was very beautiful. We were sopping wet [and] we dried ourselves by a hot open fire, then went up the river. While we were eating our lunch a rabbit jumped up from my feet. We whistled, it stopped, Louie shot it.[21]

Up in the central Rockies, a few hundred miles to the west, thirteen-year-old Walter Smith wrote letters home from Tellurium, Colorado, where he had taken a temporary job as a mine cook's helper. The miners soon had him doing jobs around the shafts. Like Luna Warner, Walter was initially homesick, especially when his mother sent him food and pressed roses, and he prayed nightly that God "may keep me out of the bad amongst these rough men." But soon those men became teachers, then something like companions in labor as they coached him in card playing, told him stories, and initiated him into the work of the mines. He wrote of his "awful appetite" in the pure mountain air and of his confidence in his growing body: "I can carry large rocks and handle the sledge, hold the drills &c and I think it makes me have more muscle. . . . " Soon he was boasting of being narrowly missed by rocks blown out by blasting: "Pretty dangerous business, ain't it?" By summer's end, Walter wrote with some sophistication of the conditions, depths, and possibilities of mines in the area and asserted that "I am getting to be a tough little mountaineer I tell you."[22] Glen Berry, who at twelve started his career wrangling and caring for tools at a Colorado mine, found by his fifteenth year that the odor of blasting powder was intoxicating: "I just love the smell of dynamite, and I love to be underground."[23]

These children quickly took on the materialistic, acquisitive drive that had spawned the camps. The youngest staked out mock claims and later sniffed out various ways to chase the dollar. "He is smart in picking up money for himself," a lawyer wrote of his son, eleven. The diary of Francis Werden, fifteen when he arrived in Montana, traces the emergence of a budding man-on-the-make. He learned to handle horses and cattle on the trip to the gold fields, jobs he continued upon arrival; he also cooked, helped build houses, and hauled logs for pay. Soon he branched out on his own, contracting to haul dirt to the sluices and trying his hand at prospecting. Then, on Christmas Day, 1864: "Today I stampeeded off after a claim. Upwards of 100 claims were taken (200 ft. each). I did not succeed in getting one [but] Heard tonight that they were made smaller, so that gives me another chance." Francis Werden was off and running for the main chance.[24]

All the while, the young were probing in detail the physical environment, their exploration fueled by experience and confidence. Scattered through their writings are precise references to the natural world, enough in some cases to provide a researcher in ecological history an excellent descriptive catalogue of the frontier's plant and animal life. In *Western Story*, Charley O'Kieffe commented on the grasses, weeds, and wild fruits of Sheridan County, Nebraska. He remarked on the value and irritations of sand cherries and pocket gophers and ascribed personalities to bobolinks and tumbleweeds. Similar passages appear in unpublished reminiscences like that of Mary Jennings, who drew a vivid and detailed picture of the New Mexico of her girlhood, with its willows and cottonwoods along trout-filled creeks, berry patches (where "people and bear met . . . occasionally"), wild hops and turkeys in the wooded canyons and draws. Luna Warner loved watching bison and antelope, and she was fascinated by the diversity of flowers. On the bluff where she gathered building stone, she found blackberry and gooseberry, verbenas, wild celery and sorrel, penny royal, and yellow violets. During her first four months after arriving, she counted 117 varieties of plants around her homestead.[25]

These working explorers learned to appreciate the land's subtleties. Around a creek near her New Mexican home, Agnes Morley found

> So many shades of green! The pine and spruce on the higher elevations, aspen a little lower down, pinions and juniper on the level stretches. So many brilliant hues of wildflowers on the valley floor! Lavender desert verbena, scarlet patches of Indian Paintbrush, great blotches of yellow snakeweed.[26]

Lillian Miller knew the colors of thrushes, curlews, finches, and swallows, as well as the blooming sequences of wild roses, lupines, phlox, shooting stars, and other wildflowers that "looked up at you like faces" from her Montana sheep pasture. Since Ellison Orr spent so much time shooing birds from the fields, his expertise leaned toward flying and feeding habits of grouse, partridges, quail, pigeons, cowlinks, and shrikes. "Almost without realizing it, the boys came to know every weed, every curious flower, every living thing big enough to be seen from the back of a horse," Hamlin Garland wrote of the young herders of his prairie days: "They enjoyed it all, too, without so much as calling it beautiful."[27]

Time surely sweetened the memories of some of these writers, but the most honeyed reminiscences, when stripped to their basics, show a close awareness and an acceptance of the place in its diversity. Adults, by contrast, were concerned more with the land's challenges and its differences from the world they had left. Breaking the land, building houses and making them "home-like," and planting eastern trees and flowers, older pioneers were less intent on observing the environment than on changing it, making of it an imitation of what they had left behind.

Children sometimes noted the difference. A mother from Ohio could see only what her youngsters had lost by their move to the Black Hills—"My poor children. . . . They know only two kinds of trees—pines and others"—while her daughter felt much the same toward her:

> We felt an unvoiced pity for her. Never as a child had she been friends with pines or climbed steep mountain sides thick with kinnikinick to come up on a divide and look down on all the world—on tumbled masses of mountains and sometimes even on clouds.

As they helped put meat on families' tables, young hunters also grew to know the land as well as or better than any adults. (Courtesy Idaho Historical Society.)

To the adult pioneer, Frank Waugh thought, "the stars above and the weeds underfoot were . . . equally nameless and therefore insignificant. . . . Every wild plant was a weed. All wild plants, like all wild animals, had to be destroyed to make way for farms." His neighbor, a successful farmer, could name only two local plants—sunflowers and cockleburrs. Frank, however, filled several pages of his memoir with comments on big and little bluestem, how rattle weed differed from compass plant, and where both stood in relation to buffalo pea, flowering thistles, wild asters, and milk weeds.[28]

There were practical reasons for these differences. Parents' work often kept them close to the house and the fields, while the children's took them into the wilder country for gathering, hunting, and herding. Yet the children's intimacy with the land was part of something more significant—the forging of their independent identities. They were naming the many parts of their surroundings; they were discovering what they could do. The two explorations continually interacted. As children shaped who they would become, they did so in a world that was, in a way, becoming more theirs than their parents'.

If much of their work pushed children out on their own, some pulled them close to the family and the household. There, too, they learned essential skills and gained confidence in themselves, though the emphasis was on cooperation and coordination. They kept their individuality in check for the good of others and themselves.

The overland trails taught these lessons well. More than most frontier experiences, the Pacific journey was a cooperative enterprise. An overlander usually pitched or broke camp in coordination with others; he watched someone else's possessions so his would be safe while he slept. Even herding, a solitary task on a farm or ranch, often was a shared responsibility over a common herd. If children had not done so before, they soon learned what it meant to work closely with others.

This made the trail a school of responsibility. Children could be pushed without warning into crises they had never imagined. When a hired man abandoned a mother and her six children on their way to Califronia, her resolution wavered:

> She seemed to be catching at straws for support [her son remembered]. For a moment she appeared to lean on her children. She asked us if we wanted to go on, and if we thought we could drive the team, and if we were afraid of the Indians. Of course we could. . . .[29]

Children generally knew nothing of the implications of such a decision, but they learned how their choices could ripple into the lives of others, sometimes with terrible effects. Mary Ellen Todd's parents, shaken by the sight of cholera victims, asked their children whether they should keep their oxen pointed westward. The family agreed: Go ahead. Then two of Ellen's sisters caught cholera along the Platte, and later she and her father lay insensible for days with mountain fever. With other travellers dying, Mary and other children were pressed into service—driving wagons, looking after infants and carrying them when needed, doing what the sick and harried adults could not. At night she thought of distant friends and grandparents, but each morning she put those thoughts aside, distilling her experience into a single lesson for facing life: "Act! Act in the living present."[30]

Moving decisively beyond mistakes, girls and boys began to take the initiative in meeting new responsibilities. Scattered among the travel accounts are references to young people stepping forward with remarkable assurance in times of crisis. Members of one company feared an Indian attack along the Humboldt River—they already had survived one near the Snake—when they found that two wagons had camped early in a dangerous canyon. A delegation tried to persuade the laggards to catch up, but the tired travelers demurred: "They were not disposed to come on, but a young girl who drove their loose stock told the guards if they would help her start the cattle, she would take them to camp. The others followed."[31]

Even the smoothest trip pressed some children into duties they usually would not have faced for years. The parents of the Kerfoot family were baffled by the most ordinary tasks of the trail, though the father did learn to fetch water, gather wood, and build a fire. In a reversal of roles, the eldest daughter stepped in to take charge. "It seems they all depend upon her," a fellow traveler wrote: "The children go to her in their troubles and perplexities, her father and mother rely on her, and she is always ready to do what she can."[32] Some parents used the crossing to initiate their young into jobs and situations they would face soon enough. Eleven-year-old Willie Ward was seldom mentioned in his mother's diary until he took his first turn at standing guard. Earlier Willie "shook and trembled like an aspen leaf" when Indians were mentioned, but despite the night's howling wolves he cared for the stock, and his mother was proud: "Willie is father's only *man*." The boy gained confidence with the miles. One night, near the journey's end, it was his father's turn on guard, but the animals had been pastured across a river, and the man could not swim:

> Willie took his place and swam the river, (which some of our young gentlemen refused to do, thinking it dangerous). . . . At twelve o'clock he re-crossed the stream and came shivering into the tent, when Frank [Frances, his sister] and I very gladly took him into our bed and warmed him. Then we all went to sleep very quietly, notwithstanding the howling of the wolves. . . .[33]

After stepping into his father's role, the eleven-year-old returned to be cuddled as a child. Responsibility forced a precocious maturity that blurred the line between boy and man.

These rites of responsibility continued after pioneers had settled into their new homes. As with hunting and herding, the young had the chance to try their hands at unaccustomed work, sometimes flexing their wills, but here they did so in a social context. Much of a farm's work was done in groups, proceeding by intricate rhythms smoothly performed. A boy

pulled a harrow to cover seeds hand-sown by his father before the wheel-
ing birds ate the grain. Children covered kernels of corn dropped a few
feet ahead by others. Teams of girls and boys thinned the closely sprouting vegetables, while others raked hay into windrows so men could gather
it into cocks and fork it into wagons. Sons and daughters worked with a
threshing crew or flayed grain in the ancient way while parents stood
waiting to winnow it. There was a clear structure to it all; children saw
boundaries of responsibility and authority clearly drawn. They learned
also how their roles would change in the years to come.

Some crises brought families together instantly, coordinating their move-
ments to avoid disaster. The most dramatic examples were prairie fires.
When a crackling wall of flame bore down on a homestead, there was no
time for hesitation, as a Kansas mother told it in her diary:

> . . . a west wind blowing briskly,—lo! a smoke off west, behold!
> —the prairie is in a blaze coming in the high grass towards
> us,—call to Wm [her brother-in-law] who said the danger was
> great,—he set fire to prairie south, 'etta, Abbie [her daughters]
> and I took water and hoes to fight the fire, Mr. A. and John [her
> husband and son] return, hitch the oxen to plow and made two
> furrows, set fire west of us, we draw water with all our might,
> run with it, and the fire had crossed the furrows direct for the
> hay. Mr. A. and Wm dashed into the flames and with the great-
> est exertion over came the fire in the most dangerous place. With
> the help of all of us danger was averted, but O! wan't we tired?[34]

Luna Warner's diary pictured the experience from the perspective of a
younger participant. In November 1871 she and her family set backfires
all night to stop blazes coming at their house from two directions. Luna's
account ended like Chestina Allen's: "We were tired." A year later another
fire moved down on the Warner homestead, and after it appeared to calm

> there came up a breeze and on it came. . . . At last it got so near
> we could hear it roar and it lighted up everything as light as day.
> We got up dressed, and went out, but shook so that we could
> hardly stand. My teeth chattered so they fairly made my tongue
> sore. . . . The fire died down all along the line . . . I kept watch
> and before long the fire was raging again as hard as ever—one
> continual line from east to west as far as we could see, and in
> some places several lines. The flames were very high. The wind

blew quite hard. . . . Five men and some boys came up with bags
to put out the fire. They set backfires along Jim's furrows and
then went to putting out the big fire. . . . After it was all out we
went to bed to freeze. Our feet ached.[35]

When a family acted as one, there was little difference in perspective
between the generations.

As children cooperated in the less dramatic tasks of farm making, they
felt the pressures and emotional demands that came with them. Nothing showed this more clearly than the diaries of the Norton family, who
arrived with modest resources to settle near Fort Larned in western Kansas in March 1877. Back in Illinois, thirteen-year-old John had pumped
water, chopped wood, and lent a hand with the turkeys, but at his new
home his role quickly expanded. He began by running business errands
for his father and uncle and negotiating herding arrangements with neighbors, an enterprise that provided most of the family income during the
first two years of homesteading. In one day's entry he wrote of negotiating egg sales and buying supplies in town, giving his promise to a neighbor for the delivery of some seed, and discussing the hay market with
his father. He became self-confident and critical, clucking his tongue at
the "loose state" of his uncle's accounting and at some of his parents'
decisions: "Pa borrowed $100 yesterday of Casset and *Mortgaged* Dick,
Pet and Fannie [horses]. It is too bad." The dreaded word, "Mortgaged,"
he bordered in heavy black. At the end of the first year, John gave a
detailed reckoning of the Nortons' situation, including the dimensions
of buildings completed, acres broken, crops planted, number of animals
raised, and farm equipment on hand. At fourteen he had become a trusted
partner in the family business.[36]

Changes among John's younger siblings were even greater. Curt,
though only two years younger, at first paid attention mainly to playing,
eating, and badgering his younger sister. "I hit Mary in the eye with a
cowturd," he wrote: "She houled like a nailer." But things were changing. Curt's responsibilities quickly expanded from herding to bone gathering and other money making. Then came the terrible drought of 1880,
no rain at all by March and hardly enough to settle the dust by June.
When his father and older brothers set off in search of work, Curt was
the eldest child at home, so now he helped with household chores and
gardening as well as the herding; he even saw that the taxes were paid.
His younger brothers also moved into new roles, and all grew acutely
aware of the crisis. They remarked on the prospects of rain, on neigh-

Branding, like planting and harvesting, taught children to work in close and intricate cooperation with others. (Solomon D. Butcher Collection, Nebraska State Historical Society.)

bors giving up, on the fortunes of absent loved ones. Even Grace, only eight, wrote in her pinched scrawl of equipment borrowed and her brothers' comings and goings.[37]

Theirs was a changing, seamless economic enterprise, the Norton children learned. For an Oklahoma girl, her family's wheat field symbolized their common fortunes. It lay outside their soddie near Cloud Chief, parched country periodically swept by tornadoes and hammered by hailstorms. She, her brothers, sisters, and parents would stare warily at the field during its sprouting and later as the grain slowly matured. They realized that without common effort, common failure was assured.[38] Margaret Archer knew this by her sixth year, when she helped plant and weed her Iowa farm. At harvest she was put atop a horse to ride around the threshing circle while her brothers raked and winnowed the trampled wheat; she would fall asleep and topple off, and they would toss her back aboard. "I rode & cryed & cryed & rode but to no avale," she wrote later. "[I] had to do my share of what I was able to do." Another girl, four, would crawl behind her brothers to thin young sugar beets, and in the fall would pile the mature beets turned up by her father's plow. Exhausted and puffy from gnat bites, she still saw the larger purpose: "We went from a sense of family solidarity, from a sense of duty or necessity, that the work was vital and must be done."[39]

This labor naturally limited what the children were allowed to do. They were regulated, even regimented, by adults. Yet this work, like the freer life of herding and hunting, also provided a sense of accomplishment. Allie Wallace's first belief in "my established capability" came when she held the reins of her father's wagon while he dug post holes and built fences. A little older, children helped with more difficult tasks that fed that sense of worth. They sat behind adults on riding corn planters and pulled the levers that released the seed. This demanded coordination, "like shooting pigeons on the wing," and done right, it testified publicly to a child's ability:

> It was an art to time the pulling of the stick to the gait of the horses, so the rows of corn would run in straight lines no matter what way you looked. . . . I was afraid of dozing off and falling in front of the sharp cutters before the runners of the machine. Even so I dropped a field for my father and one for my uncle. I was proud, indeed, when the green corn rows came up so straight that Father said there was only one man in the neighborhood who could make straighter rows than mine.[40]

Edging toward adolescence, boys and girls helped with increasingly complex work, and they gained further confidence. Samuel Boys described in detail the various steps of reaping, binding, shocking, stacking, and threshing. He declared himself an expert at pitching sheaves and a game young bulldog at the final, nastiest step of forking straw: "I tied a wet handkerchief over my face and just took to the dirt." As their pride accumulated, they felt properly boastful. Edna Matthews told of helping manage a frontier farm while her father was fighting for the Confederacy: "I repeat, they did well—a woman and three *children* working on the halves and saving enough to make payment [with] five to feed and clothe."[41]

The question of how children responded to a final type of work—that of the household—is more problematical. Two considerations make it so. As was the case throughout Victorian America, household work was much more likely to be done by females than by males. Yet because so much was to be done outside the home, frontier housework was left mostly to *adult* females. Children, both girls and boys, were pulled more into the fields, countryside, and streets; they identified more with that labor, not the tasks of their mothers. Because children envision their futures partly through their own youthful experiences and partly through the actions they see among adults, this division of labor had some important implications for the lives of pioneer children, particularly girls.[42]

Of course, the division of work by sex sometimes had to be ignored. Men who came west alone suddenly faced unfamiliar chores. "I knew nothing of woman's tasks until this season," a gold-seeker wrote his sister from California, and another cursed "what a man has to come to in this woman-forsaken Back Woods country."[43] Husbands did household labor when their wives were sick or recovering from childbirth. Women more often took up men's work, helping plant and harvest and taking a hand in emergencies like prairie fires. Misfortune left some shouldering traditional male responsibilities for years. Matilda Tomme settled in southwest Oklahoma in the 1880s with her husband, a bedridden tubercular preacher, and their four daughters. She hired a sixteen-year-old boy to help break the land for planting cotton and peanuts. All summer she cooked late into the night so she and her elder daughters could chop weeds all day. She hauled the first harvest forty miles to Quanah, Texas, only to find the bottom had dropped out of the peanut market. After buying a few necessities, she went home with the year's profit—sixty-five cents. But they stayed. She and the girls continued the same heavy labor until her husband died, and the family moved to town.[44]

Still, even when bent by the frontier's special demands, the pattern of work snapped back into its traditional shape as soon as the stress was relieved. At least among adults, the sexual division of labor held firm in the West more often than not. The point is made well in parallel documents—rare diaries kept simultaneously by both husbands and wives. Susan and Samuel Newcomb recorded their activities and thoughts while living on the Texas frontier in 1866 and 1867, first at Fort Davis and later on a nearby ranch. While in town, the schoolteacher and his wife usually wrote of similar things—their young son Gus, neighbors' comings and goings, local gossip. Then they took up ranching, and Samuel veered into a world Susan would never know. Full of bluster and brag, he wrote of a bison hunt and of sleeping on the open range "as soundly as a king in his palace on a bed of down." Soon he was noting the condition of grass and the chances of finding mavericks. But Susan's work changed little. She washed, sewed, cooked, made soap and cared for Gus while Samuel was gone for weeks herding, hunting strays, and chasing wild horses. Not surprisingly, she turned plaintive: "A man that is cowhunting with a lively crowd has no idea how long and lonesome the time passes with his wife at home. . . . A man can see his friends, hear the news and pass time . . . , while his wife is at home and sees and hears nothing until he returns from a long trip tired and worn out."[45]

Curt and Elizabeth Norton's lives were more closely intertwined on their west Kansas homestead, but Curt still wrote of little but crop conditions, finances, and climate, while Elizabeth detailed household tasks and her children's morals and family health. His mood rose and fell with what was happening outside: "Still too much snow . . . for the cattle to graze. *Mad* about the weather. Would like to *fight*. Have a slight cold— wish it was worse." Mary's sour humors came from the duties of the soddie. "I made a pair of pants for Charles today—an important event to note down," she wrote, "but that is about what my life amounts to."[46] Such differences were even more pronounced in the mining towns, where wives had little chance to take part directly in most husbands' work. In the diaries kept by Emily and James Galloway during three years in a California camp in the 1860s, Emily mentioned leaving the cabin only rarely to visit friends, gather flowers, and stroll with James, who spent his days working the tunnels and tailings, doing odd jobs, and lounging in town.[47]

The pattern appears elsewhere in endless variations. Husbands wrote of bad winters, bumper crops, and good days at the sluices; wives told of the rhythms of the household and the irritations and charms of infants. Each sex often seemed barely aware of the other's labors. Carrie Williams filled page after page of her diary without mentioning the weather in Gold Flat, California, or anything of her husband's business. Even Chestina Allen, a politically informed farm wife who came with the free soil tide to Kansas, wrote almost entirely of the difficulties and small triumphs of setting up her household; she noted her husband's work only twice in two years, frowning when cattle invaded the corn field and crowing when the crop brought a good price.[48]

Children were keenly aware of this division of labor, and they recognized the contributions their mothers made to the family's survival. Boys, especially, sympathized with the women's trials. And yet, curiously, children typically kept their emotional distance from this work. What they did *not* say was as revealing as what they did. In their comments on outdoor labor, even at its most unpleasant, there seemed an intimate connection among the work, its setting, its results, and the children's sense of value and place. But descriptions of the household tasks have little feel of excitement or pride in special achievement, little affection or involvement in the details around them.

Three reasons help explain the difference. First, many children spent relatively less time at this work than at other tasks. Especially in the early stages of settlement, when so much had to be done, most housework was shifted to mothers and young women. True, boys pitched in, and younger girls did somewhat more than their brothers, but both sons and daughters were drafted into the labors of the fields and streets—herding, harrowing, planting, weeding, guarding crops, running errands, gathering wild food, hunting, making deliveries, and peddling papers. By the time they reached adolescence, frontier children of both sexes likely had spent much more time—perhaps thousands of hours more—at this kind of work than they had at cleaning, cooking, washing, and tasks of homemaking.

Second, positive feelings about outdoor work were also reinforced through experiences with other people. Work was a series of human connections that shifted and recombined during the day and over the seasons. On the frontier, most of these connections were outside the household. Girls and boys sweated beside brothers and sisters, fathers, neighbors (usually men), and sometimes mothers. Their identification with this work was first seated, then reaffirmed through mutually endured discomforts and common enjoyment of good times. Naturally, there was much less of this human interaction in the labors of the house. Certainly young girls were much less likely than their eastern cousins to spend long stretches with older women—mothers, grandmothers, aunts, and married sisters—helping in household duties, time filled with conversation and lore tied to those tasks.

Finally, outdoor work held a special significance for children. This was the labor celebrated in contemporary tributes to "taming" the country. Breaking the land, clearing the trees, caring for the fattening herds—that was why they all had come, or so the children were incessantly told. It was an exciting process in which to take part, full of dramatic transformations, and it fed a sense that they were helping in something grand. Here also were their best opportunities to work alone, to stretch their own abilities beyond the help of others. It is no mystery, then, that girls and boys took special pride in this work. Housework was different. It was varied, difficult, complex, and productive, and by any objective standard, it was at least as important as any other in a family's struggle to survive. But it was not the stuff of boost and bluster. Independence Day orators spouted about silver bonanzas and fields of waving wheat, not soapmaking, quilts, boiling wash, and egg money. In a child's eyes, housework did not provide those startling proofs of development and "progress."

All this, in time, spelled trouble for some children, in particular daughters of the frontier. They grew up identifying more with one area of work—the outdoor labors associated mostly with men. In it they found what Allie Wallace called her "established capability." Then, as they passed into their teens, they were expected to devote most of the rest of their lives to their mothers' tasks of homemaking. The result was a refrain heard often in the writings of girls who grew to womanhood on the frontier. The distinction between men's and women's work became a source of contradiction and sometimes frustration. On her way to Oregon, Mary Ellen Todd got her first taste of this conflict. Her father, needing all the help he could get, taught her to drive the family wagon:

> How my heart bounded a few days later, when I chanced to hear my father say to mother, "Do you know that Mary Ellen is beginning to crack the whip?" And how it fell again, when mother replied, "I'm afraid it isn't a very lady-like thing for a girl to do." After this, while I felt a secret joy in being able to have the power that sets things going, there also was a sense of shame over this new accomplishment.[49]

"The power that sets things going"—the phrase caught nicely the essential image of men's work. It appeared to change the world dramatically and, it was said, for the better. Not surprisingly, some girls looked on their mothers' jobs as important, necessary—and stifling. Edna Matthews often heard her mother tell of her own early years in Tennessee, where her childhood duties of sewing, knitting, spinning, and cleaning had been impeccably feminine by the day's standards. "I thought my grandmother was the meanest woman in the world," Edna concluded, as she herself was spending her days milking, hunting, gathering fuel, and chopping weeds.[50]

Girls who moved farthest into the frontier's outdoor duties shied the most from women's work. Susie Crocket helped her brothers break and plant their Oklahoma farm, and come harvest time, she ran the thresher and binder; she also learned to trap and to tan the hides that paid for what the family could not provide for themselves. Once she found a wolf in her trap, and when her brothers taunted her, saying she would need them to help kill it, she answered, "I won't," then beat the animal to death with a tent pole. "I can see that wolf run and snarl after all these years," she remembered, "but I got the job done and skinned the carcass myself." Other work brought a different response: "I hated to see Ma come in with a big batch of sewing, for I knew it meant many long hours sitting by her side sewing seams." In the house she felt confined, and making matters worse was the unfairness of it all: "I could help the boys with the plowing or trapping, but they would never help me with the sewing."[51]

Children like Susie Crocket spoke of some frustrations. More revealing, however, was what they did not say. Those who had lived awhile with the frontier rarely referred to the fears and anxieties that bedeviled youngsters just introduced to the West. Instead of feelings of separation and helplessness, there was a sense of providing and being provided for; instead of anxiety about abandonment, there was a trust in themselves and a secure sense of contribution. Children were learning what the land could and could not do to them. They seemed at ease and in place.

This came about as the children and the new country changed each other. Most youngsters began to work extensively between the ages of five and eight, that stepping-out time when they were flexing their abilities, probing farther into the physical world, and learning to deal with others besides their parents. The coincidence of these two things—the family's economic need at a pivotal stage in the children's growth—turned work into a particularly powerful force. Through play, too, they learned of their surroundings and mastered much that seemed threatening to the uninitiated.

Despite the heavy work and frequent disappointments, children generally spoke and wrote with interest and pride of what they did. After all, everybody's work was difficult and everyone's life uncertain. "You live by comparison in this life," Hub Jones said of his years of chopping corn and herding in west Texas.[52] More than that, their difficulties left them confirmed in their own worth.

Children also were left with some conflicts. If some of what they did drew them closer to their parents, some widened the gap between the generations and tugged at the seams of families already under stress. The most rewarding work and play could have troubling implications. In a particularly sad paradox, pioneer childhood offered the most liberating possibilities to young girls, only to snatch them back as they reached their adult years.

The new country's children, living by what one would call "a discipline imposed by circumstances," carried a mixed heritage into their adult lives.[53] Out of the give and take of growing up, a new generation emerged, shaped by the opportunities and contradictions inherent in frontier life.

Charles Gallagher

Anyone who grew up along Duck Creek knew about water, land, and the spaces between people. The stream ran along the west slope of the Shell Creek Range in far eastern Nevada. By standards of the Great Basin, its valley was lush with natural forage, though eastern farmers likely would have called it a desert. A cow had to move over a lot of range to find enough to eat, so ranchers like W. C. and Ella Rowe Gallagher lived on spreads that were, by the standards of most of the world, enormous. You can stay, the country told its families, but you cannot have much company.

One of nine children, Charles Gallagher was born on his parents' ranch in 1884. His nearest friends, the McGills, lived six miles away, and the next closest were twice as far. To buy the few necessities not provided by the ranch, his father rode to Ely, about twenty miles south. The closest doctor was in Cherry Creek, more than thirty miles in the other direction. In an emergency a messenger galloped in relays, changing horses at ranches along the valley, and the doctor returned the same way. "By then the patient was either better or dead," Gallagher remembered.

The family had to find their own amusements. Children all had horses, and when not working they rode, hiked, and climbed in the hills. On winter evenings Charles's father read aloud from the family library—Dickens was a favorite—and from volumes that continuously circulated among the valley settlers.

Charles found friends among the Goshute Indians. Four lived and worked on his ranch and took the Gallaghers' name. Charles also knew the local chief, Duck Creek Charlie, and Kinemitch, or "Never Die," the sole survivor of a band slaughtered by soldiers in the 1860s. He played and fought with children with names like "Bronco" and "Squealer." He learned how Goshutes hunted deer by using modern rifles and the ancient technique of the surround. He watched them gather green pine burrs, cover them in a pit, and build a fire on top to bake them. After that, working "so fast that it made you dizzy to watch them," the Indians tapped the burrs on their hands, and the roasted nuts fell easily out.

It would have been easy to exaggerate the Gallaghers' isolation from neighbors and the outside world, however. Despite the distances, friends and passing travelers visited overnight, and then there would be evenings of hymns and folktunes sung around the organ. They sang current tunes, too, though it took a year at least for a song to be passed along from Boston to Duck Creek. A couple of times a year the family loaded their wagon with food and drove thirty miles for a dance that usually lasted three days. Through the mails came the *San Francisco Chronicle*, *London Illustrated News*, *Youth's Companion*, and *The Delineator*, from which Charles's mother took patterns for the latest eastern styles. With the outbreak of the Spanish-American War, the curious could pay a dime a day to receive telegraphic summaries of the action.

A variety of others passed periodically by the ranch. An itinerant dentist came once a year, a traveling clockmaker about as often. Children especially looked forward to the arrival of freighters who hauled in equipment and supplies unavailable in Ely. Charles sood in awe of Bob Crawford, whom he once saw drive a team of thirty-two animals with only a jerk line and shouted commands. With a spyglass Charles could spot Crawford still three days away. The sight held exotic possibilities. At fourteen he ate his first banana from a bunch brought in on Crawford's wagon.

Education also lifted Charles beyond the valley's confines. Half of each year, after the hay was cut, he attended classes in a one-room schoolhouse built by the Gallaghers and McGills. Besides basic instruction there were lessons in physics, geometry, algebra, shorthand, and bookkeeping, all taught by recitation and work on small chalkboards. Charles enjoyed it, and at sixteen, after earning a primary certificate, he began teaching at the Gallagher home. To prepare for his grammar grade exam, he rose at three each morning to study geometry, chemistry, accounting, geography, and English history. After breakfast and milking, he taught from seven until four, then did his evening chores before more study. The class of three—his sister, cousin, and a Goshute name Albert—thought he did fine.

So when Charles first left the Duck Creek valley in his twenties, he took with him a powerful curiosity and some hint of what he might find. Later, after learning aerial photography in World War I, he traveled much of the world before returning to Nevada to serve in the state legislature and work as a professional photographer in Ely. He died in 1977.

7

Family and Community

In the fall of 1873, the literary tourist Isabella Bird toured the Rocky Mountains on her way home to England from the Sandwich Islands. An accomplished horsewoman, she rode up rugged canyons and visited Estes Park, a "most romantic place." She climbed Long's Peak and gloried in her moment at the top, "fanned by zephyrs and bathed in living blue." The trip was not all pleasant, however. Most towns were wretched. Cheyenne was "God-forsaken, God-forgotten," and Golden City "showed its meanness and belied its name." She had troubling encounters with a "whiskey slave" and a profane stage driver. But something else disturbed her even more:

> One of the most painful things in the Western States and Territories is the extinction of childhood. I have never seen any children, only debased imitations of men and women, cankered by greed and selfishness, and asserting and gaining complete independence of their parents at ten years old. The atmosphere in which they are brought up is one of greed, godlessness, and frequently profanity.[1]

In a few sentences, Bird summed up a common indictment of frontier children and how they lived. The implications were troubling. In time those "debased imitations of men and women" would command the homes and institutions of the new country. The results, for both the region and the nation, could be bleak indeed.

That disaster would come, however, only if Bird was seeing pioneer society as it truly was. In fact, the frontier often deceived the casual observer. Bird's impressions, though based somewhat in fact, were

147

severely distorted. In the end, her comments best illustrate that anyone looking for the truth must reach below the surface of western life.

Bird, and many other critics, had two dire predictions about the frontier and its children. First, they believed the young were being corrupted by the West's open vices and unrestrained materialism. Scornful of traditional virtues, the rising generation would be full of impious, dollar-chasing scalawags, irresponsible men and women who ignored the rules that held proper communities together. As the years passed, western society would go morally bankrupt.

The second, more complicated warning concerned parents and families as much as the children themselves. On the frontier, Bird wrote, one could see the "extinction of childhood." By this, she meant that boys and girls were growing up without the benefits of childhood as defined in a particular fashion.[2] This definition, though commonly accepted today, was just emerging during the mid-nineteenth century. It insisted that adults think about children in a new way, rear them by new strategies, and keep them within families of a special type.

While earlier Americans tended to think of their offspring as innately depraved, parents now thought of them more as innocent. In fact, children often were described in romantic and idealized terms and were contrasted favorably with adults corrupted by a sinful world. It followed that the innocent and happy time of childhood should be enjoyed and its pleasures prolonged as long as possible; within reason, girls and boys should be encouraged to hold tight to childish things. Adults, too, could find spiritual refreshment by playing and passing time close to the natural goodness of youth.

Children eventually had to grow up, of course. It was a precarious process, and as adults paid more attention to it, they divided the years of youth into several distinct stages—infancy, earlier and later childhood, and adolescence—each with its particular problems and needs. Parents were to guide their youngsters carefully through these stages, protecting them from undue stress and dangerous temptations. Although children were to be encouraged to act independently and to think for themselves, too much freedom too soon would be disastrous. Faced with premature responsibilities, sons and daughters might suffer a crushing blow to their self-confidence. Exposure to the world's corruptions might lure them off the proper path.

Child rearing thus became a far more demanding and complex challenge. To meet it, the right kind of home and family were essential.

A close-knit family was a protected enclave where both parents, but especially the mother, could care for children and see to their moral development. Such a home naturally would be full of love, easy-going companionship, and respect for children's emotional and physical needs. More important, affection was the bond that held fathers, mothers, daughters, and sons together and persuaded the younger generation to learn from the older. Love was both the inspiration and the means for rearing children in the modern way.

So when Isabella Bird announced that childhood was extinct in the West, she was warning that the close, loving family was rarely to be found on the frontier. Without it, children were growing up ignorant or disdainful of the moral life. Frontier youths should have been encouraged to enjoy their unique time of life and initiated gradually into the world beyond the home. Instead, they were plunging into adulthood too soon and with too little supervision. The results would be lamentable, both for society and for themselves.

This indictment had germs of truth. Frontier conditions made it impossible for most parents to oversee closely their children's lives. The need for labor sent girls and boys away from their homes quite young, often as early as five or six. Curiosity and play with others also drew them out, while overworked and harried mothers and fathers had neither time nor energy to chase down their rambling offspring. The ideal of a closely watched upbringing was the one part of modern child rearing that suffered most in the developing West.

On another point, too, moral critics were correct: pioneer children inevitably had firsthand knowledge of the frontier's seedier side. It began on the overland trails. Within a hundred miles of the Missouri River, a forty-niner wrote, most of his fellows became

"cross, peevish, sullen, boisterous, giddy, profane, dirty, vulgar, ragged, mustachioed, be-whiskered, idle, petulant, quarrelsome, unfaithful, disobedient, refractory, careless, contrary, stubborn, hungry, and without the fear of God and hardly of man before their eyes."[3]

If mothers and fathers hoped their youngsters would be morally quarantined on western farms and ranches, they were often disappointed. The many army posts were occupied by men of dubious influence. The Kansas farmboy John Norton, fourteen, helped carry drunken soldiers to their barracks at Ft. Larned to keep them from freezing. Farm children passed time with local cowboys and summertime drovers; one boy brought home a crowd of Texans in their cups. The most meticulous planning did not always help. Though Jessie Newton carefully investigated part of the Texas frontier before moving his wife and children there, he found his neighbors "as wicked a family as I ever seen. Thay follow swearing, drinking, fiting, fiddleing, dancing, and hors. . . ."[4]

Farms and ranches seemed models of proper living, however, compared to the mining camps. "In the evening [we] saw Leadville by gaslight," the New England brahmin Charles Francis Adams wrote in his diary: "An awful spectacle of low vice." Observers like Sarah Royce thought that conditions there destroyed the most upright characters.[5] Participants in the fast life often agreed:

> You ask me what temptations I had [a young man wrote his sister from California]. I did not have any. If I wanted anything, I had it. If I wanted to do anything, I did it. . . . If we are very anxious to do anything that is wrong and find it very difficult to restrain ourselves from doing it, that is temptation, but when we do it, that is wicked[ness], not temptation. . . . Now do not try to refute my arguments with a long sermon.[6]

Despairing parents agreed with an Idaho schoolteacher that a typical mining town "is the hardest place to live upon principle I ever saw, and the young are almost surely to be led away."[7]

Just how and how far the young were straying, however, was not as clear as it might have seemed. Certainly children learned some alarming habits, starting with the way they spoke. Some parents worried about the rich frontier slang coming from their children's mouths. Elizabeth Fisk feared her daughter's argot would make her a *"fast western woman."* Far more disturbing was western profanity, beside which, according to the world traveler J. Ross Browne, the cursing of other lands was like "a murmuring brook to the volume and rush and thunder of a cataract." A Kansas settler found that "mere boys on the street or the farms are confirmed swearers," and an outraged Montana editor recommended extreme action: "Parents should either break [their children] of the obnoxious habit or else break their necks."[8] This concern was understandable in light of the Victorian respect for form and propriety. Yet blasphemies alone were only a superficial corruption that told little of children's guiding values.

The same could have been said about another complaint—that youngsters showed an abiding affection for gambling. Their interest was natu-

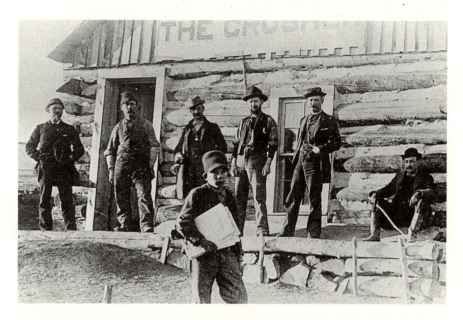

To the deep alarm of moral critics, youngsters like this newsboy outside Colorado's Crusher Saloon spent much of their time close to the West's seediest influences. (Courtesy Amon Carter Museum, Fort Worth, Texas.)

ral, especially in the mining towns, where men wager on bear baiting, burro fights, racing body lice, and scraps between dogs and a "killer duck." As youths and adults mingling on the crowded streets, men risked coins and gold dust on children's sled races and marble matches. Soon girls and boys from even the most respectable households were joining in. "We were natural born gamblers, all of us," wrote a judge's daughter.[9] On balance, however, this seems a relatively harmless amusement, one that children pursued mostly with friends their own age. Certainly there was no indication that many grew up to gamble professionally.

Neither were they necessarily corrupted by contact with another part of the demimonde. Most towns were no more than a couple of square miles in size, so it was impossible for young people to miss the prostitutes who "swarmed like bees," as one man wrote his wife from a Nevada camp. Another gold-seeker, encouraged by his sister to marry, decided to wait until he returned home, for "California women generally are women of pleasure (eather publick or private)." As a girl, Lizzie Moore gawked through knot holes in a friend's fence at the action in a saloon and in the shacks of the hurdy gurdy girls behind it. Cripple Creek students called out by name to prostitutes perched in windows along Myers Street—Mexican Jennie, French Blanche, Leo the Lion.[10] This familiarity must have allowed many adolescent males a relatively early initiation to sex. There is no hint, however, that these young men were more promiscuous than their fathers. And though children might know the whores' names, there is no evidence that their acquaintance alone drew girls from reasonably stable families into the profession.

Much that alarmed social critics, in short, apparently posed little threat to children's characters or to future order. Once more, young pioneers seem to have been tasting frontier life and adopting from it what they wished; the effects on them and on society seem to have been relatively harmless.

Yet some threats were more than illusions. Certain circumstances put families under special strains, and with that, frontier children were left vulnerable to unpleasant, and occasionally dangerous, experiences.

Pioneer life was stressful. The difficulties of uprooting, starting over, and living financially close to the edge, the rigorous work, the close confinement in drafty tents, dank dugouts, and snowbound cabins—these things chafed at the nerves. Not unexpectedly, some adults responded by lashing out at those close at hand, and the smallest and youngest were the easiest targets. Violence and child abuse usually remained behind closed doors, but enough is mentioned in reminiscences and memoirs to show that it was certainly not unknown. In *Old Jules*, Mari Sandoz recounted her father's cruel bullying within his unstable family, which included several children and four successive wives. When three-month-old Mari awoke her father with her colicky crying, he "whipped the child until she lay blue and trembling as a terrorized small animal," and years later, when she talked back to him, his answering blow broke her hand. Child and wife beating were the rule in that part of the country, Sandoz thought, and the daughter of North Dakota immigrants agreed that men found release from the pressures of frontier life by beating their sons and daughters.[11]

Another factor—the pioneers' extraordinary mobility—may have added to this threat. In these mixed and transient societies, the power of public opinion naturally was diluted. Adults who might have been restrained under the watchful eyes of neighbors and relatives felt freer to act on their impulses. This weakening of social pressure was most obvious in the most transient communities of all, the overland companies. Near Yuba City, California, the forty-niner Warren Sadler met a couple who had lived in a wagon since the birth of their daughter, now seven, traveling from

Santa Fe to Oregon and then to various points along the coast. Shortly after this meeting, the girl was kidnapped. To Sadler's astonishment, the parents made only a brief, desultory search before giving up and moving on. He eventually found the culprits and saw to the girl's safekeeping. Goldsborough Bruff also took in a boy abandoned by his father near the end of the trail.[12] The transience of these families did not cause the parents' irresponsibility. But in the come-and-go culture of the trails, a mother or father found it far easier to walk away from obligations without reprisal.

For the same reasons, husbands and wives were freer to ignore their marriage vows. The most dramatic illustrations were in the mining camps, where mobility was the greatest and men often outnumbered women by as much as ten to one. A discontented wife usually could change her situation, and if she did, few seemed to care. Martha Gally knew seven wives in the Nevada camp of Hot Creek; four eventually left their spouses. For their part, restless men might step into the moving crowds and disappear. Abandonment usually was the most common ground for divorce suits filed by wives. After hearing of five divorces in a week in her town, a young schoolteacher summed up the situation: "Husbands and wives do not live very agreeable in this country."[13]

Collapsing marriages and deaths of parents left a large number of children living in single-parent households. They were especially at risk, since they were less likely than their eastern cousins to have relatives to support and protect them. Many cases of mistreatment that surfaced in the press were in single-parent families, especially those headed by the poorest mothers, whose problems were most visible and who were watched most closely by public guardians of morality. A Nevada jury convicted a single mother of habitual drunkenness and abuse of her children; her youngest was put in an orphanage and the others sent out of state, presumably to relatives. A Deadwood judge sent the sons and daughters of a "disreputable woman" to a children's home after she refused to care for them. A surprising number of prostitutes bore and tried to rear children as they moved from cattle town to mining camp to the "hog ranches" outside military posts. These children often suffered from violence, emotional turmoil, and a high rate of illness and mortality.[14]

Alcohol was a common element in many accounts of neglected or abused children. So heavy was drinking in his town, an Idaho editor wrote, that "no man should be considered drunk . . . as long as he can make a noise." Other observers agreed that the pace of western drinking, spurred on by the pressures of frontier life and the general loosening of restraints, was far brisker than anywhere else in the nation. Alcoholism became a secondary stress on the family, encouraged by deeper difficulties but also creating ones of its own. "Uncle Howard was drunk," a young Kansan wrote in her diary. "He has been drinking 11 days. They had a terrible time." She apparently was unthreatened; others were not so lucky. Two California daughters, one visiting relatives, exchanged letters about an uncle's recent drinking bout. The absent sister was sympathetic, but, she added quickly, "I do not want to go up there and get scared to death by him. I suppose you have to run from him as we used to. . . ."[15]

Adults looking for evidence of the family's collapse might have pointed to an especially disturbing part of western life—frontier runaways. Urged by circumstance to explore the world around them, some young people simply kept going. Runaways were most common in mining and ranching regions, where work and play drew children farthest from their families and where the go-getter ethic was most celebrated. So many youngsters took off in the Comstock that a special term was coined: "little ten day bums." One of them, John Waldorf, ran away four times between his fifth and sixteenth years. Twice he returned of his own accord and once a constable hunted him down. The last time he never came back. Most were boys, but not all. A California diarist gossiped about a cigar-smoking girl who had taken up with a gambler: "How is that for Young America?"[16]

Most runaways fell into two categories illustrated by a pair of New Mexicans. By his thirteenth year, John Moses of Silver City had run away at least twice, once to join some passing freighters and again when he became infatuated with a bareback rider in a Mexican circus. Like many his age, Moses was used to taking care of himself and working independently. When the spirit moved him, he moved with it. Jack Stockbridge had the added incentive of a difficult home life. His father died before he was born, his mother seems to have been a minimal presence, and his older brother beat him vigorously and often.[17] Many other runaways mention early work on their own and turbulent home lives, often with a single parent. Leaving home was partly escape, partly a natural extension of a transient, chancy existence.

In the labor-starved West, settlers sometimes aided and protected children in their flight. After Charles DeBaud spent his early childhood with grandparents, he joined his newly remarried father as the man moved around Arizona in search of work. When Charles was fifteen, family tensions came to a head when he threw a bucket of water, and then the bucket, at his stepmother. It was time, he decided, "to paddle my own canoe." Charles openly admitted his situation as he searched for work down the road. Nonetheless, locals gave him clothes, food, and a job herding goats and driving a mule team, though he had to stand on a two-foot box to put on the bridles. A young Montanan took off from his schoolyard, enthralled by the sight of passing cowboys: the "saddle, chaps, and outfit was something wonderful to me." He quickly got a job herding. Henry Young was barely ten and "no bigger than a pint of cider" when he ran away from his ranch near Gatesville, Texas. Riding at night, dodging other travelers, he finally stopped near Colorado City, two hundred miles away. A rancher and his wife fed the boy, bought him work clothes, and hired him, though Henry told them he was on the dodge. When Henry refused to divulge his name, the rancher gave him another— Half Pint Emerson, a sobriquet he kept until he visited his parents several years later.[18]

In some ways, runaways epitomized the West's threat to the future. Their stories illustrated how the frontier's stresses, its ever-moving population, and its independence and opportunities pulled some families apart. Runaways seemed to trade the protection and guidance of a stable home for life amid the region's vices, and that, many believed, might undermine society itself. Yet in another sense, these extreme cases showed the limits of the frontier's threat. Most runaways apparently did not turn to lives of debauchery and crime. John Waldorf became a prominent journalist. Jack Stockbridge, Charles DeBaud, Half Pint Emerson, and many others grew up to be ranchers and businessmen. If these children defied parental authority, they also embraced many of Victorian America's most hallowed values, among them ambition, willingness to work, honesty, and self-reliance.

The West did have its serious delinquents, of course. One of the saddest holiday sights, a Leadville journalist wrote, was that of "half-grown lads, who staggered from saloon to saloon, asking for their New Year's drinks and cigars." A Montanan saw eight-year-old boys drinking and lounging in brothels. In 1866 Virginia City, Nevada, had two schoolyard stabbings in as many months, one by a boy of nine against another of seven. Boys in Raton, New Mexico stole black powder from a quarry and bombarded their town with rocks and debris fired from a rusty cannon they had found.[19]

Whether such incidents were more common in the West, however, is highly questionable. Frontier children, even most of those who broke the family bond, typically were after nothing but a little more personal freedom and the chance to indulge in modestly improper behavior. The runaway John Moses, who grew up to a career in ranching, explained: "I thought the biggest life in the world would be [to live] like a freighter or cowpuncher. I wanted to cuss and chew tobacco and sleep out in the mud."[20]

Critics like Isabella Bird not only misunderstood much of what they saw; they also passed over other parts of pioneer life entirely. The most unusual and disturbing aspects of the frontier scene naturally were the first noted and commented upon. After all, a blasphemous, tobacco-chewing, beer-swilling eleven-year-old tended to catch the eye. Other details went unnoticed precisely because they were so ordinary to anyone from the East; much more in the pioneers' lives, especially what happened inside their homes, was never seen by those who moved quickly and lightly across the frontier.

A closer look would have revealed that traditional values and modern attitudes toward children had been taken westward and implanted on the frontier, though conditions there sometimes demanded some modifications. The family, far from disintegrating under the pressures of the day, proved both flexible and strong. As centrifugal forces pulled at the bonds between parents and children, centripetal ones were drawing them together.

One trait of the modern family—close and attentive care of children—was especially difficult to achieve. The parents' burden of work, the youngsters' love of roaming, and the need for sons and daughters to labor on their own all stood in the way. Still, parents went to great lengths to watch over their young, at least during the crucial years of infancy. As already noted, men and women did not share this responsibility equally. Farmers went looking for work during slack times, prospectors disappeared for weeks, and businessmen traveled to tend their accounts. A study of eight Texas plains families showed that five of the men—two freighters, two cowboys, and a stage driver—were gone much of the time. It is not surprising, then, that two of the first five words spoken by a California professional's infant boy were "bye-bye," and "away," words the child learned when speaking to and about his father.[21]

Pioneer women were perpetuating the modern view that placed the responsibility of child rearing mostly with the mother, whether men were around or not. This naturally left mothers shouldering a heavy burden. They were expected to see to the thousands of details of child care while tackling the demanding jobs of frontier homemaking. Even the luckiest felt the strain. Elizabeth Fisk enjoyed the help of servants, family, and friends, though she still complained that she was rarely away from her infant daughter, even when at the sewing machine and piano. This constant closeness, with the girl's nursing, sapped her strength: "She tugs away all night long of late, and I rise in the morning more weary than when I lay down." Five years later, and with another child, Fisk wrote that sometimes "mama longs to fly."[22]

Whatever their frustrations, mothers like Fisk still had the time and resources to supervise rather closely their children's lives. The diary of eleven-year-old Edna Hedges, Fisk's cousin, shows a child of the frontier upper middle class growing up closely watched and ethically groomed. Edna was expected to work at home, but not too hard and only at the traditional tasks of womenfolk. She sewed, "held the baby," dusted, swept, and occasionally washed dishes. Only once in a year, when she walked to a bakery, was she sent on an errand alone outside the house. She took music lessons and memorized Bible verses. Her play—tea parties, croquet, skits, and rounds of "tin tin," "cross questions and crooked answers," and other parlor games—was well regulated. She also spent much time with her parents. She worked and visited with her mother; her father took her for walks and wrote Latin epigrams in her autograph album. Scattered in her diary are hints that she was learning the hundreds of lessons in the training of a proper young lady. "I am trying to be good and not snap as much," she wrote one evening. She worried about being "mean" and about giggling. "Oh! I do wish I could be decent," she scribbled in frustration.[23] By the standards of her time and social class, she was well on her way.

The poorer neighbors of the Hedges and Fisks could never direct their children's lives with such precision. With less help and more work, most mothers were hard-pressed. Those left entirely on their own had a much worse time of it. One mother, arriving friendless and broke in Oregon with a dying husband and sick baby, tried to meet expenses by selling eggs and butter, all the while worrying ("it is the worst place for children I ever saw") and trying to keep up her own failing health: "I feel hardly able to sit up to day and Alice [her daughter] is so sick and is continually calling for me. . . ." A Montana widow was caught in a similar predicament. Her daughter recalled: "I never knew how she felt, but her face was so sad that I will never forget." These women wrote of the joys of being close to their children, but on many days they paid a price. "I felt very cross & wicked & had a good cry," a ranchwoman confided in a diary bulging with notations of child care. The husband of a Dakota mother noted that after months of watching over two infants in a cramped and smoky sod house, his wife rarely spoke to others but "talked to herself in low tones and abrupt screams."[24]

But if the details of these women's lives were different, their standards were not. Scattered as it is, the evidence suggests that new attitudes and values about the family and child rearing were well entrenched among most pioneers of all classes. Many parents, it is true, found it impossible to keep close track of children beyond the age of five or so. Yet during their youngsters' infancy and earliest childhood, those first months and years crucially important to a child's sense of security and protection, the hardest-worked mothers took pains to keep their youngest children near them, even under trying circumstances. "He has not been out of my arms long at a time . . . , tho' I find my hands full I assure you," an Iowa farmwoman wrote of her son. An Arizona ranch wife insisted on taking her seven-month-old on a three-day mule trip, nestling the girl in a box set behind the saddle horn, and when a Texas sheepherder's wife lost her way looking for a stray cow, she wandered the entire night with an infant strapped to her chest and toddlers clinging to her skirts. Susan Newcomb went five weeks without leaving her house in Ft. Davis, Texas while caring for young Gus.[25] During a child's first year, the basis was laid for a relationship of intimate concern.

Other evidence reveals another trait of the modern ideal—a recognition of a child's individuality and particular needs. Parents were likely to name their infants during the first few days or weeks of life, implying that mothers and fathers already thought of their newborns as individuals and acknowledged an emotional investment in them. Though still-born children usually were buried nameless, mortality records show that the great majority who lived for a least a day were given this mark of individual identity.

The atmosphere in these homes often was one of affection and sympathy. Both mothers and fathers spent precious hours making their young children's lives more comfortable and enjoyable. A west Texas mother sewed towsacks into a small mattress she stuffed with grass cut from a riverbank to make "the sweetest smelling bed." Others made simple toys from whatever was at hand and fashioned brightly decorated clothes from flour sacks, bed ticking, and canvas torn from walls of abandoned cabins. A Kansas father sacrificed a walnut tree to make a cradle and later carried a split-bottom rocker forty miles by horseback so his children might be comforted by its sway and creak.[26]

Contrary to the common impression of parents' harsh rule, the discipline in many households was moderate, even lenient. Though there were some memories of "doses of strap oil," more striking was how seldom discipline was mentioned at all. Diaries of young people went week after

A Montana homesteader's infant rests warmly in a coffee-box pram. Hard-worked parents spent precious hours adding such touches of comfort to their children's lives. (Courtesy Montana Historical Society.)

week with no hint of heavy hands, and neither parents nor children wrote much about punishments in their reminiscences. When discipline was described, it typically was not excessive by national standards. A California diarist noted carefully the times she and her husband spanked their two-year-old—three times over two months, usually for crying fits when the child did not get his way. On the last occasion the mother promised her diary to be more restrained after her mother-in-law scolded her for this "cruel" treatment. Some relied mostly on loud reprimands. A Kansan noted that "My father once had a beautiful voice, but he's had seven children, and it is just ruined."[27]

Many recalled being spanked or switched just once or twice while growing up, usually for gross violations of the frontier code, such as letting cows into the cornfield or lying to neighbors. Though his brother once was "tapped . . . a little bit" with a switch, Ben Wallicek of west Texas claimed his parents never punished or even spoke harshly to him. His father and mother were not indulgent; he and his siblings always "watched our carefulness." They grew up knowing what was and was not allowed:

"It seemed like everything worked itself out. . . . Rules were pretty uncommon."[28] In households like this one, an intimacy was fostered in which standards of behavior were simply there, unspoken because they were clear to everyone.

Mellowing the exercise of authority was another trait fundamental to the modern family—the open expression of companionship and affection among wives, husbands, and children. Many personal documents were filled with sentiment. Some arose from extreme stress. When a Nevada saloonman's wife died while she and their son were visiting in California, the widower wrote his brother-in-law of his desperate loneliness: "I pray God you may never realize the distress—the sensation of having one half yourself suddenly taken off—the continually arresting reflection, 'Nobody to say that to. . . .' " He begged that his son be sent to him quickly, for he needed the child to help him through his grief. More often men and women turned sentimental over commonplace events. An Arizona rancher composed for his sister a doting description of his young daughter, "the nicest baby ever born." He wrote of her cooing and the twists of her mouth, her dimple and large blue eyes that shone like diamonds. When another rancher's wife and infant daughter visited family in the East, his letters were torrents of affectionate rhetoric, beginning with "Darling sweet little angel wifey my very hearts ownly love my earthly treasure my hearts pride my life my all" and concluding with a promise that he thought of "my little darlings" each hour of the day and most of the night. A west Texas sheepherder was more succinct, calling his baby daughter, the first child born in their isolated dugout, "the lily of the canyon and the rose of all the plains."[29]

Children reciprocated. A ten-year-old Kansas farmboy wrote his Quaker father, off prospecting on the Pacific coast, about family and school. There were kindnesses ("I will get thy mug and brush from the barbar shop"), promises to do the chores, and a brief word portrait of the kitchen scene as he wrote. He finished with an assurance: "When Mama read thy letter, Mon [his sister] said, we don't want to lose that letter, do we? The other day Nell was laying on the floor and she said I like papa, *I love him*." The same mix of affection and trust was suggested by other scenes described by the frontier's children. His family was fairly restrained, Ben Wallicek recalled: "We just talked kindly. . . . Soft. Just soft words. . . . We might say, 'I like you.' We didn't ever mention love. . . . But in my small way I tried to show my love by being kindly and doing favors."[30] These feelings were not limited to bonds of blood. At four, Katherine Rigelehuth came from Germany to Eureka, Nevada, after her widowed mother arranged to marry a childhood friend there. Katherine remembered her stepfather:

> He always talked to me when we were together. We sat and looked at each other. I don't know that he was interested, of course, in anything I did . . . [but] Papa seemed so proud of me. . . . Maybe he just wanted to be with me and show me off. I remember singing in company. That was all—just a little get together and singing a little German song to his accompaniment on the violin. . . . We took to one another immediately. He was a wonderful man. He was most influential in my early childhood.[31]

Implied in these moments is the message from parents that children were enjoyed and valued for themselves, that childhood was a stage of life to be appreciated, both by the young themselves and by adults who looked fondly backward. This came across during a family's leisure hours at home, usually in the evenings. More well-to-do families, as usual, had more time and more elaborate facilities for domestic intimacies. A Nevada businessman's wife described an evening's scene:

> Came to sitting room, sat on a stool near piano while Ella [her daughter, fourteen] accompanied songs by the family in chorus. Drew table in front of stove, resume reading of "Light" [an 1863 novel by Helen Modet] while children with bright happy faces filled up the gaps. Mr. H. [her husband] after playing on the floor with the two younger ones lay on the lounge and read likewise.[32]

Farmers, ranchers, and miners had less opportunity for such pastimes. From spring through autumn, as crops and herds were tended and the high country thawed enough to work, they labored hard, and by evening "there wasn't much to do but rest and be ready for the next day's work," a ranch wife explained.[33]

Then came harvest and the freezing of the sluices, and with that, long evenings at home. Clarence Kellogg, son of a California miner, passed winter nights in a one-room cabin where his mother told a mix of stories after playing "Oh, Susannah" and "The Spanish Cavalier" on her guitar. When not reading a periodical, his father whittled soft sugar pine into presents for the children—birds, bears, dishes, Bowie knives, Turkish swords, even miniature sawmills. Families made taffy, played dominoes, sang songs, asked riddles, told tales, and joked.[34] There was unselfconscious romping and wrestling between fathers and children as well as sensual gestures of love. A Kansas daughter combed her father's hair and soothed him to sleep, then twisted his beard into tight curls until he awoke and feigned anger.[35] And when relatives settled together, the chances for close, relaxed contact grew. Deep into a west Texas winter, a young widow wrote in her diary:

> Supper is over, and we are now quietly seated around our fireside. Pa is sitting in one corner, and Bettie is in the other playing her acordeon. Sallie is sitting by the table reading poetry, and ma is at my elbow chatting with pa. The men have gone down the lane to their "hall," and Gus [her son, five] has gone with them to hear Mr. Fosdick pick on his banj'O.[36]

Through these families the affectionate ideals of the modern home were implanted on the frontier. Mothers gave young children close and loving care. Fathers, even such models for the hard-bitten western male as saloonmen and ranchers, often treated their wives and children with respect, companionship, and love. In their parents' words and actions young people heard and saw that childhood was a special and valued time of life. Some unstable households, to be sure, splintered and collapsed. More typical, however, was the home described by a Colorado newlywed: "This is the happiest family I have seen since I left home. There seems to be so much sympathy between the parents and children."[37]

When children stepped away from their families, they were not necessarily swept off into the jaded corruptions of adult society. In fact, boys and girls often found as much sentimentalized affection outside the home as within it, mainly because of the frontier's crazily unbalanced demography. The West was home to huge numbers of men living without families. Many were husbands and fathers who had come west alone, hoping to make a bundle and return soon or to make a secure place before sending for wives and children. Others were single men, many of whom looked back fondly to close-knit families of young siblings, nieces, and nephews. Almost immediately some missed the children they had left behind. Contemporary ballads like "The Gold Seeker's Song" made the point:

> Then farewell to sweethearts, and farewell to wives,
> And farewell to children, the joy of our lives.[38]

Although posed and stilted, this scene still hinted of hours of relaxation that made up an important part of frontier family life. (Courtesy Montana Historical Society.)

Fathers repeatedly tried to explain why they had left. In bivouac along the Missouri, one wrote:

> Dear children,
>   I am soon going over a great big river, and then away off to a place where there ain't any people living. . . . That is the place that they call Pike's Peak. There is lots of gold there, and that is what money is made out of. I will get some when I go there, and bring some home to you and ma. . . . I look at your pictures every-day, and ma's, and Bon's and Bonpa's too. You must be good children and think about pa. You must take care of the little gen-eral. I send you a seed to plant. It is for you both.[39]

Others sent ribbons, bits of gold dust, shiny pebbles. A Montana tin-smith fashioned his coat button into a ring for his daughter. What these lonely men touched, their children would, too. Still, their letters came around to the seat of their fear—that they would be forgotten, or, as one put it, "being gone so long I will not appear natural to them again."[40] Along the California trail, the forty-niner David DeWolf wrote his wife:

> I drempt last night I was home. I thought I was mighty happy. I thought little Sis was standing in the door. I thought she had grown tremendous but I knew her. I was enjoying myself fine when I awoke & behold it was all a dream. . . . When little Sis begins to talk, learn her to call me, wont you? My God, how I want to see you both.[41]

Once settled in, these men tried to be fathers *in absentia*. In letters they lectured sons and daughters on keeping their thoughts lofty and used fellow pioneers and local Indians as illustrations of Adam's fall and Anglo Saxon superiority.[42] They worried about their children's health. Above all they dreaded hearing, as a Montanan did, of a child's death. "It is a Marriage of Sorrow," he wrote home, "but one from which there can be no divorce."

Much has been written about the emotional stress among westering women who had to meet the expanding responsibilities of modern mother-hood in the demanding environment of the frontier. But pioneer men were caught in their own Victorian dilemma—one that has gotten little atten-tion from historians. A husband was expected to compete vigorously, to raise himself up in the world and provide for his family's security. The West was a promising field of struggle. "It is one thing to be a fireside war-rior—entirely another to go into actual battle," an emigrant wrote his wife from the trail, and though he missed his family terribly, he would "not shrink when the contest thickens."[43] Yet these men also carried with them modern attitudes toward their families—an affectionate and sentimental embrace of wives and children, openly and unashamedly expressed.

The result was a tug-of-war between emotion and responsibility, with the former often winning. "O, Why did I Leave Molly and the Baby!" an east-bound Coloradan painted on the side of his wagon. At the same time, many others agreed with William Newell. How could he return, he wrote his wife, "to be a clerk, a servant of servants?" He decided to try a little longer—three years, as it turned out. The outcome of the strug-gle sometimes was pathetic. A Nevada bartender wrote guilty letters home, apologizing for his failures and expressing his love and miserable loneli-ness. Then he was shot dead by his boss in an argument over money that would have paid his way back. Of course, families might be sent for, but the trip was rough and the frontier a hazard. Pulled among the choices, many men knew the frustration of a Colorado miner. "I cannot stay away from my little family . . . ," he wrote his parents, but "neather would I like to bring them hear."[44]

Predictably, by a law of emotional supply and demand, boys and girls who were on the frontier took on a inflated value. It soared highest in the mining camps, where men vastly outnumbered children. The earliest "infant phenomena" sometimes were greeted by crowds of prospectors cheering and firing pistols into the air. Men stopped mothers on the street and asked to touch babies who reminded them of others back home. The first newborn in Empire, Colorado, was given several town lots, and children only a little older had coins and pouches of gold dust tossed at them, rewards simply for having lived five years instead of twenty-five. Syrupy songs were dedicated to "The First Baby in Camp" and "Little Feller, Child of the Sunset Country."[45]

These exiles composed some of the most idealized tributes to childhood imaginable. A diarist in Hangtown, California, wrote a gushing tribute to "those wild strains of childhood" he heard in the innocent songs from a young neighbor girl.[46] Another California miner poured out his feelings to his sister:

> I felt today for the first time for a long while like a baby. I saw a little boy passing my door, and asked him whose boy he was. His simple innocent reply was "mother's." It seemed that childhood again came over me at that one word and foolish as the world may call it, I wept. I would not, poor as I am however, exchange the sensations that that word produced for the wealth of the Indies.[47]

To put it mildly, such men expressed the view that childhood was enviable and special. Pioneer children also found among this large class of unattached males some of the most influential figures in their young lives. For the future historian Marquis James, it was Mr. Howell, a drifter who stayed for a while near the James farm on the Cherokee Strip. Howell was "the only person I knew who was always doing something interesting and would let me do it with him." The greatest men on the Comstock, according to John Waldorf, were not the bonanza kings but the older bachelors who lavished time and attention on John and his friends.

"When we were around," Waldorf wrote of the master storyteller Jimmy Anderson, "it seemed he loved the whole world."[48] There seemed to be at least one such character in almost every child's life.

From these men children learned the practical skills of woodcraft and hunting—and more, some from men that many parents considered first cousins to Satan. "A lot of things they taught us made us better boys," Edwin Bennett recalled of the profane, hard-drinking freighters who gave him unforgettable lessons in responsibility and courage. Mose Drachman, who was supporting his mother at the age of ten, knew well the gamblers of Tucson's demimonde, one of whom gave him a blistering tongue lashing after the boy's first roulette bet. Later Drachman led the city's anti-gaming crusade.[49]

More than any specific lessons, these men gave children a sense of being cared for and cared about. At work they patiently answered questions and at leisure listened to girls and boys and laughed with them. "Gathering of the little folks at our house. . . . They had a jolly time," a father on his own wrote one cold evening. Old hands told outrageous tales of Indians and grizzlies, sea voyages, and bandits, stories that "elevate the truth above the range of the familiar," as Marquis James put it. Some built playground equipment in front of their cabins; other threw parties, sometimes with hired musicians.[50]

This attention could fill a huge portion of a child's early years. Anne Ellis seemed to be growing up half-wild in Colorado camps; neither her overworked mother nor her aloof stepfather had much time for her. Through her memories, however, walked a procession of others, none of whom lived with families of their own. English bachelors loaned her books by European masters and discussed them with her. There was Si Dore, who fed her codfish and biscuits and inflated hunting stories; the drunkard "Picnic Jim," who took Anne and her siblings on camping trips and raspberry expeditions; "Uncle Pomp," who treated the children's ear aches and bellowed through his black beard verses of "The Hat Me Father Wore;" the freighter Eli, who taught her to cook; other Englishmen, who gave her chocolate, orange marmalade, and Worcestershire sauce; and Lil, a notorious woman who kept her overnight and read her "Peck's Bad Boy."[51]

Uncle Pomp, Picnic Jim, Mr. Howell, and Jimmy Anderson were not, as some parents and social critics feared, simply corrupters of the young. More often they gave boys and girls what parents found most difficult to provide—the time for attention, sympathy, and affection—and children often credited them with teaching values that parents professed to pro-

Bachelors like these near Helena, Montana taught children much about frontier life, loaned them books, and entertained them with songs and stories. (Courtesy Montana Historical Society.)

mote. In their way, these adults were among the most determined preservers of childhood and staunchest defenders of traditional upbringing.

Parents' values were taught outside the home in other ways. Each family's experiences rippled out into others. Even where societies were most transient and families most isolated, people sought each other's company, and children then saw and heard other adults speaking and acting out lessons their mothers and fathers were teaching. Frontier communities, no matter how tenuous, reinforced widely held beliefs about children and the family.

Social contact was far more extensive in some areas than in others. In recently settled country and in the drylands, where one household might need a few sections or more to survive, "to encounter a human being of any description assumed the proportions of an adventure," one mother remembered. A family might spend weeks without seeing outsiders. "Oh! I am going to meet a lady!" cried a young mother when a visitor called at her Arizona ranch, and others called their long days without company unbearable and suffocating. Children, especially teenagers, sometimes agreed. "It is so misirably lonesome here," a girl of fifteen wrote from her west Texas ranch: "I feel burried alive in this slow vally."[52]

Elsewhere social life was spirited and occasionally frenzied. Mining town families found plenty of company, and contrary to outsiders' impressions, settlers on much of the plains lived no farther from one another than in much of the rural South or Midwest. Particularly during slack work periods, pioneers crowded into each other's soddies and cabins, sitting on beds and trunks and stoves, gossiping and telling tales, singing and pulling taffy. The Norton family hosted or attended some sort of impromptu gathering on eight days out of ten during the stormy March of 1880. This meant extra work for the wives expected to feed and entertain visitors. Minnie Hodge believed her mother died before her time, exhausted by all the cooking and cleaning done for the guests who seemed always to be around their Oklahoma homestead. In what outsiders thought was a land of loneliness and isolation, this woman, in a manner of speaking, was socialized to death.[53]

Frontier children were acutely aware of those who lived around them, even when the closest neighbors were miles away. Years later, pioneer boys and girls could recall the weaving of families and single settlers, their names, origins, habits, and quirks. One woman reconstructed a roster of more than a hundred households scattered around the Montana farm of her girlhood sixty years earlier.[54] Some of a child's most influential experiences took place within this web of family and community.

The greatest public display of children's bond to the community came in holiday celebrations. Denver's parade on July 4, 1860, had two hundred youngsters marching the streets, each waving a small flag. Often boys and girls dressed symbolically to represent the states or special national virtues. Californians celebrated admission to the union with a parade featuring a young girl, dressed in white, with a banner ("The Belle of the Pacific") and a live eagle above her. Elsewhere in America children were similarly displayed, but in the frontier's infant societies, they took on added meanings—the promise of both future growth and the survival of values close to hearts of adults. Kansas settlers went so far as to celebrate Children's Day, "the frontier's spring festival," with young people singing, chanting patriotic choruses, and speaking pieces.[55]

Other social occasions focused upon religion. Children's first encounters usually came in the home, though some critics complained of the frontier's general godlessness. "The family where I board have 2 or 3 children but no Bible!" a shocked newcomer wrote from Montana. Another traveler, however, found that "a glance at the rough side-shelf [in a cabin] discloses to view the Bible or Prayer Book." There were plenty of hints that youngsters at least were drilled in religion's oral traditions. Asked to tell a story, a California six-year-old recited a series of biblical verses, starting with "Enter thou into the joy of thy Lord." When a three-year-old Kansan was shut in her room for misbehaving, she cried for a while, then began singing: "Open the door for the children/Tenderly gather them in."[56]

Slightly older youngsters received more formal instruction. "Taught children their SS [Sunday school] lesson and read to them from Pilgrim's Progress, Bible and Hugh Miller's autobiography," a high plains mother wrote in her diary. Other family records show a regular routine, like that of a Montana girl—now reading tracts received by mail, now memorizing verses from *Ecclesiastes*. Like all culture, this sometimes was translated into western vernacular. In one of their weekly sessions, some young Idahoans heard their father tell of Sampson, who "could pick up any of our horses and walk off with it. . . . He could pull a picket stake out of the ground with his teeth."[57]

Whenever feasible, settlers came out of their houses to worship together, though these services could be delayed considerably. Samuel Newcomb knew west Texans in the 1860s who married and reared children into their teens without attending a meeting. "This looks a little like heathenism," he admitted to his diary, "but here on the frontier, where the people are so scattered, it would be hardly practicable for many to attend with their families."[58] Where settlement was thicker, gatherings began almost immediately. Facilities were primitive, congregations a stew of whoever chose to attend. The first services in mining towns were held in the open and in general stores, tent theaters, even in saloons and bordellos. Plainsmen borrowed schoolhouses or sod houses. Revivals were more elaborate, with a few score families meeting at an agreed-upon spot, usually after crops were laid by. Men built a brush arbor while women cooked and children played and got acquainted. Preaching and baptisms went on for hours—"You had to have religion to sit that long," a woman recalled—and between sermons ministers visited among their flock. Half a dozen or more denominations might be represented in frontier meetings. This was no expression of an ecumenical spirit, however, and eventually a community began to sort itself out by its religious preferences.[59] As in so much of their cultural lives, pioneers were reaching forward toward what they had left behind.

Church gatherings, like this one in Nebraska in 1889, provided a chance to learn both a religious heritage and the social lessons of community life. (Solomon D. Butcher Collection, Nebraska State Historical Society.)

One thing did not change, however. From the start, parents drew their children into an emerging religious community. A newcomer to Iowa was surprised, and a little critical, to find "over a dozen little bits of things" sprinkled around the crowded congregation. When a minimal population was reached, special provisions were made for children. Chestina Allen helped organize half a dozen sabbath school classes among the first wave of Kansas Free-Soilers in 1855, and Joseph Aram's mother had scarcely unpacked when she founded California's first Sunday school near Monterey. In mining towns, special children's classes often followed hard upon the opening of the first saloons. As among adults, denominational lines were drawn as soon as possible. Town fathers in Central City, Colorado, boasted of nearly three hundred children enrolled in Methodist, Congregational, and Baptist Sunday schools in 1866.[60] These classes, however, in no sense represented a segregation of young and old. Girls and boys usually continued to attend church services and to hear the Word from parents at home.

Besides promoting particular values, religious gatherings served a useful social purpose. They offered a chance to keep up with the human ebb and flow in the transient gold and silver camps; in the rural West, they were precious opportunities to see and visit with others. For three years Sarah Duncan lived with her husband and young children in a Texas dugout, seeing virtually no women her age, no other humans for months at a time. Then came word that a Methodist circuit rider was on the way. Thirty persons from four huge counties appeared on the appointed day. For Sarah, it was a God-send, "a wonderful thing to all of us to be able to mix and mingle."[61] Scoffers remarked that the godly got religion during winter doldrums, then backslid in the busy summertime. In fact, social and religious impulses were so closely entwined that they could not be separated. As they worshiped, settlers were creating and reaffirming communities.

That was the context for one of the most common forms of pioneer entertainment—children's sabbath school programs. These were especially common on Christmas and other religious holidays, although they might be held throughout the year, especially when money was to be raised. One in Virginia City, Nevada, was typical. To a melodeon's accompaniment, young scholars sang several songs. Afterwards a boy and girl each gave an address and a visiting minister spoke about "children on a larger growth."[62] Simply by attending a performance, adults were recognizing values in common among their varied backgrounds, while before them, no doubt a bit unpolished and slightly off-key, were visible and audible proofs that those values were being projected into the future. Here were community and virtue on parade.

Just what children were learning, however, was not always clear. Many families received religious periodicals and tracts through the mail, and sabbath schools, especially in towns, often had libraries. One in the raw camp of Placerville, Idaho, in 1864 housed books imported at considerable expense from San Francisco, and the combined holdings of three schools in Central City totalled more than a thousand volumes. If some youngsters were at least potentially exposed to subtler shadings and intricate details of their faiths, most recalled being taught the general Christian principles of piety, humility before God, the value of work, love of others, and respect for elders. At least in the home, children rarely heard of their innate sinfulness. Parents emphasized memorization of Bible verses, hymns, rituals. One mother explained why she taught her four-year-old the catechism: "It kept her out of mischief and could not hurt her any, even if it did her no good."[63] Others, alarmed by the frontier's moral pitfalls, may have adopted this keep-them-out-of-trouble approach, or perhaps the recitations were a kind of assurance, summoned at an instant, that a torch was being passed.

Preaching, on the other hand, more often taught a harsher view of man's nature. Talk of God's love and His saving grace was rare, a girl recalled of her Oklahoma girlhood; sermons were full of thou-shalt-not's. This finger-wagging usually was done in a style and context children often found frightening. Crackling with emotion, filled with shouting and weeping, punctuated by persons falling into death-like trances—frontier services could be boisterous. One young minister had to abandon his sermon when he could not hear himself over the turmoil. For adults, these religious athletics were a welcome catharsis, but children were often bewildered or terrified. Ruth Clark, six, was taken from her first revival in hysterics. Andrew Davis, also six when he saw his first service, was confused and apprehensive as he felt the tempo quicken, the worshippers responding to the preacher, who shouted and paced restlessly "as though he stood on embers."[64]

Children carried away mixed feelings from their religious experiences. Especially in their worship at home, they felt comfort, spiritual strength, and a closeness to their parents. They were grateful for the chance to meet friends at church gatherings. But the dire warnings, violent preaching, and vivid descriptions of Hell's fires often left them fearful and disturbed. In time, some came to a balanced appreciation full of insights. Frank Waugh, who settled in Kansas at four, found most religion there vulgar and as arid as the land. But though revivals were "repulsive to any person of good taste," he knew these services called pioneers to better lives. They also offered a forum for the making of a community. Settlers with little else in common found religion "the solvent in which social institutions could crystallize."

Music was one tradition, full of cultural messages, that pioneers could easily carry westward. Overland accounts are full of tuneful occasions. Though the quality was uneven—George McCowen was tortured by a warbling family whose voices "varied in pitch about one note and scattered any place along"—most travelers appreciated the entertainment and easing of tension. Larger parties put together full bands from among their members. Children heard a rich mix of musical traditions—sea chanties, British and European ballads, folk tunes, and popular songs from every region of the republic. A Montana-bound company had a brass band for concerts and dances. One diarist told of a full-blown minstrel show with current songs and old favorites performed in blackface. A Colorado-bound doctor heard airs of Mozart and Beethoven at a neighboring camp, while another party went to sleep to the howling of wolves and awoke to a chorus from *The Barber of Seville* performed by nearby soldiers.[66]

Especially in the towns, musical heritages were sorted out as persons of similar origins and social backgrounds spent their leisure time together. Members of Boston's Handel and Hayden Society harmonized in a California woman's cabin, and men and women in other rough camps founded glee clubs to keep alive the more refined musical forms. But girls and boys still grew up with melodies stemming from many roots. "We had lots of music, such as it was," Charley O'Kieffe remembered of the Nebraska sand hills—hymns, verses about westering, songs carried from eastern states and some he learned phonetically from Swiss farmers ("Palta colta oxen/Swartzy broon a coo. . . .")[67]

Settlers' socializing brought children and music together often. These usually were happy occasions. The Sandoz household in northwest Nebraska, normally full of tension from the hair-trigger temper of the patriarch, Jules, always lightened when visitors and the family began to sing, first songs of separation, then martial airs, yodelled numbers, and finally sentimental favorites from distant homelands. Soon a new technology was expanding the possibilities. "Pa cleaned the music box," a teenager wrote one cold Kansas spring. "We played it all day." Jules Sandoz splurged an inheritance on an Edison phonograph and three hundred records. With that, neighbors, townsfolk, and passing grub-line riders came to hear an eclectic mix tinnily played on the "talking machine." There were "Die Kapelle" and "Listen to the Mockingbird," the sextette from *Lucia*, Straus waltzes, and minstrel tunes like "Rabbit Hash."[68]

In each verse and melody was a snippet from the past, a phrase of a larger song—the cultural traditions adults were trying to pass on toward the future.[69] Music blended bits of information with attitudes and emotional cues. Some spoke of regional and ethnic connections, from widely performed pieces like "The Irish Washerwoman" to lesser known numbers like "If I Ever Live Till the Sun Shines Tomorrow, I'll Go Back To My Alabama Again." Others looked to the West and touched on what had brought their parents there:

> Then blow, boys, blow,
> For Cal-i-forny, oh!
> There's plenty of gold in the mines, I'm told,
> On the banks of the Sac-ra-mento.

Still others affirmed political allegiances and churned up memories of recent history. There was "Just Before the Battle," "John Brown's Body," and

> My name is Charles Guiteau,
> That name I'll never deny.
> I left my aged parents
> In sorrow for to die.

Later, political and social satire might cool things down:

> Jim Blaine and Bob Ford
> Drank theirs from a gourd,
> General Grant as he smoked a cheroot;
> Lily Langtry, they say,
> Had been led astray
> By the juice of the forbidden fruit.

Many songs dwelt on the tragic. In this, the singers were transplanting a popular Victorian theme, but one child of the plains thought these verses held a special appeal among those facing difficult adjustments. Contemporary images of jilted lovers pining away, sons leaving home forever, and angelic infants called to God's bosom fit particularly well the adults' fears of loss and their sense of how fragile their accomplishments were:

> Flitting, flitting away,
> All that we cherish most dear;
> There is nothing on earth that will stay,
> For the roses must die with the year.

At dances, children picked up messages from much they saw and heard around them. Few activities were more popular, and none brought young and old together on more intimate terms. As usual, social lines sometimes were drawn. At one extreme were outright bacchanals. A family of Missourians in Boone's Bar, California, hosted a revel that included two young girls. It was a perfect rookery, a neighbor wrote, both "a ball to dance and a bawl, to cry aloud." Fueled by a stew of hot liquor, men colored the air with blasphemies and calls to the mother and girls to take a turn on the floor. At the other end of the social scale were the few "*select parties*" an early Montana governor's wife allowed her daughter to attend, chaperoned gatherings of the social elite.[70] Most, however, were respectable public affairs, many sponsored by fraternal organizations raising money for schools, hospitals, and other community needs. Drinking and offensive behavior were forbidden—at least in the open. Guests assembled about nine in the evening, broke for refreshments around midnight, then returned to the floor, often until dawn and a large communal breakfast.

Whatever the setting or the occasion, children were there. With women at a premium for dance partners, infants were accepted with the crowd; space usually was set aside to bed them down. Older children, especially girls were welcomed as participants. Edna Hedges received formal invitations to Helena dances at the age of ten. "It looked a little strange to see the married ladies hand their babies over to some friend while they went to dance," a new arrival wrote of a dance in the Montana goldfields. "There was all ages present, from the little one of four months, little boys . . ., little girls, young ladies, married ladies old and young, and men of every age from 18 to 60."[71]

Most children learned to dance on the scene, though in some towns they held practice sessions or attended classes. Parents who objected faced pressure to bend their principles, and though some held firm, most gave in or compromised. Emma Hill's mother and father finally forbid the waltz and any round dances but allowed the quadrille and Virginia reel.[72] In the end, most children took part, and for many, like this twelve-year-old, the memories would remain alive with color and movement:

> A fiddler [was] at the end of the crowded cabin, sitting with knees crossed, tapping one foot on the floor, swinging the other, nodding, swaying, now rising, gyrating, bending, bowing, always tap, tap, tapping with one foot to accentuate the rhythm of the quadrille, reel, varsovienne, schottische, polka, minuet, waltz, jig or whatever his rapid bow and nimble fingers were tearing or picking from the fiddle strings.[73]

"I think we loved dancing best of all amusements, winter and summer," another girl of the camps thought.[74]

These were more than good times. A dance was a metaphor for a whole range of occasions that blended entertainment and social education. In so much of what they did, children were learning steps. Over six or eight hours of an evening, they saw styles of converse and lines of deference. They learned to strike a balance between spontaneity and restraint and to skirt the boundary between acceptable and arrant behavior. A frontier dance was a fine display of the unspoken rules that governed how grownups moved through their days.

Children mixed easily with the crowd at frontier dances, where they learned the complex rules of adult behavior. (Courtesy Kansas State Historical Society.)

A lot in children's lives pulled them away from their families, but much drew them back. From one perspective, both girls and boys seemed to be ushered into adulthood years too soon. Working and playing, they took on a startling independence and the aggressive, money-chasing ways of the western go-getter. Some contact with the frontier's wilder side was virtually unavoidable, and children picked up habits that left moral guardians shaking their heads and clucking their tongues.

Still, there was another side of frontier life easily missed by literary tourists and social critics. The values taught in social gatherings, from casual visits to camp meetings, helped keep children's behavior within reasonably acceptable bounds. Surrogate parents reinforced those lessons and strengthened bonds between the generations. Above all, the modern companionate family flourished on the frontier. While some families fell apart, the ties of sympathy, love, and friendship in many others held children and parents together, whatever their other differences. These ways of treating one another were not fragile implants, like peonies and elms, kept alive by great effort in hostile soil. The loving, affectionate family took root and survived for the most obvious of reasons—it worked.

Mari Sandoz

The Niobrara River curves langorously out of far eastern Wyoming, through the Nebraska panhandle, and across nearly the entire length of the state before joining the Missouri. Mari Sandoz was born in 1896 in a frame shack on some grassy flatlands along the river's upper reaches.

Her mother, Mary, a German Swiss who had wed Mari's father five days after meeting him, was aloof and cold, caught in an unhappy, sometimes violent marriage. The dominant force in Mari's early years was her father, Jules Ami Sandoz. A well educated Swiss, he had been among the first settlers on Mirage Flats, and his shuffling, crippled walk and sharp blue eyes were as familiar to locals as his foul temper. Jules was a cynic about human beings and an obsessive optimist about the region's future. He was a seasoned trapper and crack marksman, tough, manipulative, boastful, an effective booster who was quick to feud with many of his new neighbors. Guilty of gargantuan selfishness and frequent cruelties, Jules was largely innoncent of baths, the shaving razor, and fresh underwear. He was the sort of pioneer that historians later would call "colorful."

Mari was a shy, lonely, thin child whose body and face seemed all angles. As the eldest of six children, she often went with Jules when he surveyed homesteads for settlers he had lured west with his letters. She was with him when, struck by a diamondback, he saved his life by blowing away the envenomed top layer of his hand with his shotgun. Jules told her of his early days of the flats, his passing time with Indians, and his scrapes with cowboys. He described the sandstone hills and grasslands as he had first seen them. She heard how he had crushed his foot in a fall and had lain for two weeks before a cavalry patrol found him.

His were not the only tales. In the evenings she would sit for hours in the wood box and listen as neighbors and passing travelers spun out their stories. She heard Indians like Old Cheyenne Woman and the Oglala Sioux, Bad Arm, remember the recent wars and life on the plains before the whites flooded in.

But always, with and without Jules, there was the land, the valley of the river that Indians called the Running Water. Between doing much of the housework and chopping weeds in the garden and orchards, she explored the low hills covered with bunch grass, the rockier knobs and buttes, and the white river cliffs full of fossils. A favorite thinking spot was Indian Hill, rich with arrowheads and dotted with ash pits of old signal fires. In 1910 Jules grabbed a homestead in the harsher, drier sandhills to the southeast. To hold the claim Mari and her brother James lived on it alone that summer, prowling the hills and sleeping in a windowless shack.

Not until a truant officer threatened Jules did he send Mari to school. She was nine, and she spoke only a few words of English. Within a year she was speaking and writing the new language, and reading had become her passion. No printed word was safe. She devoured local newspapers, agricultural bulletins, and the socialist journal, *Appeal To Reason*. She smuggled home fiction from trash novels to *Toby Tyler* to the continental masters. Joseph Conrad was her favorite.

To Jules, reading and writing, if they did nothing to build up the country, were worse than useless. When a proud Mari, eleven, showed the family her first publication, a short story published in the *Omaha Daily News*, her enraged father beat her and sent her to the cave-dark cellar, where she crouched for hours, trembling, thinking of the snakes she knew were there. But she kept writing, though for years she used pseudonyms, and her independence increased with her skill.

Her world expanded steadily, but the river and sandhills remained its center; pulling away from home, she drew from it what she needed. After teaching school briefly, she lived for years in Lincoln, researching, attending the university when she could, always writing. In 1926, two years before Jules died, she sent him notice of her honorable mention in a national short story competition. He returned it with a note scribbled at the bottom: "You know I consider writers and artists the maggots of society."

Mari Sandoz would write twenty-one histories and novels, most of them set on the plains and high country. Her first success came in 1935 with *Old Jules*, a biography of her father, whom she called "a prophet . . . a sort of Moses working the soil of his Promised Land." She told also of cattlemen, trappers, hide hunters, sodbusters, Cheyenne, and Sioux. She wrote in a lyrical, sensual, utterly original voice, a stew of accents and rhythms that her editors, try as they might, could never much dilute. When she died in 1966, she was buried on a hillside overlooking the sandhills homestead.

8

A Great School House

Shortly after Melissa Everett's family arrived in Cook County, Texas, they were joined by some immigrants from Tennessee, among them a preacher named Davis. After some persuasion, Davis agreed to hold classes in a log schoolhouse that hopeful settlers had already built. "Oh, I was so glad," Everett remembered. "My father told me he wanted me to go every day & I wanted an education so bad." School began on schedule, but when the teacher's family sickened, he suspended classes to nurse them. Then his baby died, and he took the survivors back East. Melissa's formal education ended ten days after it began: "Now I have pulled through this long life in ignorance."[1]

In Everett's story many parents would have seen one of their deepest fears confirmed. At least a little schooling was considered as essential as transplanting moral values. The two tasks were closely entwined, in fact. Both were seen as necessary for individual fulfillment and the making of an orderly society.

Bringing education to the frontier, however, proved a frustrating job. Western conditions, including some attitudes of the settlers themselves, continuously worked against the efforts of those trying to establish a system of schooling. Given these difficulties, the accomplishments were all the more impressive. At a heavy cost of time and effort, parents taught their sons and daughters fundamentals of reading, mathematics, and other subjects. Schools were operating remarkably early in most areas, and community activities reinforced lessons learned there. Most children approached their education with interest, and many sought it out with determination.

"You could learn a great many things here," a California miner wrote a boy back East: "You could learn to work for a living, [and] you could

179

learn human nature, for this country is a great school house."[2] Laboring to make a new society, learning something of human strengths and corruptions, girls and boys also grew up with at least some exposure to more formal education. No part of frontier life illustrated better the frustrations of adults who hoped to transplant their mother culture; none showed more clearly their perseverance and their children's receptiveness to their efforts.

By at least one standard western children acquired skills fundamental to an educated society. In most of the West the literacy rate among youngsters over the age of ten was barely below that of the Ohio Valley and slightly above that of New England, regions that took great pride in the spread of learning.[3] Melissa Everett, after all, could write about her lack of classroom training. Even where schools were unavailable, most children could read and write at a modestly competent level. For that, parents were largely responsible. Home instruction was the earliest form of education for most frontier youngsters. For some it would be their best.

To teach their children, parents relied on the published word. Although newcomers occasionally described the West as a literary wasteland—a Montanan in 1864 doubted there were a hundred books in the territory—the number and range of published works was remarkable for societies still in their infancies.[4] As was so often the case, technological changes in the East speeded the transmission of culture to the frontier. A rapidly expanding publishing industry was producing more and cheaper books and periodicals. Westering families found it increasingly easy to buy reading materials to take with them; those already settled could send away for what they needed.

Books were not monopolized by the elite. A judge's daughter browsed among shelves sagging with works by Plato and Burns, Shelley and Thoreau, Carlyle, Macaulay, Froude and Byron, and a Montana editor's wife wrote casually of reading several excellent translations of recent German novels.[5] These families' choices were broader than most, yet all but the poorest households typically had at least a few volumes. Even when they lacked the wherewithal, parents did what they could to increase their holdings. One widow amassed a substantial library for her children by salvaging books and magazines thrown away by others. Adults often lent children what they had. In many towns other opportunities quickly arose. Within five years of its founding, Central City, Colorado, had a library association and reading room, and the small camp of Montezuma, Colorado, boasted a collection of three hundred volumes brought from Boston by a local mining company. Finally, as early as the 1880s parents could order books by mail. A mother of the Texas high plains told her diary of sending ten dollars to "Library Revolution," a New York City book club, and another received works by Dickens, Scott, and Lew Wallace through the Sears, Roebuck and Company catalogue. Some of the best examples of the democratizing influence of mass publishing were in the Far West.[6] At least some reading material was available to almost any frontier child.

Because they realized their children's earliest education would come from home libraries, parents chose works that blended moral uplift with a taste of their literary and cultural heritage. The first woman to settle in Ouray, Colorado, carried with her the Bible, Shakespeare's complete works, and Rollin's *Ancient History*. On the way to the Rockies, Emma Hill's parents let her read a few romantic novels as long as she also passed time with a hymnal and, appropriately, *Pilgrim's Progress*.[7]

Despite loud protests from their parents, boys and girls grabbed up cheap adventures, especially those set in the West. A Colorado lad liked *The Boy Emigrants*, set on the overland trail; an Iowa farmboy leaned more toward tales featuring Old Neversleep, Moccasin Mose, and Squint-Eyed Bob. Generally, however, children mixed these among the works of the literary masters. Edward Dale, son of a Texas rancher, loved trash fiction and pulse-pounders like H. Rider Haggard's *King Solomon's Mines*, but he also bought or borrowed Longfellow's and Coleridge's poems as well as volumes by Dickens, Scott, Hawthorne, Cooper, Eliot, and Bulwer-Lytton. The young were particularly fond of Sir Walter Scott and Charles Dickens, grand storytellers of an idyllic past and an urban, industrial present. Over only a few months Luna Warner read *Martin Chuzzlewit*, *Nicholas Nickleby*, *Dombey and Son*, and *David Copperfield*.[8]

Tourists like Fitz Hugh Ludlow, expecting a cultural desert, were impressed:

> It was a perpetual surprise to me to hear girls whose whole life ·had been spent on the Plains or in the backwoods talk of Longfellow and Bryant, Dickens and Thackeray, Scott and Cooper when they came in from milking, and sat down in their plain calicoes to knit the masculine stockings or mend the infantile pinafores. Nobody could talk more understandingly, criticize more justly, or appreciate more fully everything in their authors that related to natural feeling. . . .[9]

He would have found much the same throughout the region. Growing up poor in the Colorado camps, Anne Ellis never went beyond a third-grade reader in class, but outside school she could choose from a literary feast, first dime novels, then *Don Quixote*, Plutarch's *Lives* and works by Dumas, Sand, and Zola. "The greatest influence in my life has been books," she would write later, "good books, bad books, and indifferent ones."[10]

Periodicals also were found in most of the West. The number and circulation of daily newspapers and inexpensive magazines were growing fantastically during these years. Pioneers carried them to the new country, and with the first mail service, larger towns offered an impressive selection. A vendor in Virginia City, Nevada, in 1866 sold issues of *Harper's, Leslie's, Ballou's,* and *Demorest's Monthly* as well as the *London Illustrated Times* and the *Knoxville Whig*. Parents among the poorest families, thirsty for news from home, sometimes could not resist subscribing. "I do not care for the price, but I am determined to have something to read," a working class Colorado mother told her diary.[11]

Though periodicals were slower to arrive in the most isolated regions— "What an event in our stunted lives!" a woman remembered of the first she saw—most children grew up around at least some journals. A three-year-old Kansan was asked to recite an Ursula Bailey verse:

> I want to be an angel
> And with the angels stand,
> A crown upon my forehead,
> A harp within my hand.

He devised his own version:

> I want to be an angel
> With a town upon my head
> And a *Harper's Weekly* in my hand.[12]

Children pored over the attractive illustrations, literary pieces, and contemporary commentaries in national periodicals. Big city daily newspapers, more atuned to current affairs, offered more direct opinion on political and social issues. Horace Greeley's *New York Tribune*, the *St. Louis Republic*, and others with more local focus, such as *Pennsylvania Grit*, were found throughout the region. Girls and boys were eager to read them all. J. W. LaSeur and his brother would stand on their heads to read the illustrated newspapers pasted upside-down as insulation on the walls of their Arizona cabin.[13] These were windows onto a larger world.

Some young people were enthusiastic enough to publish newspapers of their own with the help of small presses available through the mail by the 1880s. Scores of these publications, with titles like *Prairie Breezes, Alkali,* and *The Little Pioneer,* spoke of both the youngsters' regional loyalties and the broadening rim of vision their reading gave them. Editors, most in their teens, took up their elders' boosterism. "That Dakota is the greatest agricultural country in the world has been conceded by all who have ever visited it," one wrote. With such items were reprints of sentimental stories, tales of adventure, commentaries on local and national events, and literary tidbits of special meaning to the young, like James Whitcomb Riley's "A Boy's Mother."[14]

Wealthier parents, as usual, had the advantage of time to use these books and periodicals to teach their children. "You should see what a literary family we are this morning," a railroad official's wife wrote her mother from Montana.

> While I am writing, Eleanor is studying and printing her lesson and Katie is trying to follow her example and has established herself with a book at her little table and is muttering away at herself, seemingly entirely absorbed in her task.

Women like her started their children's education early—Eleanor was five, Katie two—and for years they spent a sizeable portion of their daytime hours at the task. On a typical day Elizabeth Fisk directed her children at some light housekeeping, helped them study for an hour, listened to their recitations, and oversaw writing exercises and sewing practice. After an hour or so of play, it was time for supper.[15]

Yet far less affluent mothers and fathers somehow found time for instruction. Lucinda Dalton was only three when her father, "determined that his children should not be ignorant as well as poor," began teaching her each evening after work in the California diggings. Bennett Seymour's father conducted candlelit sessions in California Gulch, Colorado, for his children and nine neighborhood youngsters. Reinforcements were recruited when available, often from the many single men on the frontier. One such New Mexican helped Jack Stockbridge learn the alphabet after the boy's mother whipped him and withheld his supper for consistently forgetting E and M. Another bachelor taught the fatherless Martha Collins her letters by printing them on a smooth shake and making her a pencil from melted bar lead. Though it meant plenty of expense and work, a plains mother entertained and fed as many travelers as possible specifically so her children could listen and learn from them.[16]

Results varied, of course, but most children later would give high marks to home schooling. Some scattered evidence backs them up. The Montanan Charles Draper had been in a classroom only twenty-three months of his sixteen years when he applied to enter the state's normal school; nonetheless, he qualified easily and was graduated ahead of schedule. When Alma Kirkpatrick and her sister came to teach in Montana's Beaverhead valley in 1879, they found that most children had read extensively on their own and had cultivated a wider range of knowledge than most midwestern youngsters.[17] On balance, frontier home education was better than adequate.

This training was reinforced through community activities—public events that spoke both of a commitment to learning and the children's prominent place in their elders' social life. A spelling match was popular and easily organized. A considerable crowd of forty to fifty persons attended the weekly contests begun by Frank Waugh's father.[18] Competition sometimes was individualized, with players eliminated until only the error-free champion was left. At other times teams stood against opposite walls and spelled "fructify" or "gelatinous" at each other over the spectators' heads. Beyond the obvious purpose of promoting literacy, a spelling bee offered the interplay and conflict of familiar personalities, and usually there was a chance to see the proud brought low. Most who attended would have agreed with the young Kansas diarist: "Had a jam-up good time."[19]

Literary societies, or "literaries," were more elaborate in performance and more complex in purpose. Especially on the plains frontier, these were a prominent part of settlers' social life. The literary was descended from the lyceum movement, born in the Jacksonian period, dedicated to moral uplift and the diffusion of useful knowledge. The lyceum's primary tool, the public lecture, could be heard in plains towns. Citizens of early Lawrence and Leavenworth, Kansas, attended talks on phrenology, the geology of the Andes, and "Japan and the Jesuits."[20]

In the countryside, where professional lecturers were rare and community needs different, the emphasis shifted. The literary became more an occasion for visiting and entertainment, especially during the long winter months. Organizers competed to arrange the most amusing programs, and some published papers outlining performances on the horizon. Beyond that, literaries were meant to educate children and initiate them into adult society. A typical evening began with recitations, dialogues, and musical numbers by both adults and young scholars. Most selections taught moral lessons, particularly the values of perseverance, honesty, and piety. After an intermission came the highlight, a debate. It might address a local issue, but opponents usually squared off over some aspect of national politics or a timeless moral dilemma, from Chinese immigration and women's suffrage to the relative nobility of giving and receiving. One frequently debated question was especially pertinent to frontier settlement: "Resolved, that there is more pleasure in pursuit than possession." More socializing followed, often over a communal dinner, before the crowd dispersed.[21]

Children in the audience saw and heard familiar figures perform bits of their literary heritage, with humorous pieces like "Darius Green and His Flying Machine" included for leavening. When they themselves took part, the young had their cultural allegiances affirmed and deepened by their elders' broad smiles and hearty applause. Some drills assured audiences that the future was in safe hands. A favorite was "Choice of Trades." Each child carried before the crowd a tool of a respectable occupation and promised in verse a useful adulthood:

> When I am a man, a man I'll be.
> I'll be a doctor if I can, and I can.
> My pills and powders will be nice and sweet,
> And you can have just what you want to eat,
> When I am a man.

When an older child took part in a debate, he entered public life with at least the appearance of equality with adults. His performance—a blend of oratorical flourish, the persuasive arts, and a boastful celebration of democracy—acted out public values hallowed on the western fringe of Victorian America. An English settler on the plains agreed that "the American is born into the world with 'Fellow Citizens' in his mouth, and leaves it with 'One more word [and] then I'm done.' " Even so, he was startled that children adopted so faithfully their parents' self-confident bombast: "It is astonishing to see a young boy get up and rattle off a speech, presenting his side of the question, or picking holes in the weak points of the armour of his opponent," he wrote after visits to a local literary. "Even these striplings do not 'concise their diction or let their sense be clear,' but wander off willfully into wordiness."[22] The literaries' style and content caught the spirit and tensions of frontier child rearing. Children were taught an outspoken, think-on-your-feet independence but drilled to accept traditional moralisms. They were preached to—and taught to preach—about self-help and competition even as they were channeled into particular behaviors and nudged toward certain lines of work.

Most parents agreed, however, that community exercises and home education were not enough. Yet it took time for territorial governments to organize educational systems, and even then many families lived isolated from public schools. To meet this problem, settlers usually turned to the subscription school. This was a typical mingling of eastern and western traditions—in this case the private academy, common throughout the country since colonial days, and the pioneers' collective response to frontier deficiencies. The subscription system had many variations. In far west Texas, where ranches were many miles apart, each family first hired its own teacher. When horses became more plentiful and the Indian danger eased, children from several ranches met at one house. Next a subscription teacher presided over her own schoolhouse. Only in the 1920s did public schools appear in all parts of the region. Under those conditions an extended family or network of friends had an advantage. The Black family, a web of households with twenty children, set down near Breckenridge, Texas, in 1877. One man, put in charge of schooling, supervised construction of a log house, hired a passing tubercular as a teacher, and got classes quickly underway.[23]

Usually, however, parents joined with strangers and recent acquaintances to establish these experiments in free-market education. A group in White Pine, Colorado, circulated a subscription paper until they had enough pledges for three months' salary; in one busy morning, Jerry Riordan raised $150 among his Texas panhandle neighbors, enough to begin classes the next day. Teachers' pay varied considerably. Some instructors adopted a pay-as-you-go policy. Dora Bryant and her nine siblings each carried a nickle a day to class in western Oklahoma. Such a rate was a substantial outlay for families strapped for cash, and some teachers found the terms of payment suddenly changed. Near Cimarron, Oklahoma, Mary England took on twenty-five students at fifty cents per month each, but after four months, she had received two dollars, six chickens, a pig, and a quarter of beef. In the towns, where cash flow was greater and cost of living higher, teachers were paid as much as a dollar a week per child—four to eight times the rate in the countryside.[24]

Parents often had to search frantically for teachers. A group in one mountain town had to persuade the best educated woman they could find to quit her lucrative job—as piano player in the local saloon. Ranchers advertised in eastern newspapers and periodicals. Desperate organizers of Denver's earliest school first noticed Oliver J. Goldrick when he

This dugout school was more commodious than many during the first years of settlement in western Kansas. (Courtesy Kansas State Historical Society.)

arrived in town wearing a Prince Albert coat and cursing his mules in Greek, Latin, and Sanskrit; when he told them he was a graduate of the University of Dublin, they hired him immediately. In other cases freelance teachers took the initiative, moving in quickly to exploit a vigorous and growing market. In Portland, Oregon, Aaron J. Hyde traded two pups for a town lot and offered the settlement's first classes in 1848. When Abner Brown learned that Boulder, Colorado, in 1860 had forty children and no school, he promptly quit his prospecting party, built and furnished a frame building, and advertised his services.[25]

B. F. Dowell, one of these educational entrepreneurs, first tried farming for a few months in the Willamette Valley. Then, in July 1851, he "made up a school."[26] Twenty-six students initially paid eight dollars apiece for a three-month term, though in that fluid society enrollment first dipped, then rose to thirty-nine in early August. Dowell's performance must have been acceptable, for he attracted customers until he took off to hunt gold along the Rogue's River in April 1852. Though he paid for his students' books, his personal expenses were minimal, since his pay included board, lodging, and laundry. Nothing in his journal suggests dedication, or even much interest, in teaching *per se*; his prime incentive apparently was his comfortable income of sixty dollars a month. Dowell was a man on the make, looking for quick money while awaiting the next opportunity. A few months after leaving the classroom, he was selling cigars and whiskey to miners.

However else they might educate their children, most parents agreed that a publicly funded common school system was the ultimate answer. As everywhere in the country, public school education was to accomplish two broad goals. Students were to acquire a fundamental acquaintance with reading, writing, mathematics, and the nation's historical and literary heritage. Universal schooling also was to instill certain values— Christian piety, respect for authority, loyalty to the nation and its institutions, and a faith in free enterprise and the rewards of hard work. At a time of sweeping economic development, rapid social mobility, blurring of class distinctions, and an unprecedented immigrant influx, American education was to provide a measure of social control and a uniformity of belief.[27] The pioneers' determination to implant traditional values in the new land gave this second goal a special urgency.

In the developing West, however, organizers faced formidable problems. Many childless settlers were not eager to spend the taxes and time needed to get a school system underway. The frontier's transient society also left organizers with a shifting, uncertain base with which to work, while great surges of population complicated attempts at planning and adjustment. When the wet years of the late 1870s brought a wave of hopeful farmers onto the plains, for example, Nebraska's school-age population soared by almost 13 percent in a year, from 92,161 to 104,030. Although nearly two hundred new schools were organized, only nineteen schoolhouses were built, and to instruct nearly twelve thousand new potential students, the teaching force grew by six.[28]

Complicating matters in the Southwest were tensions between new arrivals and native Hispanics. To many Anglo-American pioneers, education of Spanish-speaking residents seemed pointless. "Socially, the Mexicans are below par, and little can be done with them mentally or morally," a Colorado official wrote the U.S. Commissioner of Education in 1870. But, he added, "Mexicans cannot stand civilization, and will soon give way to enterprising Americans. So, in school matters, better times are at hand."[29]

In New Mexico and Arizona, huge Hispanic majorities remained well into the twentieth century. A deadlock quickly developed in these states between territorial governments and the Catholic Church. Advocates of public education generally wanted tax-supported, non-denominational schools; Catholic leaders insisted that tax income also go to parochial schools and that clergy be allowed to teach in public classrooms. Neither side would give way. For decades students attended either parochial schools or poorly funded public classes created by county initiative. The struggle between church and state continued for generations, though Arizona had a centralized, tax-based, non-sectarian system operating parallel to parochial schools by 1875. New Mexico did not follow suit until 1891.[30]

The availability of public schools, then, varied widely from some states and territories to others [Table 2]. In 1870 Nevada had only thirty-eight schools, or about seven for every thousand school-age children. No public schools were operating in Arizona and only five in New Mexico. Yet elsewhere the accomplishments of organizers were remarkable. Colorado could boast of fourteen schools per thousand potential students—the same as in Massachusetts. The figures for Montana and Nebraska, even after recent leaps in population, were among the highest in the nation. By 1880 thousands of schools had blossomed across the region, more than keeping up with the growth in population. At least by this simple measure—the ratio of schools to youngsters of the age to attend them—public education was more accessible in the West than in any other part of the nation.

When schools were available, however, parents found themselves in a dilemma. As an exasperated Wyoming official complained, too many mothers and fathers believed "that a little learning is a (more) dangerous thing . . . than blasting in a mine, driving an ox team, or taking in washing and marrying early."[31] He exaggerated, but the family's heavy burden of labor tempted many parents to keep their youngsters at home, at least during the busiest seasons. The situation was worse in some areas than in others. Town children could fit their chores around school hours, but on farms and ranches all hands usually were needed to work the land from early spring until snowfall. Harsh, unpredictable weather then kept many at home. Margaret Archer was nearly eleven before she was large enough to pull on copper-toed boots and break her way through the Iowa snows to get to school. Many faced round trips of up to fifteen miles.[32]

Under the circumstances attendance was surprisingly high, and it increased substantially between 1870 and 1880, though the situation varied greatly within the region [Table 3]. In the more urbanized states and territories, such as Montana and Idaho, the percentages of school-age children attending classes were among the highest in the nation. Where farming and ranching reigned, as in the Dakotas, the figures dipped considerably, and in the most thinly populated reaches, like Wyoming, the

Table 2
Extent of Public Schools

	Number of Public Schools		Schools per 1,000 School-age Persons	
	1870	1880	1870	1880
U.S.	125,059	225,917	10	15
West				
Arizona	0	101	0	13
California	1,342	3,446	9	16
Colorado	124	600	14	17
Dakota	34	508	10	15
Idaho	21	128	12	17
Kansas	1,663	6,148	15	20
Montana	45	159	20	24
Nebraska	781	3,286	23	24
Nevada	38	185	7	16
New Mexico	5	162	.2	5
Oregon	594	1,068	20	21
Utah	0	383	0	8
Washington	154	531	24	26
Wyoming	4	55	5	15
Northeast				
Connecticut	1,635	2,601	12	17
Massachusetts	5,160	6,604	14	15
Pennsylvania	14,107	18,616	13	15
South				
Alabama	2,812	4,629	8	11
Arkansas	1,744	2,768	10	10
Midwest				
Indiana	8,871	11,623	16	19
Michigan	5,414	8,608	15	19
Missouri	5,996	10,329	10	15

Data from: Ninth Census of the U.S., 1870, vol. 1, 452, 618; Tenth Census of the U.S., 1880, vol. 1, 646, 916.

Table 3
School Attendance: 1870 and 1880

| | % School-Age Persons Attending School | | Average Months Schools in Session |
	1870	1880	1880
U.S.	52	66	6.4
West			
Arizona	0	53	7.3
California	55	75	8.3
Colorado	50	80	6.4
Dakota	36	42	4.8
Idaho	62	78	4.7
Kansas	53	78 .	6.0
Montana	74	70	5.0
Nebraska	49	75	5.3
Nevada	35	79	7.5
New Mexico	.6	13	5.6
Oregon	a	75	4.8
Utah	0[b]	54	7.0
Washington	74	72	5.0
Wyoming	20	77	6.0
Northeast			
Connecticut	64	76	9.0
Massachusetts	65	74	9.0
Pennsylvania	69	75	6.9
South			
Alabama	22	45	3.9
Arkansas	44	41	3.9
Midwest			
Indiana	79	83	6.8
Michigan	71	78	7.7
Missouri	55	69	5.7

[a]statistics from published census, showing 101 percent of school-age children attending class, obviously are in error.

[b]schools organized by the Church of Jesus Christ of the Latter Day Saints apparently were not classified as public schools.

Data from: Ninth Census of U.S., 1870, vol. 1, 452, 618; Tenth Census of the U.S., 1880, vol. 1, 646, 916–18.

numbers lagged well behind even those in the most educationally deprived region, the South. On most of the frontier, school terms were briefer than in other parts of the U.S., though once again there were great differences in how long these schools remained in session. In two-thirds of the states and territories, classes were held less than half the year in 1880—well below the national average.

In many parts of the West a day's ride would educate a traveler on the erratic, spotty record of frontier schooling. The percentage of school-age children attending class in Montana in 1867–68 ranged from 80 percent in the mining country to 27 percent among the farms and ranches. As late as 1910 a fourth of Montana districts held classes only four months a year or less. The average term among Arizona's urban schools in that year was 174 days; that in rural areas was 105 days.[33]

Frontier education was also expensive. Organizers were starting from scratch, building and furnishing schoolhouses at a time when everything from lumber to books cost more than in the East. Among widely scattered families, furthermore, only a handful of children could be brought together for a class; some school districts covered a thousand square miles. Nevertheless, each cluster of students needed its schoolhouse and teacher. The pattern of settlement thus demanded an extremely high expenditure per student (and taxpayer). In addition, many officials felt obliged to pay teachers high salaries to lure them into the classroom. They reasoned that the cost of living was high, wages in other jobs were good, and school terms brief. High wages for teachers, in turn, quickly exhausted a district's funds. The result was a mischievous cycle. Short terms mandated high wages, which left only enough money for short terms.[34]

Although the situation varied from place to place, generally teachers' salaries were well above the national average, while western taxpayers paid as much as or more than easterners for each school [Table 4]. With fewer people to pay the bills, that left pioneers struggling under the heaviest financial burden in the nation [Table 5]. In 1880 the West spent $2.41 per capita on education, nearly a dollar above the national average; the gap was even wider forty years later.

Congress had a plan to help meet these costs. In most territories income from the sixteenth and thirty-sixth sections of each township was to go into a permanent fund, with interest used to establish and maintain public schools. It was a typical expression of frontier optimism. The new country was expected to help pay for changing itself; a cultural wilderness would generate its opposite.

Yet the system never worked that way. Settlers almost always were on

Scrubbed and brushed, pupils in Choteau County, Montana stand with their teacher before their school in a "car-roof" homestead cabin. (Courtesy Montana Historical Society.)

the scene, waiting for schools, long before land was surveyed, much less leased and developed. Seven years after Idaho was organized, fewer than a million acres out of fifty-five million had been surveyed.[35] Even when available for leasing, the more arid and mountainous country usually went begging. Public use of resources also clashed with the exploitive, individualistic spirit of the day. Some mountain states allowed prospectors to file on school lands, and everywhere there were complaints that school sections ended up in the hands of speculators.

Such a system could never pay for frontier schooling. In 1878, in fact, ten western states and territories reported no income at all from their permanent funds.[36] Administrators turned instead to taxpayers, but among the footloose frontier population, tax collection was a frustrating enterprise indeed. In addition the most reliable taxable resource, land, remained largely in government hands, while most private holdings were still being developed and thus were low in value.

In the face of all this, some educators pleaded for outside help. Cornelius Hedges, Montana's first superintendent of public instruction, argued

Table 4
School Expenditures and Teacher Salaries: 1880

	Expenditures Per Public School	Average Teacher Salary Per Month
U.S.	$ 352	$36.39
West		
Arizona	606	76.58
California	880	76.99
Colorado	982	61.91
Dakota	361	32.31
Idaho	300	54.73
Kansas	296	27.56
Montana	428	63.21
Nebraska	329	31.38
Nevada	1,147	89.45
New Mexico	179	30.67
Oregon	297	38.63
Utah	446	42.48
Washington	212	35.97
Wyoming	518	60.23
Northeast		
Connecticut	513	40.36
Massachusetts	715	58.49
Pennsylvania	392	33.52
South		
Alabama	93	21.66
Arkansas	138	37.62
Midwest		
Indiana	388	38.90
Michigan	362	29.05
Missouri	299	36.33

Data from: Tenth Census of U.S., 1880, vol. 1, pp. 916–17.

Table 5
Regional Per Capita Expenditures

	1870–1871	1879–1880	1889–1890	1899–1900	1909–1910	1920
U.S.	1.75	1.56	2.24	2.84	4.64	9.80
North Atlantic	2.38	1.97	2.76	3.99	5.53	9.99
South Atlantic	.63	.68	.99	1.24	2.20	5.25
North Central	2.14	2.03	2.81	3.27	5.52	12.36
South Central	.73	.55	.97	1.07	2.42	5.67
West	2.15	2.41	3.37	4.21	7.27	15.44

Robert H. Bremner, ed. *Children and Youth in America: A Documentary History* (Cambridge: Harvard University Press, 1971), vol. 2, 1103.

that the federal government should invest in his territory's education system. He pointed out that Montana miners had pumped millions in gold and silver into the national economy, while under the Morrill Act territorial land helped pay for agricultural colleges elsewhere. Montana was a "subjective province." Thus far, Hedges complained, Washington had given westerners only bland assurances that it would bless them with benefits when they grew up.[37] Requests like these went unanswered, however. Organizers had to patch together whatever income they could to meet expenses.

School organizers accomplished more than might be expected, given the obstacles before them. Behind the statistics, furthermore, was much to be learned about frontier families and their grappling with problems of education. If some mothers and fathers kept their youngsters home to work, others made considerable sacrifices to put their children in classes. Some remained in unpromising areas to keep their sons and daughters near schools. A core of such families wintered in Meadow Lake, California, in 1866–67, though the camp was withering fast. One of the schoolchildren appreciated what was given up: "It was a dreary winter for our parents . . . , left in this land of lost dreams to watch their fortunes dwindle away." More often families abandoned prospering country to move within reach of schools. Some migrated annually. Ella Irvine spent her summers among the Montana placer mines of Pioneer and Yam Hill, where her father was a ditch superintendent, and her winters near the classrooms of Deer Lodge Valley. This pattern was especially common in the ranchlands, where some parents maintained two homes and others moved to town so their children could attend school for several years before returning to the countryside. An entire settlement of west Texas ranchers disappeared for want of a classroom. "It is a serious and sad affair to break up a community or group of friends," one of them wrote, "but our children are our first consideration and we take the consequences."[40]

Other children were boarded close to schools. Older scholars earned their way, but parents usually had to pay for younger ones. Sarah Hively of Denver boarded Ida Cropper, eight, for $4.50 a week in 1864. Many youngsters lived with their teachers. The woman in charge of Pleasant Valley, Nebraska's first school had up to eleven students living in her oat bin during school terms, five of whom stayed until they married. Other children commuted, hopping trains and stages early in the morning and returning by late evening.[41] Parents of these children paid twice, once to board or transport their children and again by losing the young workers' earning power.

Other young people were schooled by a different pattern. Moving often, taking full part in family labors, they attended class when they could, sometimes after they had left home. Elisha Brooks had three terms of school behind him when he went from Michigan to California at eleven. Six years later, after working as a free-lance hunter, sawmill laborer, and milk delivery boy, he decided that he "knew a whole lot of things that were not so, and very little else," and he returned to school for several years. Many followed a similar course. A young Coloradan worked in California Gulch before returning for a year of classes in Iowa, then he bounced back to clerk in a grocery and to freight produce before attending school regularly in another gold town. He was then thirteen.[42]

This pattern—education by "broken doses," one man called it—was most common among boys and young men. Presumably because sons were more likely to be kept at home to help at heavy labor, girls often outnumbered boys among students under twelve. By sixteen or seventeen, daughters were expected to assume full domestic duties, while males at that age lived with increasing independence. Thus older students were almost all young men. Girls, in short, usually went to school early if at all, while boys sometimes jumped back and forth from the classroom to the working world from the age of six until their twenties or even later.

This stuttering system helps explain the remarkable range of ages often found in frontier classrooms. A rare class census from Montezuma, Colorado, shows twenty-one students, the youngest six and the eldest nineteen. In his first teaching assignment, James Bushnell of Oregon presided over two small children and "a wild and frolicsome set of boys," all nearly grown. Most of young Susie Crocket's Oklahoma classmates wore beards, and six-year-old Charley O'Kieffe's desk-mate was thirty-four. Some financially harried administrators saw in this an opportunity. The Madison County, Montana, school board ordered each scholar over the age of twenty to pay a dollar a week in tuition.[43]

In education, as in so much of frontier life, the line between childhood and adulthood blurred, here in particular among males. First they were nudged into adult responsibilities, then expected to stay within traditional bounds of children, in this case under a teacher's instruction and discipline. They shifted among these roles increasingly by their own choice. Raleigh Wilkenson turned to forking in the sluices when he arrived in Alder Gulch at thirteen. A few years and several jobs later, he decided to return to studying math, surveying, and classical languages: "From being almost a man, [I] became once more a boy."[44]

Both children and their parents showed a strong and persistent interest in public education; both, however, were reaching for compromises between that interest and the frontier's demands and opportunities. Given this, frontier attendance figures were even more impressive. If 50 or 60 percent of school-age children were enrolled at the moment a census-taker counted them, a much greater proportion attended classes at one time or another. Pioneer schooling certainly was choppier and less consistent than elsewhere, but a large majority of young westerners had at least some exposure to it.

When parents and officials set out to open a school, their first step was to find a teacher. Organizers offered infrequent employment at a frustrating task. In exchange they often got instructors who had turned to teaching as a last resort. Daniel White wrote in his diary of a disappointing search for fortune in California in 1855, first prospecting, then investing in claims, working at odd jobs, and "laboring under the most discouraging circumstances." Finally, in despair: "Wrote to Hamilton to get a School." Some schools were staffed for years by such frontier floaters, "men . . . too lazy to work, who hadn't the ability to gamble and who couldn't scrape a little on the fiddle," as a California veteran described them.[45]

There were alternatives. Idaho's first school board persuaded a local man's wife to emigrate from Ohio for a salary of a hundred dollars a month. Older daughters and cousins were imported from back East. Local wives and husbands sometimes stepped forward, some out of concern for the children, others to help themselves through hard times. William Holden's father gave up on his drought-stricken Texas farm and took over a school for four terms. It brought in $160, "and so we ate that year," his son remembered.[46]

Everywhere on the frontier officials recruited instructors from the large, continuously replenished supply of young single women. For all the job's frustrations, teaching had its attractions for pioneer daughters. As they approached their mid-teens, these young women were expected to abandon the wide variety of labors and play they had known as children and devote most of their time to strictly domestic tasks. Some were unhappy with this change. For them, teaching was an option offering a unique combination of independence and respectability. When Ada Vrooman's family moved to the Cherokee Outlet, the sixteen-year-old chafed at spending her time tending the house and watching her younger brother. When the county superintendent told her that she could start a school if she passed an examination and found a place to hold classes, she persuaded a bachelor to loan his dugout, and classes commenced.[47] The record is full of similar spur-of-the-moment offers to adolescent daughters. School-mistresses of fifteen were commonplace, thirteen-year-olds not unknown. A vigorous demand and an appealing freedom probably explains why the ranks of western teachers came to be dominated by women even more than elsewhere in the nation.

Whatever its source, the teaching force was extremely unstable. Unattached men were the most itinerant of all pioneers. Older family members usually taught as a temporary expedient, while single women married or moved from district to district searching for better pay. Students grew used to seeing a new face at the front of the class each term. Sarah Black's thirty-year tenure in Tubac, Arizona, would have been unusual anywhere in the nation; in the West it was astounding. More typical was the case of two Oklahoma districts, which hosted seventeen teachers in sixteen years.[48]

Teaching quality was erratic. A minister found the Remini, Montana, schoolmistress intelligent and competent, "the only 'civilized' being in town"; in a nearby camp trustees had to resolve officially that "the teacher must not get drunk in school hours." A Helena, Montana, instructor in 1867 tutored his students in Latin orations and Shakespearean dialogues; in the same year and town a churchman found another teacher "indolent and incompetent and uninterested and *dirty*." At least some of these men and women went on to distinguished careers. Mose Drachman's first teacher in frontier Tucson later was Mexico's ambassador to the United States, and three years after A. E. Joab left a classroom in Lake City, Colorado, he was chairman of the mathematics department at the University of Chicago. Yet a gold camp mother refused to send her children to school, for "they would learn so many *bad things* that would injure them more than all the good. . . ." Teaching quality varied everywhere in America, but social conditions in the new West made the choice of instructors even more hit-and-miss. "Getting a teacher was sort of like getting married," a Texas mother observed: "You didn't know what you'd got until you'd gotten it."[49]

Facilities also varied enormously. Residents of affluent mining camps sometimes raised funds for a school that was, in one editor's words, "an ornament to the town"—in this case a two-room frame building outfitted with the latest styles in school furniture. By 1866 Virginia City, Nevada, boasted a large schoolhouse with wainscoted hardwood walls and new blackboards running the width of the room. With less fluid capital, rural pioneers usually had to float bonds or vote district taxes, then rely on volunteer labor. Nonetheless, some made the commitment. The sturdy schoolhouse of Strawberry Valley, Arizona, the pride of local parents, had wallpaper, blackboards, ceiling lamps, factory-made desks, maps, a globe, and a dictionary.[50]

These showpieces, however, were exceptions. In many areas classes convened in abandoned soddies and dugouts, defunct saloons, and space rented in private dwellings. When busy settlers got around to building the first schoolhouses, the results usually were more primitive than their homes. "A hole in the ground . . . covered with poles was our school," an Oklahoma girl remembered. An Arizona mother sent her boy to a hovel with three walls and a brush roof: "The children sit on the ground or [on] boxes from the store. If it is cold they have embers in an old bucket which is moved from one to another." In colder regions students crowded into cramped, stuffy, dimly lit rooms. The Cripple Creek cabin where Mabel Barbee met had a "dank mushroomy odor" and a decrepit stove that drove children outdoors when snow clogged its chimney. In a decade of teaching in several districts of three Kansas counties, Martha Byrne knew only three schools with anything but dirt floors.[51]

Children often provided their own seats and desks, and if not, they might sit for hours on unplaned, backless wooden slabs. A "recitation bench" usually sat near the front of a classroom, and sometimes a chest-high writing shelf ran along one wall. A simple desk or table for the teacher completed the furnishings. In the corner was a bucket of water and a dipper. Only the best-equipped schools had outhouses; most children found limited privacy behind a tree or large rock. As for educational tools, a blackboard typically consisted of two or three painted planks; chalk often was picked up from nearby streambeds. Students commonly used slates to practice writing and arithmetic and studied simple charts illustrating the alphabet. Instructors had to invent any further teaching aids. One used lima beans, pins, and dyed toothpicks for number work, while an Oklahoman "called books" with a megaphone made from a polished cow horn. These, however, were minor improvements to appalling facilities. After touring Montana in 1873 an official found the majority of school-houses "a terror to behold."[52]

In such classrooms students were to learn basic academic skills and principles of moral life. The earliest school laws usually laid out a fundamental curriculum. Montana's included reading, writing, orthography, arithmetic, geography, grammar, United States history, and bookkeeping. Children did not always hear much about debits and credits, but certain subjects—reading, spelling, grammar, and mathematics—were invariably taught, while penmanship, geography, physiology, history, and literature usually were at least touched upon. Occasionally there was more. A Helena schoolgirl had extensive lessons in Greek mythology, and a county superintendent reported scholars at work in Latin, Greek, and advanced mathematics.[53]

The Montana school law also called for instruction "in manners and morals and the laws of health." In particular teachers were to drill their students in principles of truth and justice, divert them from paths of idleness and falsehood, and "train them up to a true comprehension of the rights, duties, and dignity of American citizenship." The Madison County school board backed up this tall order by warning their teachers never to tolerate lying, profanity, cruelty, or any form of vice, while principals were empowered to expel any pupil whose conduct or character besmirched a school's reputation. At least some teachers took the goals of moral uplift quite seriously. "I . . . desired not only to instruct [the girls of her classes] in books but in their personal habits of cleanliness, neatness, order, courtesy," a New Englander wrote of her school near Santa Cruz, California, in 1852.[54]

Formidable obstacles, however, stood in the way of meeting the two responsibilities. Children rarely worked from the same texts. Teachers and parents occasionally sent back East for spellers, readers, and texts on arithmetic, geography, history, and physiology. Some of these books were held by school districts, others passed on informally from older to younger students. More often textless teachers asked students to bring whatever reading matter happened to be at home. The result was a motley collection, from almanacs to Balzac, so some teachers turned to the one source most likely to be at hand. Martha Collins's schoolmistress had her charges pick out words from pages torn from the Bible.[55]

Even with up-to-date texts, a teacher faced an imposing challenge. Somehow a group of students of various ages, diverse backgrounds, and different levels of learning had to be taught the basics of several subjects and trained in moral fundamentals. The result was a system recalled by nearly all veterans of one-room schoolhouses. A teacher first classified students into several groups according to their skills and progress, a task made especially difficult by short school terms and the rapid turnover of children and teachers. A conscientious schoolmistress might spend three weeks out of a twelve-week term evaluating students before they began their push through the course of instruction. Teaching then proceeded by a rotating scheme of study and testing. One group of children was called to the front, usually to sit on a "recitation" or "clause" bench. There they were drilled while the majority, supposedly practicing and poring over their lessons, waited their turn to perform.[56]

Testing combined memorization, fundamental skills, and the imprinting of moralisms, some general and others more particularly patriotic. Multiplication problems might be followed by drills on the rivers of Europe, or bones of the body, or the Jackson administration. That was surely distracting to those who sat studying. On the other hand, one student explained, children learned three ways. They listened, at the back of their consciousness, to reciters before them; they gave their own answers; they heard their lessons reinforced by the following group. Like public literary entertainments, recitations also boosted children's self-confidence, cultivated skills at public speaking, and deepened their understanding of language. A Kansas teacher had her class read stories backward to focus upon each word, enunciate it correctly, and define those they did not know. Shuttling teams of students gave an instructor maximum control, while the children, starting from different points and moving along at different rates, all were advancing toward a common goal. Given the limitations within which teachers worked, the system was commonsensical and reasonably effective.

In spite of teachers' best efforts frontier conditions posed some nagging problems in keeping to this educational progression. Like all parents

Idaho schoolchildren have brought outside the basic tools of instruction—books, benches, a desk, and a duncecap. (Courtesy Idaho Historical Society.)

pioneers were quick to give advice on what should be taught and how. Their rich mix of backgrounds, however, made their opinions unusually diverse. On the Montana plains Violet Alexander's classmates were "Irish, French-Chippewa, Norwegian, Missourian, Hoosier, and what-have-you." Though settlers typically could find some broad consensus of goals and approaches, sometimes even that was impossible. An Arizona teacher found her town

> filled up with people of all grades, from the most ignorant Arkansas family to San Francisco "hoodlums." One class of parents wish for speaking. Another does not. One wishes the children to march in good order, & the children taught good manners, & another set of people, just the opposite. The only way I know of is to pay no attention to this talk, but go on & do what one's experience & observation teaches to be best for the children's good.[57]

Among the students, normal difference of personality and temperment were heightened immeasurably by the range of ages and experiences.

A girl of five might sit by a lad of sixteen who had been moving in and out of classrooms for years, splicing lessons in Asian geography and the Spencerian system with others in herding and hauling ore. Many older students were living on their own, while those slightly younger likely had been playing and working for years with little supervision.

In such a class a teacher also was supposed to impose a single set of moral principles. Not surprisingly, many found this an uphill struggle. Various devices were tried. Some teachers had students memorize moralizing verses. A Texas schoolmaster tacked inspirational aphorisms on the wall—"Education is wealth," "Knowledge is Power"—and had scholars search books at home for others they would sing out at morning roll call. A daughter of a California camp wrote essays on "Gamboling" [*sic*], "Tobacco," and "Things I Do Not Like," explaining, a little self-righteously, why she scorned vices that many of her friends embraced. Instructors often devoted part of each day to mini-sermons on proper conduct and respect for parents. A teacher in Diamond City, Montana, took his youngsters to view an unexpected demonstration of the wages of sin—the dangling corpse of a man lynched the night before.[58]

Rather than producing model citizens, however, some teachers struggled simply to keep order. "The worst set of children I ever saw or heard tell of," a Montana schoolmistress called her students: "[I] am almost afraid that I never can bring them under subjection." An Arizonan called hers "hard game," and a west Texas schoolmaster found girls and boys in his classroom "very rude and wild [and] unacquainted with school discipline." Teachers occasionally went to extraordinary lengths to maintain control, especially over older students. One locked his worst boys in a coal house, while another asserted command by periodically shooting a moose head hanging at the rear of the room. A New Mexican wore a pistol beneath his swallowtail coat, but even then a boy crept behind him and knocked him senseless with a logging chain.[59]

Extreme circumstances like these presented officials with yet another dilemma. To maintain control, superintendents hired heavy-handed teachers, who in turn had to be disciplined if they got too rough. Spanking students was permissible, but an early Kansas schoolmaster was dismissed for "swinging Jimmy Adams by the ear." When two boys neglected to greet a west Texas teacher politely, she beat them three times a day for several days. Trustees then demanded she resign. She refused, barricading herself in the school, and when an official tried to crawl in a window, she struck him on the head with a log. The Leadville, Colorado, Board of Education would not fill a vacant post in 1881 because none of the applicants was tough enough. Not long afterwards, board members urged the prosecution of an instructor for "shooting at scholars."[60]

Nonetheless, cases of extreme violence and disorder were rare. Frontier students probably were somewhat rowdier than elsewhere, but teachers need not have feared for their lives and limbs. Instances of gross misbehavior, like young runaways, do suggest a broader tendency of frontier childhood, however. Children's varied experiences and their in-again, out-again attendance made them exceptionally independent and reluctant to accept the close regulation of a tightly disciplined schoolroom. Yet most were interested, even eager, to learn. Older students, for instance, usually singled out as troublemakers, often had chosen freely to come back to school. They also chose what behavior was appropriate and what lessons were most important and useful. Some genuine delinquents doubtless attended classes, but much of what teachers considered unrestrained wildness was only another case of young people answering in their own way the frontier's difficulties and opportunities.

Whatever their causes, problems of discipline and the many other frustrations of frontier schoolteaching naturally tested the instructors' patience. Many found their feelings drifting between dedication and despair. The Kansas schoolmistress Clara Conron wrote in her diary of minor victories, from successful recitations to days free of misbehavior, but she complained more of her drafty classroom with its smoky stove, the poor attendance of working children, and her own heavy household labors on weekends and between terms. Sarah Herndon left similar impressions of her life in the gold camp of Virginia City, Montana. To bitter winters and stifling summers were added the irritations of leaky roofs and flirtatious bachelors visiting school. Herndon found deep and genuine fulfillment in her students' progress. How pleasant it was to know "that seed has been sown, bread cast upon the waters," she wrote after an especially good day. Soon, however, she was fretting about unruly children, erratic attendance, and "this tedious, tiresome life." In the end, it was "High Ho! I am free once more. Our school is closed today."[61]

High officials hoped to solve the problems of frontier education by pursuing four elusive goals—finding money to improve schools, bringing all school-age children into the classroom, improving teaching, and standardizing what was taught. Since no help was available from the outside, most states and territories spread out the financial burden among the various levels of government. By 1867 California had a state tax of eight cents on each hundred dollars of valuation, a county tax equal to at least three dollars for each school-age child, and a district tax of up to

Minnie Bridges, mistress of a west Texas ranch school, gives a lift to John Prude, later a prominent rancher of the region. (Courtesy John Prude and Sul Ross State University.)

thirty-five cents per hundred dollars to pay for construction. Districts could also levy taxes up to fifteen cents per hundred dollars for other purposes. Any income from school lands would be distributed among the state's districts. This system worked so well—the Yale educator Benjamin Silliman later called California's common schools the best of any English-speaking people—that several other legislatures adopted it, though some added their own wrinkles. Nevada placed 2 percent of toll road receipts into its common fund, and it and other states included fines paid for penal offenses. In exchange for support from above, districts usually were required to hold classes at least three months a year. A superintendent was responsible for visiting districts, apportioning income, and making sure minimum requirements were met.[62]

But most responsibility stayed at the local level. By law, for instance, a school should have been funded when a certain number of children had moved into a newly settled area. In South Dakota the minimum was seven youngsters living at least three miles from an existing school. In North Dakota an additional school was permitted where nine children lived more than two and a half miles from an older one; a new school was required when a dozen youngsters were so situated. In practice, however, nothing happened unless parents petitioned for action. Once a school was authorized, district and county officers were expected to build, furnish, and improve facilities. And despite promises of state revenue, local property owners usually ended up paying most of the bills. In Colorado state and county contributions paid for only a fourth of school expenses; district taxes covered the rest.[63] As had been true from the first, the quality of education, and whether schools existed at all, depended on the initiative of the local settlers.

Nonetheless, all states and territories eventually passed laws requiring school attendance. Some parents answered that children were needed for the family labors or that they lived too far from schoolhouses. Others argued, with some justification, that they could better instruct their sons and daughters at home. So legislators hedged. They limited compulsory enrollment, usually to twelve weeks, then added a list of acceptable excuses for children to stay home. As a result, one superintendent complained, laws "contain[ed] so many reasons why a child should not be compelled to attend school that no reasonable person can see why they should."[64]

The answer, obviously, was to provide teaching of such quality that parents would willingly enroll their youngsters. That depended on making the business more desirable for competent, dedicated professionals, but for reasons already noted, officials could do little to increase pay, improve working conditions, and provide longer, more reliable employment. Instead, they manipulated what they could—the standards applied to those asking to teach. Competency examinations were required almost from the beginning. The earliest tests, however, usually were composed and administered by county superintendents worried about finding someone—anyone—to fill an open job. The result was predictable. When Frank Fuller volunteered to teach in a remote Arizona camp, a grateful superintendent hired him after two questions: "Can you spell 'Bob'?" and "Can you spell it backwards?" An exasperated territorial official summed up the problem: "We cannot afford to experiment with scapelings who want to become teachers because they fail in all other pursuits."[65]

The answer, some argued, was a system of examinations imposed from above. Governments eventually adopted three-tiered tests like those used in the East. The third-grade exam, usually taken by those just starting in the profession, certified applicants for a year or two. The other tests were progressively more difficult, and the first-grade exam, which allowed survivors to teach at all levels, was rigorous. Rose Hattich, at sixteen a recent graduate of the Tombstone, Arizona, schools, toiled for several hours over her first-grade exam. There were problems in arithmetic, grammar, geography, history, physiology, natural philosophy, teaching methodology, and educational law. Besides calculating the number of acres in a field with a diagonal of 42.43 rods, she wrote brief essays on the mound builders and the financial troubles of the Van Buren administration, then traced a water route from St. Louis to Peking. She described the excretory organs and diagrammed an imposing sentence: "The merit of poetry, in its wildest forms, still consists in its truth conveyed to the understanding, not directly by words, but circuitously by means of imaginative associations, which serve as its conductor."[66]

To help teachers meet these standards, most states and territories encouraged or required attendance at annual institutes of one to four weeks, usually held in counties with more than a few districts. There instructors received intensive training in required curricula and in "the science and art of teaching." The capstone of this system was the public normal school of the type that first appeared in New England around 1840. By 1900 every western state and territory except Wyoming and Nevada, those with the smallest student populations, had such institutions. Iowa had five of them, California and Oregon four each. That in Emporia, Kansas, had nearly two hundred students in 1870, and despite troubles down the road—it was struck by a tornado in 1878, then burned to the ground a few months later—its enrollment had grown seven times over by the turn of the century. Colorado governor Job A. Cooper predicted graduates of his state's normal school would be "wide-awake, practical, keen-sighted, [and] thoroughly trained." Whether or not he was overly enthusiastic, the students' commitment of time, effort, and money implied they looked on teaching as a long-term enterprise, perhaps even a profession for life. Graduates in Colorado and several other states, in fact, were granted lifetime certification. By 1900 a large and growing class of professional teachers, most of them women, was staffing western classrooms.[67]

State-controlled certification, annual institutes, and normal schools all built toward the final goal—standardization of education. Those who passed examinations and were graduated from normal schools would teach the same curricula in similar ways; presumably they also would embrace kindred values. All governments, furthermore, eventually passed laws requiring certain courses to be taught and certain textbooks to be assigned. Ideally, these texts were to be issued free to students, though the cost, like most, usually was passed on to the districts. These laws, and all the lofty goals of administrators, conspired to the same end. All children were to work their way through a common course of instruction taught by qualified and dedicated teachers who themselves had received similar training.

Western conditions continued to frustrate each part of this formula, however. Professional training certainly raised standards and improved the overall quality of teaching, and in more affluent areas, especially the towns, a growing portion of children were attending classes under conditions far better than during the first stages of settlement. But the pace of change was slowest where the need was greatest, particularly in the most sparsely settled regions where work was most likely to keep children from school. In the most isolated areas classes remained tiny and the per capita tax burden correspondingly large. As late as 1922 there were 144 districts in eastern Washington with fewer than four students enrolled in each. These areas had little to attract good teachers. Institutes were rare and standards loose. Sparse resources and rapid turnover in the teaching force undermined attempts to standardize curricula and methods. Nearly a decade after Nebraska required a uniform list of texts, for instance, barely half the state's districts used any of the titles, and only 75 of 2,690 provided free books for students.

The primitive state of public education in these parts of the West was symbolized by the condition of schoolhouses. Even at the end of World War I, 224 claim shacks and 54 ranch houses still were used for classes in Montana. Nine out of ten South Dakota schools had no indoor plumbing. Only 7 percent had wells; 20 percent had no drinking water at all. The typical rural school on the northern plains, the U.S. Bureau of Education concluded in 1918, was little different from a country school of the 1840s.[68]

Alice Polk Hill, a child of the Rockies, quoted John Greenleaf Whittier to sum up her parents' goals in coming to the frontier:

> The riches of our commonwealth
> Are free, strong minds and hearts of health;
> And more to her than gold or grain
> The cunning hand and cultured brain.[69]

The verse touched on pioneer society's most painful dilemma. Moving west in search of a better life, many settlers feared they were also turning their backs on their cultural birthright. Public education was meant to reconcile that conflict. As children learned fundamental skills and something of their society's inheritance, they would also learn the values of patriotism, moral rectitude, and an individualism tempered by respect for order, property, and dominant political and social institutions. The dilemma would be resolved. Reaching toward a better future, pioneers still could save the best of the past.

Unfortunately the conditions that allowed the first purpose always worked against the second. Cheap land was another name for a pitifully thin tax base incapable of supporting the most modest school system. Undeveloped resources demanded dawn-to-dusk workdays with no time for classes. Where people were forever pursuing grand possibilities, populations surged and shrank; try as they might, planners could never keep up. The most aggressive families pushing farthest into the new country found that the cost of schooling each child was higher than elsewhere and facilities much worse. Throughout the West, children were lured away by opportunities around them.

"We could outlive our destitution, & everything else of the kind, but we could not get an education so easily," wrote Martha Minto, who attended class only three months during her girlhood in early Oregon. When schools were available, another child of the West complained, they were "mixed and ill-regulated." Compared to eastern institutions, she thought, those she had known were like a weak crutch to a strong leg. The Englishman James Price's opinion was more balanced. He was impressed that all prairie children he knew could at least read and write; the only illiterates he knew had come to Kansas from his own country. But, he quickly added, schoolchildren's training was erratic: "I could not think that these Americans are *thorough* in anything."[70]

Price summed up the successes and failures of frontier education. Schools were established quite early and always at significant sacrifice. The great majority of children passed at least some time in classrooms. Above all, formal schooling was supplemented by the stubborn commitment of parents and communities to educate their young. Still, conditions inherent to the developing West continually worked against efforts to provide a well-rounded education and rigorous moral indoctrination.

In the end it was up to the children to push themselves beyond what was required. Many did so. Borrowing books, turning back to school after working the placers or chasing cattle, pursuing some lessons and ignoring others—children found much room to maneuver in that space between their elders' intentions and accomplishments. As in so much of frontier childhood, the story of education showed the limits of adults' control and the power of children to make what they would of themselves and their futures.

Lillian Miller

Lillian Miller was six when she, her mother, and her twelve-year-old brother, Louie, took the Great Northern Railroad from Iowa to Chinook, Montana. They came to join her father and two older brothers, Henry and Chris, on a sheep ranch bought the previous year in the Bear's Paw Mountains, north of the Missouri River breaks. Nearby Chief Joseph's people had finally been run to ground in their dash toward Canada in 1877, fifteen years before Lillian made her own way into the country.

At first Lillian found the country a little disturbing. Gazing from the train and from the wagon seat on the long trip from Chinook to the ranch, she thought the land was bleak and barren. She saw her first Indians, whose round, fleshy faces and braided hair were alien and whose staring children seemed hopelessly beyond reach of her words. Their sod-roofed cabin was gloomy, despite her mother's efforts to brighten it. With the autumn rains water came through the ceiling in noisy, muddy streams.

She felt more in place after she could name some of her new life's pieces. With Louie she watched the lizards and snakes populating the small spring-fed reservoir her father had made. They plotted the blooming patterns of wild roses, primroses, lupines, and various cacti. They learned the plains birdsongs. Lillian, a specialist in chicken sounds, eventually could crow in all keys. They collected curlew eggs—and with them, lice that their mother battled for weeks, scrubbing the children and setting their bed posts in cans of kerosene, before the house was free of the scourge. On the hills they found colorful rocks they carried to a rise behind the house to build miniature ranches and castles.

Evenings were given over to other imaginings. After dinner Lillian's father would tell of his boyhood in Husum, a small town on the North Sea, and how he made his way to America as a galley slave. Her mother recalled her childhood trip from Germany to Iowa and of growing up to meet the handsome German she would marry. The Millers collected a good library, though it was not always quiet enough to read, since Henry, a music lover, eventually traded among herders for a zither, violin, banjo, guitar, and phonograph with a morning glory horn.

Lillian and Louie learned to ride on a crafty, moon-eyed horse their father bought from nearby Indians. Nig was lazy. Catching and saddling him was an enterprise of guile. That done, it took great effort to goad him into a walk. Their father built the children a cart, a dandy sight with its cushioned seat, black body, and yellow wheels. When Nig pulled them seven miles to their one-room schoolhouse, they made a proud procession. At the plodding pace, they surveyed the countryside for hours a day, sometimes meeting Indians and usually seeing jackrabbits, rattlesnakes, cattle, and prairie chickens.

Louie died that winter. When the boy complained of stomach pains, a neighbor rode twenty-five miles to Chinook for a doctor, who fought his way back through snowdrifts, only to find that Louie's appendix had ruptured. He lived nearly a week longer. His father took the boy's body, wrapped in blankets and packed in charcoal, back to Iowa for burial. "Why did we come out here?" Lillian's mother often would ask. And her father always answered: "We should not have."

They all had further doubts when a land dispute set the family against some neighbors. Until the courts upheld the Miller's claim seven years later, there were cut fences, trampled crops, poisoned chickens and sheep, and a few threats of worse.

The Millers stayed, and eventually they established a firm foothold. They did so through absolute fidelity to what Lillian would call the first law of sheep ranching: "Everything and everyone . . . takes second place to the sheep." By the time she began boarding in Chinook to be near better schools, she had learned much about the business. She sympathized with sheepherders, "a strange lot" who held up well in spite of hard work, loneliness, and a diet of hard biscuits, burnt oatmeal, and barely recognizable coffee. She knew intimately the sheepman's tools, perils, and essential tricks. She watched shed-men skin a stillborn and put an orphaned lamb in the hide so the mother would accept the stranger's suckling; she saw her father warm chilled, apparently dead newborns back to life in the family oven.

Henry and Chris eventually took over the operation their father had begun with a quarter section homestead. They began buying cattle, and when they sold out in 1958, their ranch, at nearly half a million acres owned and lease, was one of Montana's largest. Lillian moved back to Iowa in 1909. She visited the ranch only rarely after that, but at eighty-two, when she wrote of what had shaped her life, it was of the Bear's Paw and its people.

9

Suffer the Children

Dr. Charles Clark found the overland trip to Colorado grueling. The blustery, erratic spring of 1860 had the New York physician shivering one day, parched and pinked the next. Nonetheless, he held up well. Others did not. "The little children were objects of pity, harmless and helpless as they were," he wrote. Confined for hours to their wagons, buffeted by the weather and often hungry and thirsty, they were the greatest sufferers of the journey. For Clark this answered emphatically the question of whether boys and girls should be subjected to the frontier at all. "Any man who removes his family from a comfortable home, packed away like so many 'dry goods' . . . with nothing but an 'expectancy' for their maintenance," he concluded, "[is] suffering from aberration of the mind."[1]

His diagnosis was common. Many agreed that parents were crazy to take their children into the new country, despite the West's reputation as a place where the weak would grow strong and the ill regain their health. Besides economic uncertainties, pilgrims feared Indians, ferocious animals, murderous storms, and wilderness where a child might lose his way and, with it, his life. Talk of these things was common among anxious relatives before departure and from travelers along the road.

Despite such fears there is no statistical evidence that children were more at risk on the frontier than elsewhere in the nation. They may have been safer. Unsettled western conditions made mortality figures somewhat suspect; deaths there perhaps were less likely to be reported. Even so, there is nothing to suggest that the West devoured its young more hungrily than other regions.[2]

That said, the threats that did await the children were grim enough. Accidents, sickness, and death gave adults plenty to worry about. Their particular fears, however, were often misdirected. As they watched for danger from one quarter, it struck from another. And as always, parents' perceptions of what was happening, and their ideas of what it all meant, could be very different from those of their sons and daughters. In this sense, the saddest and happiest times told a strikingly similar story. The children's dying, like their living, measured distances—the gap between expectations and reality, and the different meanings that young and old drew from frontier life.

As in so much else, life on the trails, in this case its tragic side, anticipated that elsewhere on the frontier. Children and their parents rarely encountered the dangers they expected. Indians helped emigrants more often than they harmed them, and wild animals were virtually no threat at all. Though rattlesnakes were a familiar sight—one party, routed from sleep by swarms of them, killed fourteen under their wagon wheels as they fled—snakebites were rare.[3]

Fears of extreme hunger and thirst were also generally unfounded. The most celebrated cases depended on a terrible coincidence of errors and bad luck. The Donner-Reed party, delayed by quarrels and a poor choice of routes, straggled late into the Sierra Nevada and were trapped by early storms. Among the forty dead were several children. Some young survivors ate their dog, Cash, hide and all, and later, thirteen-year-old Virginia Reed wrote her cousin, "thay was 10 days without any thing to eat but the Dead."[4] A large party of Mormon pilgrims in 1856 left Iowa late and were caught by October snows four hundred miles short of Salt Lake City. Of more than a thousand who began, about two hundred, many of them children, perished before help arrived. One girl died as she raised a piece of cracker to her mouth; another awoke in agony to find a man chewing her fingers.[5]

Less famous overlanders suffered because of similar mistakes. Argonauts reported women and babies sucking on rawhides and pork rinds after squandering food earlier in the trip. Untested shortcuts turned into nightmares. Joseph Lyman left his starving wife and children while he searched for help, getting by on meals of a wolf and woodpecker—"hard eating, I assure you." After an Oregon-bound widow and her nine offspring had devoured their last ox, "the children all would . . . smoke the Wood mice out of the Logs and Rost and Eat them."[6]

Yet these incidents were exceptional. Most emigrants carried plenty of food, and in any case private businesses and government posts were selling provisions along the main roads by the mid-1850s.[7] Sensible travelers who planned reasonably well, kept to a timetable and to tested routes, and enjoyed average luck generally avoided catastrophes.

Some unpleasantness was unavoidable, of course. Young Mary Boatman found the clouds of alkali dust "almost unbearable," and children's faces and hands stayed swollen for weeks from the bites of mosquitoes and sand flies. Bad fortune brought difficulties even to the scrupulously careful. An unseasonal blizzard might catch travelers on the high plains. One gold hunter found refuge in a small cabin after a late spring howler filled his blankets with sleet, but nearby a party with many small children had no shelter: "How they passed the night is better known to themselves." Near the end of the Oregon trail, some lost their last supplies while floating the Columbia's rapids or were made miserable by autumn weather. "I carry my babe and lead, or rather carry, another through the snow, mud, and water, almost to my knees," Elizabeth Geer wrote in her diary. "There was not one dry thread on one of us—not even my babe."[8] Yet the same chances, twisting differently, left others in fine shape. "Kate is fat as a pig," a father boasted at trail's end, and though William Warner's daughter had been sickly at the start, by August he claimed the girl at sixteen months, was as large as a three-year-old and could trot beside the wagon for an hour at a time.[9]

That was a dangerous way to travel, however, for by far the most common injuries were to youngsters who fell beneath the wheels of moving wagons. These accidents, in fact, surpassed all others combined.[10] Nervous mothers and fathers at first tried to keep their young inside the wagons, but confining restless girls and boys in so small a space was like trying to hold grasshoppers in a soup bowl. Soon curious children were hopping in and out, and inevitably some tripped and hit the ground just before the wheels groaned over them. A farm wagon crammed with barrels, trunks, tools, and people weighed more than a ton, yet many victims, pressed down into the sand and dust that lay shin-deep in places, suffered only bruises. Anna Fish popped up, with the mark of the wheels across her head, crying out, "Am I killed?" John Haskins Clark met a boy playing happily the day after a wagon had rolled over his head. "It did not quite kill him," his grandmother explained, "but it made the little rascal holler awfully."[11]

Others were not so lucky. At best a broken leg or hip left a child confined for weeks to a wagon's stifling heat and painful jolt and sway. Improperly treated, an injury meant crippling or worse. Edwin Bryant, asked to examine a boy's broken leg, found a festering compound fracture had turned the limb gangrenous from the knee down. When Bryant refused to amputate, another man set to work with a butcher knife, handsaw, and carpenter's awl. The boy died near the end of the operation.[12]

Rivers posed another threat. While fetching water or playing along the banks, children might fall into streams churning and muddy with the spring runoff. Edward Ayer heard the cries—"Doddie's in the river!"—and jumped into the Platte in time to save his friend's son, but other youngsters were swept to their deaths. Crossing the Platte or Green River presented "a scene far surpassing any thing the imagination ever conceived," one diarist thought, and another asked his friends to "imagine a dark and turbid stream . . . with a sand bottom which slides away and sinks the moment the foot touches it." Men pulled and lashed at the oxen while women and children huddled in wagon beds that shuddered with the current's weight against the sides. When wagons capsized, children usually were saved, though some were washed more than a mile downstream; others, however, drowned beneath the wrecks or were lost in the flood.[13]

There was an assortment of relatively ordinary mishaps to worry about—wagons overturning, runaway horses, and guns discharged by accident—as well as exotic dangers, such as plunging into boiling springs. At all times, the perils of living in close quarters were unpredictable. "One of the Davidson girls got considerably hurt by one of the men," a traveler told his journal: "He threw a club at a hog and hit her just below the eye."[14]

Sickness, however, killed many more children than starvation, exposure, and accidents combined. The overland migration, a congested human stream, was in some ways a superb breeding ground for diseases. Because parties traveled at various rates, many camped near different outward-bound groups almost every night, and they met others who were heading eastward. Never before or again would most pioneers come into contact with so many people in so short a time. In camp pilgrims often were greeted with refuse, dead draft animals, and human waste, "The stench is sometimes unendurable," one diarist lamented.[15] Inevitably some excrement seeped into streams that all used for drinking and cooking water. On the desert pioneers and their animals drank together from sluggish pools wriggling with microscopic killers. High on the North Platte, A. H. Cutting found that "the water is stagnant, . . . a dirty reddish color and tastes no one can know how till they try it."[16]

Children were more vulnerable than their elders to these conditions, for many had not yet had "childhood diseases" to which most adults were immune. The young were more in danger from intestinal disorders, since their smaller bodies dehydrated more rapidly. The nutritional needs of growing girls and boys were especially great, so the young likely used up vitamins at a greater rate. Given the menu of the trail, with few greens and virtually no fresh fruit, many youngsters were starved of certain essentials, especially vitamins C and D, that would have helped them combat infection and recover from illness.

Nearly all identifiable illnesses fell into three categories. The first—measles, scarlet fever, smallpox, and typhus, all communicated mainly through personal contact—usually appeared during the first few weeks of the trip. Probably they were carried by some children and adults into the bivouacs on the Missouri and the crowded camps of the trip's first leg. Measles was most common. Its high fever could kill, especially when victims were exposed to the cold of early spring, and so stopping for rest and recovery was important. Elisha Brooks recalled lying in a tent with five other stricken siblings "while six inches of snow covered all the ground and the trees were brilliant with icicles."[17]

The worst conditions were on the steamboats carrying emigrants to Ft. Benton, there to head overland to the Montana gold fields. Measles or typhus moved like brushfire through the crowded decks, with the sick sweltering in stuffy state rooms while mothers bathed them to keep the fever down. Measles in one family quickly spread to virtually every child on the boat that carried Sallie Davenport. No doctor was among the passengers, and army surgeons who came aboard had little experience with the disease. Though most children lived, one mother saw a daughter die and a son blinded, and Sallie's brother died minutes after his father met the boat at Benton.[18]

The second category included intestinal diseases, mostly dysentery and Asiatic cholera. These were most common on the first third of the journey, though dysentery, or "the flux," might strike farther down the road. They were spread through contact with victims or with infected clothes, bedding, and water. Cholera was particularly dangerous; outbreaks of it occurred mostly between 1849 and 1852, above all in that last year.

Cholera gave those who witnessed it their most terrifying time of the trip, if not of their lives. Cholera bacteria destroyed the intestinal lining, leaving the victim unable to absorb food or water; with this came high fever, cramping, vomiting, and unstoppable diarrhea. Victims suffered a maddening thirst, cracked lips, swollen tongues, and often delirium. Robust men died less than two days after they first sickened, and children, because they dehydrated so quickly, even sooner. One man witnessed the death of a seven-year-old who "was taken at twelve oclock and at four she was a corpse."[19] The disease spread easily within a company or family, so while some groups escaped it, others were devastated. An overlander saw "one woman and two men [lying] dead on the grass & some more ready to die." Travelers passed graves of brothers and sisters taken the same day. Ezra Meeker met a party of eleven wagons, all driven by women; every man had died.[20] This was a recipe for panic. One diarist told of "men . . . running about through the crowd hunting Physicians [and] enquiring for medicine." East Owen's trail mates spooked and bolted from one camp, driving nearly until midnight, "but where shall we stop, for its all crowd for the next five hundred miles?"[21]

Stopping, however, was exactly what stricken companies should have done. Since travelers had little idea of the disease's cause or cure, it was largely up to the victim to hold on until the illness had run its course. Some parents doctored their young with pills and salts, while others tried frequent bathing. Some gave liberal draughts of water, others denied it entirely. Yet the best results came from letting the sick rest in an isolated, comfortable place and treating the fever symptomatically. The majority of child victims survived, but the toll was still terrible, particularly in families that pressed on out of fear or to keep on schedule. "The trubel was, they wood not stop to docter thar sick," a father wrote: "They wood kep a roling on."[22]

An unusually detailed account of one boy's trials confirms this lesson.[23] Twenty-year-old Vincent Hoover kept a diary of his trip to California with his parents and brother, Jonathan, twelve. Late in the afternoon of July 14, a Thursday, "Johnnie" complained of fatigue, and that evening he doubled up with cramps and diarrhea. He worsened so quickly that Vincent had to carry him to the wagon. When they broke camp next morning the boy was "reduced down to a skeleton . . . [and] had you met him you would not have known him." Two miles later, Vincent asked his father to halt. Johnnie improved during that day's rest, though he still could not stand. The Hoovers were on the road again Saturday and Sunday, and Johnnie held his own, but that night he crawled from his bed for a long pull at the water jug, and immediately the diarrhea began anew. At ten the next morning, the boy called out, begging his father to stop. A halt was called, but Jonathan sank quickly. By four he was delirious. He "would rol and kick the cover off . . . and upon Father putting it on him, he would hollow and say that there was a dead man and a dead ox in the sheet." At five he stopped speaking; his breathing was labored, his eyes set. By six, four days almost to the hour from the first symptoms, he was dead. His family buried him at sunset and carved an epitaph on a pine board: "Rest in Peace, Sweet Boy, Thy Troubles Are Over."

Suddenly, five or six hundred miles up the road, the threat eased. By Independence Day, overlanders were almost entirely free of cholera, and the rate of dysentery slackened. Just then, however, cases appeared from the third category—fevers, vaguely defined and of uncertain origin. Most were called "mountain fever." Many victims doubtless suffered from Rocky Mountain spotted fever and Colorado tick fever, debilitating infections contracted from the bite of ticks indigenous to an area between Colorado and the Sierra Nevada—precisely the corridor of travel.[24] This label may also have covered a range of other illnesses and infections. By now, the resistance of the tired travelers was likely low, especially considering their vitamin-poor diet, and a host of infections could have moved in on them.

Like cholera, mountain fever came on quickly and caused its victims to do "all sorts of unseemly things," as one girl wrote.[25] In this case she watched a delirious man try to cut his son's throat. Again multiple family victims were common. The parents of W. A. Hockett, nine, died within a week of each other, as did an entire family of his friends, before he himself fell unconscious for days. Mothers and fathers tried to make sick children as comfortable as they could, but at this stage of the trip supplies and time were running short, and few stopped for long. "We found it a hard place to be sick," a woman wrote of the flushed youngsters who lay in wagons jolting over the journey's roughest terrain—fields of stones, steep mountains, rugged canyons, and kiln-hot deserts. Parents did their best. Advocates of hydropathy, who bathed the ill and packed them with wet cloths, may have saved some before the fever cooked their brains. In any case most of the young lived, though they came through the ordeal exhausted and emaciated. Part of young Hockett's spine and hip wore through his skin.[26]

Once pioneers had settled they found once again that many of their deepest fears proved virtually groundless. Many thought the new land threatened their young with all sorts of accidents, but a survey of child mortality in the farms and ranch country of western Kansas and in several mining counties in Colorado and California shows a different picture [Tables 6, 7, and 8]. Accidents were responsible for only about one child death out of twenty.

Furthermore, only a few accidental deaths had any direct connection with the landscape, weather, or wild creatures [Table 9]. Mothers and fathers were especially terrified of poisonous snakes, and at first glance, their anxiety seems reasonable. There were thick-bodied water moccasins in river bottoms east of the drylands and copperheads in the woods of the plains' eastern fringe. Nearly all the West, particularly the plains and Southwest, fairly writhed with millions of rattlesnakes. A Kansas farmer killed 127 on his land in 1878; his neighbor slew 133. When settlers

Table 6

All Child Deaths: *Mining, Farming, Ranching Regions*

Stillborn[a]	45	5%
Diphtheria	177	22%
Pulmonary	147	18%
Intestinal	103	13%
Spinal/Brain	94	11%
Typhoid	35	4%
Measles	30	4%
Scarlet Fever	29	4%
Other	70	7%
Accidents	40	5%
Unknown	54	7%
TOTAL	824	100%

[a]Includes infants dying during first month of complications of birth.

Calculations based on manuscript mortality schedules from the following counties: Kansas, 1880: Edwards, Ford, Hodgeman, Meade, Ness, Decatur, Graham, Norton, Rawlins, Rooks, Sheridan, Buffalo, Ellis, Foote, Hamilton, Lane, Gove, Pawnee, Rush, Trego, Sequoyah, Wallace. Colorado, 1870 and 1880: Clear Creek, Gilpin, Lake. California, 1860 and 1870: Tulare and Tuolumne.

in South Dakota dynamited a den of rattlers, 300 were killed, but an estimated 3,000 escaped. One newcomer kept a long stick by his bed to drive away the poisonous reptiles that frequently slithered through holes in his plank floor.[27] Working and playing, running around barefoot, children saw plenty of these snakes. Many had close scrapes, and some were taught to carry small cords to use as tourniquets in case they were struck.[28] And yet in the counties examined, only six children, all in Kansas, died of snakebite. Only one of these was older than six, and half were under three years. Older girls and boys knew the land and its fauna well, and they and the snakes seem to have given each other ample room. The few deaths probably were chance encounters by the least experienced young.

Venomous snakes, moreover, were by far the most dangerous wild animals. Though wolves were plentiful, there is no reliable evidence that they posed any significant threat. Luella Newman recalled of her girlhood that the beasts would dash into her cabin clearing and snatch food

Table 7
West Kansas Farm and Ranch Counties, 1880

	M	F	Still Born	Diphtheria	Pulmonary	Intestinal	Spinal/ Brain	Measles	Scarlet Fever	Typhoid	Other	Accident	Unknown
BIRTH to 1 mo.	49	35 (84)	39	2	6	5	1	1	1	—	2	3	23
2 mo. to 1 yr.	90	69 (159)	—	17	31	51	15	7	2	5	15	3	14
2–5 years	57	62 (119)	—	49	12	7	7	7	12	6	7	8	3
6–10 years	31	30 (61)	—	24	5	2	3	2	3	6	7	9	—
11–15 years	17	12 (29)	—	9	6	1	1	—	2	10	1	2	—
TOTAL	244	210 (454)	39	101	60	66	27	17	20	27	32	25	40
% of Total Deaths		9	9	22	13	15	6	3	4	6	7	6	9

Table 8
California and Colorado Mining Counties, 1860–80

	M F / Still Born	Diphtheria	Pulmonary	Intestinal	Spinal/ Brain	Measles	Scarlet Fever	Typhoid	Other	Accident	Unknown
BIRTH to 1 mo.	25 15 / 40 / 6	3	3	7	3	1	—	—	12	—	5
2 mo. to 1 yr.	89 76 / 165 / —	39	27	42	18	7	4	2	16	4	6
2–5 years	60 56 / 116 / —	25	37	17	10	5	2	3	8	6	3
6–10 years	17 19 / 36 / —	6	15	1	5	—	2	2	1	4	—
11–15 years	9 4 / 13 / —	3	5	—	1	—	1	1	1	1	—
TOTAL	200 170 / 370 / 6	76	87	37	67	13	9	8	38	15	14
% of Total Deaths	2	24	20	18	10	4	2	2	10	4	4

Table 9
Accidental Child Deaths

	Farm/Ranch	Mining	Both
Drowned	2	6[a]	8
Snakebite	6	—	6
Kicked by Horse	2	2	4
Burned	2	2	4
Run Over	1	2	3
Smothered	3	—	3
Poisoned	1	1	2
Gunshot	1	1	2
Blow to Head	1	1	2
Lightning	2	—	2
Fell Into Well	1	—	1
Scalded	1	—	1
Frozen	1	—	1
Tornado	1	—	1
TOTALS	25	15	40

[a]Three of these drownings were in mine shafts or coal pits.

from her hands without harming anyone. Bear attacks were extremely rare, and occasional stories of panthers carrying away babies were almost surely apocryphal. "We never heard of a case of unprovoked attack upon human beings by a wild animal," Agnes Cleaveland wrote of her New Mexico childhood. "We wandered as far from home as our enterprises called for."[29]

In this wandering the children had little to fear from another parental worry—becoming lost. Some of the plains and deserts, slashed suddenly with gullies, were covered with high grass and thick brush. Newcomers often became disoriented. Those walking the wooded hills around the mining towns were cut off quickly from familiar landmarks. But because children spent much of their time out in this terrain, they soon adjusted. It they did find themselves lost, it was rarely for more than a couple of hours. More frequently they used their knowledge of the country to lose themselves, running away from their elders and hiding in the arroyos and fields until they chose to be found or to go home.[30]

Fears about losing children to the new country and its beasts, one of them the biblical symbol of evil, may reflect parental uneasiness about breaking with their past and bringing loved ones into a place largely beyond their control. If so, it is especially ironic that children were much more likely to fall victim to accidents connected with their elders' attempts to gain mastery over the land.

Some fatalities were from falls, though hardly ever tumbles from cliffs or into canyons. On the plains, some of the continent's flattest terrain, the children fell *into* the earth—down uncovered wells their parents had dug as much as two hundred feet deep. The mining regions, where, according to Carolyn Palmer, every child expected to find a gold mine, were wormed through with open shafts and prospect holes that "merely whetted our zest for the elusive search." The result was predictable: some youngsters were killed, many more injured. A Nevada editor reported that two-year-old Tommy Roark looked "happy and rugged and tough" several months after he and his dog had lain for thirty-six hours at the bottom of a hundred-foot shaft. (The dog, having recently thrown nine pups, presumably was also fine.)[31]

Similarly, most deaths from burnings came not from the famous prairie and forest fires but from children stumbling into fireplaces or having their clothes ignited as they crouched too close to campfires. The youngest sometimes took fatal spills into washtubs of boiling water.[32] Most child drownings occurred near mining camps, where the stripping of the hillsides of trees greatly increased the flow of the frigid streams. The threat was considerable and the danger was seldom far from mothers' minds. A woman in Globe, Arizona, noticed her two-year-old was absent when her brood returned from a walk. She ran immediately to the creek, "always our first thought when one of the children was missing," just in time to snatch her daughter from the rushing water.[33]

Another danger was much closer to home. In crowded frontier houses, youngsters too often found medicines and poisons within easy reach. "Elick . . . has not had a Sick Spell since he stole the Bottel of Coperas and honney and eat it up," a California mother wrote home.[34] Elick was luckier than others, who did not survive their tastes of laudanum or iodine. A more common poisoning was connected with the household chore of soapmaking. When water was poured over ashes kept in a sloping trough, or "hopper," the seepage that trickled out was liquid lye that made a strong, abrasive soap when mixed with animal fat. If a curious child should drink from the lye bucket, however, the result was severe injury or a slow, excruciating death. A young Montanan lingered for three years and near the end was fed through small tubes forced down his swollen throat. A woman present at his death saw that "on one of [the tubes], the last used, were the prints of his little teeth where he had bitten it in his agony."[35]

Many accidents were directly related to the children's work. As on the trails, they fell under the wheels of wagons essential to the labor of farms, ranches, and mines. Given that a girl or boy might spend hundreds of hours a year herding and riding, it is not surprising that many were hurt or killed when they fell from or were kicked by horses.[36] Many children were playing with guns and rifles and hunting to supply food and income as early as their sixth year, and they sometimes made painful or fatal errors. One mother told her journal that her young son George had been shot in the head when he and a friend were playing "duel." A Texas lad's hands were mangled when he knocked two shotgun shells together—an insight into the playthings of the time—and probably was saved from death when his mother plunged his hands into a flour barrel to stanch the flow of blood.[37] Many new farm tools, with their whirling, slicing blades, took a toll. A California mother wrote relatives that her son had survived a difficult week. First a friend with a shotgun accidentally had peppered him with birdshot, then a hay-cutter had taken off the first joint of the boy's right index finger—"his most important finger!"[38]

Mining towns were far more dangerous than the farms. Besides runaway wagons, rushing streams, and occasional shots fired in drunken anger or celebration, children lived close to the many pitfalls of an unregulated industry. A boy or girl risked being run over by ore carts, crushed by rock blasted from the earth, or flung high into the air by the twirling crank of a slipped windlass. Many mining sites were so littered with blasting caps that the explosives were picked up as trash and thrown into a stove. "When the blast went off, so much excitement," one girl recalled of it happening in her house. Though Luther Johnson, eleven, lost four fingers when a cap with which he was playing exploded, his local editor predicted that "the boy will be sufficiently recovered to offer another digital sacrifice by the Fourth of July." A few months later in the same town, another boy was blinded after friends dared him to hold a match to a cap.[39]

Small wonder, then, that a woman called Rich Bar, California, "an awful place for children . . . Nervous mothers would 'die daily.' " A man who had grown up on the Comstock agreed: The experience was "as full of thrills and wounds and scars as going to the wars." He believed survivors deserved medals.[40]

Some children never had a chance to cope with these dangers. Stillbirths and deaths within the first month accounted for about one child fatality in twenty. Frontier conditions cannot be blamed for all these. Modern caesarian deliveries were unknown in the most advanced eastern hospitals, and deaths from the grosser birth defects and many from complications of labor likely would have been unavoidable anywhere in the country.

Neither were pregnant pioneers necessarily deprived of the care and support so important to their health and to that of the children they carried. Many lived near female relatives and friends who gave help and the benefits of their experience. Mary Curtis wrote of her mother sterilizing Mary's birthing clothes by treating them with carbolic acid and baking them in the oven on their Arizona ranch.[41] On the trails most expectant mothers could expect help from women in their parties and from nearby camps, and while some impatient overlanders insisted on pushing on only a few hours after delivery, others responded differently:

> I saw a lady where we nooned today, who had a fine son three days old. The arrival of the little stranger had made it necessary for his friends to go into camp for a week or more, and they had settled down to make themselves at home, quietly and patiently awaiting the time that they might resume their march. The lady was comfortably situated and in good spirits.[42]

New arrivals often were greeted warmly and given special care. A young bachelor wrote of one who "took his place behind *Formable* [formidable] *Breast works in the wagon* and claimed protection of the company," and a mother told of her friends happily passing her newborn around and naming him "the young Captain."[43]

As further evidence of the companionate marriage on the frontier, many husbands shifted the day's burdens from their wives during pregnancy, gave them added attention around birthing time, and in general showed a loving concern. Some overlanders, like Virginia Ivin's husband, hired companions to help pregnant wives with chores and child care.[44] Some husbands in the settlements sent wives to relatives or moved everyone temporarily back east when time for delivery neared. Flora and Sam Heston stayed on their Kansas homestead, but he took over the washing and heaviest house chores. Flora rested and waited: "The bees are ready to swarm . . . but you know you can't *rush the thing.*" A new Montana mother would have given anything to have her own mother near, she wrote her sister, but she added quickly that her husband "did everything in his power for me and is the very best of nurses."[45]

Unfortunately these conditions always were in tension with others that heightened pregnancy's dangers. Many women did break bonds of blood and friendship when they took the trip west. If a wife's husband would not help with the frontier's heavy load of work, the unborn child could suffer. A physician in Hodgeman County, Kansas, attributed the still birth of twins to "overwirk [sic] and exposure of Mother."[46] Where the population was most transient, mothers-to-be could not always depend on support from other females, as Martha Gally learned when she and a neighbor, Mrs. Shafer, helped a woman who began an early labor after her husband had left her in the remote mining camp of Hot Creek, Nevada:

> I went in and found her in great pain. . . . It was the first time I had witnessed, much less assisted at the great mystery of birth. . . . Mrs. F. [the expectant mother] sent for her friend, Mrs. Smith, who declined coming. Mrs. Shafer then went for a Mrs. Potter who also refused to come, so we were all alone.[47]

Without advice of friends and relatives, women might know little of hygiene or the niceties of prenatal procedures. A letter from another Nevada mining town makes the point well:

> Mary Jane has busted. Got a real prettly little fat girl. Mrs. Church and Dr. Neal were the only ones that were there with her when she had it. . . . Cad [Mrs. Church] said [Mary Jane's] feet were so dirty that she had to put clean stockings on her before the Dr. came. She said Mary J. dint have any thing prepared. They couldn't find the soap and she didnt have a bit of sweet oil or a piece of old linen in the house. Dr. said (after he's looked all over the house for the soap) Guess you wasnt expecting so soon. "O Lord yes." [She] said she had been expecting for the past two weeks. I think the Dr. must have weakened. She says the soap is in there on the floor, I guess. George [her husband] had it washing his feet.

In treating more than 2,500 pregnant women, Dr. Rollin Fillmore of Kansas lost only two to infections, and in each case the houses were filthy. In one, a pig lived in the kitchen.[48]

Male physicians everywhere in American were assuming from midwives the care of expectant mothers. Some frontier doctors were competent and experienced, but many charlatans passed themselves off as professionals. Dr. Theophilus Degan became a regional legend in the Pacific Northwest, reportedly delivering three thousand babies success-fully. But a California woman found the physicians around San Jose "briefless, . . . losing healthy patients frequently," while nurses were filled with superstitions about infant care. Some pregnant women consulted manuals on the subject, but others would have agreed with a Colorado mother: "If there had been any books on the 'do's and don'ts' during pregnancy and prenatal care, I knew nothing of them."[49]

Self-appointed experts often did more harm than good. Nationally, the practice of medicine was in transition. Patients might find able veterans, trained in excellent schools, or, as an observer noted,

> allopaths of every class of allopathy; homeopaths of high and low dilutions; hydropaths mild and heroic; chronothermalists, Thom-sonians, Mesmerists, herbalists, Indian doctors, clairvoyants, spir-itualists with healing gifts, and I know not what besides.[50]

The worst as well as the best practices made their way westward, as Joseph Fish's wife discovered. When she complained of a headache after child-birth, her midwife gave her a powerful emetic that left her semiconscious and in hourly spasms for a day and a half. Next, sweating was tried, but the overheated rocks put in her bed scorched a leg and burned the end off a toe. Two "specialists" then began a duel of strategies: the first, a Thomsonian, prescribed more emetics, and when the spasms returned, the second bled the woman heavily from the ankles. Eventually, after everyone gave up, the patient gradually improved.[51]

Finally, some westerners' isolation frustrated the best intentions and most elaborate plans. If labor began early, while her husband and other helpers were gone, a wife delivered her own child. Even when friends were at hand, complications that might have been manageable with proper help turned into disasters. Bertha Andersen's labor began one Saturday night. By Monday evening, Bertha was exhausted, her hands were blis-tered and bleeding from pulling. Only then was a doctor summoned. He arrived late Tuesday by stage and took the dead infant, in breach posi-tion, with instruments the next day. "It was like a butchering," a neigh-bor said.[52]

Parents almost always tried to isolate children from their mothers' labor and birthing, sending them to stay with neighbors or at least in another room, the barn, or a wagon. But when no one else was available to help, the young, as in so much else, had to assume without warning the place of adults. A daughter of the Texas frontier remembered a time when her father had gone on a trip for supplies:

> Mother awakened me in the night and had to have assistance. She gave birth to a baby—stillborn. She had to get a little box that we had, and we placed the baby in it, and in the morning before the other children were awake, she sent me out to bury it not far from the house. I was about twelve years old at the time. I tried to carry out my mother's instructions. Father returned a day or two later and he reburied the little baby. . . . Such is pioneer life.[53]

For children born alive, the greatest threat ahead was that of disease. As was true everywhere in the nation, the first five years were the most treacherous [Tables 7 and 8]. Some frontier conditions encouraged the spread of diseases. Except for dwellers of eastern slums, pioneer families probably were packed more densely into living spaces than any other Americans. Public sanitation in mining camps was appalling, and doctors told horror stories of the farming regions, especially among immigrants from eastern Europe. One family packed manure a foot thick beneath their floor, for instance. But other observers were emphatic that family dwellings were typically well scrubbed and living conditions no more unsanitary than in Ohio or the Carolinas. Rural Americans generally were battling diseases more effectively because they were eating more and better food.[54] Frontier families, as already seen, sometimes went hungry, but most ate reasonably well.

If there was a pattern to illnesses and fatalities, it reflected the West's geographical and social diversity. Like almost everything else, how the pioneers suffered was dictated by differences of climate, migratory trends, the nature of settlement, and chance.

Malarial fevers were most common in parts of Iowa, Kansas, and Texas swarming with mosquitoes and settled by people already shivering with "the quakes" or "the ague." A child described the onset of an attack as a "snake-like wiggle up your spine," followed by galloping, chattering chills that loosened the teeth, then fever that gnawed into the veins—all of it leaving one "limp and heartless." Granville Stuart remembered trying to put food into his mouth during chills, but "I would nearly put it in my ear."[55] Parents gave youngsters quinine in whiskey, coffee, and dried apples, but the assaults still could be devastating. Often fevers struck family members simultaneously. Then, even in moments of supreme joy or sorrow, victims lay helpless. A young Kansas girl saw the results:

> The day Albert Jordan [her brother] was born, everyone in the house had a chill, except one of the little boys. Sister Sarah came to help us and she had a chill. My chill came on before I got up in the morning and continued till late at night. We heard that Helen Hall, age ten, had died. I was the only one who could go there, so I got on a horse and went. I found them in a sad plight. Mrs. Hall was so weak that she could just walk by holding on to things. She had dressed the little girl by wrapping her in a sheet. One neighbor, an old bachelor, had gone to town for a coffin, and when he came in he lay right down on the floor because he would not stay up any longer. The neighbors buried her without a funeral.

Another plains mother told her journal of her husband, parents, and two daughters lying helpless around their one room. "Just three months to-day since we left home," she wrote in her diary: "Mark the contrast!"[56]

Though children rarely died from malaria, the debilitating disease surely hobbled their development. Its effects on the very young were pitiable. Johnnie Cushing's father wrote from Iowa that the fifteen-month-old "has lost his flesh [and] his legs look all pined away. He crys nearly one half of the night. . . . He will chill and look as blue and then he will Vomit and look as pale as can be." Johnnie lived at least to the age of eight, but one wonders of his health at fifteen and at thirty.[57]

West of the malaria belt, on the high plains and in the mountains, pulmonary diseases, above all pneumonia, were among the worst killers of the young. Both viral and bacterial in nature, pneumonia was most common during the cold of winter and early spring, especially in wetter regions like the mountains. In the dank and crowded dugouts of the plains, where many thousands of settlers huddled between November and April, the disease flourished and moved easily from person to person. Parents rightfully feared the fever's flush, the dry cough, and labored respiration. "Baby quite sick last night. Feared Pnemonia," a west Texas mother worried in her diary: "Such short quick breathing."[58] Survival depended not on the outlandish remedies—onion poultices, "Indian Primp" tea, and boiled corn nestled next to the body—but on luck, rest, and escape from the cold and damp. Such care often came too late. Near Weed, New Mexico, one of a pair of stricken children died soon after a doctor arrived. Neighbors were making a small coffin when word came of the second's death, so they broke down their work and made it double-size.[59]

A variety of other ailments stemmed not mainly from environmental conditions but from living among other humans. Some diseases were passed through contact with infected excrement, refuse, and especially fouled water. Mining towns, where people lived crowded together with virtually no health regulations, were splendid breeding grounds for cholera, dysentery, and other intestinal disorders. "No one can form the most faint conception of the filth, lice, fleas, bugs, reptiles, etc., by which we are surrounded," a Californian wrote home. Another described Sacramento as "one great cesspool," and a father found that city full of "*filth,* [and] *dead animals in abundance.*"[60] Less obvious was how easily these diseases could spread in the farm and ranch country. Children of the arid lands, like those Mary Jane Alexander brought to the Texas panhandle, sickened after drinking from stagnant pools. Everywhere in the rural West families settled near streams whenever possible. These watercourses could distribute bacteria from one family to the next quite efficiently.[61]

Because children were particularly vulnerable to dehydration, many died from diseases physicians called the bloody flux, inflammation of the bowels, and cholera infantum, a term that seems to have included almost anything that produced diarrhea and vomiting among infants, especially in the summer. "Baby had sickened . . . Nothing would stay on his stomach," a mother wrote from along Oklahoma's suspiciously named Boggy Creek. "[He] was burning up with fever. . . . Nothing relieved him." Soon he was dead.[62] The symptoms—and the outcome—were familiar. Thomas Conger was one of many parents who carried their children safely the length of the overland trail only to watch them die of these common killers in the camps of California. The course of such diseases often was rapid. A young relative of Elizabeth Fisk held on for more than a week, in the end rousing only occasionally from a stupor, before he succumbed to dysentery.[63]

The death of this boy, part of a prominent Montana family, illustrated that wealth offered children little protection. The mining frontier's well-to-do could separate themselves more from the contagion around them, but virtually everyone drew upon the same polluted water sources, and in any case all lived in common ignorance of the diseases' causes. The elite could better afford a doctor's care, but that was a dubious advantage. "My great misfortune lay in getting *well meaning* but *ignorant* Physicians," Thomas Conger wrote.[64] For dysentery doctors often prescribed

The clutter and filth in streets and alleys of towns like Butte, Montana posed grave threats of accidents and disease to youngsters who played there. (Courtesy Montana Historical Society.)

aromatic powders of doubtful value and calomel, a powerful purgative also used to expel worms. The latter's effect, of course, was simply to accelerate children's fluid loss. Thus richer and poorer children sometimes played apart, often were schooled differently, and usually looked ahead to different economic opportunities, but death took them democratically.

A final set of diseases included several borne through the air and contracted through contact with contaminated items like utensils or clothes. The most dangerous of these, smallpox, had been all but banished from the eastern states through vaccination programs, and it was extremely rare among westering pioneers. (Not so, however, in the Hispanic Southwest, where smallpox accounted for seventy of Tucson's eighty-three child deaths in 1870.)[65] Several other diseases still plagued the young, among them meningitis (or "brain fever"), whooping cough, measles, and scarlet fever. Together these usually accounted for about a fifth of the fatalities.

Like intestinal diseases, these killers may have spread more easily in the towns, but only in the southwest ranchlands, where contact among families was limited, did isolation provide significant protection. The author Helen Hunt Jackson stayed the night with a woman in a cabin perched high and alone up the Arkansas River in the Colorado Rockies. Two of her three children had died during the past month, one from scarlet fever and the other from meningitis. "How do such viruses reach such incredible heights and isolated victims?" a Telluride mother asked: "Nobody knows."[66] In most of the West the population density needed to support these diseases was reached early, especially given the settlers' passion for socializing. Commentators agreed that even under quarantine, these illnesses spread with appalling speed. The danger apparently depended on whether a contagion was introduced at all and whether it made enough connections to set off its hungry geometric progression. If emigrating parents hoped to find a safe harbor for their children, charting a course would have been chancy indeed.

Nowhere was this better demonstrated than in the case of the frontier's greatest child killer—laryngeal diphtheria, which accounted for nearly one in four deaths, more than measles, scarlet fever, meningitis, and typhoid combined. The diphtheria bacillus was passed easily through the air, by touch, or by the merest handling of a victim's clothes or playthings. Forty percent of boys and girls taken by diphtheria had brothers or sisters who died with them. The Willis family of Arizona had three sons and a daughter down at once:

> Merrill was burning with fever, Trying to climb out of the window. He surely was Sick. Samuel one morning jumped from his bed, running around with Dyphtheare Croup, could not breathe. Lilly lay propped up in bed with pillows, picking big white chunks from her throat and handing them to her father.[67]

Most children who died of pulmonary or intestinal diseases did so during their first five years, but diphtheria attacked persons up to ten or even older, so a grateful parent might watch one child after another pass through early childhood, only to see them die within days at nine or thirteen.

The symptoms were horrifying. First came a headache and lethargy, then high fever and a painful swelling of the throat; soon air passages were heavily coated with a fibrous yellow-to-white membrane. The victim's cough was persistent, his breath fetid. As the membranes thickened, breathing grew increasingly labored, and death came from suffocation or from strain on a system overtaxed by the symptoms. The fever, and perhaps oxygen deprivation, brought hallucinations and triggered bizarre behavior. A young Kansan suffered "indescribable pain" and dreams of animals and snakes that filled all space, writhing, in constant motion, coming closer to me, but never quite in on me. . . . The horror of it all was very real and for months those dreams returned, causing me to wake in a cold sweat.[68]

Death usually came within a few days, sooner among the youngest. Lydia Hadley was alone on her Iowa farm when her only son, seven months old, showed the first signs. "He was toock sick one evening about dark and died the next morning about eight oclock," she wrote a friend.[69]

Doctors occasionally tried tracheotomies. Some used fishhooks to hold the incisions open. One girl's physician "burned my throat with a vitriol pencil until the blood ran." Other doctors swabbed victims' throats with diluted sulphuric acid and concoctions of salt, pepper, alum, vinegar, and nitrate of potash. Not surprisingly, some fathers and mothers trusted to fate and refused to allow these painful treatments. In Leadville after four of the Corum children died, Dr. J. J. Smith scribbled angrily on the mortality record that "the parents [said] they could not cruilize the children but would *Rather them Die*."[70]

It would have been impossible to predict which part of the frontier was safest from this terrifying disease. While diphtheria was somewhat less common south of the thirty-seventh parallel, it generally struck some areas terrible blows and left others alone, seemingly at random. The 1880 census noted that three Arizonans died of diphtheria, while Utah, with three times as many people as its southern neighbor, reported 808 fatalities. One California mining county suffered a single death; another of about equal population had forty-five.[71]

The randomness probably resulted partly from the happenstance of who settled where. An upsurge of diphtheria around mid-century struck hardest in cities of the Atlantic coast. Many people, exposed to small doses of the bacillus, likely developed a natural resistance. By 1860, one authority suggests, some cities had become vast "reservoir[s] of immunity," but their denizens still could carry the pestilence to others never exposed to it.[72] These city dwellers, heading West to be scrambled among the many thousands from Europe and rural American, carried more than their hopes with them.

A close look at western Kansas in 1880 illustrates the dappled pattern of diphtheria outbreaks. A published census map showed that Missouri and eastern Kansas were far freer of diphtheria than the area just to the west, a region of farms, ranches, small towns, and military posts. Yet the situation was not so simple.[73] Southwestern Kansas was untouched. Twenty miles north of Dodge City, the first diphtheria deaths were recorded—a pair in Hodgeman County, five in Pawnee—and in the next tier of counties, the numbers jumped. Thirty percent of child deaths in Rush County were from the sickness. Then, mysteriously, the figures dropped again to the west and directly northward.

The worst, however, was not confined to that band of country between the villages of Kinsley and Nicodemus. Huddled against the Nebraska border were Decatur and Norton Counties. In the first diphtheria took nearly four of ten children who died, and in battered Norton County forty-five of eighty-five. Nearly twice as many girls and boys died of diphtheria in Norton County that year than in all Montana Territory. Move closer: In the western third of the county, twenty-four children died, all but one from the disease. Step closer, into the houses: Clara and Archie Blake, six and eight, both died in mid-summer. In the fall the Fairbanks family lost Eva, Elva, and Lawrence. The Hudsonpillars, Railsbacks, Lindsays, and Watsons each lost a pair. In Rooks County to the southeast, Mr. and Mrs. Jones saw six of their children die in September—their twin four-year-olds, Cora and Dora, Daniel (seven), Nancy (nine), George (thirteen), and Sarah (fourteen).

The emotional blow of these and other child deaths must be understood in the context of the westward movement and of the choices pioneer parents had made. Diphtheria epidemics and other contact diseases also struck randomly in the East. Statistically, frontier children were not unusually in danger. In 1880 four times as many children died in Montgomery County, Alabama than in Nevada, and infants were twice as likely to die in Hartford, Connecticut than in the wilds of west Texas.

But in the sod houses of Norton County things surely looked different. There are stories in the methodical notes of the census takers. The Proctor girl, three, and her parents had been born in Scotland. Having crossed an ocean and half a continent, they had lived in western Kansas three weeks when she died. The Railsbacks' journey had been more modest. The mother, Maria, was from Missouri; she and her Hoosier husband had been in Kansas two years. One boy had been born there, but for the other's birth, Maria had returned to Missouri, presumably to be among relatives. The precaution came to nothing, for diphtheria took both sons in September, five months after Maria had died of consumption. There was always the hopeful movement, the reaching for the better chance, the gestures of protection, then the sudden chop of death. And when the dying began, it must have seemed everywhere.

No aspect of frontier childhood is more difficult to penetrate than the inner response of pioneers, older and younger, to the children's deaths.

The collective responses of neighbors were most visible. Their cooperative, communal impulses did not always hold up during an epidemic. When Alice Carnow and three of her children were down with diphtheria, their friends shunned them, refusing to bring food or to finish washing clothes that had been boiled vigorously. Alice's husband was alone when he buried a daughter.[74] Usually, however, neighbors brought food and gathered to lay out the small body, build a coffin, and perhaps blacken it with soot. Wealthier mothers gave linen and velvet dresses for corpses that in life had worn flour-sack underwear. "There is something about death here that draws men's hearts together," an Englishman wrote of a child's wake and funeral on the plains: "People drop work, dress neatly and come to attend."[75] Once more, settlers were creating community through common traditions—in this case, by means of the rituals of mourning.

Those closest to the dead typically kept their feelings veiled. A Kansas farmwife wrote in her diary:

> Sept 13 [1883]: [This] day your little baby Davied was very sick with the hooping cough he died this afternoon 1/4 past 5 o clock.
> Sept 14: [This] day was buried in Arvonia Cemetery 4 of Clock this evening.
> Sept 15: i was sick in bed Mrs. Jones Cumbu went home this afternoon.
> Sept 16: Sunday morning. i got up today Rees Jones came over to see us.
> Sept 17: John [her husband] was busy cutting corn and father to.
> Sept 18: fine day John busy cutting Corn and father to. i took the children out on top of the hills.[76]

The use of the second person ("your little baby"), the visits, the prostration and quick return to routine, and finally the elevating moment with surviving children—the terse entries suggest emotional pain and rituals to ease them.

When parents were more articulate, they most often expressed deep guilt. *"Be calm my friends; don't censure me for what I have done,"* Thomas Conger began his letter home telling of his son's and wife's deaths. The reason was never far below the surface. "Ma thinks if we had been at home, he neednt have died," a teenager confided to her journal of her brother's death. The wound was sometimes raw and open. In Placerville, California, in 1850 an argonaut heard a woman's keening in a tent. "Oh, my child is dying!" she cried. She had taken the infant west against relatives' advice, "but now he is dead. How can I go home without him[?] . . . I can't go."[77]

They felt a special anguish over putting children into alien ground. Couples occasionally packed corpses in charcoal and sent them back to relatives, though most had to bury the dead quickly, wherever they were. Worst of all were burials on the trail, for the young would remain far from family now scattered east and west, lying in country seen as wild and desolate, abandoned in what one called "this boundless city of the dead." Sympathetic strangers lay flowers and small gifts by the children's graves and built protective barriers.[78] In the settled regions many sorrowing families eventually had to move on, some leaving a trail of plots across the West. Even when they stayed many were troubled that the resting places were so different from the settings of their own pasts. The New Englander Endicott Peabody spoke for these parents after attending a three-year-old's funeral in Tombstone:

> I pitied the poor mother and father very much indeed. It really does not matter where one's body rests when the spirit has left it—but I should like to be where there is something green—where nature is beautiful—or else in the deep—but to be left in a perfectly sterile soil with only rocks and lime over one seems to me incomparably dreary.[79]

To help cope with these feelings, parents reminded themselves of what remained. "God took him to His fold, this one pet lamb," a Denver wife wrote of her stillborn son, but she added quickly that "we dare not murmur at our loss, . . . for *my* life was spared."[80] As she did, mothers and fathers emphasized their child's sure ascent into heaven. They drew assurance from the moment of death, for "dying well" was proof of entry into the kingdom of eternal glory:

> Calmly, peacefully, the little soul left the earthly tenement, and as it entered on the new life, a little of the radiance of the heavenly glory settled on his face and the look of weariness and suffering passed away.[81]

In turn, this was linked to the living child's innate goodness. Following the sudden death of her two-year-old, "the center of our universe," Sarah Martin looked back and saw the signs: he had loved to put his head in her lap and ask her to sing about Jesus. " 'That little boy is too sweet to

The Andrews family at the grave of Willie, son and sibling who died at nineteen months on their ranch in Cedar Canyon, Nebraska. (Solomon D. Butcher Collection, Nebraska State Historical Society.)

live,' " a visitor remarked. "That does not seem an exaggeration now," Martin wrote: "The next Sunday we buried him."[82]

Similar sentiments were carved on tombstones. The parents of the three Richards children, who died within four days during a diphtheria epidemic in Caribou, Colorado, consoled themselves by seeing their lost offspring pioneering celestial territory:

> Gone before us
> oh our children
> To the better land.
> Vainly wait we
> for others in
> Your places to stand.[83]

More elaborate were poems of faith and consolation published in frontier newspapers. The *Globe* of Dodge City, Kansas, offered these thoughts on the death of Lyda Anthony, four:

> Gone from the beautiful eyes the light;
> Mama's darling is dying tonight.
> Faintly and sweetly yielding her breath;
> Plague-stricken cherub! Pitiless death!
> Hide up the toy-things—the shoes put away;
> Lambs from Christ's bosom go never astray.[84]

The time and place of this poem—the boom year of what was supposedly one of the frontier's wildest towns—illustrates how easily some traditions and contemporary trends were carried westward.[85] These private statements and public displays were expressions of two Victorian developments—the sentimentalizing of rituals for the dead of all ages and the increasingly romantic view of childhood. Images of children as cherubs and a faith in the "good death" comforted parents who had reached hopefully for a new life only to see their young die in alien country. A child might be left by the road or on a stopover farm, but in "the better land" the scattering would be gathered and guilt's weight set down. Once more, adults found that recent changes in family culture served well the special needs of the fringe of American settlement.

As for surviving children, little was done to shield them from the deaths of others. The older ones seem to have accepted matter-of-factly the passing of those not close to them. Within two months, Edna Hedges, eleven, mentioned in her diary that a schoolmate had died and that "Poor Lily, Mrs. Paynter's girl, is dead with pneumonia." The entries sit calmly beside notes of the ordinary. The teenaged Luna Warner wrote that a neighbor's "little Burton is dead. Genelia and I went over afterwards . . . Louie shot a wild goose out on the prairies."[86] Younger pioneers expressed more emotion, especially if the loss was of a friend or sibling. Although Frances Moore claimed that death held no terrors for her as a child, she recalled feelings of desolation watching dirt shoveled onto a casket and unease when her twin brother died: "To a child, [death] is so dark and forbidding, so unreal and seemingly impossible." Allie Wallace's more frightening memories began with the "glassy, sightless eyes" of slaughtered hogs that so recently had been full of life. Then her infant sister died of dysentery: "I was overwhelmed, stunned, shocked." She ran terrified to her devastated mother, who gave neither comfort nor explanation.[87]

These were classic reactions of children everywhere—alarm at dead animals and their changes, anxiety over the implications for loved ones and themselves, puzzlement, and sometimes great fear at an irreversible separation. But nothing suggested that the frontier gave death any special meaning. Their responses differed from those of adults in what was not said. Whether writing at the time or years later, these children expressed no anguish that siblings and friends had died in alien country and had been buried in "sterile" soil; neither did they portray their loss as the passing of angelic innocents into gloryland.

Their descriptions of the last moments and burials instead are images, straightforward and unadorned, of those they love being set into land they know well and accept:

> When little brother died there was no one near us [on their Oklahoma homestead] but some cowboys in a line camp about ten miles away. The cowboys came and dug the grave and made a box to lay him away in. The cowboys sang a song and my grandfather James prayed a prayer and that was all.[88]

More revealing was Augusta Dodge's memory of the death of her brother, Osseon, twelve, on the Kansas plains. When their mother saw the boy was dead, "her cry of agony was not human. Then it seemed she would never get her breath again." The father at first just stared, then began shaking and sobbing. Augusta, ten, was exceptionally close to her brother, and this was one of her life's greatest sorrows. Years later, when she described the wake and funeral, she moved abruptly into the present tense: "Now they are putting him in the hack." After Osseon was buried, the family stayed several days nearby with her grandparents. When at last they walked back toward their dugout, Augusta felt guilty because she was so anxious to see the house and the country around it. Then, as they topped the last rise, she stood stunned: her father had pulled the logs from the roof, broken down the walls, and plowed over the ruins and all around.[89] To him the place was a reminder of his pain and, it is implied, a symbol of recrimination. To Augusta the dugout and its land were home, a comfort, a part of herself.

Accidents, sickness, and death were a common enough part of children's lives, even if the young were no more in danger on the frontier than elsewhere in America. These trials are also essential to understanding the inner, emotional history of pioneering. The decision to go west, usually the most momentous that parents would ever make, was taken in precarious balance. On one side was a faith in their good fortune and their talents at making the land pay; on the other, an unease about the loss of the past and about threats, especially to their children, they imagined ahead. As it happened, parents' fears—of Indians, wild beasts and serpents, and space that swallowed the young—proved largely illusory. But their own ambitions could turn upon them in terrible ways.

Mothers and fathers brought most of their death with them. Nearly all fatal accidents happened while children were working the land or helping make a home. Children usually died not from what the wilderness did to them but from what they did to it. Diseases that emigrants imported and cultivated with impressive efficiency were more dangerous than the frontier environment. On the grimmer side of the frontier lottery, parents came trusting to luck, then saw their sons and daughters die from the chance of where they landed. Determined to keep tradition alive, they made their houses into preservers of the past; their children then infected one another between the close walls of clapboard and wild sod. Confident in their power to make over the environment, men and women saw youths killed by the tools of development. The settlers met the enemy, and it was themselves.

Not surprisingly, these parents felt a special grief mixed with guilt and self-doubt. Yet the children who survived did not carry that load of blame, for their emotional surroundings were not those of their elders. To the young, death was a frightening, mysterious force that took people they knew. When they grieved, it was not because brothers, sisters, and friends had died where they had. If anything, that gave them solace. Children's first responses to the West had deepened differences between them and their elders, as had part of their work, play, and even their education. And so, finally, did these tragedies.

When frontier sons and daughters grew up to bear and lose children of their own, a cycle was finished. Anne Ellis, having married young and left the Colorado gold camps of her childhood, was in Goldfield, Nevada, in the summer of 1906 when her daughter died of diphtheria and was buried in a pauper's grave. A few weeks later, Ellis stole a stone from a building site, chiseled her daughter's name on its face, and with her last seventy-five cents hired a freighter to haul it past Tex Richter's saloon and over the railroad tracks to the cemetery. Before he left, the man helped her plant the stone, level and square. As she tells it in her memoir, Ellis then

> found more rocks and built around it, and, as the sun came up,
> it saw her kneeling there beside her child's grave. At the head
> was a white headstone with the name "JOY" carved in it. She
> was smiling.
> Now she must hurry back to work, and, as she walked the mile
> and a half, she wondered what the builders of the Sundog School-
> house thought—when they missed their white stone step?[90]

Ellis's words, full of sentiment and affection, show no guilt or remorse; her act was an affirmation. Surrounded by mines, mills, schools, businesses, and other monuments to pioneer accomplishments, the stone she raised had a simple, resonant message about her daughter: She had been there.

Owen McWhorter

It was full dark and Owen was in bed when he heard the horse, stamping and snuffling like it was tired. The boy had his pants on and was out the door just as his father was asking the rider to come in for some food and rest. No, much obliged, but he'd best not. He'd be thankful, though, for something to eat while he rode.

By then Owen was standing by the stirrup, and he looked down into the man's boot: It was full of blood. The man explained that his horse had spooked and thrown him. He had managed to climb back into the saddle, but the bones of his lower leg had splintered and broken the skin. He knew that when he got down now, he would be a long time getting up. Owen's mother fried two eggs, put them on some bread, and gave them to the horseman, who went on. His farm was sixty miles off, he said, and his wife would be looking for him.

Few visits were that dramatic, but all, even the grim ones, were welcome. The McWhorters lived along the seams of three frontiers. Several miles south was the village of Lubbock, seven years old when Owen was born in 1897. To the east a few farmers were trying to coax mesquite land into corn, cotton, and hay fields. West of the McWhorters' small ranch was the much larger Slate spread. Counting the open range around the Slates, there were more than twenty-five thousand acres that were home to cattle, antelope, coyotes, some wild horses, and a scattering of bachelor cowboys in line camps.

That made it lonesome sometimes, especially for his mother, but Owen was born into the country and loved it. As a crawler he played with horse bones and stuck his fists into the hollowed hooves to clop and gallop in the dirt around the house. A few years later he was in the saddle for real, chasing varmints and acting the man. Once, when a blizzard drove a few hundred antelope into a fenced corner of pasture, several dozen froze. Owen and his friends rode over for a mock roundup after the thaw, "branding" the carcasses with sticks and cutting ranch marks into the ears.

From his parents Owen learned to think about the two persistent questions of plains life: "What do we drink?" and "What do we burn?" The worst summers cooked the grass, dried up the creek's trickle, and made the family wonder. Storms were welcome visitors, polite and gift-bearing. Whenever one came at night, Owen's father, a little awed, would wake him with a soft shake and a whisper ("Oh! It's raining . . ."), and they would listen to good news pounding the roof.

A winter storm was a rude thief, but even when it took a lot, it left a little behind. In deep snowfalls, the thinner cattle got "on the lift." Man and boy would look for them in the coldest snaps. Owen would hold a fistful of grass in a cow's face while his father hoisted at the rump, heaving and encouraging. Sometimes a tired cow would rise up and live to graze on springtime beeweed; many gave in and died. In the worst winters, as in 1906, with the last fuel gone or too soggy to use, Owen would search out the low, gentle mounds of snow, pull out the bones, and take them home to burn: "Course, all the food tasted like bones, smelled up the house, but we had to have something."

Still, the signs were clear enough that the newcomers were winning. Only a few mustangs were left, small and wily and a little treacherous, worthless for anything but sport. Louis Hutchins caught one of the last. He and Owen's father spent a day and a half maneuvering the tough, tangle-haired scrapper to a corral. Several men were there to get their ropes on for the final pull. Then, all of a sudden, the horse was loose and twirling, free of all but Hutchins' rope and bolting for open country. When it hit the end of the tether, it broke its neck, a hanged outlaw. A few years later Hutchins was killed, hit in the head when a wind gust spun the vane of a windmill he was repairing.

In 1907 Owen's family moved to Lubbock so he could go to school. Soon a few automobiles were reeling drunkenly down county roads; after a five mile journey, the first car to reach town arrived on a tire and three rims. Farmers had more than a foothold, and some ranchers kept second houses in town. Owen had read a lot at home, and he did well in his classes. He studied law at the University of Texas and afterwards returned to work in the county tax office.

There he learned that the saddle-bound nester had made it home. The man came in one day to pay his taxes, a lot smaller than McWhorter recalled, but even after seventeen years, the face was clear in Owen's memory. He had been two days getting home, the farmer said, and two months more on his back, but "I been going ever since, kid." The man showed McWhorter his twisted leg, and the two talked crops and cattle.

McWhorter spent his life both in town and on the land around it. In 1929 he began farming on the side, and with his partner, L. S. Howard, he developed a nationally respected breed of milking shorthorns. In Lubbock he served two terms as county attorney and in 1933 began his own law practice. In that he would prosper, attain the elusive status of civic father, and be elected president of the Texas State Bar Association. He died in 1986.

10

Children and the Frontier

Until its children are heard, the frontier's history cannot be truly written. The story of westward expansion has been a national inspiration and a global entertainment. It is a key to understanding America's precocious rise to power; from it, our people have taken their most enduring myths. But since its first telling, the story has been incomplete, and thus distorted. In all the human striving, failure, and accomplishment, a large portion of the actors have been left out.

Historians have ignored those who knew the far western frontier best. The lifetime of children born on the frontier spanned the greatest era of western development. When young Matilda Sager crossed the plains to Oregon in 1844, her new home was, by her terms, a wilderness. A handful of missionaries and a few hundred Anglo-American farmers lived in country dominated by British trappers and more than a score of Indian tribes. When she died in 1929, the Pacific Northwest was an empire of great cities and vast farmlands, enjoying the benefits and plagued by the troubles of a modern industrial state. Many thousands of others throughout the Far West lived through that extraordinary time of change, when a baby born in Nebraska or Arizona might frolic around oxcarts and live to vote for Lyndon Johnson.

Pioneer children helped accomplish this last, and most rapid, westward expansion. As they did, their values, visions of the future, and perceptions of themselves emerged. The growth of the two cannot be separated. We must take the children into account when describing the settlement of America's final frontier, and only through the frontier's evolution can we hope to understand those last generations born of three centuries of pioneering.

Western history looks very different when the children are included in it. Their story demands a drastic rewriting of the most familiar episodes of frontier history—those of conquest and economic development. In a typical textbook the traditional drama unfolds in an orderly march, chapter by chapter. Indians are subdued and imperial rivals whipped or hoodwinked; tracks are laid to carry steam-belching locomotives into the continent's outback; precious metals are discovered and extracted; great herds of cattle are brought up on the grasslands; prairies and plains are transformed into farms.

This story has been written far too narrowly. For one thing, the leading actors have been almost all men. The reader assumes women and children were there, yet their roles are described so vaguely that, as one critic has suggested, the West might as well be labeled "Hisland" on the traditional historical map.[1] Men did, of course, direct many of these great changes and did some of the most visible work—that of military conquest, diplomacy, and town building, for instance. To tell this story as primarily an enterprise of adult males, however, is absurd.

Children and women played an important part in much that is credited to their fathers and husbands. A new agricultural technology allowed boys, girls, and women to help with the arduous jobs of plowing, planting, and harvesting. Children handled much of the tedious but essential work of caring for growing crops; child herders were a common sight. On the thousands of smaller ranches and stock farms they were often the only ones in the field.

Moreover, the usual descriptions leave out as many tasks as they include. Children who hunted, gathered wild plants, and tended gardens in many cases fed the men who farmed, ranched, and mined. When parents bought some item they could not make for themselves, they used cash earned by sons and daughters who helped make butter and gather eggs for sale and who herded neighbors' cattle, clerked in stores, hawked newspapers, and delivered laundry. Weary fathers ate and rested in homes where women and children did the cooking, cleaning, canning, and washing.

The frontier economy was like the grasses carpeting the Great Plains, where what was seen on the surface was sustained by roots much lengthier, grasping for nourishment in stingy soil. So, too, unseen and unheralded by standard histories, the remarkable range of labor done by youngsters and women was as important as the visibly dramatic business of fighting Indians and building railroads. Children, in fact, were the frontier's most versatile workers. They gave their families what was needed most—an impressive adaptability. They eased the adjustment to new economic settings, took on new tasks demanded by changing circumstances, and helped their parents through hard times. Some sons and daughters provided virtually the full support for mothers and fathers who lost spouses or were struck down by sickness.

Most of all, the children remind us that the West was transformed through a complex economy of mutual dependence. A pioneer mother put it well:

> When all is said and done, man alone never settled a country, never built an empire, never even stayed "put" unless accompanied by wife and children. . . . The unconquerable spirit of man may subdue, but it never yet has settled a new country; the family does that.[2]

Yet even when it is broadened, the traditional view of the frontier remains badly distorted. This approach emphasizes economic development above all else, and by implication, it portrays pioneers as moving with a single-minded motivation to profit by making over the land. A typical adult pioneer, to be sure, was an optimist inspired by dreams of gain. Yet pioneers did more than transform the country, and certainly they worried about more than making profits. They went west also determined to build what they considered a proper social order. The focus of that was not the field and the mine but the family, the home, and the children.

This concern shaped both the pioneers' grander decisions and their daily grind. Many parents chose their destinations according to the opportunities—educational and social as well as economic—for their sons and daughters, and among the most common reasons for moving around the new country was the desire to be near schools or to escape social corruptions. Pioneer mothers spent precious energy beginning their children's educations and directing their moral growth.

Outside the home, children formed the center of social and political life. In popular entertainments like spelling matches, school programs, and lyceums, they provided a welcome source of diversion and amusement. These gatherings, in fact, were public statements that children were valuable and their rearing important to a community's purpose. The point was made in holiday parades, when girls and boys rode and marched, waving flags and wearing garb symbolic of venerated values. The young were celebrated as the hope of the future and a measure of the new land's

The primary force behind westward expansion—the family. (Solomon D. Butcher Collection, Nebraska State Historical Society.)

social maturity. The young were an encouragement to politicking. Often their parents' first collective action was to organize subscription schools, and once educational systems were established by law, local districts often were the arena of public life where participation was the broadest and interest the most persistent.

All this was as much a part of westward expansion as discovering bonanzas and driving longhorns up the Chisholm trail. Pioneers' dreams, fears, and obsessions were complex and sometimes contradictory. They conceived their goals and measured their successes and failures far more broadly than the tale is typically told. Only when we widen our angle of vision to include children and the family will we see this larger picture.

The children's story also reminds us what stubborn conservatives the pioneers were. To say this is to run against the most hallowed tradition in writing western history—that associated with Frederick Jackson Turner. "American social development has been continually beginning over again on the frontier," Turner announced in his famous address of 1893. His genius was to emphasize how things had changed in the developing

West. To the master and his disciples, the westering story was one of "perennial rebirth."[3]

Turner's sweeping statements, meant to goad scholars in a new direction, were bound to stimulate a reaction, however. In an essay nearly as influential as Turner's, Earl Pomeroy argued that the most striking fact of pioneer life was how little it changed: "The Westerner has been fundamentally an imitator rather than innovator. . . . He was the most ardent of conformists." To make his point, Pomeroy pointed out the many continuities in western law, religion, economic structures and business practices, governments, and constitutions.[4]

Pomeroy's was a healthy rebuttal, well argued and long overdue. But he failed to mention probably the most conservative area of frontier life—the family, its behavior, its rituals, and the attitudes associated with it. Pioneers poured physical and emotional energy into trying to transplant and nurture traditions in the frontier's fresh soil. Their houses were monuments to that purpose. Like a ship at anchor along the Atlantic coast in the seventeenth century, a pioneer home was a depository crammed with carefully chosen artifacts from the place that had sent it forth. Many of these details held no economic benefit. Photographs, chromos, clocks, mirrors, delicate dishes, tablecloths, books and parlor organs, vines and flowers and shade trees were meant to speak, especially to children, of the way things ought to be, of places left behind and values carried forward. Here parents, especially mothers, spent hours teaching the lessons and telling the stories that made up the complex creation of a family's ordinary homelife. Social occasions—dances, informal visiting, holiday celebrations, and others—also perpetuated beliefs and styles of behavior and decorum. Together they added up to an extraordinary effort, the dogged replanting of ways of life.

The powerful educational impulse, centering on children and the family, by its nature involved the westward transfer of information, values, and culture. Hard-worked mothers made time for teaching the basics of reading and mathematics. Fathers and mothers established common schools remarkably early, considering the trying circumstances, and educational officials argued for standardized curricula and instruction in good manners and patriotism as well as the "three R's." On many parts of the frontier, children could attend sabbath schools within the first years of settlement. Lyceums, literaries, and spelling matches stressed moral homilies almost as much as knowledge and fundamental skills. All this was a wave of tradition, east to west.

These public gestures went beyond their obvious, immediate purposes.

Frontier society was a slumgullion stew, its population the most diverse and transient in the nation. Settlers were looking for something to pull themselves together—some first, tentative step from *pluribus* to *unum*. Through education, strangers found that common ground. Specific goals were less important than that most people could agree on them. Pioneers may have come from all over the nation and Europe, from Hoosierland to Hesse, but they could get together on the need for systematic education. A commitment to schooling became a useful tool in the pioneers' search for community, present and future.

Children also were conservatives in their way. They brought westward the rich lore of childhood—rhymes, word puzzles, songs, jokes, and games, some from a couple of centuries in the past. These spoke to the special concerns of the young; in laughing and playing, boys and girls used time-tested devices to amuse and soothe themselves in ways they knew best. Games, like some of what their parents did, created instant communities. With the rules and choreography of age-old contests, youngsters recognized a common heritage, and through the scrap and scramble, they introduced themselves. They used the traditions of their own complex culture to knit together this younger level of society.

In this transfer of eastern ways, one fact, puzzling on the face of it, stands out. When adult pioneers carried with them modern attitudes about children and the family, they found that many of these ideals made the transition to the new country with surprising ease. The frontier was receptive, for instance, to the modern romanticized view of childhood. Where adults greatly outnumbered children, the social and emotional value of youngsters increased, and lonesome, nostalgic men doted on the frontier's children, giving them gifts and special favors, reading to them, offering them advice and instruction. Most parents—not only those of the elite but also poorer farmers, ranchers, sheepherders, and saloonkeepers—showed their children affection and loving concern. Western children grew up with the message that their time of life was precious and to be prolonged as much as possible.

The stresses and idiosyncrasies of frontier life apparently encouraged, not threatened, these attitudes among pioneers of all classes. The typical frontier family, after all, relied heavily on itself, not just for economic support but for its emotional needs as well. Children were valuable, both as workers and as sources of amusement and companionship. Yet these boys and girls also enjoyed a remarkable independence and ease of movement. Under the circumstances, parents may have unconsciously hedged their bets, lessening the chances of runaways by making homelife as pleasant as possible by letting their children know they were appreciated. Whatever the reasons, a warm and affectionate regard for children seemed a natural, rewarding part of pioneer life.

In the darkest times, when death took their children, parents found comfort in another modern ideal. They faced the loss of sons and daughters with the new styles of mourning increasingly common in the East. These rituals proclaimed a sentimentalized vision of innocent youth. They spoke with assurance of children's heavenly ascent and of a family's rendezvous in paradise. These consolations soothed the special guilt of mothers and fathers who learned pioneering's blackest joke—that most children died, not at the hands and claws of savages and beasts, but through their parents' confident fantasies of controlling the land.

The children's story, then, teaches us a fascinating irony never noted by those who have studied how tradition and innovation have woven together into a new western culture. At work here was something like the evolutionary principle of pre-adaptation. The companionate family and idealized views of children did not develop in response to frontier conditions; they were brought westward from elsewhere in Victorian America. But these imported values—and, presumably, others—did not run against the Turnerian grindstone. The new country did not wear them down or change them dramatically. On the contrary, these attitudes and modes of living flourished because, quite by chance, they were splendidly suited to a setting for which they were never intended—the peculiar world of the frontier West.

No pioneer, however, could duplicate absolutely what had been left behind. Turner was correct. American society did change in the developing West, largely because of the physical and social environments that usually have received the credit and the blame. But historians have again missed the clearest examples—the rising generations touched by the new country from their earliest years.

Sooner or later, anyone interested in western children comes around to certain questions. How did the frontier's peculiar conditions shape its children? Did this heritage alone make western childhood distinctive? How did their early years prepare children for facing the challenges of adulthood? And how, finally, have frontier children left their mark on the modern West?

Children inevitably were influenced by conditions beyond their parents' control. The children's reality—their ideas of what the future held, their beliefs and attitudes, the ways they saw themselves—were formed partly through contact with surroundings that were different from those their elders had known. Work took them out into that environment—encouraging exchanges with it, helping them master their fears, and posing a variety of challenges and responsibilities. Play became another means of exploring the world around them, and through it they also learned to cope with anxieties and problems of frontier life. Around the children was a diverse, mobile society strikingly different from that to the east. Youngsters took on its aggressive, optimistic ways, even as they learned other lessons from its wide range of human types.

Not surprisingly, these children showed certain attitudes and behaviors long associated with the frontier. Ray Allen Billington has summarized the most distinctive traits encouraged by life in pioneer America, traits that in turn contributed to a unique national character. Among these were an optimistic individualism—a faith in one's own ability to rise upward in society and generally to improve one's life—and a tendency to hit the road if those hopes were not soon realized. The work ethic was no abstraction; pioneers equated long, strenuous labor with normal living. Because some of that work required the help of others, the frontier inspired a cooperative spirit. But even more basic was the pioneer's inner-directedness, a determination to achieve fueled not by the opinions of others but by the heady reward that came to those who wrestled with the environment and won. Akin to these attributes were a pragmatism and an impatience with authority, especially if arbitrarily exercised.[5]

These traits have become part of a shimmering, heroic ideal of the western character. When the sentiment is stripped away, however, it is clear that some of these characteristics were firmly grounded in the day-to-day realities of frontier childhood. Growing up in the West, girls and boys naturally acquired independent, self-motivated, confident, even brash personalities. Hard work was a given, for in Edna Clifton's words, "there was no life without it." As children matured, they were often eager to move on in search of better things. Many squinted hard at parents, teachers, and anyone else who tried to direct their lives too closely. Children likely acquired other, far less admirable traits linked to frontier life. Among these were an all-too-easy acceptance of violence, an exploitive frame of mind, a compulsive restlessness, and an unappeasable inner drive toward accomplishment and control of physical surroundings.

But when these traits are added up, they still fall short of describing the children's characters. Responding to the peculiar nature of the frontier, boys and girls were also absorbing what has already been noted—surviving traditions, the teaching of parents, the persistence of ideals from other places. Every generation has its mix of messages; because the world changes, parents' points of view always differ from their children's. But on the frontier, these normal differences were vastly exaggerated.

Paradoxically, then, the key to understanding the uniqueness of pioneer childhood is not in the children's special kinship with the new country. Nor is it in their elders' obsession with passing on their own values. Rather, it is in the mingling of these two powerful, contrasting influences.

Out of this mingling came what was, in the end, the most distinguishing characteristic of western childhood—its ambiguity. Children were told, through words and actions, that childhood was precious and should be prolonged as long as possible, then they were expected to play adult roles and to take on the tasks of men and women. They were admonished to tend to their studies and their moral betterment and then pushed into a society renowned for its open corruptions and its lusting for the almighty dollar. Look to your parents and obey them, they were urged, even as they were forced into situations bound to make them independent and emotionally self-reliant. Powerful bonds of love, affection, and respect drew families close together, while the generations' different perspectives and experiences, as well as the children's bonds among themselves, eroded family unity. The diary entry of a twelve-year-old girl in Helena, Montana, captures this jumble of impressions. It is a Sunday in 1865:

> At two o'clock in the morning a highway Robber was hung on a large pine tree. After breakfast we went to see him. At ten o'clock preaching, at one o'clock a large auction sale of horses and cattle. At two o'clock Sunday school. At three o'clock a foot race. At seven o'clock preaching. The remainder of time spent by hundreds of miners in gambling and drinking.[6]

More than anything else, this—a garbling of messages, the push and shove of conflicting influences—set frontier childhood apart.

For elsewhere in the nation, the course of childhood was moving in quite a different direction. A new approach to child rearing was emerging, one that would evolve into that of today. Now parents were to think of their children in a new way and treat them with greater affection, respect, and sensitivity. As already seen, these attitudes took root on the frontier because, in their way, they were practical.

But parents were also supposed to control their children's lives far more closely. A protected home was to be a school for moral guidance. Girls were to be trained to behave and work a certain way, boys in another. Children were not supposed to take on too much too soon; independence

Within this family portrait were hints of youthful independence and a different view of the world—standing on horseback and aiming off-camera. (Courtesy Colorado Historical Society.)

was to come in deliberate, calibrated steps. New public institutions appeared—the Y.M.C.A., juvenile courts, kindergartens, National Child Labor Committee, and the American Playground Association, to name a few—meant to segregate the young from society and to minister to children's unique needs. Homelife and public policy worked to the same end. Ideally, growing up would be a lovingly ordered march from infancy to adulthood.

That, however, was impossible on the frontier. Parents found their economic needs were great and their days crowded. Young children were pushed into heavy responsibilities and left to play and explore mostly on their own. To say the least, social controls were imperfectly enforced, and girls and boys grew up close to the West's famous vices and its sizable population of rakehells and shady characters. Theirs was no protected, choreographed upbringing.

This way of life was out of step with much of the nation, but it was not unprecedented. The children's lives resembled those in another anomalous part of America—the poorest sections of the teeming cities of the northeast and midwest, another culture of rapid change where children grew up much by their own devices.[7] A closer comparison can be made to the nation as a whole during the early nineteenth century. During that time of quickening change, youngsters enjoyed a remarkable freedom and economic opportunity. They took part in adult activities and entertainments and moved easily across the blurred boundaries between their world and that of adults. Observers commented on their precocity, self-confidence, and arrogance. In a dynamic and unsettled America, the child's role was shifting and imprecise.[8]

Here was one of the most delicious ironies of the children's story. What some described as a new and disturbing trend in the West actually was a recurrence of an earlier social arrangement. As they moved forward in space, westering pioneers, in a sense, were travelling backward in time.

No wonder so many adults worried about frontier children. At first glance, western childhood seemed an afront to the modern ideal. How could the future hold anything but trouble? Today's parents, too, might wonder about the later lives of boys and girls brought up so differently from our own sons and daughters.

Specifically, critics warned that children were bound to be corrupted. They need not have been concerned. The frontier did not produce a generation of moral anarchists. Mose Drachman roamed Tucson's streets and passed time with monte dealers. Later, as mayor, he fought to close saloons and gambling halls. Caesar Brock's daughter, Helen, grew from her wide-roaming, bronc-busting childhood to be a highly regarded rancher. Most children would mature not into outlaws and reprobates but responsible citizens respectful of institutions and prevailing values.

Another threat at first seems more serious. At an early age, far earlier than most youngsters today, frontier children were expected to deal with the demands and pressures of adulthood. They were given heavy responsibilities and exhausting work in some of the most difficult environments the country could offer. Many were expected to make important, even vital decisions. Frequently they saw the fruits of their efforts destroyed by natural disasters and human error, often their own. Then came hard times: short meals or outright hunger, scrambling to survive, or moving to another chance. This might seem to threaten a child's sense of himself and his ability to face the future. Frances Moore watching the hoppers eat the corn from her mother's arms, Owen McWhorter trying to coax freezing cattle from the snow, John Norton praying for rain that came too late—the stories make depressing reading. The lessons seemed to be of children's inadequacies, life's insurmountable difficulties, the likelihood of losing.

Yet these lessons were balanced by others. Under the right circumstances, hardships could have other, much more positive effects, as a provocative line of recent research suggests. Psychologists have studied children who matured under even more trying adversities, among them psychotic parents, disrupted homes, the turmoil of war, even the Holocaust. These experiences did produce some young people unable to cope with life's challenges. Many others, however, emerged with faith in themselves and their ability to form stable families of their own.

Three circumstances apparently set this second group apart. Even those with emotionally disturbed parents received love and encouragement from mothers, fathers, or siblings during infancy and early childhood. Outside their families, these children got added emotional support from other adults; they also developed close contacts with other youngsters and found hobbies and interests of their own. Finally, at some point in their early years, these boys and girls faced threatening situations that demanded they assume difficult responsibilities essential to their families' well being. Of course, that put them under stress, but even when they failed, the experience gave them two things—a sense of "required helpfulness" that bolstered their self-esteem and a belief that even when life is hard, "things *will work out.*"[9]

These conditions describe well the lives of most pioneer children. The companionate family was alive and healthy on the frontier, and most parents treated their young with concern and an awareness of their emotional needs. Mothers especially gave them affection and close attention during infancy and early childhood, those first two years of life most crucial to their emotional security. Children also made lives for themselves away from their families, cultivating close friendships with others their ages and making their surroundings into playgrounds. They enjoyed the affection, advice, and encouragement of adults outside the home, surrogate parents like Anne Ellis's Uncle Pomp and Marquis James's Mr. Howell. Certainly youngsters grew up with a sense of their "required helpfulness." When a child had such sources of emotional support, formidable challenges, even when followed by failure, became sources of strength.

So what worried many critics most—the confused and unpredictable nature of growing up, its harsh demands and grave responsibilities—could be frontier childhood's finest virtue, not its greatest threat. Most children grew up reasonably acquainted with their parents' heritage and strengthened by their families' affection and care. However trying, their lives gave them a secure sense of worth and capability. Boys and girls entered adolescence aware of life's adversities and of how people usually survived them. They learned to adjust and to overcome, or at least endure, unexpected difficulties. They gained a healthy appreciation for human personalities and oddities. Even those who moved often among the West's many settings earned an intimate understanding of the country around them. Children may have known only imperfectly from where they had come, but by any measure they knew just where they were.

Unfortunately, the question of how the frontier prepared its children for the future cannot be tied up so neatly. As the young matured, their ambiguous beginnings sometimes turned back upon them. The results could be troubling. The most obvious examples had to do with gender and sexuality, in particular how girls and boys identified with their elders and perceived their futures as women and men. Though frontier daughters worked and passed leisure time among women, much of their labor was alongside boys and men in the fields, countryside, and boomtown streets. Their feelings of accomplishment came largely from helping with men's work—those transforming tasks and celebrated changes linked to a grand national purpose. Their play, too, was mostly out-of-doors, away from the houses that were their mothers' domain. In short, they often identified less with women than with fathers, brothers, and uncles. That left them freer to question the attitudes and roles that defined—and in many ways limited—their mothers' lives, and it may have contributed to a strong sense of independence and self-confidence among girls who grew up western. "To look for liberation," an historian of western women wrote recently, "is to look to the second generation of the frontier."[10]

As these daughters approached womanhood, however, they were expected to retreat from much of the life they had known and to perform instead the traditional roles of wives and mothers. The result was an emotional confusion suggested in some of the most famous literary works by women influenced by the frontier as children. Mari Sandoz's *Old Jules*, Jean Stafford's *The Mountain Lion*, and Willa Cather's *My Ántonia*—a biography and memoir, a novella, and a novel—all celebrate accomplishments of the man's world. In all of them, young heroines find their greatest pleasure and sense of value while at work and at play with men and male friends. In contrast to the extraordinary contributions most mothers actually made, the ones in these books are either vague, insignificant characters or repressive figures resentfully portrayed. Even Cather's Ántonia Shimerda, ostensibly a fictional tribute to pioneer womanhood, grows up with an unappealing, almost shrewish mother. Ántonia "loved her father more than anyone else" when she was a girl and "stood in awe" of her older brother. She is most at home plowing and wandering through

On a Montana homestead, a girl and young woman sit amid reminders of their childhoods and of the life that awaits them as adults. (Courtesy Montana Historical Society.)

the meadows and along the creeks. "I like to be like a man," she tells the novel's narrator.[11] Less famous reminiscences often suggest the same ambivalence of allegiance, even of sexual identity. Sometimes the titles alone make the point. Agnes Cleaveland called her memoir *No Life for a Lady*. Oello Martin chose "Father Came West," though it is obvious from the story that her mother was at least as responsible for their family's survival and achievements.[12]

Boys also identified with the work and amusements of men. Yet they knew that they would continue in these roles as adults, and this, ironically, allowed them to appreciate and sympathize more openly with their mothers. Frequently, in fact, they overstated the bleakness of pioneer women's lives. Hamlin Garland's angry memory of his mother's sacrifices is well known: "All her toilsome, monotonous days rushed through my mind with a roar like a file of gray birds in the night—how little—how tragically small her joys, and how black her sorrows, her toil, her tedium."[13]

Frontier boys grew up to face their own contradictions, however. They naturally pictured a future of westering, developing new country, continuing a process through which their characters had been shaped. Their experiences prepared them for that life; public tributes to pioneering affirmed their inclinations. Garland wrote of his Iowa youth: "All the boys he knew—all the young men talked of 'the west,' never of the east; always of the plains, of the mountains and cattle-raising and mining and Indians." By the time Edward Dale was five, the word "West" instantly summoned visions of "a mighty, mysterious land" of exotic savages, wild and beautiful beasts, exciting frontiersmen. The impressions seemed confirmed by visits from his more itinerant relatives, especially Uncle Ike, a widower who lived in a wagon as he drifted from one part of the plains to another. Young Ed used all his senses to conjure up his frontier dream. Climbing onto the wagon box to greet his hero, he smelled Arbuckle coffee, brown sugar, dried apples, mule sweat, and oiled leather—"a delightful odor," he thought, "which must be that of the West itself!"[14]

Yet many boys would live through the country's frontier stage to find themselves in a different West, a region of narrowing limits, where dwindling resources were pulled beyond their reach or kept firmly in the grasp of others. They saw a natural landscape that had seemed uniquely their own changed irrevocably into something else, transformed through a process in which they themselves had played a prominent part.

In a larger sense, all children faced this dilemma. Girls and boys grew up with the same presumptions—that their surroundings were full of grand potential, that there would always be more awaiting, and that they would be free to make of it what they could. Then, in the postfrontier West, they would confront the limits of the pioneer dream. Abuse of an abundant land led to ecological catastrophes; apparently boundless riches could be exhausted; government stewardship followed in the wake of a virtually unregulated pursuit of wealth. "The West was like a harlot who bore children," wrote a mother who reared two daughters on a Montana homestead, only to see them driven away by the dust bowl and the government's closing of land to new settlement: "We had brought them to the hard country. . . . They had grown up in the Badlands, knew what they could do there, but they were not allowed to."[15]

The frustration of those daughters suggests the children's final lesson. Students today study the West both as frontier and as region. The first, at heart, is the story of a process, the interaction between invaders and the land invaded. The second is the story of a place—a part of the continent that, despite its diversity, has a few unifying elements, including natives who think of the West and westerners as a unique land and society. Historians are particularly curious about how the one experience became the other, how from conquest and settlement a distinctive part of the nation emerged with its own identity.

This book has been about the frontier. The children's story, however, also has obvious implications for the study of the West as a region. As we try to understand how one era became the next, we should look to the lives of those who were shaped from their own beginnings by both the pioneering experience and the country's enduring nature.

The frontier is gone. It would be misleading, however, to suggest, as Avery Craven did nearly half a century ago, that the modern West shows the traces of the pioneer era only "as a landscape reveals the action of glaciers in ages long passed."[16] No neat, precise line can ever be drawn between frontier and region, for the two eras have slid over one another, like sleeves of a spyglass, as pioneer youngsters have matured. Precisely because they were young, children were the persons most influenced by the frontier; as children, they had the most years ahead of them to live out the implications of that influence.

The contours of the recent West have been shaped by many forces. Among the most obvious have been a massive wave of new immigrants, especially since 1945, the reach of outside capital and technology, the continuing interaction among the region's various ethnic communities, and the weight of myth, the world's expectations of what the West ought to be. At least as important, however, have been those persons who matured as the new country was being settled. As adults, during the transitional decades of the early twentieth century, tens of thousands of these men and women helped determine the outlines of the modern West. As a new region emerged, they were most of its political and business leaders, educators and ministers, skilled workers and day laborers, housewives and merchants, criminals and drifters. They helped build new western institutions; more than any others, perhaps, they were responsible for regional attitudes and limitations.

Certainly the children can help us understand the most intriguing trait of the modern West—its deeply conflicted personality. Children grew up pulled between two sets of influences, their identification with the land about them and their parents' dogged efforts to instill values and traditions from another world. "I am a product of the American earth," Wallace Stegner would write of his boyhood on the plains just north of the Montana border, "and in nothing quite so much as in the contrast between what I knew through the pores and what I was officially taught."[17] So

A frontier success story: the trees are up, the fields broken and plowed, the soddie standing square. Children like these of Custer County, Nebraska would play prominent roles in the making of the modern West. (Solomon D. Butcher Collection, Nebraska State Historical Society.)

westerners are fiercely loyal to their region and condescending toward outsiders who cannot understand and cope with the country; they are also excessively defensive about their lack of "culture"—defined, of course, in eastern terms. They are inordinately fond of art and fiction that romanticize frontier experiences unique to the West, yet they obsessively imitate alien architectural forms, building Cape Cod cottages and plantation-style banks against backdrops of buttes and craggy mountains. Growing up steeped in the virtues of free-wheeling enterprise and intimate with the natural setting, children matured into a region where individual opportunity was diminishing and the wilderness was under siege. Out of this dilemma has come the familiar harangue of modern westerners, who chafe at restraints and demand a free hand in development even as they wax nostalgic about the vanished beauty of an increasingly crowded land.

The frontier experience, we are told, gave Americans their greatest strengths and noblest virtues. Surely, however, this heritage has its troubled side. Westward expansion, Jackson Putnam has observed, "generated its own internal dynamic of ungratified aspiration." Driven by contradictory values, the character forged in the process was necessarily frustrated.[18] Putnam's melancholy thought seems truer than ever when we consider the history of pioneer children and their passage to adulthood.

Just as surely, the frontier left a happier heritage. A child's life in the developing West encouraged traits especially useful in the contemporary world. Among these were a resilient strength, a self-reliance and sense of worth, and a tested understanding that hard times can be endured. Most children must have taken into their adult lives a faith in the family and its ability to adjust to trying circumstances. In the particulars of pioneer childhood were grounded qualities commonly associated with the modern West, among them an openness toward strangers, a confidence in dealing with fresh challenges, a kinship with what remains of the natural setting, and a pride—albeit an often grudging pride—in its contrariness.

Whatever the frontier's mark upon the children, their story, both the good and bad of it, is essential to understanding the region today. Only when we consider their history can we reconstruct what one writer recently called "the unbroken past of the American West."[19]

"How could any writer . . . know the details of our daily life?" asked Lee Whipple-Haslam seventy years after she began her time on the frontier. There is much to learn by trying to answer her question. Children were not passive observers of the making of western history. Just as the young always were far more in control of their own lives than their elders realized, so they shaped the course of western settlement in ways historians have ignored almost entirely. Their influence—and that of the pioneer experience—have not wholly disappeared. Long after the close of the frontier, its shaping force has survived, carried into our own day by those who grew up with the country.

Key to Notes

AHS: Arizona Historical Society, Tucson, Arizona
Ban: Bancroft Library, University of California, Berkeley
Be: Beinecke Library, Yale University
CHS: California Historical Society, San Francisco, California
CHSS: Colorado State Historical Society, Denver, Colorado
DPL: Denver Public Library, Denver, Colorado
HEH: Henry E. Huntington Library, San Marino, California
IHS: Idaho Historical Society, Boise, Idaho
KSHS: Kansas State Historical Society, Topeka, Kansas
MSH: Montana Historical Society, Helena, Montana
MSU: Montana State University Library, Bozeman, Montana
Newberry: Newberry Library, Chicago, Illinois
OHS: Oklahoma State Historical Society, Oklahoma City, Oklahoma
UNev: University of Nevada Library, Reno, Nevada
UNMex: University of New Mexico Library, Albuquerque, New Mexico
SWC/TT: Southwest Collection, Texas Tech University, Lubbock, Texas

Notes

Preface

1. Lee Whipple-Haslam, *Early Days in California: Scenes and Events of the '50s as I Remember Them* (Jamestown, Cal.: S.n., 1925), 4 and *passim*.

2. Anyone interested in the history of children in the United States should begin with an excellent collection of evaluative essays: Joseph M. Hawes and N. Ray Hiner, eds., *American Childhood: A Research Guide and Historical Handbook* (Westport, Conn.: Greenwood Press, 1985). For surveys of literature on the history of children and the family, see Lawrence Stone, "Family History in the 1980s," *Journal of Interdisciplinary History* 12:1 (Summer, 1981): 51–87; Barbara Finkelstein, "Tolerating Ambiguity in Family History: A Guide to Some New Materials," *Journal of Pyschohistory* 11:1 (Summer, 1983): 117–28; Mary P. Ryan, "The Explosion of Family History," *Reviews in American History* 10:4 (December, 1982): 181–95; David J. Rothman, "Documents in Search of an Historian: Toward a History of Childhood and Youth in America," *Journal of Interdisciplinary History* 2:2 (Autumn, 1971): 367–77.

3. The only lengthy analytical study of frontier children is Mary Anne Norman Smallwood, "Childhood on the Southern Plains Frontier," (Ph.D. diss., Texas Tech University, 1975). J.E. Baur, *Growing Up With California: A History of California's Children* (Los Angeles: Will Kramer, 1978) is often interesting but is unanalytical and highly anecdotal. A few articles have appeared, though some of them treat children's history not for its own sake but as an aspect of women's history: Ruth Barnes Moynihan, "Children and Young People on the Overland Trail," *Western Historical Quarterly* 6:3 (July, 1975): 279–94; Annette White Parks, "Children's Work and Play on the Northwest Frontier," *Henry Ford Museum and Greenfield Village Herald*, November 1, 1986; Elliott West, "Heathens and Angels: Childhood in the Rocky Mountain Mining Towns," *Western Historical Quarterly* 14:2 (April, 1983): 145–64; Georgia Willis Read, "Women and Children on the Oregon-California Trail in the Gold-Rush Years," *Missouri Historical Review* 39:1 (October, 1944): 1–23; Robert L. Munkres, "Wives, Mothers, Daughters: Women's Life on the Road West," *Annals of Wyoming* 42:2 (October, 1970): 191–224; Carol Fairbanks, "Lives of Girls and Women on the Canadian and American Prairies," *International Journal*

of Women's Studies, 2:5, 452–72; Elaine Siverman, "In Their Own Words: Mothers and Daughters on the Alberta Frontier, 1890–1929," *Frontiers* 2:2, 37–44.

4. Greeley's "palpable homicide" quotation is from John D. Unruh, *The Plains Across: The Overland Emigrants and the Trans-Mississippi West, 1840–60* (Urbana: University of Illinois Press, 1979), 11; James F. Meline, *Two Thousand Miles on Horseback* (New York: Hurd and Houghton, 1867), 28.

Chapter One

1. East S. Owen journal, May 13, 1852, Be.

2. Samuel Frances diary, April 19, 20, 1853, Be.

3. Samuel Bowles, *Our New West* (Hartford: Hartford Publishing Co., 1869),v.

4. For an excellent description of western physiography, see Charles B. Hunt, *Natural Regions of the United States and Canada* (San Francisco: W.H. Freeman, 1973).

5. Frank D. Hughes reminiscence, SC1482, MHS.

6. May G. Flanagan, "A Frontier House," SC1236, MHS.

7. Fitz Hugh Ludlow, *The Heart of the Continent: A Record of Travel Across the Plains and In Oregon With an Examination of the Mormon Principle* (New York: Hurd and Houghton, 1871), 131.

8. Emma Shepard Hill, *A Dangerous Crossing and What Happened on the Other Side* (Denver: Press of the Smith-Brooks Co., 1914), 45; Estelline Bennett, *Old Deadwood Days* (New York: J. H. Sears and Co., 1928), 16.

9. Aurelia Tipton Diary, July 23, 1878, SC853, MHS; Whipple-Haslam, *Early Days in California*, 8.

10. S. T. Hauser to sister, June 17, 1862, S. T. Hauser Letters, Newberry.

11. James P. Price, *Seven Years of Prairie Life* (Hereford, England: Jakeman and Carver, 1891), 19.

12. Abigail Smith to brother and sister, March 9, 1844, Alvin T. Smith Letters, Be; Charles Athearn to wife, June 22, 1855, Charles Athearn Letters, Be.

13. Alden Brooks diary, 1859, end note, 45, Newberry,

14. Pearl Daniel autobiography, SC58, MHS.

15. Adrietta A. Hixon, *On to Oregon! A True Story of a Young Girl's Journey Into the West*, ed. Waldo Taylor (Weiser, Idaho: Signal-American Printers, 1947), 7; Glenda Riley, ed., "Family Life of the Frontier: The Diary of Kitturah Penton Belknap," *Annals of Iowa*, 44:1 (Summer, 1977): 44.

16. Quoted in Roxanna C. Foster, "The Foster Family, California Pioneers of 1849," reminiscence, 43–44, Be.

17. Thomas D. Sanders reminiscence, 16, DPL; Mrs. Frank B. Johnson autobiography, SWC/TT.

18. Melissa Everett reminiscence, 2, SWC/TT; Eliza Rudd reminiscence, 5, AHS.

19. Mrs. Mary L. Neely interview, SWC/TT; J. Henry Brown autobiography, 1, Ban; Edward Everett Dale, *The Cross Timbers: Memories of a North Texas Boyhood* (Austin: University of Texas Press, 1966), 163; Benjamin Franklin Bonney, *Across the Plains by Prairie Schooner* (Eugene, Ore.: Koke-Tiffany Co., 192–), 1; F. M. McCarty autobiography, SC409, MHS.

20. Chester Dutton to Rodman, June 20, 1878, Yale Class Records, 1938, Manuscripts Archives Division, Yale University Library.

21. For works emphasizing the loss of support systems and women's reluctance to go west, see Lillian Schlissel, *Women's Diaries of the Westward Journey* (New York: Schocken Books, 1982) and "Frontier Familes: Crisis in Ideology," in Sam B. Girgus, ed., *The American Self: Myth, Ideology and Culture* (Albuquerque: University of New Mexico Press, 1981), 155–65, and John Mack Faragher, *Women and Men on the Overland Trail* (New Haven: Yale University Press, 1979).

22. Elizabeth Dixon Smith Geer, "Diary, 1847," *Oregon Pioneer Association, Transactions*, 1907.

23. Eleanor Knowlton reminiscence, 52, CHS; Elizabeth E. O'Neil reminiscence, Mary Ann Busick Collection, MSU; Albert Simpson Neighbors reminiscence, Charles M. Wood Collections, Box 2, AHS; Augusta Dodge Thomas, "Praire Children: An Autobiography," 10, KSHS; Mary Jane Hayden, *Pioneer Days* (San Jose: Murgotten's Press, 1915), 7–8.

24. Frank Waugh, "Pioneering in Kansas," 148–49, KSHS; Thomas D. Sanders reminiscence, 16, DPL; John C. Van Gundy, *Reminiscences of Frontier Life on the Upper Neosho in 1855 and 1856* (Topeka: College Press, 1925), 7–8; Wallace Wood reminiscence, KSHS; Effie Conwell reminiscence, Jessie K. Snell Collection, KSHS.

25. All accounts of the overland migration discuss its human makeup. Among the best are John D. Unruh, Jr., *The Plains Across: The Overland Emigrants and the Trans-Mississippi West, 1840–60* (Champaign: University of Illinois Press, 1979); David Lavender, *Westward Vision: The Story of the Oregon Trail* (New York: McGraw-Hill Book Co., 1963); George R. Stewart, *The California Trail: An Epic With Many Heroes* (New York: McGraw-Hill Book Co., 1962). The figures from the Ft. Laramie register are from Henry S. Bloom diary, June 14, 1850, Ban. For other specific counts of the overland city, see Louise Barry, *The Beginning of the West: Annals of the Kansas Gateway to the American West, 1540–1854* (Topeka: Kansas State Historical Society, 1972), 1008, 1084, 1158; Lucian Wolcott journal, June 14, 1850, HEH; William Dresser to Sarah, May 29, 1850, Dresser Family Papers, and William Hampton diary, June 3, 1852, Ban. For counts of travelers to Montana and Colorado, see C. Adelia French reminiscence, SC782, MHS and Le Roy R. Hafen, ed., *Colorado Gold Rush: Contemporary Letters and Reports, 1858–1859* (Glendale: Arthur H. Clark Co., 1941), 316.

26. Calculations are from *Report on Population of the United States at the Eleventh Census: 1890, Part 1* (Washington, D.C.: Government Printing Office, 1895), 398–99; *Twelth Census of the United States, . . . 1900. Population, Part I* (Washington: United States Census Office, 1901), 575–608, 736–95. See also Frederick C. Luebke, "Ethnic Minority Groups in the American West," in Michael P. Malone, ed., *Historians and the American West* (Lincoln: University of Nebraska Press, 1983), 387–413.

27. William P. Daingerfield to "J," August 18, 1850, William P. Daingerfield Letters, Ban; *San Francisco Bulletin*, November 13, 1862, quoted in William J. Trimble, *The Mining Advance in the Inland Empire* (Madison: University of Wisconsin, 1914), 140.

28. *Tenth Census of the United States: Population, 1880* (Washington, D.C.: Government Printing Office, 1883), 428, 431, 438, 439; Ralph Mann, *After the Gold Rush: Society in Grass Valley and Nevada City, California, 1849–1880* (Stanford: Stanford University Press, 1982), 229; Elliott West, "Five Idaho Mining Towns: A Computer Profile," *Pacific Northwest Quarterly* 73:3 (July, 1982): 108–20.

29. Waugh, "Pioneering in Kansas," 26–27.

30. Mann, *After the Gold Rush*, 225.

31. For demographic studies of far western communities, see Sherman L. Ricards, Jr., "A Demographic History of the West: Butte County, California, 1850," *Michigan Academy of Science, Arts, and Letters* 46 (1961): 469–91; David J. Wishart, "Age and Sex Composition of the Population of the American Frontier," *Nebraska History* 54:1 (Spring, 1973): 107–19; George M. Blackburn and Sherman L. Ricards, "A Demographic History of the West: Nueces County, Texas, 1850," *Prologue* 4:1 (Spring, 1972): 3–20; William Bowen, "The Oregon Frontiersman: A Demographic View," in Thomas Vaughan, ed., *The Western Shore: Oregon Country Essays Honoring the American Revolution* (Portland: Oregon Historical Society, 1975), 181–97; D. Aidan McQuillan, "The Mobility of Immigrants and Americans: A Comparison of Farmers on the Kansas Frontier," *Agricultural History* 53:3 (July, 1979): 576–96; Jack E. Eblen, "An Analysis of Nineteenth-Century Frontier Populations," *Demography* 2 (1965): 399–413; Duane A. Smith, "The San Juaner: A Computerized Portrait," *Colorado Magazine* 52:2 (Spring, 1975): 148; West, "Five Idaho Mining Towns;" Mann, *After the Gold Rush*.

32. McQuillan, "Mobility of Immigrants and Americans."

33. Mrs. E. A. Van Court reminiscence, Be; Dora Miller interview, 36/272, IP; Melissa Everett reminiscence, SWC/TT.

34. W. T. Parker diary, February 2, 1851, HEH.

35. Wishart, "Age and Sex Composition."

36. William Bowen, "The Oregon Frontiersman;" F. L. Kirkaldie to wife, July 23, 1865, F. L. Kirkaldie Letters, MSU.

37. Rebecca Ketcham, "From Ithaca to Clatsop Plains: Miss Ketcham's Journal of Travel," Leo M. Kaiser and Priscilla Knuth, eds., *Oregon Historical Quarterly* 62:3 (September, 1961): 237–87.

38. Nancy A. Hunt, *By Ox-team to California* (San Francisco: 1916), 10; Louise Amelia Knapp Clappe, *The Shirley Letters From California Mines in 1851–52* (San Francisco: T. C. Russell, 1922), 323–24.

39. Christopher J. Huggard, "The Role of the Family in Settling the Cherokee Outlet," (Master's thesis, University of Arkansas, Fayetteville, 1987), 24–44; Venola Lewis Bivens, ed., "The Diary of Luna E. Warner, A Kansas Teenager of the Early 1870s," *Kansas Historical Quarterly* 35:3,4 (Autumn and Winter, 1969): 276–311 and 411–441; Lula Black Veale reminiscence, SWC/TT; Luella Newman interview, 37/569, Indian-Pioneer Collection, OHS.

40. Sallie Reynolds Matthews, *Interwoven: A Pioneer Chronicle* (College Station: Texas A&M University Press, 1982); Lena Martin interview, SWC/TT; Zella Hunter Mills reminiscence, KSHS.

41. William Bowen, "The Oregon Frontiersman."

Chapter Two

1. Ward G. and Florence Stark De Witt, eds., *Prairie Schooner Lady: The Journal of Harriet Sherill Ward, 1853* (Los Angeles: Westernlore Press, 1959), 91.

2. For works I found most useful in understanding the development of children's perceptions, see Jean Piaget, *The Child's Conception of the World* (New York:

Harcourt, Brace, and Co., 1929); Barry J. Wadsworth, *Piaget's Theory of Cognitive and Affective Development* (New York and London: Longman, 1984); David Elkind, *The Child's Reality: Three Developmental Themes* (Hillsdale, N.J.: Lawrence Erlbaum Associates, 1978); William C. Crain, *Theories of Development: Concepts and Applications* (Englewood Cliffs: Prentice-Hall, Inc.); Boyd R. McCandless and Ellis D. Evans, *Children and Youth: Psychological Development* (Hinsdale, Ill.: The Dryden Press, 1973); Theodore Lidz, *The Person: His and Her Development Throughout the Life Cycle* (New York: Basic Books, Inc., 1976); Robert M. Liebert, et al., *Developmental Psychology* (Englewood Cliffs: Prentice-Hall, Inc., 1974).

3. Addison Crane Diary, June 1, 1852, HEH.

4. Sarah Hively Journal, May 10, 1863, DPL; Helen Stewart Diary, June 5, 1853, Lane County Historical Society, Eugene, Oregon; Ward, *Prairie Schooner Lady*, 60–61; Kate Dunlap, *The Montana Gold Rush Diary of Kate Dunlap*, ed. S. Lyman Tyler (Denver: Fred A. Rosenstock, Old West Publishing Co., and University of Utah Press, 1969), B-5; Agnes Stewart Diary, May 21, 1853, HEH; John Clark Journal, July 12, 1852, Be; Solomon Gorgas Diary, May 24, 1850 and Solomon Gorgas to Mary F. Gorgas, May 27, 1850, Solomon Gorgas Letters, HEH; Henry S. Bloom Diary, June 30, 1850, Ban; David DeWolf to Matilda, May 15, 1849, David DeWolf Letters, HEH; Addison Crane Diary, June 17, 1852, HEH.

5. Ward, *Prairie Schooner Lady*, 86, 110, 112; Addison Crane Diary, May 15, 1852, HEH; Angeline Ashley Diary, June 20, 1852, HEH.

6. Ward, *Prairie Schooner Lady*, 147; Basil Longworth Memorandum, July 22, 1853, HEH; James Clyman Diary, June 19, 1844, HEH; John N. Jones Diary, May 26, 1850, KSHS; Daniel White Diary, May 15, 1854, HEH; Helen Stewart Diary, May 1, 1853, Lane County Historical Society, Eugene, Oregon.

7. For examples see Isaac Foster Journal, June 13, 1849, HEH; John Clark Journal, July 29, 1852, Be; Samuel Handsaker Diary, August 5, 1853, HEH; Philip Condit Diary, June 4, 1854, HEH; Alden Brooks Diary, June 19, August 12, 1859, HEH; Vincent Hoover Diary, June 22, 1849, HEH; James Owen Journal, July 17, 1860, Newberry; Mary Stuart Bailey Diary, June 16, 1852, HEH.

8. Glenda Riley, ed., "Pioneer Migration: The Diary of Mary Alice Shutes," Part I, *Annals of Iowa*, 43: 7 (Winter, 1977): 491–92.

9. Catherine Sager Pringle Reminiscence, 2, HEH.

10. Nancy M. H. Bogart, "Reminiscences of a Journey Across the Plains in 1843 . . . ," 1–2, Fred Lockley Collection, Box 14 (3), HEH; Martha Ann Morrison Minto, "Female Pioneering in Oregon," 3, Ban; D. B. Ward, *Across the Plains in 1853* (Seattle: Ward, 1911), 10; Sarah A. and A. W. Wisner, "A Trip Across the Plains in 1866", 14, Newberry; Julia S. Lambert, "Plain Tales of the Plains," *The Trail* 8:8 (January, 1916), 1.

11. Jesse Applegate, *Recollections of My Boyhood* (Roseburg, Ore.: Press of Review Publishing Co., 1914), 21.

12. *Ibid.*, 13–18.

13. Catherine Thomas Morris interview, in Fred Lockley, *Conversations With Pioneer Women*, ed. Mike Helm (Eugene, Ore.: Rainy Day Press, 1981), 137; Hixon, *On To Oregon!* 11.

14. Applegate, *Recollections*, 17, 55; Ward, *Across the Plains*, 18–19.

15. Mary L. Boatman Reminiscence, SC444, MHS; Thomas D. Sanders Remi-

niscence, 29, DPL; Barsina Rogers French, *Journal of a Wagon Trip from Evanston, Indiana to Prescott, Arizona. 1867*, August 6, 1867.

16. Applegate, *Recollections*, 14–15.

17. Ward, *Across the Plains*, 21; C. Adelia French Reminiscence, SC782, MHS.

18. Bennett Seymour Reminiscence, 5, CSHS; Robert P. Thoroughman Reminiscence, MSU; Ada Millington Jones Journal, May 24, 1862, Ban; Lambert, "Plain Tales," II, 7–8.

19. Barsina Rogers French Journal, August 11, 1867, HEH; Ada Millington Jones Journal, March 10, 1862, Ban; Elisha Brooks, *A Pioneer Mother of California* (San Francisco: Harr Wagner Publishing Co., 1911), 11; Hixon, *On to Oregon*, 32; Ward, *Across the Plains*, 19.

20. I found the following sources most useful in summarizing the recent research on childhood fears: Adah Maurer, "What Children Fear," *Journal of Genetic Psychology* 106 (1965): 265–77; David H. Bauer, "An Exploratory Study of Developmental Changes in Children's Fears," *Journal of Child Psychology and Psychiatry* 17 (1976): 69–74; Suzanne Bennett Johnson, et al., "Assessment and Treatment of Children's Fears," in Benjamin B. Lahey and Alan E. Kazdin, *Advances in Clinical Child Psychology*, vol. II (New York: Plenum Press, 1979), 108–139; Robert Eme and Dwight Schmidt, "The Stability of Children's Fears," *Child Development* 49 (1978): 1277–79.

21. John L. Johnson Journal, April 2, 1851, Be.

22. Brooks, *A Pioneer Mother of California*, 26–27; Thomas D. Sanders reminiscence, 27–28, DPL; David M. Adams biographical file, AHS.

23. Hixon, *On to Oregon*, 28; Bonney, *Across the Plains by Prairie Schooner*, 57; Mrs. Matthew P. Deady, "Crossing the Plains to Oregon in 1846," *Transactions of the Oregon Pioneer Association*, 1928, 57.

24. Hixon, *On to Oregon*, 22–23; John Clark Journal, May 11, 1852, Be; Samuel Handsaker Diary, May 11, 1853, HEH; Joseph W. Wood Diary, June 8, 1849, HEH; Charlotte Pengra Diary, June 1, 1853, HEH; Esther Hanna Journal, May 19, 1852, HEH; Agnes Stewart Diary, June 13, 1853, HEH.

25. John Bowlby, "Separation Anxiety," *International Journal of Psycho-Analysis* 41 (1960): 89–113.

26. Ward, *Across the Plains*,, 43; Charles R. Parke Diary, June 4, 1849, HEH; Alden Brooks Diary, July 29, 1859, HEH.

27. L. William Thavis, *Pioneering in Kansas: Iowa to Kansas in an Ox Wagon* (Washington, D.C., 1917), 11; Nancy A. Hunt, *By Ox-team to California*, 13; George Belshaw Diary, June 22, 1853, HEH; Ward, *Prairie Schooner*, 44; Margaret Ann Frink, *Journal of the Adventures of a Party of California Gold-seekers* (Oakland, 1897), 82; Brooks, *Pioneer Mother*, 18–19.

28. Anne Ellis, *The Life of an Ordinary Woman* (Lincoln: University of Nebraska Press, 1980); Glenda Riley, "The Specter of a Savage: Rumors and Alarmism on the Overland Trail," *Western Historical Quarterly* 15: 4 (October, 1984): 436; Lucy H. Fosdick, "Across the Plains in '61," reminiscence, Be; Emma Shepard Hill, *A Dangerous Crossing and What Happened on the Other Side* (Denver: Press of the Smith-Brooks Co., 1914), 10.

29. Unruh, Jr., *The Plains Across*, 117–58.

30. Deady, "Crossing the Plains," 57; Minto, "Female Pioneering," 4–5; Apple-

gate, *Recollections*, 28; Robert P. Thoroughman Reminiscence, MSU; W. A. Hockett, "Experiences . . . on the Oregon Trail," Reminiscence, 9, KSHS; John L. Johnson Journal, June 28, 1851, Be.

31. Whipple-Haslam, *Early Days in California*, 8; Applegate, *Recollections*, 26–27; Frink, *California Gold-seekers*, 68; Minto, "Female Pioneering," 24; Ada Millington Jones Journal, June 18, 1862; Perry Kline Reminiscence, 41, CSHS; Robert Thoroughman Reminiscence, MSU.

32. Brooks, *Pioneer Mother*, 22–25.

33. Ellis, *Life of Ordinary Woman*, 11–12; Juliette Fish Reminiscence, 13, HEH.

34. Hill, *Dangerous Crossing*, 28.

35. Unruh, Jr., *The Plains Across*, 345–50.

36. On children's perceptions and attitudes toward death, I found these sources most useful: Sylvia Anthony, *The Discovery of Death in Childhood and After* (London: Allen Lane, 1971); Marjorie Edith Mitchell, *The Child's Attitude Toward Death* (New York: Shocken Books, 1967); Robert Kastenbaum, "Childhood: the Kingdom Where Creatures Die," *Journal of Clinical Child Psychology* 3 (Summer, 1984): 11–14.

37. Virginia Reed to Mary C. Keyes, May 16, 1847, in Dale Morgan, *Overland in 1846: Diaries and Letters of the California-Oregon Trail* (Georgetown, Cal.: Talisman Press, 1963), I, 279–87; Silas Newcomb Journal, August 14, 1850, HEH; Esther Hanna Journal, August 31, 1852, HEH; Israel Lord Journal, September 16, 1849, HEH; Brooks, *Pioneer Mother*, 20; Mary E. Ackley, *Crossing the Plains, and Early Days in California's Golden Age* (San Francisco: Privately Printed, 1928), 29.

38. Whipple-Haslam, *Early Days*, 20; Harriet P. Sanders reminiscence, SC1254, MHS; C. Adelia French reminiscence, SC782, MHS; Fannie Forbes Russell Reminiscence, SC165, MHS; Hill, *Dangerous Crossing*, 15–16; Applegate, *Recollections*, 29–30; Ada Millington Jones Journal, June 13, 1862; Hixon, *On to Oregon*, 37.

39. Eli and Mary Bloyed to W. M. Tigand, November 13, 1852, Eli and Mary Bloyed Letters, Special Collections, University of Arkansas Library.

40. John Clark Journal, June 28, August 20, 1852, Be; Charlotte Pengra Diary, August 5, 1853, HEH; Brooks, *Pioneer Mother*, 17.

41. Enos Ellmaker Autobiography, 15, HEH; John Clark Journal, June 1, June 28, August 20, 1852, Be; Lester Hulin Journal, June 14, 1847, HEH; W. T. Parker Diary, May 1, 1850, HEH; Basil Longworth Memorandum, May 27, 1853, HEH; Joseph Wood Diary, June 14, 1849, HEH; Eleanor Knowlton Reminiscence, 64, CHS; Lorenzo Sawyer, *Way Sketches; Containing Incidents of Travel Across the Plains* (New York: Edward Eberstadt, 1926), 27; Joseph Batty, *Over the Wilds to California* (Leeds: J. Parrott, 1867), 23, Agnes Stewart Diary, May 27, June 6, 1853, HEH; Helen Stewart Diary, May 23, 1853; John L. Johnson Journal, May 5, 1851, Be.

42. For a few examples, see Angelina Smith Crews Reminiscence, HEH; H. A. Anable Diary, August 28, 1852, HEH; Dr. John Smith Diary, June 28, 1853, HEH; Esther Lyman Letter, HEH; Elizabeth Stewart Letter, HEH; Addison Crane Diary, May 26, June 10, June 24, 1852, HEH; Elizabeth Dixon Smith Geer, "Diary, 1847", *Transactions of the Oregon Pioneer Association* (1907), 157, 164.

43. John H. Clark Diary, June 11, 1852, Ban; C. Westover to wife, November 10, 1852, Be; Luella Dickenson, *Reminiscences of a Trip Across the Plains in 1846 and Early Days in California* (San Francisco: Whitaker & Ray Co., 1904), 8–9; Addison

Crane Diary, June 3, 1852, HEH; Susan T. L. Parrish, "Following the Pot of Gold," Reminiscence, 2, HEH; Hixon, *On to Oregon*, 36–41; Washington Henry Chick Reminiscence, 8, KSHS.

44. Ackley, *Crossing the Plains*, 24–25.

45. John H. Clark Diary, June 30, 1852, Ban.

46. Hockett, "Experiences," 6–7; Catherine Sager Pringle Reminiscence, 4–6, HEH; Ackley, *Crossing the Plains*, 23–24.

47. Richard Owen Diary, June 14, 1864, SC613, MHS; Stewart, *California Trail*, 327; Esther Hanna Journal, June 24, 1852, HEH; Addison Crane Diary, June 21, 1852, HEH; C. Westover to wife, November 10, 1852, Be; Silas Newcomb Journal, July 26, 1850, HEH; Whipple-Haslam, *Early Days*, 9; David Maynard Diary, September 17, 1850, HEH.

48. John H. Clark Diary, May 29, 1852, HEH; Angelina Smith Crews Reminiscence, 16–17, Fred Lockley Collection, Box 14 (7), HEH.

49. Effie Wood Conwell Reminiscence, KSHS; Katherine Williams Woodin, *Recollections of My Childhood on the Nebraska Pioneer Prairie Camp*, ed. Marthalene Filley McGill (N.P.: Privately Printed, 1975), 20–21; Frances Moore Reminiscence, 20, KSHS; Mary Hembree Reminiscence, KSHS.

50. Cedenia B. Willis Journals, 7, AHS; Mary Gardner Kane Reminiscence, AHS.

51. R. L. Jones, ed., "Folk Life in Early Texas: The Autobiography of Andrew Davis," *Southwestern Historical Quarterly* 43:3 (January, 1940): 329–30; Maggie L. B. Holden interview, Oral History Collection, SWC/TT.

52. J. B. Harper interview, Indian-Pioneer Collection, OHS.

53. Grace Snyder, *No Time on My Hands*, (Caldwell, Idaho: Caxton Printers, 1963), 15–16; Augusta Dodge Thomas, "Prairie Children," Reminiscence, 11, KSHS.

54. Oello Ingraham Martin, "Father Came West," Reminiscence, 49, KSHS; Louise M. Kreipie, "Reminiscences of the Early Settlers," 1, KSHS.

55. Walter Posey interview, Walter S. Posey File, SWC/TT.

56. Georgellen K. Burnett, " 'We Just Toughed It Out': Women Heads of Households on the Llano Estacado, 1880–1925," (Master's thesis, Texas Tech University), 1982, 25; Charles Greer interview, Indian-Pioneer Collection, OHS; Ralla Banta Pinkerton, "Pioneer Days in the Beaver Creek Community," Reminiscence, 1, R. J. Bradley Collection, SWC/TT; Effie Wood Conwell Reminiscence, KSHS; Alma Carlson Roosa, "Homesteading in the 1880s: The Anderson-Carlson Families Cherry County," *Nebraska History*, 58:3 (Fall, 1977): 377; Thomas, "Prairie Children," 67.

57. George Hockderffer Autobiography, 24–27, KSHS.

58. Owen McWhorter interview, Oral History Collection, SWC/TT.

59. Mary Ronan, *Frontier Woman: The Story of Mary Ronan as Told to Margaret Ronan*, ed. H. G. Merriam (Missoula: University of Montana Press, 1973), 1.

Chapter Three

1. For some especially helpful works on interpreting houses and their interiors, see Dale Upton, "The Power of Things: Recent Studies in American Vernacular Architecture," in Thomas J. Schlereth, ed., *Material Culture: A Research Guide*

(Lawrence: University Press of Kansas, 1985), 57–78; Simon J. Bronner, *Grasping Things: Folk Material Culture and Mass Society in America* (Lexington: University Press of Kentucky, 1986), 23–86; Clifford Clark, Jr., "Domestic Architecture as an Index to Social History," *Journal of Interdisciplinary History* 7 (Summer, 1976): 35–56; Gwendolyn Wright, *Building the Dream: A Social History of Housing in America* (Cambridge: MIT Press, 1983). For examples of various applications of this approach, see Henry Glassie, *Folk Housing in Middle Virginia* (Knoxville: University of Tennessee Press, 1975); Sally McMurry, "Progressive Farm Families and Their Houses, 1830–1855: A Study in Independent Design," *Agricultural History* 58:3 (July, 1984): 330–46; Gwendolyn Wright, *Moralism and the Model Home: Domestic Architecture and Cultural Conflict in Chicago, 1873–1913* (Chicago: University of Chicago Press, 1980); Dell Upton, "Toward a Performance Theory of Vernacular Architecture in Tidewater Virginia," *Folklore Forum* 12 (1979): 180–84.

2. Frank Waugh, "Pioneering in Kansas," 20, Reminiscence, KSHS.

3. William J. Petersen, "The Pioneer Cabin," *Iowa Journal of History and Politics* 36:4 (October, 1938): 387–409; Mildred Sharp, "Early Cabins in Iowa," *Palmpest* 2:1 (January, 1921): 16–29.

4. Donald W. Meinig, *The Great Columbia Plain: A Historical Geography, 1805–1910* (Seattle: University of Washington Press, 1968), 298; Georgellen K. Burnett, " 'We Just Toughed it Out' " 32; Alexander Family interviews, Panhandle-Plains Historical Museum, Texas Western University.

5. Harold Kirker, *California's Architectural Frontier: Style and Tradition in the Nineteenth Century* (New York: Russell and Russell, 1960), 29–43, 59. The author estimates that at least three-fourths of all structures in California of the 1860s were of frame construction.

6. Roger L. Welsch, *Sod Walls: The Story of the Nebraska Sod House* (Broken Bow, Neb.: Purcells, Inc., 1968); Cass G. Barns, *The Sod House* (Lincoln: University of Nebraska Press, 1970); John I. White, "That Zenith of Prairie Architecture—The Soddy," *American Heritage* 24:5 (August, 1973): 33–35; Flora Dutcher, "A Sod House," *Journal of Geography* 48:9 (December, 1949): 353–62.

7. Andrew Guilliford, "Earth Architecture of the Prairie Pioneer," *The Midwest Review* 7, second series (Spring, 1986): 1–25; Michael Koop and Stephen Ludwig, *German-Russian Folk Architecture in Southeastern South Dakota* (Vermillion, S.D.: State Historical Preservation Center).

8. J. B. Harper interview, Indian-Pioneer Collection OHS; Julie Roy Jeffrey, *Fronier Women: The Trans-Mississippi West, 1840–1880* (New York: Hill and Wang, 1979), 53; Pauline Neher Diede, *Homesteading on the Knife River Prairie*, ed. Elizabeth Hampsten (Bismark: Germans From Russia Heritage Society, 1983), 24; Albert D. Richardson, *Our New States and Territories* (New York: Beadle and Co., 1866), 42–43.

9. J. Ross Browne, *Crusoe's Island: A Ramble in the Footsteps of Alexander Selkirk* (New York: Harper and Brothers, 1864), 372.

10. For examples of these houses, see Lillie May Shane Reminiscence, part 2, 3–4, Frank Forman Collection, Olive Bascom Reminiscence, KSHS; Lena Martin interview, Oral History Collection, SWC/TT; Mrs. John H. Smith Reminiscence, 9–10, CHS; Emeline Day Journal, October 20, [?], Ban; B. Pearl Conner Reminiscence, SC 6, Sue Howells Reminiscence, 15, SC 88, William H. Laubach Autobi-

ography, 6, SC 1455, Frank D. Hughes Reminiscence, SC 1482, MHS; Elizabeth E. O'Neil Reminiscence, Mary Ann Busick Collection, MSU.

11. For interiors, see Alice Carnow, "My Journey With Tom," 35–37, AHS; D. E. Counsil and C. F. Patton Reminiscence, Jessie K. Snell Collection, Olive Bascom Reminiscence, Oello I. Martin, "Father Came West," 9–10; Lillie May Shane Reminiscence, 3–4, Frank Forman Collection, KSHS; Clarence W. Kellogg, "Early Day Life in California Mining Camps," Ban; Mary L. Boatman Reminiscence, SC 444, MHS; Mrs. John H. Smith Reminiscence, 9–10, CHS; Frances E. Albright, "A Child in Virginia City, Montana, in 1863," in H. G. Merriam, ed., *Way Out West: Recollections and Tales* (Norman: University of Oklahoma Press, 1969), 187–92; Lizzie Moore Sisk Reminiscence, IHS; Elizabeth O'Neil Reminiscence, Mary Ann Busick Collection, MSU; Sarah Day Duncan Reminiscence, Arthur B. Duncan Papers, Blanche T. McCullough and Lena Martin interviews, Oral History Collection, SWC/TT.

12. William H. Taylor to Eliza Taylor, March 27, 1869, Mitchell Family Papers, HEH.

13. Mrs. Fred Goosman, "Early Days in Nebraska," Nebraska Territorial Pioneer Association, *Reminiscences and Proceedings*, vol. 1, 21–22; Elizabeth Dixon Smith Geer, "Diary, 1847," *Oregon Pioneer Association Transactions*, 1907, Nov. 30, 1847, 172; Owen P. White, *A Frontier Mother* (New York: Minton, Balch and Co., 1929), 57; Sallie Davenport Davidson Reminiscence, SC 606, Bessie K. Monroe Reminiscence, SC 1503, and Bertha J. Anderson Autobiography, 27, SC 360, MHS; Chestina Allen Diary, November 25, 1854, Olive Bascom Reminiscence, and Wallace A. Wood Reminiscence, KSHS.

14. Jorgen Jorgensen Autobiography, 46, SC 178, MHS; Lucy H. Fosdick, "Across the Plains in '61," 21, Be; Walter Posey interview, Walter Posey Collection, SWC/TT.

15. Mary E. Norton, March 26, 1880, in Norton family Diaries, KSHS; Susan Newcomb Diary, January 6, 19, February 14, 1866, SWC/TT.

16. Charles Oliver interview and Mrs. Luna Smyer Maxes to Sylvan Dunn, Estacada, Texas file, SWC/TT; Chestina Allen Diary, March 15, 1855, KSHS; Minnie Prey Knotts, "Nebraska and Its Pioneers," in Nebraska Territorial Pioneer Association, *Reminiscences and Proceedings*, 1907, vol. 1, 26; Carnow, "My Journey," 113–14.

17. Sue Summers Reminiscence, AHS; Francis I. Sims Fulton, *To and Through Nebraska* (Lincoln: Journal Co., 1884), 52–53; Dutcher, *Sod House*, 354; Olive Bascom reminiscence, KSHS; Job E. Green, "Pioneering in Boone County," Nebraska Territorial Pioneers Association, *Reminiscences and Proceedings*, vol. 2, 36–37; Bertha J. Anderson Autobiography, 29–30; Waugh, "Pioneering," 19; Diede, *Homesteading*, 37.

18. C. F. Patton Reminiscence, Jessie K. Snell Collection, KSHS.

19. Kellogg, "Early Day Life," 34–36; Fitzgerald, "Life in Moore's Flat," Madison Loring Collection, AHS; Mrs. John Smith Reminiscence, 13; Sallie Davenport Davidson Reminiscence, SC 606, MHS.

20. Charley O'Kieffe, *Western Story: The Recollections of Charley O'Kieffe, 1884–1898* (Lincoln: University of Nebraska Press, 1960), 62; Ellis, *Life of Ordinary Woman* 42.

21. Albert Reed interview, Indian-Pioneer Collection, OHS; Ella Irvine Mountjoy reminiscence, Wiley and Ella Mountjoy Collection, SC 545, MHS; Carrie Strong Kay Robbins Journal, March 4, 1887, KSHS.

22. Barbara Welter, "The Cult of True Womanhood: 1820–1860," *American Quarterly* 18 (1966): 151–74; Nancy Cott, *The Bonds of True Womanhood: "Woman's Sphere" in New England, 1780–1835* (New Haven: Yale University Press, 1977); Kathryn K. Sklar, *Catherine Beecher: A Study in American Domesticity* (New Haven: Yale University Press, 1973), especially 158–67.

23. Isabel L. Eckles interview, 6–7, Pioneer Foundations Collection, UNMex.

24. Sarah Royce, *A Frontier Lady: Recollections of the Gold Rush and Early California* (New Haven: Yale University Press, 1932), 8–9; Rebecca Woodson Reminiscence, Ban; Harriet Fish Backus, *Tomboy Bride* (Boulder: Pruett Press, 1969), 213; James L. Thane, Jr., ed., *A Governor's Wife on the Mining Frontier: The Letters of Mary Edgerton From Montana, 1863–1865* (Salt Lake City: Tanner Trust Fund, 1976), 63; Ronan, *Frontier Woman*, 35; Evelena M. O'Neal Reminiscence, SC 169, MHS; Agnes Morley Cleaveland *No Life For a Lady* (Lincoln: University of Nebraska Press, 1977), 30.

25. Fitzgerald, "Life in Moores Flat," Madison Loring Collection, AHS; Ronan, *Frontier Woman*, 35; Carnow, "My Journey," 35–37; Dutcher, *Sod House*, 360; Irene A. Myers Reminiscence, HEH; D. E. Counsil Reminiscence, Jessie K. Snell Collection, and Augusta Dodge Thomas, "Prairie Children: An Autobiography," 13, KSHS.

26. Sarah D. Duncan, "Recollections of a Pioneer Mother," Arthur B. Duncan Papers, SWC/TT.

27. Snyder, *No Time On My Hands*, 17; Francis D. Haines, Jr., ed., *A Bride on the Bozeman Trail: The Letters and Diary of Ellen Gordon Fletcher, 1866* (Medford, Ore.: Gandee Printing, 1970), 82.

28. Percy G. Ebbutt, *Emigrant Life in Kansas* (London: Swan Sonnenschein and Co., 1886), 81; Fitzgerald, "Life in Moores Flat;" Isabella L. Bird, *A Lady's Life in the Rocky Mountains* (Norman: University of Oklahoma Press, 1960), 157.

29. Lucy Rutledge Cooke, *Covered Wagon Days: Crossing the Plains in 1852* (Modesto, Cal.: Privately Printed, 1923), 72.

30. Charles Davis to Martha Ellis Davis, January 9, 1851, Charles Davis Letters, and Philo ———— to sister, November 10, 1850, Philo ———— Letters, Be; Thomas Conrad to Mary, January 1, 1865, Thomas Conrad Papers, Collection #30, Box 1, folder 8, MHS; William H. Taylor to Eliza Taylor, February 17, February 21, 1896, Mitchell Family Papers, HEH; William H. Kidd, *Glittering Gold; Or, Pencillings About Pike's Peak* (St. Louis: Missouri Democrat, 1860), 9–10.

31. Royce, *Frontier Lady*, 129–30.

32. Olive Bascom Reminiscence, KSHS; Cleaveland, *No Life*, 35; Julia S. Lambert, "Plain Tales of the Plains," *The Trail*, 8:8 (January, 1916): 1–2; Mrs. James Kirkpatrick, "Early Life in Beaverhead County," SC 940, MHS; Elinore Pruitt Stewart, *Letters of a Woman Homesteader* (Boston: Houghton Mifflin Co., 1913), 124–25.

33. Ellis, *Life of Ordinary Woman*, 102.

34. Kenneth L. Ames, "Material Culture as NonVerbal Communication: A Historical Case Study," *Journal of American Culture* 3:4 (Winter, 1980): 619–25.

35. Mary Lillian Faeth, *Kansas in the 80s. Being Some Recollections of Life on Its Western Frontier* (New York: The Procyon Press, 1947), 18; Jeff Jenkins, *The Northern Tier; Or, Life Among the Homestead Settlers* (Topeka: Kansas Publishing House, 1880), 151.

36. Price, *Seven Years of Prairie Life*, 19; Fulton, *To and Through Nebraska*, 95; Fitzgerald, "Life in Moores Flat;" Mary E. Blake, *On the Wing. Rambling Notes of a Trip to the Pacific* (Boston: Lee and Shepard, 1883), 24; Ward G. and Florence Stark DeWitt, *Prairie Schooner Lady: The Journal of Harriet Sherill Ward, 1853* (Los Angeles: Westernlore Press, 1959), 170–71; Josephine Moorman Reiley, " 'I Think I Will Like Kansas': The Letters of Flora Moorman Heston, 1885–1886," *Kansas History* 6:2 (Summer, 1983): 93; Ellison Orr, "Reminiscences of a Pioneer Boy," *Annals of Iowa* 40:7 (Winter, 1971): 544–46; Mary E. Norton, April 25, 1880, in Norton Family Diaries, KSHS; Miller, "I Remember Montana," 64–65, SC1404, MHS; Emma Teller Tyler Reminiscence, Lynn Perrigo Collection, Western Historical Collections, University of Colorado Library.

37. Roosa, "Homesteading in the 1880s," 374.

38. Muir, *Elam Bartholomew, Pioneer, Farmer, Botanist*, 40.

39. Thane, ed., *Governor's Wife*, 63.

40. Hill, *A Dangerous Crossing and What Happened on the Other Side*, 47–48.

41. DePew, "William A. Hamill," 266–279.

42. William H. Taylor to Eliza Taylor, February 17, 1869, Mitchell Family Papers, HEH.

43. Rodman W. Paul, ed., *A Victorian Gentlewoman in the Far West*, 175–78.

44. Bennett, *Old Deadwood Days*, 6.

45. Elizabeth Fisk to Mother, September 17, 1871, Fisk Family Papers, Collection #31, Box 6, Folder 5, MHS.

46. Richard G. Lillard, ed., "A Literate Woman in the Mines," *Mississippi Valley Historical Review* 31:1 (June, 1944): 88.

47. C. Aubrey Angelo, *Sketches of Travel in Oregon and Idaho* (New York: By the Author, 1866), 143.

Chapter Four

1. Edna Matthews Clifton Reminiscence, I, 12, and *passim*, SWC/TT.

2. Viviana A. Zelizer, *Pricing the Priceless Child: The Changing Social Value of Children* (New York: Basic Books, 1985), 73–112. Though the situation has varied with families' occupations and economic status, the undeniable trend of this century has been toward parents' spending more on children, who in turn contribute less, directly and indirectly, to their families' incomes. On the complexities of calculating economic contributions of children, see Moni Nag, "Economic Value of Children in Agricultural Societies: Evaluation of Existing Knowledge and an Anthropological Approach," in James T. Fawcett, ed., *The Satisfactions and Costs of Children* (Honolulu: East-West Center, 1972), 58–98. Generally the contributions of children have declined more rapidly in urban areas. But by mid-century, according to one estimate, American farm children did not pay their way through their work until their late teens. See James D. Tarver, "Costs of Rearing and Educating

Farm Children," *Journal of Farm Economics* 38:1 (February, 1956): 144–53. For a recent estimate of the costs of child rearing, see Thomas J. Espenshade, *Investing in Children: New Estimates of Parental Expenditures* (Washington, D.C.: Urban Institute Press, 1984).

3. For a discussion of the sexual division of labor among midwestern farming families, see John Mack Faragher, *Women and Men on the Overland Trail* (New Haven: Yale University Press, 1979), 433–59.

4. Joseph M. Reed to brother, January 11, 1863, Joseph M. Reed Letters, Kansas Collection, Spencer Library, University of Kansas.

5. Linnaeus B. Rauck interview, 41/158–59, Indian-Pioneer Collection, OHS; Cedenia B. Willis Journal, 12, AHS.

6. Fannie L. Eisele, "We Came to Live in Oklahoma Territory," *Chronicles of Oklahoma*, 38:1 (Spring, 1960): 59–61; Orr, "Reminiscences of a Pioneer Boy," 40:7 (Winter, 1971): 552; Van Gundy, *Reminiscences of Frontier Life*, 14–16; Mrs. J. L. Ealum interview, 23/194–95, Indian-Pioneer Collection, OHS; Meda Perry and Lena Martin interviews, Oral History Collection, SWC/TT; Hiram M. Drache, *The Challenge of the Prairie* (Fargo: North Dakota Institute for Regional Studies, 1970), 195.

7. W. H. Laubach Autobiography, 12, MHS; Lucy Stocking Diary, October 2, 1873, SC142, MHS; Ebbutt, *Emigrant Life*, 90.

8. Van Gundy, *Reminiscences*, 14–15; Margaret E. Archer Murray, "Memoir of the William Archer Family," *Annals of Iowa* 39:5 (Summer, 1968): 356; Samuel E. Boys, *My Boyhood In the Flint Hills of Kansas, 1873–1893* (Plymouth, Indiana: By the Author, 1958), 30; Louis Williams and J. G. Duncan interviews, 23/54, Indian-Pioneer Collection, OHS; Augusta Dodge Thomas, "Prairie Children," 115–16; Louis M. Kreipie, "Reminiscences of the Early Settlers," KSHS; Ralla Banta Pinkerton, "Pioneer Days in the Beaver Creek Community," R. J. Bradley Collection, SWC/TT.

9. Hamlin Garland, *Boy Life on the Prairie* (Lincoln: University of Nebraska Press, 1926), 64; Edna Clifton Matthews Reminiscence, I, 14, SWC/TT.

10. Ebbutt, *Emigrant Life*, 90; Glen R. Durrell, "Homesteading in Colorado," *Colorado Magazine* 51:2 (Spring, 1974): 98–101; Hub Jones interview, Oral History Collection, SWC/TT; Anne Jones Davies Diary, June 2, 6, 13, 14, 16, 1888, KSHS; Edna Clifton Matthews Reminiscence, I, 13, SWC/TT; Linnaeus B. Rauck interview, 41/158–59, Indian-Pioneer Collection, OHS; Orr, "Reminiscences," 551.

11. Diede, *Homesteading on the Knife River Prairies*, 67–70; Pinkerton, "Pioneer, Days," 4–5; Maggie L. B. Holden Reminiscence, Maggie Lee Bullion Papers, SWC/TT; Oello Ingraham Martin, "Father Came West," 21–22, KSHS; Sadye Drew Autobiography, SC1532, MHS.

12. O'Kieffe, *Western Story*, 86–87; Durrell, "Homesteading," 98–101; Orr, "Reminiscences," 594–95; Boys, *My Boyhood*, 32–34; Murray, "Memoir," 364.

13. J. G. Duncan interview, 23/54, Indian-Pioneer Collection, OHS; Boys, *My Boyhood*, 9–10; Andrew D. Crofut, "Diamond Valley Dust," 90–104, Oral History Collection, UNev; James A. Young, "Hay Making: The Mechanical Revolution on the Western Range," *Western Historical Quarterly* 14:3 (July, 1983): 315, 320–21.

14. Emma Jane Davison Reminiscence, IHS; Ronan, *Frontier Woman*, 21–22; J. Milton Barnhart Reminiscence, SC396, MHS; Lizzie Moore Sisk Reminiscence, IHS; Theodore Taylor Johnson, *Sights in the Gold Region, and Scenes By the Way*

(New York: Baker and Scribner, 1849), 183; F. M. McCarty Autobiography, SC409, MHS.

15. Lewis Carstairs Gunn, *Records of a California Family*, ed., Anna Lee Marston (San Diego: Privately Printed, 1928), 213, 233–34; Abby F. Mansur to sister, November 21, 1852, Mansur Family Letters, Be.

16. Frank A. Crampton, *Deep Enough: A Working Stiff in the Western Mine Camps* (Norman: University of Oklahoma Press, 1982), 18–24; Robert A. Lewis Reminiscence, AHS; Walter A. Smith to parents, May 25, June 6, 9, 12, 1878, Walter T. Smith Letters, Western History Collection, DPL.

17. Mabel Stoll Brown, "Mabel Stoll Brown: Prairie Child," *South Dakota Historical Collections* (Pierre: South Dakota Historical Society, 1979), 168–71.

18. Frank Albert Waugh, "Pioneering in Kansas," 114–115, KSHS; Maggie L. B. Holden Reminiscence, SWC/TT; Mrs. Clayton Carter interview, Oral History Collection, SWC/TT; J. S. Bird, *Prairies and Pioneers* (Hays, Kan.: McWhirter-Ammons Press, 1931), 34; Arthur J. Dickson, ed. *Covered Wagon Days: A Journey Across the Plains in the Sixties. . . .* (Cleveland: Arthur H. Clark Co., 1929), 129; Christoper James Huggard, "The Role of the Family in Settling the Cherokee Outlet," (Master's thesis, University of Arkansas, 1987), 68–69; O'Kieffe, *Western Story*, 36–37.

19. Charles Wesley Wells, *A Frontier Life* (Cincinnati: Jennings and Pye, 1902), 31–32; Orr, "Reminiscences," 616–24; William Holden, James W. Mayfield, Sam Crawford, James E. Black, C. M. Randal, Sr., Mrs. Hawley Allen interviews, Oral History Collection, SWC/TT; Pinkerton, "Pioneer Days," 4–5, 17; Lucy H. Stocking Diary, November 20, 1873, SC142, MHS; Vallie McKee, "Passing of the West," 8, George Cork Reminiscence, Jessie K. Snell Collection, KSHS; Venola Lewis Bivens, ed., "The Diary of Luna E. Warner, A Kansas Teenager of the Early 1870s," *Kansas Historical Quarterly* 35:3 (Autumn, 1969): 283, 294, 308.

20. John H. Clark Diary, May 29, 1852, Ban; Josephine Moorman Reiley, ed., " 'I Think I Will Like Kansas': The Letters of Flora Moorman Heston, 1885–1886," *Kansas History* 6:2 (Summer, 1983): 79; Mr. and Mrs. Charles Littell Reminiscence, Jessie K. Snell Collection, KSHS; Clayton Carter, Owen McWhorter, Lena Martin interviews, Oral History Collection, SWC/TT; Edna Matthews Clifton Reminiscence; O'Kieffe, *Western Story*, 25–26.

21. D. E. Counsil, William M. Menkins, Mrs. C. D. Gillespie Reminiscences, Jessie K. Snell Collection, KSHS; Lydia Louise Mooar interview, Mooar Family Papers, SWC/TT; O'Kieffe, *Western Story*, 34–35, 96; Thomas, " Prairie Children," 13; Fred C. Moore biographical sketch, Madison Loring Collection, AHS.

22. Martha Ann Morrison Minto, "Female Pioneering in Oregon," 2–5, Ban; Ada Millington [Jones] Journal, May 4, August 31, 1862; Mary Eliza Warner Diary, May 1, 1864, Ban; Hixon, *On to Oregon!*, 45–6; Bennet Seymour Reminiscence, 5, CSHS; John L. Johnson Journal, June 23, 1851, Be; James Wilkins Diary, June 15, 1849, Thomas Crawford Reminiscence, HEH; Robert P. Thoroughman Reminiscence, MSU; Bill Gay Reminiscence, SC52, Raleigh F. Wilkinson Reminiscence, SC983, MHS; Elisha Brooks, *A Pioneer Mother of California* (San Francisco: Harr Waggner Publishing Co., 1922), 29–30.

23. Garry L. Nall, "The Farmers' Frontier in the Texas Panhandle," *Panhandle-Plains Historical Review* 45 (1972): 1–20.

24. Jim Lanning and Judy Lanning, *Texas Cowboys: Memories of the Early Days* (College Station: Texas A&M University Press, 1984), 17, 45, 61, 70, 87, 108; Walter Posey interview, Walter Posey Collection, Lula M. Veale Reminiscence, Mrs. J. W. Jackson interview, Oral History Collection, SWC/TT; David Hilger Reminiscence, SC854, "The Nuttings," SC1239, MHS; Mary Jennings reminiscence, AHS.

25. Fulton, *To and Through Nebraska*, 42; Helen Brock interview, Pioneer Foundations Collection, UNMex; Cleaveland, *No Life for a Lady*, 56–57; Mrs. Mary L. Neely interview, Oral History Collection, SWC/TT.

26. Garland, *Boy Life*, 94.

27. Kreipie, "Reminiscences," and Clara Frost reminiscence, KSHS; Katie Bell Crump, Meda Perry, Ima C. Jennings, and Hub Jones interviews, Oral History Collection, SWC/TT; Ebbutt, *Emigrant Life*, 97–106; Bertha Anderson Autobiography, 41, SC360, MHS; John Ise, *Sod and Stubble: The Story of a Kansas Homestead* (Lincoln: University of Nebraska Press, 1970), 212–23.

28. Edward Teachman interview, Indian-Pioneer Collection, OHS; Bertie Lord Reminiscence, 2, SC395, MHS; John T. Norton Diary, May 6, September 5–19, 1877, January 12, March 13, 30, 1878, Norton Family Diaries, KSHS.

29. Anne Jones Davies Diary, September 15, 1882-March 1, 1883, KSHS. See also Bertha Anderson Autobiography, 13–14, SC360, MHS.

30. John T. Norton diary, January 26, February 6, 15, 27, 28, March 7, 1878, Norton Family Diaries, KSHS; Susie Crocket interview, 21/220, Indian-Pioneer Collection, OHS.

31. Bennett Seymour Reminiscence, 13, CSHS; Ellis, *Life of Ordinary Woman*, 40–41; J. Milton Barnhart Reminiscence, SC396, MHS.

32. Ronan, *Frontier Woman*, 26–27; Martha E. G. Collins Reminiscence, HEH; Martin G. Wenger, *Recollections of Telluride, Colorado, 1895–1920* (Mesa Verde, Co.: Gilbert R. Wenger, 1978), 23; Glen Berry interview, Oral History Collection, SWC/TT; James W. Harrison, "Pioneer Story" in Charles M. Wood Collection, AHS; J. Milton Barnhart Reminiscence, SC396, MHS.

33. Cornelius Hedges to parents, March 8, 1870, Hedges Family Papers, box 2, folder 11, Collection #33, MHS; Charles H. Draper Reminiscence, SC642, MHS; Dorothy M. Johnson, "Helena's Past As Seen Through Teen-Age Eyes and Newsprint," *Montana, The Magazine of Western History* (Winter, 1962): 11; Bennett, *Boom Town Boy*, 57; Wenger, *Recollections of Telluride*, 23–25; Brooks, *Pioneer Mother*, 43.

34. Cornelius Hedges to parents, April 18, 1868 and March 8, 1870, box 2, folder 11, Hedges Family Papers, Collection #33, MHS.

35. Olive Bascom Reminiscence, KSHS.

36. Margaret Ferris to mother, February 20, 1874 and September 24, 1878, Mrs. Eddy F. Ferris Collection, MSU.

37. Edna Hedges Diary, October 7, 15, 1878, January 6, April 16, 18, 26, 1879, box 11, folder 27, Hedges Family Papers, Collection #33, MHS.

38. Lydia Walker to mother, October 2, 1872, Walker Family Papers, Be.

39. Hixon, *On to Oregon*, 43. See also Joseph Fish, "Autobiography," Joseph Fish Collection, AHS and J. Goldsborough Bruff, *Gold Rush: The Journals, Drawings, and Other Papers of J. Goldsborough Bruff*, ed. Georgia Willis Read and Ruth Gaines (New York: Columbia University Press, 1949), 218; "Those Early Years," SC1740,

David Hilger Reminiscence, SC854, Bertha Anderson Autobiography, SC360, Matovich Family Reminiscence, SC457, MHS; Thomas, "Prairie Children," 40.

40. Meda Perry and Irey Harrison interviews, Oral History Collection, SWC/TT; Mary Jennings Reminiscence, AHS; Edna Matthews Clifton Reminiscence, *passim*, SWC/TT; Lillian Miller, "I Remember Montana," 26–29; Bivens, ed., "Diary of Luna Warner," 299.

41. Burnett, " 'We Just Toughed it Out'," 69; Mary Jennings Reminiscence, AHS; Thomas, "Prairie Children," 35, Martin, "Father Came West," 11–12, 29.

42. See, for instance, the entry in the diary of M. A. Bowie: "Annie [her younger sister] and I have all we can do with the washing, milking, and cooking. While I do all the sewing for the family of seven." M. A. Bowie Diary, November 1, 1872, Barker.

43. Esther Brakeman Lyman Letter, typed copy, Esther and Joseph Lyman Papers, HEH; D. B. Ward, *Across the Plains in 1853* (Seattle: Ward, 1911), 50–51.

44. Octavius M. Pringle, "Experiences of an Emigrant Boy in 1846," in *Magic River Deschutes* (N.p., n.d.); Virgil Pringle Diary, November 3–6, 1846, in Dale Morgan, ed., *Overland in 1846: Diaries and Letters of the California-Oregon Trail*, I (Georgetown, Cal.: Talisman press, 1963), 185–86.

45. M. E. Dyer interview, Oral History Collection, Walter M. Posey interview, Walter Posey Collection, SWC/TT.

46. Louisa Walter to brothers and sisters, June 18, 1864, Louisa Walters Letters, IHS; Marvin Lewis, *Martha and the Doctor: A Frontier Family in Central Nevada*, ed. B. Betty Lewis (Reno: University of Nevada Press, 1977), 77.

47. Angelina Smith Crews Reminiscence, 13–15, HEH; Blanche McCullough interview, Oral History Collection, SWC/TT.

48. Mary Olive Gray interview, Pioneer Foundations Collection, UNMex; Thomas Conger to parents, April 9, 1851, Conger Family Letters; Mamie Rose Harbottle interview, Pioneer Foundations Collection, UNMex.

49. R. T. Alexander Reminiscence and Alexander Family interview, Panhandle-Plains Historical Museum, Canyon, Texas.

50. Martha E. G. Collins Reminiscence, Fred Lockley Collection, HEH; Mose Drachman Reminiscence, 5–9, AHS; Joseph F. McDonald, "The Life of a Newsboy in Nevada," 14–15, 20, 26, 36–37, Oral History Collection, UNev.

51. Mary R. Brophy to Kate Welborn Beson, April 1, 1867, Brophy-Beeson Collection, HEH.

Chapter Five

1. Applegate, *Recollections of My Boyhood*, 24–5.

2. Irene Athey, "Contributions of Play to Development," in Thomas D. Yawkey and Anthony D. Pellegrini, *Child's Play: Developmental and Applied* (Hillsdale, N.J.: Lawrence Earlbaum Associates, 1984): 9–28; Roberta R. Collard, "Exploration and Play," in Brian Sutton-Smith, ed., *Play and Learning* (New York: Gardner Press, Inc., 1979): 45–68; C. Hutt, "Exploration and Play in Children," in Dietland Muller-Schwarze, *Evolution of Play Behavior* (Stroudsburg, Penn.: Dowden, Hutchinson & Ross, Inc., 1978): 328–48.

3. Philip Condit Diary, May 26, 1854, HEH; Helen Stewart Diary, June 16, 1853, Lane County Historical Society, Eugene, Oregon; Bruff, *Gold Rush*, 199.

4. Lucy H. Fosdick, "Across the Plains in '61," Reminiscence, Be; Mary L. Boatman Reminiscence, SC444, Harriet P. Sanders Reminiscence, SC1254, MHS; Harriet Wright Reminiscence, AHS; Lavinia H. Porter, *By Ox-team to California: A Narrative of Crossing the Plains in 1860* (Oakland: Oakland Enquirer Publishing Co., 1910), 112; Julia S. Lambert, "Plain Tales of the Plains," *The Trail* 8:8 (January, 1916): 2–3.

5. Reiley, " 'I Think I Will Like Kansas'," 78; Owen McWhorter interview, Oral History Collection, SWC/TT; Allie B. Wallace, *Frontier Life in Oklahoma* (Washington, D. C.: Public Affairs Press, 1964), 79; Frank Dean, "Pioneering in Nebraska, 1872–1879," *Nebraska History* 36 (June, 1955), 113.

6. Alice Carnow, "My Journey With Tom," Reminiscence, 89–90, AHS.

7. Ella Irvine Mountjoy Reminiscence, Wiley and Ella Mountjoy Collection, SC545, MHS.

8. Ronan, *Frontier Woman*, 18; Edwin Lewis Bennett, *Boom Town Boy* (Chicago: Sage Books, 1966): 17–18; Carolyn H. Palmer, "Reminiscences of Early Days in Boise," MS/224, IHS.

9. John H. Smith Reminiscence, 2, CHS; Mrs. W. H. Hathaway Reminiscence, AHS; Glen Berry interview, Oral History Collection, SWC/TT.

10. Erikson, *Toys and Reasons*, 17.

11. Annette White Parks, "Children's Work and Play on the Northwest Frontier," *Henry Ford Museum and Greenfield Village Herald* 15:1 (November 1, 1986): 34; Ise, *Sod and Stubble*, 213; Martha E. G. Collins Reminiscence, HEH.

12. John Norton Diary, September-October, 1877, and January 26, 1878, Norton Family Diaries, KSHS.

13. Dora Bryant interview, 17/207–08, Indian-Pioneer Collection, OHS; Ben Wallicek interview, Oral History Collection, SWC/TT; Jack Stockbridge interview, #387, Pioneer Foundations Collection, UNMex; Bivens, ed., "The Diary of Luna E. Warner," 416; Frank Albert Waugh, "Pioneering in Kansas," Reminiscence, 68–9, 189,. KSHS.

14. Ellis, *Life of Ordinary Woman*, 99; Martin, "Father Came West," Reminiscence, 19, KSHS; Emma Jane Davison reminiscence, IHS.

15. I. R., *A Lady's Ranche Life in Montana* (London: W. H. Allen and Co., 1887), 54–55; Cleaveland, *No Life for a Lady*, 66, 68; Ursula Haskell to sister, August 4, 1848, Ursula B. H. Haskell Letters, Be.

16. Ise, *Sod and Stubble*, 213; Katie Bell Crum interview, SWC/TT; Jennie E. Ross, "A Child's Experiences in '49," *Overland Monthly*, 63, second series (April, 1914): 406;

17. Bivens, ed., "Diary of Luna Warner," 424, 436.

18. Garland, *Boy Life on the Prairie*, 95.

19. Alice Barker Reminiscence, 12, AHS; Irene A. Meyers Reminiscence, HEH; George Cork Reminiscence, Jessie K. Snell Collection, Myrtel Smith Reminiscence, 14; Augusta Dodge Thomas, "Prairie Children: An Autobiography," Reminiscence, 47–8, KSHS; Frank T. Alkire, "Little Lady of Triangle T. Ranch," reminiscence, appendix I, AHS; Clayton Carter interview, Oral History Collection, SWC/TT; Cleaveland, *No Life for a Lady*, 68–9; Wallace, *Frontier Life in Oklahoma*,

61; Bayard Taylor, *Colorado: A Summer Trip* (New York: G. P. Putnam and Son, 1867): 21.

20. Edward Everett Dale, *The Cross Timbers: Memories of a North Texas Boyhood* (Austin and London: University of Texas Press, 1966): 74–6; Hill, *A Dangerous Crossing*, 53–4; Cleaveland, *No Life for a Lady*, 50; Ellis, *Life of Ordinary Woman*, 111–21.

21. Jean Piaget, *Play, Dreams and Imitation in Childhood* (New York: W. W. Norton, 1951): 142–46; Frank and Theresa Caplan, *The Power of Play* (New York: Anchor Books, 1973): 61–85; Rivka R. Eifermann, "Social Play in Childhood," in R. E. Herron and Brian Sutton-Smith, eds., *Child's Play* (New York: John Wiley and Sons, 1971): 270–97; Susanna Millar, *The Psychology of Play* (New York: Jason Aronson, 1974): 188–90.

22. Of the scores of diaries and reminiscences that mention and discuss children's games, I have relied on the following for my impressions of how these games were played, their functions, and the relative popularity of some over others: Vera Tepe, Veta Harris, Lena Martin and Katie Crump interviews, Oral History Collection, and Lula M. Veale and Anna Wilkinson Reynolds reminiscences, SWC/TT; Fred C. Moore biographical sketch, Madison Loring Collection, AHS; Emma Teller Tyler Reminiscence, Lynn Perrigo Collection, Western History Collections, University of Colorado Library; Edna Hedges Diary, Hedges Family Papers, Collection #33, Box 11, folder 27, MHS; Robert E. Steiner, "Children in Early Alder Gulch," MSU; Bennett, *Boom Town Boy*, 68; Boys, *My Boyhood in the Flint Hills of Kansas*, 20; Eisele, "We Came to Live in Oklahoma Territory," 543 and 595; Glen R. Durrell, "Homesteading in Colorado," *Colorado Magazine* 51:2 (Spring, 1974), 103.

23. Iona and Peter Opie, *Children's Games in Street and Playground* (Oxford 1969) and *The Lore and Language of Schoolchildren* (Oxford 1960), and John Opie, "The Tentacles of Tradition," in *Advancement of Science* 20 (September, 1963), 235–44.

24. Dale, *Cross Timbers*, 90.

25. Opie, *Lore and Language of School Children*, 2.

26. May V. Seagoe, "Children's Play as an Indicator of Cultural and Intracultural Differences," *Journal of Educational Sociology* 35: 6 (February, 1962), 278–83. For an application of this approach, see David K. Wiggins, "The Play of Slave Children in the Plantation Communities of the Old South, 1820–60," *Journal of Sport History* (Summer, 1980), 21–39.

27. Brian Sutton-Smith, "The Two Cultures of Games," in *The Folkgames of Children* (Austin and London: University of Texas Press, 1972): 295–311.

28. Brian Sutton-Smith and B. G. Rosenberg, "Sixty Years of Historical Change in the Preferences of American Children," in Sutton-Smith, *Folkgames of Children*, 258–94.

29. Thomas, "Frontier Children," 41; Ben Wallicek interview, Oral History Collection, SWC/TT; Grace Snyder, *No Time on My Hands* (Caldwell, Idaho: Caxton Printers, Ltd., 1963): 25; Dale, *Cross Timbers*, 82–3, 91; Virginia City, Nevada *Territorial Enterprise*, April 15, 1865.

30. Millar, *Psychology of Play*, 136–57.

31. Applegate, *Recollections*, 19.

32. Mrs. W. H. Hathaway Reminiscence, AHS.

33. Thomas, "Prairie Children," 58–9.

34. Catherine Garvey, "The Natural History of the Smile," in *Play* (Cambridge: Harvard University Press, 1977): 17–24; Thomas R. Shultz, "Play as Arousal Modulation," in Sutton-Smith, *Play and Learning*, 7–22.

35. See, for instance, Bernard Wishy, *The Child and the Republic: The Dawn of Modern American Child Nurture* (Philadelphia: University of Pennsylvania Press, 1968) and Dominick Cavallo, *Muscles and Morals: Organized Playgrounds and Urban Reform, 1880–1920* (Philadelphia: University of Pennsylvania Press, 1981).

36. Hixon, *On to Oregon!*, 8; Glenda Riley, ed., "Family Life on the Frontier: The Diary of Kitturah Penton Belknap," *Annals of Iowa* 44:1 (Summer, 1977), 49.

37. Gunn, *Records of A California Family*, 162.

38. Thomas, "Prairie Children," 6–7; Wallace, *Frontier Life*, 64–5; Snyder, *No Time on My Hands*, 21; Minnie Hodge interview, 62/162 and Florence Woods interview, 50/394, Indian-Pioneer Collection, OHS; Mrs. W. H. Hathaway Reminiscence, AHS; Gunn, *California Family*, 169.

39. Abigail Emigh Reminiscence, G. Donald Emigh Collection, MS2/361, IHS; Martin, "Father Came West," 12; Maggie L. B. Holden Reminiscence, SWC/TT; Craig Miner, *West of Wichita: Settling the High Plains of Kansas, 1865–1890* (Lawrence: University Press of Kansas, 1986): 51.

40. Parks, "Children's Work and Play," 35–36.

41. Mary Elizabeth Norton in Norton Family Diaries, January 26, 1880, KSHS.

Chapter Six

1. For a selection of studies I found most helpful in understanding the relationship of work to children's development, see Erik H. Erickson, *Childhood and Society* (New York: W. W. Norton and Co., 1963), 258–61; Barnard Goldstein and Jack Oldham, *Children and Work: A Study of Socialization* (New Brunswick, N.J.: Transaction Books, 1979); Walter W. Emmerick, "Young Children's Discrimination of Parent and Child Roles," *Child Development*, 30 (September, 1959): 403–19; Robert J. Havinghurst, "Youth in Exploration and Man Emergent," in Henry Borow, ed., *Man in a World of Work* (Boston: Houghton, Mifflin and Co., 1964), 215–36; Dale B. Harris, et al., "The Relationship of Children's Home Duties to Responsibilities," *Child Development* 25 (March, 1954): 29–33; Kurt Danziger, "Children's Earliest Conceptions of Economic Relationships," *Journal of Social Psychology* 47 (May, 1958): 231–34; Mary Ellen Goodman, *The Culture of Childhood: Child's-Eye View of Society and Culture* (New York: Teachers College Press, 1970), 67–70; Mary Engle, et al., "Orientation to Work in Children," *American Journal of Orthopsychiatry* 38 (January, 1968): 137–43.

2. John Taylor Waldorf, *A Kid on the Comstock: Reminiscences of a Virginia City Childhood* (Palo Alto: American West Publishing Co., 1970), 132–33.

3. Woodin, *Recollections of My Childhood*, 16–17; Frances Moore Reminiscence, 5, Augusta Dodge Thomas, "Prairie Children: An Autobiography," 20–25, KSHS.

4. Wallace A. Wood Reminiscence, 9, KSHS.

5. John T. Norton Diary, May 8, 1878, Norton Family Diaries, KSHS; Ise, *Sod and Stubble*, 217; Wallace, *Frontier Life in Oklahoma*, 30.

6. Edna Matthews Clifton Reminiscence, I, 19–20, SWC/TT.

7. Lucy H. Fosdick, "Across the Plains in '61," 22, Be.

8. Huggard, "The Role of the Family in Settling the Cherokee Outlet," 66; William Holden interview, Oral History Collection, SWC/TT; C. F. Patton Reminiscence, Jessie K. Snell Collection, CSHS; Dollie E. Jones interview, 31/347 Indian-Pioneer Collection, OHS; Edna Matthews Clifton Reminiscence, I, 3, SWC/TT.

9. T. W. Dobbs Reminiscence, 16, Elijah Dobbs Collection, AHS.

10. Frank Albert Waugh, "Pioneering in Kansas," *passim*, KSHS.

11. Diede, *Homesteading on the Knife River Prairies*, 22–25, 36–39, 62.

12. Thomas, "Prairie Children," 25.

13. Wallace A. Wood Reminiscence, 3, Oello Ingraham Martin, "Father Came West," 24, KSHS.

14. Cliff Newland interview, Oral History Collection, SWC/TT.

15. Ebbutt, *Emigrant Life in Kansas*, 100–104; Ise, *Sod and Stubble*, 213–214; Boys, *My Boyhood in the Flint Hills of Kansas, 1873–1893*, 14–15; John T. Norton Diary, January 12, 1878, Norton Family Diaries, KSHS.

16. Ralla Banta Pinkerton, "Pioneer Days in the Beaver Creek Community," 16, R. J. Bradley Collection, SWC/TT; Marvin Powe interview, Pioneer Foundations Collection, UNMex.

17. Joe Pearce, "Line Rider," 16–20, AHS; Pinkerton, "Pioneer Days," 16.

18. Homer Thomas to Isabella Thomas, December 14, 1864, Homer Thomas Collection, MHS; Bennett, *Boom Town Boy*, 12–13; Bennett, *Old Deadwood Days*, 2, 23.

19. Milton J. Barnhart Reminiscence, SC396, MHS; Clarence W. Kellogg, "Early Day Life in California Mining Camps," 70–71, Ban; Bennett, *Boom Town Boy*, 48; Joseph McDonald interview, Oral History Collection, UNev.

20. Wilhelm, *Last Rig to Battle Mountain*, 49; Frances E. Albright, "A Child in Virginia City, Montana, in 1863," in H. G. Merriam, ed., *Way Out West: Recollections and Tales* (Norman: University of Oklahoma Press, 1969), 189–90; John Moses interview, tape 211, Pioneer Foundations Collection, UNMex; Andrew Crofut interview, 41–46, Oral History Collection, UNev.

21. Bivens, ed., "The Diary of Luna E. Warner," 280, 281, 294, 301.

22. Walter Smith to Parents, May 6, 30, June 2, 4, 6, July 15, 1878, Walter T. Smith Letters, Western History Collection, DPL.

23. Glen Berry interview, Oral History Collection, SWC/TT.

24. Cornelius Hedges to Parents, April 18, 1868, Hedges Family Papers, box 2, folder 9, Collection #33, MHS; Frances Werden Diary, September 24, October 17, 28, November 10, 17, December 25, SC971, MHS. See also Homer Thomas to Isabella Thomas, December 14, 1864, Homer Thomas Collection, MHS; *Frontier Woman: The Story of Mary Ronan as Told to Margaret Ronan*, ed. H. G. Merriam (Missoula: University of Montana Press, 1973), 16; Mose Drachman Reminiscence, 8, AHS.

25. O'Kieffe, *Western Story*, 36–38, 44–57; Mary E. Jennings Reminiscence, AHS; Bivens, ed., "Diary of Luna Warner," 283, 288.

26. Cleaveland, *No Life for a Lady*, 44.

27. Lillian Miller, "I Remember Montana," 21–25, SC1404, MHS; Orr, "Reminiscences of a Pioneer Boy," 556–57, 600–14; Garland, *Boy Life on the Prairie*, 95.

28. Bennett, *Old Deadwood Days*, 15–16; Waugh, "Pioneering in Kansas," 65–71, 80–85, KSHS.

29. Brooks, *A Pioneer Mother of California*, 15–16.

30. Hixon, *On to Oregon!*, 24–27, 37–42.

31. Juliette G. Fish and Emeline L. Walker, "Crossing the plains in 1862," 10–11, HEH.

32. Sarah Raymond Herndon, *Days on the Road: Crossing the Plains in 1865* (New York: Burr Printing House, 1902), 116.

33. DeWitt and DeWitt, *Prairie Schooner Lady*, 46, 83, 89, 109, 130, 140, 150.

34. Chestina Allen Diary, April 3, 1858, KSHS.

35. Bivens, ed., "Diary of Luna Warner," 295, 431.

36. John T. Norton Diary, November 18, 1876–January 24, 1877, August 15, 19, February 6, March 6, 25, 30, 1878, February 15, 1879, Norton Family Diaries, KSHS.

37. Curt Norton Diary, October 2, 1877, March 31, 1879; family diary entries, May 20, 22, July 14, November 2, 1880, Norton Family Diaries, KSHS.

38. Wallace, *Frontier Life*, 81.

39. Vera Best interview, 15/84, Indian-Pioneer Collection, OHS; Murray, "Memoir of the William Archer Family," 364; Clara Hilderman Ehrlich, "My Childhood On the Prairie," *Colorado Magazine* 51:2 (Spring, 1974): 125.

40. Wallace, *Frontier Life*, 13; Orr, "Reminiscences of Pioneer Boy," 551.

41. Boys, *My Childhood*, 32–34; Edna Matthews Clifton Reminiscence, SWC/TT.

42. Ruth E. Hartley, "Children's Conceptions of Male and Female Roles," *Merrill-Palmer Quarterly* 6 (Summer-Fall, 1960): 83–91; N. K. Schlossberg and J. Goodman, "A Woman's Place: Children's Sex Stereotyping of Occupations," *Vocational Guidance Quarterly*, 20 (June, 1972): 266–270.

43. George Girdley to Charlotte, November 3, 1851, George Girdley Letters, Ban.

44. Matilda Tomme interview, 47/225–30, Indian-Pioneer Collection, OHS.

45. Susan and Samuel Newcomb Diaries, SWC/TT. See entries for fall, 1865 and summer, 1866, particularly those in each diary for September 6, 12, 29, October 17, 25–26, November 7, December 11, 1865, and January 6, 21, February 8, 1866. See also Samuel's diary for December 21–22, 1865 and Susan's for December 22–25, 1865, October 19, 1866, and March 13, May 5, 20, June 4–22, 1867.

The letters of B. W. and Mary Curtis, ranchers in Arizona's Gila River valley, describe a similar situation. Though they spent more time together than did the Newcombs, this husband still wrote of long periods away from home, and his concerns were dominated by range conditions, long hours working cattle, and the weather—none of which is mentioned at all by Mary, who wrote of the looks, accomplishments, and illnesses of their children. See B. W. Curtis to Gussie, December 9, 1889, March 22, 1891; Mary Curtis to Gussie, February 12, 1891, June 3, 1891, Elizabeth McPhail Collection, AHS.

46. Norton Family Diaries, 1879–1880, *passim*, and particularly January 9, 11, February 7, 27–March 11, 1879, April 22, May 1, 15–August 1, 1880. Quotations are from January 16 and February 25, 1879.

47. Emily and James Galloway Diaries, 1862–65, *passim*, Ban.

48. Carrie Williams Diary, November 26–December 6, 1858, January 11, January 22, February 18, 21, March 5, 1859, Be; Chestina Allen Diary, 1855–57, *passim*,

and especially March-July, 1855, January 3, October 5, 1857, KSHS.

49. Hixon, *On to Oregon!*, 45–46.

50. Edna Clifton Matthews Reminiscence, I, 21–22, SWC/TT.

51. Susie Crocket interview, 21/221–29, Indian-Pioneer Collection, OHS.

52. Hub Jones interview, Oral History Collection, SWC/TT.

53. Cleaveland, *No Life for a Lady*, 86.

Chapter Seven

1. Bird, *A Lady's Life in the Rocky Mountains*, 67.

2. The following comments are drawn from an extensive literature on the changing status of the child in the nineteenth century. The curious reader will discover that there are varying viewpoints and some disagreement among these sources. See Wishy, *The Child and the Republic*; Carl N. Degler, *At Odds: Women and the Family in America from the Revolution to the Present* (New York: Oxford University Press, 1980); Cott, *The Bonds of Womanhood*; Joseph Kett, *Rites of Passage: Adolescence in America: 1790 to the Present* (New York: Basic Books, 1977); Robert McGlone, "Suffer the Children: The Emergence of Modern Middle-Class Family Life, 1820–1870," (Ph.D. diss., University of California, Los Angeles, 1971).

3. Israel Lord Journal, August 13, 1849, HEH.

4. John T. Norton Diary, February 13, 1879, Norton Family Diaries, KSHS; Bivens, ed., "The Diary of Luna E. Warner," 304–305; Jesse Newton to brother and sister, July 21, 1857, Frederic Stafford Papers, Special Collections, University of North Carolina Library.

5. Quoted in Robert G. Athearn, "A Brahmin in Buffaloland," *Western Historical Quarterly 1:1 (January, 1970): 30*; Sarah Royce, *A Frontier Lady: Recollections of the Gold Rush and Early California* (New Haven: Yale University Press, 1932), 109.

6. Edward Austin to sister, September 21, 1849, Edward Austin Letters, Ban.

7. Louisa Walters to "Dear Friends," May 17, 1865, Louisa Walters Letters, IHS.

8. Elizabeth Fisk to mother, February 5, 1871, box 6, folder 4, Fisk Family Papers, Collection #31, MHS; Browne, *Crusoe's Island*, 307; Reiley, " 'I Think I Will Like Kansas'," 79; Ouray, Colorado *Solid Muldoon*, April 2, 1880.

9. Virginia City *Montana Post*, May 6, 1865; Waldorf, *A Kid on the Comstock*, 123–24, 130; Bennett, *Old Deadwood Days*, 24.

10. William H. Taylor to Eliza Taylor, March 31, 1869, Mitchell Family Papers, HEH; William D. Dixon to Mary Pendleton, March 20, 1852, Holliday-Pendleton Papers, Special Collections, University of North Carolina Library; Lizzie Moore Sisk Reminiscence, IHS; Mabel Barbee Lee, *Cripple Creek Days* (Garden City, N.Y.: Doubleday and Co., 1958), 27.

11. Mari Sandoz, *Old Jules* (New York: Blue Ribbon Books, 1935), 215–16; Diede, *Homesteading on the Knife River Prairies*, 84.

12. Warren Sadler Reminiscence, 19–172, Ban; Bruff, *Gold Rush*, 241–85.

13. Lewis, *Martha and the Doctor*, 140; Sarah Herndon Diary, February 17, 1866, MHS. For two insightful recent studies on divorce in two western settings, see Robert L. Griswold, *Family and Divorce in California, 1850–1890* (Albany: State University of New York Press, 1983) and Paula Petrik, "If She Be Content: The Devel-

opment of Montana Divorce Law, 1865–1907," *Western Historical Quarterly* 18:3 (July, 1987): 261–91.

14. Virginia City, Nevada *Territorial Enterprise*, June 30, 1866; Bennett, *Old Deadwood Days*, 211–14; Anne M. Butler, *Daughters of Joy, Sisters of Misery: Prostitutes in the American West, 1865–90* (Urbana and Chicago: University of Illinois Press, 1985), 35–41.

15. Silver City, Idaho *Owyhee Avalanche*, February 3, 1866; Bivens, "Diary of Luna Warner," 295; Ella Mitchell to Emma Mitchell, April 3, 1877, Mitchell Family Papers, HEH.

16. Waldorf, *Kid on the Comstock*, 162; Charles R. Parke Diary, April 25, 1850, HEH.

17. John Moses and Jack Stockbridge interviews, Pioneer Foundations Collection, UNMex.

18. Charles DeBaud, "Seventy-one Years of Experience of My Life," Charles DeBaud file, AHS; "My Memories of Early Days," SC95, MHS; Lanning and Lanning, *Texas Cowboys*, 111–17.

19. Leadville, Colorado *Daily Democrat*, January 3, 1880; *Creede* (Colorado) *Candle*, February 24, 1893; Virginia City *Montana Post*, December 3, 1864; Virginia City, Nevada *Territorial Enterprise*, April 15, May 15, 1866; Jack Stockbridge interview, Pioneer Foundations Collection, UNMex.

20. John Moses interview, Pioneer Foundations Collection, UNMex.

21. Burnett, " 'We Just Toughed it Out'," 34–35; Helen Nye to sister, January 21, 1855, Helen Nye Letters, Be.

22. Elizabeth Fisk to mother, March 6, 1870, box 6, folder 2, Elizabeth Fisk to mother, March 22, 1875, box 6, folder 10, Fisk Family Papers, Collection #31, MHS.

23. Edna Hedges Diary, September 19, October 7, 15, November 4, 13, December 12, 31, 1878, March 17, 23, April 17, 19, 25, 26, 28, 1879, box 11, folder 27, Hedges Family Papers, Collection #33, MHS.

24. Sister to George Underwood, November 17, 1850, August 31, 1851, George Underwood Letters, Be; Elizabeth E. O'Neil reminiscence, Mary Ann Busick Collection, MSU; Mary Curtis to Gussie, February 13, 1891, Eliza MacPhail Collection, AHS; Mrs. J. E. Riordan Diary, June 30, 1881, Riordan Family Collection, SWC/TT; Diede, *Homesteading on the Knife River Prairies*, 61.

25. Glenda Riley, ed., "The Morse Family Letters: A New Home in Iowa, 1856–1862," *Annals of Iowa* 45 (Winter, 1980): 226; Frank Alkire, "Little Lady of Triangle T Ranch," 33–35, AHS; Sarah Day Duncan, "Recollections of a Pioneer Mother," 6, Arthur B. Duncan Papers, SWC/TT; Susan Newcomb Diary, January 14, 1866, SWC/TT.

26. Duncan, "Recollections," 5; Margaret Marshall Reminiscence, 14–15, KSHS.

27. Carrie Williams Diary, Be; Margaret Marshall Reminiscence, 16, KSHS.

28. Oello Martin, "Father Came West," 18, KSHS; Frances Moore Reminiscence, 7, KSHS; Mrs. J. Raymond George Reminiscence SWC/TT; Ben Wallicek interview, Oral History Collection, SWC/TT.

29. William Forbes to William Taylor, October 16, 1870 and October 24, 1870, Mitchell Family Papers, HEH; B. W. Curtis to sister, September 8, 1886, Septem-

ber 30, 1886, October 28, 1886, November 24, 1887, Elizabeth MacPhail Collection, J. K. Brown to Olive Brown, August 14, 1881, September 15, 1881, December 2, 1881, E. W. Davis Collection, AHS; Duncan, "Recollections," 5.

30. Charles F. Stubbs to Salmon P. Stubbs, December 5, 1883, Mrs. C. F. Stubbs Papers, SWC/TT; Ben Wallicek interview, Oral History Collection, SWC/TT.

31. Katherine Rigelehuth reminiscence, Oral History Collection, UNev.

32. Lillard, ed., "A Literate Woman in the Mines," 85.

33. Mrs. W. H. May interview, Oral History Collection, SWC/TT.

34. Clarence W. Kellogg, "Early Day Life in California Mining Camps," 45–49, Ban. See also Carrie Williams Diary, January 1, 1859, Be; Annie Taylor interview, Oral History Collection, SWC/TT; Martin, "Father Came West," 13–14.

35. Augusta Dodge Thomas, "Prairie Children," 56–57, KSHS.

36. Susan Newcomb Diary, January 31, 1871, SWC/TT.

37. Mollie Dorsey Sanford, *Mollie: The Diary of Mollie Dorsey Sanford in Nebraska and Colorado Territories, 1857–1866* (Lincoln: University of Nebraska Press, 1959), 157.

38. LeRoy R. Hafen, ed., *Colorado Gold Rush: Contemporary Letters and Reports, 1858–1859* (Glendale, Cal.: Arthur H. Clark Co., 1941), 305.

39. Anonymous to Harry and Metta, n.d., Harry Faulkner Collection, Western History Collection, DPL.

40. Thomas Conrad to Mary, March 19, 1865, box 1, folder 8, Thomas Conrad Papers, Collection #30, MHS; C. Westover to wife, November 10, 18??, Be.

41. David DeWolf to Matilda, June 17, 1849, David DeWolf Letters, HEH.

42. Jotham Varney to Edwin Varney, September 10, 1850, Jotham Varney Letters, CHS; Charles Davis to Martha Ellen Davis, January 5, 1850, Charles Davis Letters, Be; William Dresser to Albert and Charles Dresser, October 29, 1850, May 13, 1853, Dresser Family Papers, Ban; Theodore Richmond to wife, July 24, 1864, Theodore Richmond Papers, Special Collections, University of North Carolina Library.

43. Addison Crane Diary, May 26, 1852, HEH.

44. Harlow C. Thompson, "Across the Continent On Foot," 21, Newberry; William Newell to Mary Newell, February 4, 1851, Pownall Collection, HEH; C. S. Hinman to father, February 3, 1861, C. S. Hinman Letters, Western History Collection, DPL.

45. Mrs. John H. Smith Reminiscence, 6, CHS; Louise Amelia Knapp Clappe, *The Shirley Letters From California Mines in 1851–52* (San Francisco: T. C. Russell, 1922), 159–60; Georgia Burns Hills, "Memories of a Pioneer Childhood," *Colorado Magazine*, 32:2 (April, 1955): 113; Ellen Fletcher to mother, November 26, 1867, Ellen Fletcher Letters, SC78, Mary E. Booth reminiscence, SC1492, MHS; Royce, *Frontier Lady*, 80–81; William P. Bennett, *The First Baby in Camp* (Salt Lake City: Rancher Publishing Co., 1893), 6–8; Robert Van Carr, *Black Hills Ballads* (Denver: Reed Publishing Co., 1902), 13–16.

46. Henry S. Bloom Diary, February 23, 1851, Ban.

47. William Dangerfield to sister, February 14, 1853, William Dangerfield Letters, Ban.

48. James, *The Cherokee Strip*, 7–8; Waldorf, *Kid on the Comstock*, 69–70.

49. Whipple-Haslam, *Early Days in California*, 11, 16; Bennett, *Boom Town Boy*, 20–21; Mose Drachman Reminiscence, 13–14, 18, AHS.

50. "Plummer Jeffries," Madison Loring Collection, AHS; Mrs. John H. Smith Reminiscence, 1–12, CHS; Whipple, *Early Days*, 16; Henry S. Bloom Diary, February 22, 1851, Ban; James, *Cherokee Strip*, 24; George A. Root Reminiscence, George A. Root Collection, CSHS; Elizabeth Crider interview, 0–42/C868, Oral History Collection, CSHS.

51. Ellis, *Life of Ordinary Woman*, 30–34, 58–59, 67–76, 100–02, 122–23.

52. Alice Barker Reminiscence, 18, AHS; M. A. Bowie Diary, October 11, 1872, Barker.

53. Norton Family Diaries, March 2–11, 1880, KSHS; O'Kieffe, *Western Story*, 58–59; Minnie Hodge interview, 62/163, Mrs. J. L. Ealum interview, 23/198, Indian-Pioneer Collection, OHS.

54. Frank D. Hughes Reminiscence, SC1482, MHS.

55. Barney, *Letters*, 87–88; Danker, ed., *Mollie*, 132; Virginia City *Territorial Enterprise*, July 6, 1865; Elizabeth E. O'Neil Reminiscence, Mary Ann Busick Collection, MSU; John H. Clark Diary, May 1, 1855, Ban; Phineus Blunt Diary, October 29, 1850, Ban; William H. Laubach Autobiography, 11, MHS; Bird, *Prairies and Pioneers*, 35.

56. John Blanchard to Milton Badger, August 22, 1864, John Blanchard Collection, SC442, MHS; Angelo, *Sketches*, 143; Gunn, *Records of a California Family*, 233; Thomas, "Prairie Children," 68.

57. Mrs. J. E. Riordan Diary, July 10, 1881, Riordan Family Papers, SWC/TT; Edna Hedges Diary, September 22, 1878, April 17, 20, 1879, box 11, folder 27, Hedges Family Papers, Collection #33, MHS; Wilhelm, *Last Rig*, 63–65.

58. Samuel Newcomb Diary, August 26, December 24, 1865, SWC/TT.

59. D. E. Counsil Reminiscence and Chris Jasperson Reminiscence, Jessie K. Snell Collection, Frank Albert Waugh, "Pioneering in Kansas," 157–61, KSHS; Melissa Everett Reminiscence, 5, Mrs. Hawley Allen, Mary Dunn, Meda Perry, Annie Henderson interviews, Oral History Collection, SWC/TT.

60. Glenda Riley, ed., "Eighty-six Years in Iowa: The Memoir of Ada Mae Brown Brinton," *Annals of Iowa*, 45:7 (Winter, 1981): 553; Chestina Allen Diary, May 27, 1855, KSHS; Biographical information, James and Sarah Ann Aram file, Ban; Nelle Frances Minnick, "A Cultural History of Central City, From 1859 to 1880, In Terms of Books and Libraries" (Master's thesis, University of Chicago, 1946), 50–51.

61. Duncan, "Recollections," 3, SWC/TT; Ralla Banta Pinkerton, "Pioneer Days in the Beaver Creek Community," 12, SWC/TT; Mary Kelly, Mary Dunn, James Mayfield interviews, Oral History Collections, SWC/TT; Wallace, *Frontier Life in Oklahoma*, 35; Margaret Marshall Reminiscence, 15, Waugh, "Pioneering in Kansas," 156–61, KSHS.

62. Virginia City *Territorial Enterprise*, May 1, 1866.

63. Louisa Walters to Brothers and Sisters, June 18, 1864, Louisa Walter Letters, IHS; Elizabeth Fisk to mother, March 30, 1873, box 6, folder 6, Collection 31, MHS.

64. Wallace, *Frontier Life*, 35; Ruth Clark interview, 51/278, Indian-Pioneer Collection, OHS; R. L. Jones, ed., "Folk Life in Early Texas: The Autobiography of Andrew Davis," *Southwestern Historical Quarterly* 43:3 (January 1940): 337–39.

65. Waugh, "Pioneering in Kansas," 160–65.

66. George McCowen Diary, August 11, 1853, James Clyman Journal, May 26, 1844, Addison Crane diary, May 12, 1852, HEH; Wesley Tonner to "Dear Friends,"

September 11, 1854, with Mary Burrell Diary, Be; Rose Bell Diary, May 7, 1862, CSHS; David Hilger Reminiscence, SC854, MHS; Ralph P. Bieber, ed., "Diary of a Journey to the Pike's Peak Gold Mines in 1859," *Mississippi Valley Historical Review*, 14:3 (December, 1927): 366; James Abbey, *California, A Trip Across the Plains in 1850* (New Albany, Ind.: Jno. R. Nunmacher, 1850), 7; James F. Meline, *Two Thousand Miles on Horseback* (New York: Hurd and Houghton, 1867), 298.

67. DeWitt and DeWitt, *Prairie Schooner Lady*, 169; O'Kieffe, *Western Story*, 73.

68. Sandoz, *Old Jules*, 335–38; Bivens, ed., "Diary of Luna Warner," 289.

69. For some examples of songs, see Maggie L. B. Holden Reminiscence, SWC/TT; Wallace, *Frontier Life* 105–07.

Chapter Eight

1. Melissa Everett Reminiscence, Carl Coke Rister Papers, SWC/TT.

2. Samuel Few to T. C. Steele, February 8, 1855, California Gold Rush Letters, Ban.

3. U.S. Bureau of the Census, *Twelfth Census of the United States, 1900, Population*, Vol. II, ci-cii, cxv-cxvi.

4. John Blanchard to Milton Badger, August 22, 1864, John Blanchard Letters, SC442, MHS.

5. Bennett, *Old Deadwood Days*, 47; Elizabeth Fisk to mother, March 22, 1875, Fisk Family Papers, box 6, folder 10, Collection #31, MHS.

6. Burnett, " 'We Just Toughed It Out'," 71; Minnick, "A Cultural History of Central City, Colorado," 30–72; Verna Sharp, "Montezuma and Her Neighbors," *Colorado Magazine* 33 (January, 1956): 16–41; Mrs. J. E. Riordan Diary, January 25, 1881, Riordan Family Collection, SWC/TT; Mrs. Albert Taylor statement, Pioneer Women tapes, Oral History Collection, SWC/TT.

7. Stella Fairlamb interview, Pioneer Foundations Collection, UNMex; Hill, *A Dangerous Crossing*.

8. Orr, "Reminiscences of a Pioneer Boy," 597; Dale, *The Cross Timbers*, 47–61; Bivens, ed., "The Diary of Luna Warner," 289–92, 299–300.

9. Ludlow, *The Heart of the Continent*, 29–30.

10. Ellis, *Life of Ordinary Woman*, 122–24.

11. Virginia City *Territorial Enterprise*, June 5, 1866; Sarah Hively Journal, February 4, 1865, Western History Collection, DPL.

12. Edna Matthews Clifton Reminiscence, SWC/TT; Norton Family Diary, January 30, 1879, KSHS.

13. Dale, *Cross Timbers*, 73; J. W. LaSueur Autobiography, AHS; Bivens, ed., "Diary of Luna Warner," 424; Roosa, "Homesteading in the 1880s," 379; Myrtle Smith Reminiscence, 27, KSHS; Frank Albert Waugh, "Pioneering in Kansas," 180–81, KSHS; Walter T. Smith to parents, May 4, 1878, Walter T. Smith Letters, Western History Collection, DPL.

14. For several hundred issues of these newspapers, see Amateur Newspaper Collection, American Antiquarian Society, Worcester, Massachusetts.

15. Margaret Ferris to mother, September 10, 1880, Mrs. Eddy F. Ferris Collection, MSU: Elizabeth Fisk to mother, March 22, 1875, Fisk Family Papers, box 6, folder 10, Collection #31, MHS.

16. Dalton, *Autobiography*, 3–4; Bennett Seymour Reminiscence, 9, CSHS; Jack Stockbridge interview, Pioneer Foundations Collection, UNMex; Martha E. G. Collins Reminiscence, Fred Lockley Collection, HEH. For other instances, see Carolyn H. Palmer Reminiscence, IHS; Mrs. John H. Smith Reminiscence, 4, CHS; Anna Wilkinson Reynolds Reminiscence, Anna Wilkinson Reynolds Collection, AHS; Minnie Uto interview, 48/5, Indian-Pioneer Collection, OHS.

17. Charles H. Draper Reminiscence, SC642, MHS; Alma C. Kirkpatrick, SC940, MHS.

18. Waugh, "Pioneering in Kansas," 195–96.

19. Will Norton in Norton Family Diary, January 20, 1880, KSHS.

20. Lawrence A. Cremin, *American Education: The National Experience* (New York: Harper and Row, 1980), 312–318; Carl Bode, *The American Lyceum:Town Meeting of the Mind* (New York: Oxford University Press, 1956); Calvin W. Gower, "Lectures, Lyceums, and Libraries in Early Kansas, 1854–1864" *Kansas Historical Quarterly* 36:2 (Summer, 1970): 176–79.

21. For descriptions and comments on literaries, see Dale, *Frontier Ways*, 171–85; Glen R. Durrell, "Homesteading in Colorado," *Colorado Magazine* 51:2 (Spring, 1974): 105; Mr. and Mrs. Charles Littell Reminiscence and D. E. Counsil Reminiscence, Jessie K. Snell Collection, KSHS; Vallie McKee Reminiscence, KSHS; Mrs. Irving Hunt Statement, Pioneer Women tape, Oral History Collection, SWC/TT.

22. Price, *Seven Years of Prairie Life*, 40.

23. John G. Prude, "The Early Ranch Schools of the Fort Davis Area," (Master's Thesis, Sul Ross State Teachers College, 1942), 86; E. M. Anthony Reminiscence, 27, Ban; Lula M. Veale Reminiscence, 5–6, SWC/TT.

24. George A. Root Reminiscence, 1889, George A. Root Collection, CSHS; Mrs. J. E. Riordan Diary, March 28, 1881, SWC/TT; Boise Basin file, Cornelius Brosnan Collection, Special Collections, University of Idaho; G. W. W. Yates to G. W. Martin, October 6, 8, 1904, G. W. W. Yates Letters, KSHS; Dora Bryant interview, 17/207, and Mary England interview, Indian-Pioneer Collection, OHS; Elizabeth Fisk to mother, January 19, 1868, and Elizabeth Fisk to Fannie, January 25, 1868, Fisk Family Papers, box 5, folder 12, Collection #31, MHS.

25. O. J. Goldrick, "The First School in Colorado," *Colorado Magazine* 6:2 (March, 1929): 72–74; Joseph Emerson Smith, "Personal Recollections of Early Denver," *Colorado Magazine* 20:1 (January, 1943): 7; Thomas Crawford Reminiscence, HEH; Carrie Williams Journal, March 7, 1859, Be; Mahan, "Education in Colorado," 1153.

26. B. F. Dowell Journal, *passim*, HEH.

27. The history of American education in the nineteenth century has attracted much attention from historians recently. For a sense of the wide range of opinions and interpretations among these works see Cremin, *American Education: The National Experience*; Michael B. Katz, *The Irony of Early School Reform: Educational Innovation in Mid-Nineteenth Century Massachusetts* (Cambridge: Harvard University Press, 1968); David Nasaw, *Schooled To Order: A Social History of Public Schooling in the United States* (New York: Oxford University Press, 1980); David J. Rothman, *The Discovery of the Asylum: Social Order and Disorder in the New Republic* (Boston: Little, Brown and Co., 1971); Bernard Bailyn, *Education in the Forming of American Society: A Reinterpretation* (Chapel Hill: University of North Carolina

Press, 1960). For an essay stressing the goal of shaping and standardizing the values of pioneer children through education, see Ronald E. Butchart, "Education and Culture in the Trans-Mississippi West," *Journal of American Culture* 3:2 (Summer, 1980): 351–73.

28. *Report of the Commissioner of Education* in *Report of the Secretary of the Interior*, 45th Congress, 3rd session, 1880, House Ex. Doc. 1, Part 5, 149.

29. *Commissioner of Education*, 1870, 319.

30. Howard Roberts Lamar, *The Far Southwest, 1846–1912: A Territorial History* (New York: W. W. Norton and Co., 1970), 89, 167–69, 187–89, 442, 459–60; Dianna Everett, "The Public School Debate in New Mexico, 1850–1891," *Arizona and the West* 26:2 (Summer, 1984): 107–34; Jay J. Wagoner, *Arizona Territory, 1863–1912: A Political History* (Tucson: University of Arizona Press, 1970), 106–13.

31. *Report of the Commissioner of Education* in *Report of the Secretary of the Interior*, 41st Congress, 3rd session, 1870, House Ex. Doc. 1, Part 4, 334–35.

32. Murray, "Memoir of the William Archer Family," 366.

33. *Commissioner of Education*, 1870, 322, 325; Mary W. M. Hargreaves, "Rural Education on the Northern Plains Frontier," *Journal of the West* 18:4 (October, 1979): 28; Ronald E. Butchart, "The Frontier Teacher: Arizona, 1875–1925," *Journal of the West* 16:3 (July, 1977): 65, 10n; Wayne E. Fuller, "Country Schoolteaching on the Sod-House Frontier," *Arizona and the West* 17:2 (Summer, 1975): 121–40.

34. George Lubick, "Cornelius Hedges: Frontier Educator," *Montana, the Magazine of Western History* 28:2 (April, 1978): 31.

35. Robert H. Bremner, ed., *Children and Youth in America: A Documentary History*, II, Part 8 (Cambridge: Harvard University Press, 1971), 1103.

36. *Commissioner of Education*, 1870, 336.

37. *Commissioner of Education*, 1880, 308–09.

38. Lubick, "Cornelius Hedges," 31; *Commissioner of Education*, 1870, 323–34.

39. U.S. Bureau of the Census, *Tenth Census of the United States. Population*, Vol. I, 646, 918.

40. Plummer Jeffries Reminiscence, 18–19, Mary Gardner Kane Reminiscence and Fred C. Moore biographical sketch, all in Madison Loring Collection, AHS; Ella Irvine Mountjoy Reminiscence, Wiley and Ella Mountjoy Collection, SC545, MHS; Lydia Louise Mooar interview, Mooar Family Papers, Maggie L. B. Holden Reminiscence, Ruth Sheldon and Mrs. Eppie Barrier interviews, Oral History Collection, SWC/TT.

41. Sarah Hively Journal, August 29, September 3, 1864, Western History Collections, DPL; Mrs. W. H. Hathaway Reminiscence, AHS; Glen Berry interview, Oral History Collection, SWC/TT; Sarah Blackbourne interview, 66/22, Indian-Pioneer Collection, OHS; Job E. Green, "Pioneering in Boone County," Nebraska Territory Pioneers Association, *Reminiscences and Proceedings* Vol. II, 37; Susan Tucker Shanstrom interview, Prowers County, Colorado Writers Project Papers, CSHS.

42. Brooks, *A Pioneer Mother of California*, 43; Bennett Seymour Reminiscence, 15, CSHS.

43. School records, Montezuma, Colorado Collection, CSHS; James Bushnell Autobiography, 29, HEH; Susie Crocket interview, 21/226, Indian-Pioneer Collection, OHS; O'Kieffe, *Western Story*, 65; Madison County School District Records,

March 25, 1867, MHS. See also Wright L. Liles Reminiscence, SC385, MHS; Rilla Jarvis Denison Reminiscence, Jessie K. Snell Collection, KSHS; Thomas, "Prairie Children," 59, KSHS; Orr, "Reminiscence," 543; Hub Jones interview, Oral History Collection, SWC/TT.

44. Raleigh Wilkenson Reminiscence, SC983, MHS.

45. Daniel White Diary, February 2–22, 1855, HEH; E. M. Anthony Reminiscence, 29–30, Ban.

46. F. A. Fenn to C. J. Brosnan, F. A. Fenn file, Cornelius Brosnan Collection, Special Collections, University of Idaho Library; Oello Ingraham Martin, "Father Came West," 19; Willa Jarvis Denison Reminiscence, Jessie K. Snell Collection, KSHS; William Holden interview, Oral History Collection, SWC/TT.

47. Ada Vrooman Ferguson Reminiscence, box 57, Edna P. G. Hatfield Collection, Western History Collections, University of Oklahoma. See also Myrtle Smith Reminiscence, 16, KSHS; Martin, "Father Came West," 19, 56, Vallie McKee Reminiscence, 25, KSHS.

48. Anna Wilkinson Reynolds Reminiscence, SWC/TT; Dayton and Prairie Creek School District Records, 1894–1910, Edna P. G. Hatfield Collection, Box H-34, Western History Collection, University of Oklahoma.

49. Rollin L. Hartt to mother, November 2, 1896, Rollin L. Hartt Letters, MHS; Alma C. Kirkpatrick Reminiscence, SC940, MHS; Ronan, *Frontier Woman*, 38; Daniel Tuttle to wife, August 27, 1867, Daniel Tuttle Letters, MHS; Katie Bell Crump interview, Oral History Collection, SWC/TT; Mose Drachman Reminiscence, 5, AHS; Thompson, "Social and Cultural History," 45; Mary Edgerton to sister, November 20, 1864, in Thane, Jr., ed., *A Governor's Wife on the Mining Frontier*, 102; Mrs. J. C. McNeill interview, Oral History Collection, SWC/TT.

50. Virginia City *Territorial Enterprise*, May 22, 1866; Mrs. D. C. Martin, "Memories of Strawberry School," AHS.

51. Susie Crocket interview, 21/225–26, Indian-Pioneer Collection, OHS; Alice Barker Reminiscence, 18–19, AHS; Lee, *Cripple Creek Days*, 26; Martha Byrne Reminiscence, KSHS.

52. Emma Teller Tyler Reminiscence, Lynn Perrigo Collection, Western History Collection, University of Colorado Library; Goldie R. Gilbert Reminiscence, Edna P. G. Hatfield Collection, Western History Collection, University of Oklahoma; Stuart, *Forty Years on the Frontier*, 26–27; Katie Bell Crump interview, Oral History Collection, SWC/TT; Edna Matthews Clifton Reminiscence, SWC/TT; Mrs. W. H. Hathaway Reminiscence, AHS; Susie Crocket interview, 21/225–26, Indianioneer Collection, OHS; Lubick, "Cornelius Hedges," 31.

53. Emmet J. Riley, *Development of the Montana State Educational Organization, 1864–1930* (Washington, D. C.: Catholic University of America, 1931), 34; Report of Superintendant of Schools, Lewis and Clark County, SC623, MHS; Dale, *The Cross Timbers*, 140; Edna Hedges Diary, April 22, 1879, box 11, folder 27, Hedges Family Papers, Collection #33, MHS; Mary L. Boatman Reminiscence, SC444, MHS; Abigail Emigh Reminiscence, G. Donald Emigh Collection, IHS; Erasmas L. Anthony Reminiscence, SC364, MHS; Louisa Walters to Emma, July 29, 1864, Louisa Walters Letters, IHS; Ronan, *Frontier Woman*, 38; Martin, "Father Came West," 56–57.

54. Riley, *Montana Educational Organization*, 35; Rules and regulations, Madison County School District Records, MHS; Georgiana Kirby Diary, December 14, 1852, CHS.

55. Martha E. G. Collins Reminiscence, Fred Lockley Collection, HEH.

56. Wenger, *Recollections of Telluride, Colorado*, 10–12; Erasmus L. Anthony Reminiscence, SC364; Alice Carnow, "My Journey With Tom," 133, AHS; Ben Wallicek interview, Oral History Collection, SWC/TT.

57. Violet Alexander, "School Days in Kelly's Granary," SC358, MHS; M. H. Sherman to Mr. Burmister, May 23, 1877, M. H. Sherman biographical file, AHS.

58. Dale, *Cross Timbers*, 138; School essays in Mitchell Family Papers, HEH; Sallie Davenport Davidson Reminiscence, SC606, MHS.

59. Sarah Herndon Diary, March 5, 1866, MHS; Samuel Newcomb Diary, March 13, 1865, SWC/TT; Lula Veale reminiscence, 6, R. B. Wood and Sam Crawford interviews, Oral History Collection, SWC/TT.; J. W. LaSueur Autobiography, AHS; Mrs. Victor Culberson interview, 9–10, Pioneer Foundation Collection, UNMex.

60. G. W. W. Yates to G. W. Martin, October 6, 1904, G. W. W. Yates Letters, KSHS; Prude, "Early Ranch Schools," 64–65; Eugene Floyd Irey, "A Social History of Leadville, Colorado, During the Boom Days, 1877–1881," (Ph.D. diss., University of Minnesota, 1951), 320.

61. Clara Conron Diary, October 4, 29, 31, November 4, 11, December 23, 1884, January 21, February 15, March 15, 1885, KSHS; Sarah Herndon Diary, April 3, May 25, 28, 29, July 13, 25, August 10, 17, 1866, MHS.

62. William Warren Ferrier, *Ninety Years of Education in California, 1846–1936* (Berkeley: Sather Gate Book Shop, 1937), 10–12. Summaries of common school legislation are found in *Commissioner of Education*, 1870 and 1880. See also Riley, *Montana Educational Organization*, 36–37; Mahan, "Education in Colorado," 1155–58.

63. Hargreaves, "Rural Education," 25; Mahan, "Education in Colorado," 1168; *Commissioner of Education*, 1880, 308–09.

64. Riley, *Montana Educational Organization*, 55.

65. D. C. Martin, "Memories of Strawberry School," AHS; Riley, *Montana Educational Organization*, 48.

66. Teacher's examination, Cochise County, William and Rose Hattich Papers, AHS.

67. *Commissioner of Education*, 1880, 24, 70, 77–78, 151, 202, 271, 285, 293; *Statistical Abstract of the United States. 1900* (Washington, D. C.: Government Printing Office, 1901), 410; Kathleen Underwood, "The Pace of Their Own Lives: Teacher Training and the Life Course of Western Women," *Pacific Historical Review* 55:4 (November, 1986): 518.

68. John Fahey, *The Inland Empire: Unfolding Years, 1879–1929* (Seattle and London: University of Washington Press, 1986), 73; *Commissioner of Education*, 1880, 150; Hargreaves, "Rural Education," 26–27.

69. Alice Polk Hill, *Tales of the Colorado Pioneers* (Denver: Pierson and Gardner, 1884), 64.

70. Martha Ann Morrison Minto, "Female Pioneering in Oregon," 15, Ban; Dalton, *Autobiography*, 4; Price, *Seven Years of Prairie Life*, 36–37.

Chapter Nine

1. Clark, *A Trip to Pike's Peak*, 19.

2. In the more transient culture of the frontier, deaths arguably were more likely to go unreported, thus making that region appear less dangerous than it actually was. Even so, the rate of death among the very young, at least, seems exceptionally low in the West. According to the census of 1880, for instance, the rate of infant mortality in the Pacific northwest, the Rocky Mountains and the western plains was the nation's lowest. See *Report on the Mortality and Vital Statistics of the United States as Returned at the Tenth Census. Part 1.* (Washington, D.C.: Government Printing Office, 1885), xxvii-xxx. The census calculated infant mortality only for children under one year, however, so western mortality rates for older children cannot be compared with other parts of the nation. More sophisticated modern studies concentrate almost entirely on the twentieth century. See Sam Shapiro, et al., *Infant, Perinatal, Maternal and Childhood Mortality in the United States* (Cambridge: Harvard University Press, 1968); Robert Morse Woodbury, *Infant Mortality and Its Causes* (Baltimore: Williams and Wilkins Co., 1926); Ernst Christopher Meyer, *Infant Mortality in New York City* (New York: Rockefeller Foundation, 1921).

3. Joseph Francl, *The Overland Journal of Joseph Francl* (San Francisco: William P. Wreden, 1968), 44.

4. George R. Stewart, *Ordeal By Hunger: The Story of the Donner Party* (Boston: Houghton Mifflin Co., 1936); Virginia Reed to Mary C. Keyes, May 16, 1847, in Morgan, ed., *Overland in 1846*, I, 279–87.

5. Wallace Stegner, *The Gathering of Zion: The Story of the Mormon Trail* (New York: McGraw-Hill Book Co., 1964) 248, 254.

6. George R. Stewart, *The Opening of the California Trail: The Story of the Stevens Party from the Reminiscences of Moses Schallengerger* (Berkeley: University of California Press, 1953), 77; C. Hawkins, *The Argonauts of California* (New York: Ford, Howard and Halbert, 1890), 107–08; Ross, "A Child's Experiences in '49," 304; Joseph Lyman to mother, November 11, 1853, Joseph and Esther Lyman Letters, HEH; Angelina Smith Crews Reminiscences, 11–21, Fred Lockley Collection, box 14(7), HEH.

7. Joseph R. Conlin, *Bacon, Beans, and Gallantines: Food and Foodways on the Western Mining Frontier* (Reno: University of Nevada Press, 1986), 39–67; John D. Unruh, Jr., *The Plains Across: The Overland Emigrants and the Trans-Mississippi West, 1840–60* (Champaign: University of Illinois Press, 1979), 219–51; Jean Webster, "The Myth of Pioneer Hardship on the Oregon Trail," *Reed College Bulletin* 24:3 (April, 1946): 27–46.

8. Mary L. Boatman Reminiscence, SC444, MHS; Mary L. Kelley Reminiscence, SC920, MHS; Jerry Bryan, *An Illinois Gold Hunter in the Black Hills: The Diary of Jerry Bryan* (Springfield, Illinois: Illinois State Historical Society, 1960), 15; Nancy Bogart Reminiscence, 3, HEH; Elizabeth Dixon Smith Geer, "Diary, 1847," *Oregon Pioneer Association Transactions* (1907), 172.

9. T. J. Ables to mother and father, October 12, 1857, Ayer Collection, New-

berry; William Warner to mother, September 23, 1853, California Gold Rush Letters, Ban.

10. For some of the many such incidents, see Mary Ringo, *The Journal of Mary Ringo* (Santa Ana, Cal.: Privately Printed, 1956), 4; William S. Haskell Diary, June 21, 1864, SC806, Samuel Word Diary, June 13, 1863, SC284, MHS; Eleanor Knowlton Reminiscence, 58–9, CHS; Bennett Seymour Reminiscence, 5, Bennett Seymour Collection, CSHS; J. Henry Brown Autobiography, 8, and William Hampton Diary, June 27, 1852, Ban; John L. Johnson Journal, April 12, 1851, Be; Catherine Washburn Journal, May 21, 1853, Catherine Pringle Reminiscence, 4, and Basil Longworth Memorandum, June 11, 1853, HEH.

11. Joseph Fish Autobiography, 23, AHS; Louise Barry, ed., "Overland to the Goldfields of California in 1852," *Kansas Historical Journal* 11 (1942): 255–56.

12. Ellen Fletcher to ———, June 9, 1866, Ellen Fletcher Letters, SC78, MHS; Mary C. Ackley, *Crossing the Plains, and Early Days in California's Golden Age* (San Francisco: Privately Printed, 1928), 24; James Bennett, *Overland Journey to California* (New Harmony, Ind.: Times Printing, 1906), 36; Edwin Bryant, *What I Saw in California* (London: Richard Bentley, 1849), 70–71.

13. Edward E. Ayer Reminiscence, 4, Joseph E. Wood Diary, June 23, 1849, Addison Crane Diary, May 22, 1852, E. A. Tompkins Reminiscence, 82, HEH; Eleanor Knowlton Reminiscence, 57, CHS; Julia C. Stone Diary, June 30, 1865, Frank L. Stone Collection, MSU; Ada Millington Jones Journal, August 23, 1862, Ban; Ackley, *Crossing*, 26; Mrs. Lula W. Brooks Reminiscence, SC472, MHS.

14. Joseph Batty, *Over the Wilds to California; or Eight Years from Home* (Leeds: J. Parrott, 1867), 25; Joe H. Sharp, "Crossing the Plains in 1852," *Oregon Pioneer Association Transactions* (1895), 92; Catherine Pringle Reminiscence, 4, A. H. Cutting Journal, June 24, 1863, Charlotte Pengra Diary, May 19, 20, 1853, Vincent Hoover Diary, August 10, 1849, Catherine Pringle Reminiscence, 3, 6, Medorem Crawford Journal, July 17, 1842, HEH; Eleanor Knowlton Reminiscence, 77, CHS; George McCowen Journal, May 1, 1857, Newberry.

15. Charlotte Pengra Diary, August 14, 1853, HEH.

16. A. H. Cutting Diary, June 7, 1863, HEH.

17. C. Adelia French Reminiscence, SC782, MHS; Brooks, *A Pioneer Mother of California*, 13. See also Angeline Ashley diary, June 2, 5, 1852, W. T. Parker Diary, May 1, 1850, Addison Crane Diary, May 28, 1852, William S. Haskell Diary, April 28–May 2, 1864, MHS.

18. Sallie Davenport Davidson Reminiscence, SC606, MHS. For a similar account of a typhus attack on a Missouri River boat, see Elizabeth Fisk to mother, July 4, 1875, Fisk Family Papers, Collection #31, box 6, folder 10, MHS.

19. Vincent Hoover Diary, June 20, 1849, HEH.

20. C. Westover to wife, November 10, 1852, Be; James Wilkins Diary, August 9, 1849, David Maynard Diary, June 6–8, 1850, Soloman Zumwalt Letter, Soloman Zumwalt Autobiography, HEH; Unruh, *Plains Across*, 88.

21. John Clark Journal, May 14, 1852, Be; Mrs. Elizabeth Lord, *Reminiscences of Eastern Oregon* (Portland: Irwin-Hudson, Co., 1903), 51–53; East S. Owen Journal, May 30, June 2, 1852, Be.

22. Soloman Zumwalt Autobiography, 17, HEH.

23. Vincent Hoover Diary, June 14–18, 1849, HEH.

24. Georgia Willis Read, "Diseases, Drugs, and Doctors on the California-Oregon Trail in the Gold Rush Years," *Missouri Historical Review* (April, 1944): 267.

25. Hixon, *On to Oregon!*, 36–38.

26. Rebecca Woodson Reminiscence, Ban; Hixon, *On to Oregon*, 37; Charlotte Pengra Diary, August 18, 24–28, 1853, Esther Lyman Letter, HEH; Eleanor Knowlton reminiscence, 78, CHS; W. A. Hockett Reminiscence, 10–14, KSHS.

27. Miner, *West of Wichita*, 151; Paul Corey, "Bachelor Bess; My Sister," South Dakota Historical Society, *Collections* 37 (1975), 16; Mrs. Miriam Davis Colt, *Went To Kansas; Being a Thrilling Account of an Ill-fated Expedition to That Fairy Land and Its Sad Results* (Watertown: L. Ingalls and Co., 1862), 104.

28. Maud Pittman interview, 40/120, and James A. Bannister interview, 13/280, Indian-Pioneer Collection, OHS; David Hilger Reminiscence, SC854, MHS; Charles S. Reed, "Life in a Nebraska Soddy," *Nebraska History* 39:1 (March, 1958): 65.

29. Luella Newman interview, 37/575, and Mary E. Engle interview, Indian-Pioneer Collection, OHS; Cleaveland, *No Life For A Lady*, 50.

30. See, for instance, Ralla Banta Pinkerton, "Pioneer Days in the Beaver Creek Community," R. J. Bradley Collection SWC/TT, and for a mention of a girl hiding from her parents, Anne Davies Diary, August 5, 1887, KSHS.

31. Abbie Hall interview, 63/272, and Fannie Borden interview, 15/494–97, Indian-Pioneer Collection, OHS; Carolyn H. Palmer, "Reminiscences of Early Days in Boise," MS2/224, IHS; Waldorf, *A Kid on the Comstock*, 51–53; Glenn Berry interview, Oral History Collection, SWC/TT; Virginia City *Territorial Enterprise*, June 12, 1866.

32. Sarah Hively Journal, May 31, 1863, DPL; John V. Smith, *Incidents and Events in the Life of John V. Smith* (Salem: Ross E. Moores and Co., 1893), 20.

33. Manuscript mortality schedules, Ada County, Idaho, 1870, National Archives; Mary Jennings Reminiscence, AHS.

34. Mrs. Willard to son, July 24, 1865, Be.

35. Miriam L. Clayton Reminiscence, 24–25, KSHS; Elizabeth Fisk to mother, April 20, 1873, Fisk Family Papers, Collection #31, box 6, folder 6, MHS.

36. Mary Jennings Reminiscence, AHS; Lula M. Veale reminiscence, 12, SWC/TT.

37. Alexander Family interview, Panhandle-Plains Historical Museum, Canyon, Texas; Carrie Williams Journal, April 11, 1862, Be; George A. Root Reminiscence, 1892, CSHS.

38. Gunn, *Records of a California Family*, 226–27.

39. Bennett, *Boom Town Boy*, 13; Mary Jennings Reminiscence, AHS; Cripple Creek *Daily Press*, July 4, 1899, June 22, 24, December 9, 1900.

40. Louise Amelia Knapp Clappe, *The Shirley Letters From California Mines in 1851–52* (San Francisco: T. C. Russell, 1922), 75; Waldorf, *Kid on the Comstock*, 50.

41. Mary Curtis, "The Night of Your Birth," in Elizabeth MacPhail Collection, AHS.

42. Mrs. Frances H. Sawyer Journal, August 6, 1852, Ayer Collection, Newberry. In another party, on the other hand, three babies were born along the way, and "in every instance, after the birth, we traveled right along the next day, mothers and babes with the rest of us." See Nancy A. Hunt, *By Ox-team to California* (San Francisco: 1916), 13.

43. John L. Johnson Journal, May 10, 1851, Be; Mary Burrell Diary, July 16, 1854, Be; Roxanna Foster Reminiscence, 45, Be.

44. Virginia Wilcox Ivins, *Pen Pictures of Early Western Days* (N.p., 1905), 65.

45. Frank T. Alkire, "Little Lady of Triangle T Ranch," 19–20, AHS; Olive Bascom Reminiscence, 7, KSHS; Sarah Martin Reminiscence, 12–13, AHS; Frank D. Hughes Reminiscence, SC1482, MHS; Reiley, " 'I Think I Will Like Kansas'," 92; Ellen Fletcher to Blanche, January 11, 1870, Ellen Fletcher Letters, SC78, MHS. For other instances of husbands and families arranging for help and for midwives, see Thomas Wildman to mother, September 27, 1861, Augustus and Thomas Wildman Letters, Be; Carrie Williams Journal, March 6, 1861, Be; Chestina Allen Diary, April 27, 1855, KSHS; Wallace A. Wood Reminiscence, 10, KSHS; Anna Wilkinson Reynolds reminiscence, Anna Wilkinson Reynolds Collection, Meda Perry interview, Oral History Collection, SWC/TT; M. A. Bowie Diary, January 10, 1877, Barker; Bertha J. Andersen Autobiography, 20, SC360, MHS.

46. Manuscript mortality schedules, 1880, Sterling, Hodgeman County, Kansas, National Archives.

47. Lewis, *Martha and the Doctor*, 142.

48. Mary Forbes to Eliza Taylor, August 29, 1869, Mitchell Family Papers, HEH; Rollin S. Fillmore, *Life and Experience of a Country Doctor in Kansas* (Long Beach, Cal.: Privately Printed, 1934), 36.

49. Richard Dunlop, *Doctors of the American Frontier* (Garden City N.Y.: Doubleday and Co., Inc., 1962), 122; Georgiana Kirby Diary, February 13, 1853, CHS; Harriet Fish Backus, *Tomboy Bride* (Boulder: Pruett Press, 1969), 107.

50. Quoted in George Rosen, *The Structure of American Medical Practice* (Philadelphia: University of Pennsylvania Press, 1983), 15.

51. Joseph Fish Autobiography, 65, AHS.

52. Eleanor Knowlton Reminiscence, 114, CHS; Bertha J. Andersen Autobiography, 35–36, SC360, MHS.

53. Pinkerton, "Pioneer Days," 11.

54. Robert Higgs, "Mortality in Rural America, 1870–1920: Estimates and Conjectures," *Explorations in Economic History* 10:2 (Winter, 1973): 177–96.

55. Frances Moore Reminiscence, 18, KSHS; Pinkerton, "Pioneer Days," 10; Oello I. Martin, "Father Came West," 26, KSHS; Stuart, *Forty Years on the Frontier*, 28.

56. Georgiana Packard, "Leaves From the Life of a Kansas Pioneer," 20–21, KSHS; Mrs. Colt, *Went To Kansas*, 99–100.

57. John Cushing to sister, November 6, 1877, Cushing Family Papers, Special Collections, Duke University Library.

58. Mrs. J. E. Riordan Diary, March 21, 1881, Riordan Family Collection, SWC/TT.

59. Mrs. Mary L. Neely interview, Oral History Collection, SWC/TT. On remedies, see Wallace A. Wood Reminiscence, 14, KSHS; May E. Murphy, "Our Pioneer Mother," 3–4, KSHS; Sarah Hively Journal, October 1, December 2, 1864, DPL.

60. William Daingerfield to "J," August 18, 1850, William P. Daingerfield Letters, Ban; J. S. Holliday, *The World Rushed In: An Eyewitness Account of a Nation Heading West* (New York: Simon and Schuster, 1981), 321; Thomas Conger to parents, April 9, 1851, Conger Family Papers.

61. Burnett, " 'We Just Toughed It Out'," 68–69.

62. Fannie K. Borden interview, 15/498–90, Indian-Pioneer Collection, OHS.

63. Thomas Conger to parents, August 4, 16, 1850, Conger Family Papers; Elizabeth Fisk to mother, August 19, 1875, Fisk Family Papers, Collection #31, box 6, folder 10, MHS.

64. Thomas Conger to parents, April 9, 1851, Conger Family Papers.

65. Manuscript mortality schedules, Pima County, Arizona, 1870, National Archives.

66. Helen Hunt Jackson, *Bits of Travel at Home* (Boston: Roberts Brothers, 1887), 269; Backus, *Tomboy Bride*, 95.

67. Cedenia B. Willis Journal, 15, AHS. Though diphtheria and croup are different diseases, their symptoms are so similar that it is impossible to distinguish between them in contemporary descriptions. In this discussion, I have lumped them together with cases of "membranous croup" and "putrid sore throat," two other terms apparently synonymous with the others.

68. Augusta Dodge Thomas, "Prairie Children," 66, KSHS.

69. Lydia and Joshua Hadley to Sarah Stafford, May 1, 1849, Frederick Stafford papers, Special Collections, University of North Carolina Library,

70. Dunlop, *Doctors of the Frontier*, 2; Thomas, "Prairie Children," 66; Caroline Gale Budlong, *Memories of Pioneer Days in Oregon and Washington Territory* (Eugene: Picture Press Printers, 1949), 26–27; Manuscript mortality schedules, Lake County, Colorado, 1880, National Archives.

71. The California counties are El Dorado and Tulare. *Report on Mortality . . . Tenth Census*, 11, 16–17, 157.

72. John W. Florin, *Death in New England: Regional Variations in Mortality* (Chapel Hill: University of North Carolina, 1971).

73. Ibid., xxxviii–xlv. The following is based on Kansas manuscript mortality schedules cited for Tables 6–9.

74. Alice Carnow, "My Journey With Tom," 144–49, AHS. For similar instances, see Dr. Bert Foster, *A Rocky Mountain Parson* (Upland, Cal.: 1940), 20–21; Lee, *Cripple Creek Days*, 22–23; Bertha Andersen Autobiography, 49–50, SC360, MHS.

75. Price, *Seven Years of Prairie Life*, 50. For other examples of this communal ritual in various settings, see Nellie Buchanan interview, Kit Carson County, Colorado Writers Project Collection, CSHS; Chestina Allen Diary, November 22–25, KSHS; Roosa, "Homesteading in the 1880s," 386; William Dolman Reminiscence, 131–32, HEH; Frank D. Hughes Reminiscence, SC1482, MHS.

76. Anne Davies Diary, September 13–18, 1883, KSHS.

77. Thomas Conger to parents, August 16, 1850, Conger Family Papers; Ada Millington Jones Journal, August 16, 1862, Ban; Horace M. Ballew to wife, September 8, 1850, Horace Ballew Letters, Ban.

78. Quotation is from Clappe, *Shirley Letters*, 322. See also S. Lyman Tyler, ed., *The Montana Gold Rush Diary of Kate Dunlap* (Denver: Fred A. Rosenstock, Old West Publishing Co., and University of Utah Press, 1969), B–16; C. Adelia French reminiscence, SC782, MHS; Samuel Word Diary, June 15, 16, 1863, SC284, MHS.

79. Endicott Peabody Journal, February 24, 1882, Endicott Peabody biographical file, AHS.

80. Sanford, *Mollie: The Journal of Mollie Dorsey Sanford*, 157.

81. Elizabeth Fisk to mother, August 19, 1875, Fisk Family Papers, Collection #31, box 6, folder 10, MHS.

82. Sarah Martin Reminiscence, 12, KSHS.

83. David H. Stratton, "The Rise and Decline of Caribou," *Colorado Magazine* 30 (April, 1953): 118.

84. Dodge City *Ford County Globe*, January 1, 1878.

85. For changing attitudes toward death and in mourning rituals, see David E. Stannard, *Death in America* (Philadelphia: University of Pennsylvania Press, 1975), especially 49–68; James J. Farrell, *Inventing the American Way of Death, 1830–1920* (Philadelphia: Temple University Press, 1980); Margaret M. Coffin, *Death in Early America* (Nashville and New York: Thomas Nelson, Inc., 1976); Lewis O. Saum, "Death in the Popular Mind of Pre-Civil War America," and Robert W. Habenstein and William M. Lamers, "The Pattern of Late Nineteenth-Century Funerals," in Charles O. Jackson, ed., *Passing: The Vision of Death in America* (Westport, Conn.: Greenwood Press, 1977), 65–90, 91–102; Karen Halttunen, *Confidence Men and Painted Women: A Study of Middle-Class Culture in America, 1830–1870* (New Haven: Yale University Press, 1982), 124–52.

86. Edna Hedges Diary, February 4, March 28, 1878, box 11, folder 27, Hedges Family Papers, Collection #33, MHS; Bivens, ed., "The Diary of Luna E. Warner," 307–08.

87. Frances Moore Reminiscence, 10, 21, 23, KSHS.

88. Wallace *Frontier Life in Oklahoma*, 79–80, 145; Susie Crocket interview, Pioneer-Indian Collection, OHS.

89. Dodge, "Prairie Children," 94–105.

90. Ellis, *Life of Ordinary Woman*, 263–66, 281–83.

Chapter Ten

1. Susan Armitage, "Through Women's Eyes: A New View of the West," in Susan Armitage and Elizabeth Jameson, eds., *The Women's West* (Norman: University of Oklahoma, 1987), 9.

2. Margaret Marshall reminiscence, 1, KSHS.

3. Frederick Jackson Turner, *The Frontier in American History* (New York: Holt, Rinehart and Winston, 1962), 2.

4. Earl Pomeroy, "Toward a Reorientation of Western History: Continuity and Environment," *Mississippi Valley Historical Reivew* 41:4 (March, 1955): 579–600.

5. Ray Allen Billington, *America's Frontier Heritage* (New York: Holt, Rinehart and Winston, 1966), *passim* and especially pp. 219–35.

6. Julia C. Stone diary, July 30, 1865, Frank L. Stone Collection, Montana State University Library.

7. David Nasaw, *Children of the City at Work and at Play* (Garden City: Anchor Press/Doubleday, 1985).

8. Kett, *Rites of Passage*, 11–108; Rowland Berthoff, *An Unsettled People: Social Order and Disorder in American History* (New York: Harper and Row, 1971), 214–17; David J. Rothman, *The Discovery of the Asylum: Social Order and Disorder in the New Republic* (Boston: Little Brown and Co., 1971), 216–71.

9. Emmy E. Werner and Ruth S. Smith, *Vulnerable, But Invincible: A Longitudinal Study of Resilient Children and Youth* (New York: McGraw-Hill, 1982); Norman Garmezy, "Stressors of Childhood," in Norman Garmezy and Michael Rutter, eds., *Stress, Coping and Development* (New York: McGraw-Hill, 1983); J. Block, "Growing Up Vulnerable and Growing Up Resilient: Preschool Personality, Pre-Adolescent Personality and Intervening Family Stresses," in Charlotte D. Moore, ed., *Adolescence and Stress* (Washington, D.C.: Government Printing Office, 1981); Sarah Moskovitz, *Love Despite Hate; Child Survivors of the Holocaust and Their Adult Lives* (New York: Schocken Books, 1983); Louise Murphy and Alice Moriarty, *Vulnerability, Coping, and Growth From Infancy to Adolescence* (New Haven: Yale University Press, 1976); Emmy E. Werner, "Resilient Children," *Young Children* (November, 1984): 68–72.

10. Paula Petrik, *No Step Backward: Women and Family on the Rocky Mountain Mining Frontier, Helena, Montana, 1865–1900* (Helena: Montana Historical Society Press, 1987), 96.

11. Sandoz, *Old Jules;* Jean Stafford, *The Mountain Lion* (New York: Harcourt, Brace and Co., 1947); Willa Cather, *My Ántonia* (Boston: Houghton Mifflin Co., 1918), 90, 138.

12. Cleaveland, *No Life For a Lady;* Oello Ingraham Martin, "Father Came West," KSHS.

13. Garland, *A Pioneer Mother,* 18.

14. Garland, *Boy Life on the Prairie,* 90; Dale, *The Cross Timbers,* 160–61.

15. Pearl Daniel autobiography, SC58, MHS.

16. Avery Craven, "The 'Turner Theories' and the South," *Journal of Southern History* 5:3 (August, 1939): 296.

17. Wallace Stegner, *Wolf Willow: A History, a Story, and a Memory of the Last Plains Frontier* (Lincoln: University of Nebraska Press, 1980), 23.

18. Jackson K. Putnam, "The Turner Thesis and the Westward Movement: A Reappraisal," *Western Historical Quarterly* 7:4 (October, 1976): 402–04.

19. Patricia Nelson Limerick, *The Legacy of Conquest: The Unbroken Past of the American West* (New York: W. W. Norton, 1987).

Bibliography

Oral History Collections

Colorado Writers Project. State Historical Society of Colorado, Denver, Colorado.
Indian-Pioneer Collection. Oklahoma Historical Society, Oklahoma City, Oklahoma.
Oral History Collection. Southwest Collection, Texas Tech University, Lubbock, Texas.
Oral History Collection. State Historical Society of Colorado, Denver, Colorado.
Oral History Collection. University of Nevada Library, Reno, Nevada.
Pioneer Foundations Collection. University of New Mexico Library, Albuquerque, New Mexico.

Government Documents

Manuscript Mortality Schedules. 1860 (California and Colorado), 1870 (Colorado, Idaho, Kansas, Montana, Texas), 1880 (Arizona, Idaho, Kansas, Montana, Texas). National Archives.
Tenth Census of the United States: Population, 1880. Washington, D.C.: Government Printing Office, 1883.
Report of the Commissioner of Education. In *Report of the Secretary of the Interior.* 41st Congress, 3rd Session, 1870. House Ex. Doc. 1, Part 4.
Report of the Commissioner of Education. In *Report of the Secretary of the Interior,* 45th Congress, 3rd Session, 1880. House Ex. Doc. 1, Part 5.
Report on Population of the United States at the Eleventh Census: 1890, Part 1. Washington, D.C.: Government Printing Office, 1895.
Report on the Mortality and Vital Statistics of the United States as Returned at the Tenth Census. Part 1. Washington, D.C.: Government Printing Office, 1885.
Twelfth Census of the United States. . . . 1900. Population, Part 1. Washington, D.C.: Government Printing Office, 1901.

Unpublished Primary Sources

Ables, T.J. Letter. 1857. Ayer Collection. Newberry Library, Chicago, Illinois.

Adams, David Maddux. Reminiscence. Arizona Historical Society, Tucson, Arizona.

Albright, Mabel W. Reminiscence. Montana Historical Society, Helena, Montana.

Aldrich, J. Frank. Diary. 1876. Henry E. Huntington Library, San Marino, California.

Alexander Family Papers. Interviews and Reminiscence of R. T. Alexander. Panhandle-Plains Historical Museum, Canyon, Texas.

Alexander, Violet. "School Days in Kelly's Granary." Reminiscence. Montana Historical Society, Helena, Montana.

Alkire, Frank T. Reminiscence. Arizona Historical Society, Tucson, Arizona.

Allen, Chestina Bowker. Diary. 1854. Kansas State Historical Society. Topeka, Kansas.

Allen, Sallie Fox. Reminiscence. Arizona Historical Society, Tucson, Arizona.

Amateur Newspaper Collection. American Antiquarian Society, Worcester, Massachusetts.

Ames, P.G. Letter. 1852. Henry E. Huntington Library, San Marino, California.

Anable, H.S. Diary. 1852. Henry E. Huntington Library, San Marino, California.

Anthony, E.M. "Early Days in Siskiyou." Reminiscence. Bancroft Library, University of California, Berkeley.

Applegate, Pearl. Reminiscence. Montana Historical Society, Helena, Montana.

Aram, Joseph and Sarah Ann. Biographical Sketch. Bancroft Library, University of California, Berkeley.

Ashley, Angeline. Diary. 1852. Henry E. Huntington Library, San Marino, California.

Athearn, Charles G. Letters. 1855. Beinecke Library, Yale University, New Haven, Connecticut.

Austin, Edward. Letters. 1849–51. Bancroft Library, University of California, Berkeley.

Ayer, Edward A. Reminiscence. Henry E. Huntington Library, San Marino, California.

Bailey, Mary Stuart. Diary. 1852. Henry E. Huntington Library, San Marino, California.

Baldwin, Caryl A. "An Account of the Baldwin Family." Reminiscence. Southwest Collection, Texas Tech University, Lubbock, Texas.

Ballew, Horace Madison. Letters. 1850–51. Bancroft Library, University of California, Berkeley.

Barker, Alice Lee. Reminiscence. Arizona Historical Society, Tucson, Arizona.

Barnhart, J. Milton. Reminiscence. Montana Historical Society, Helena, Montana.

Barrier, Effie. Reminiscence. Southwest Collection, Texas Tech University, Lubbock, Texas.

Bascom, Olive J. L. and S. J. Bascom. Reminiscence. Kansas State Historical Society, Topeka, Kansas.

Bayne, Martha. Reminiscence. Kansas State Historical Society, Topeka, Kansas.

Belshaw, George. Diary. 1853. Henry E. Huntington Library, San Marino, California.

Berry, Glenn. Reminiscence and Interview. Southwest Collection, Texas Tech University, Lubbock, Texas.

Biertu, R. Journal. Arizona Historical Society, Tucson, Arizona.

Bishop, Leander Hackney. Diary. 1850. Bancroft Library, University of California, Berkeley.

Black, Sarah M. Reminiscence. Arizona Historical Society, Tucson, Arizona.

Blanchard, John. Letters. 1864. Montana Historical Society, Helena, Montana.

Blood, James A. Diary. 1850. Newberry Library, Chicago, Illinois.

Bloom, Henry S. Diary. 1850–52. Bancroft Library, University of California, Berkeley.

Bloyed, Eli and Mary. Letters. 1852. Special Collections, University of Arkansas Library, Fayetteville, Arkansas.

Blunt, Phineas W. Diary. 1849–52. Bancroft Library, University of California, Berkeley.

Boatman, Mary L. Reminiscence. Montana Historical Society, Helena, Montana.

Bogart, Nancy M. H. "Reminiscences of a Journey Across the Plains in 1843." Fred Lockley Collection. Henry E. Huntington Library, San Marino, California.

Bowie, Margaret Armstrong. Diary. 1872–77. Eugene C. Barker Library, University of Texas at Austin.

Brooke, T. Warwick. Letters. 1848–74. Bancroft Library, University of California, Berkeley. Transcript at Newberry Library, Chicago, Illinois.

Brooks, Alden F. Diary. 1859. Henry E. Huntington Library, San Marino, California.

Brooks, Lula W. Reminiscence. Montana Historical Society, Helena, Montana.

Brophy-Beeson Families. Papers and Letters. Henry E. Huntington Library, San Marino, California.

Brosnan, Cornelius. Collection. Special Collections, University of Idaho Library, Moscow, Idaho.

Brown, J. Henry. Autobiography. Bancroft Library, University of California, Berkeley.

Brown, J. K. Letters. 1881. E. W. Davis Collection. Arizona Historical Society, Tucson, Arizona.

Burrell, Mary. Diary. 1854. Beinecke Library, Yale University.

Bushnell, James Addison. Autobiography. Henry E. Huntington Library, San Marino, California.

Busick, Mary Ann. Collections. Special Collections, Montana State University Library, Bozeman, Montana.

Byrne, Martha. Reminiscence. Kansas State Historical Society, Topeka, Kansas.

California Gold Rush Letters. Bancroft Library, University of California, Berkeley.

Carnow, Alice. "My Journey With Tom." Reminiscence. Arizona Historical Society, Tucson, Arizona.

Carpenter, William. "A California Pioneer of the Fifties." Reminiscence. Newberry Library, Chicago, Illinois.

Carruth, James H. and Jane G. Carruth. "Life Pictures in Kansas." Reminiscence. Kansas State Historical Society, Topeka, Kansas.

Castleman, Philip F. Journal. 1849. Beinecke Library, Yale University, New Haven, Connecticut.

Chapman, William Wesley. Diary. 1849. Henry E. Huntington Library, San Marino, California.

Chick, Washington Henry. Reminiscence. Kansas State Historical Society, Topeka, Kansas.

Chillson, Lorenzo D. Diary. 1859. Henry E. Huntington Library, San Marino, California.

Choteau County School District, School Census. 1884. Montana Historical Society, Helena, Montana.

Clark, John. Journal. 1852. Beinecke Library, Yale University, New Haven, Connecticut.

Clark, John H. Diary. 1852. Bancroft Library, University of California, Berkeley.

Clayton, Miriam Lawton. Reminiscence. Kansas State Historical Society, Topeka, Kansas.

Clifton, Edna Matthews. Reminiscence and Notebooks. Southwest Collection, Texas Tech University, Lubbock, Texas.

Clyman, James. Journals. 1844, 1845, 1846. Henry E. Huntington Library, San Marino, California.

Collins, Martha E.G. Reminiscence. Fred Lockley Collection. Henry E. Huntington Library, San Marino, California.

Condit, Philip. Diary. 1854. Henry E. Huntington Library, San Marino, California.

Conger Family. Letters. 1849–51. Copies in author's possession.

Connelly, Cyrus B. Letters. California Historical Society, San Francisco, California.

Conner, B. Pearl. Reminiscence. Montana Historical Society, Helena, Montana.

Conrad, Thomas. Letters. 1864–65. Montana Historical Society, Helena, Montana.

Conron, Clara L. Diary. 1884–85. Kansas State Historical Society, Topeka, Kansas.

Conwell, Effie Wood. Reminiscence. Kansas State Historical Society, Topeka, Kansas.

Cooke, Lucy Rutledge. Letters. California Historical Society, San Francisco, California.

Cowden, James S. Diary. 1853. California Historical Society, San Francisco, California.

Crane, Addison Moses. Diary. 1852. Henry E. Huntington Library, San Marino, California.

Crawford, Medorem. Journal. 1842. Henry E. Huntington Library, San Marino, California.

Crawford, Thomas H. Reminiscence. Fred Lockley Collection. Henry E. Huntington Library, San Marino, California.

Crews, Angelina Smith. Reminiscence. Fred Lockley Collection. Henry E. Huntington Library, San Marino, California.

Curtis, Benjamin W. Letters. Elizabeth MacPhail Collection. Arizona Historical Society, Tucson, Arizona.

Curtis, Mary. "The Night of Your Birth." Reminiscence. Elizabeth MacPhail Collection. Arizona Historical Society, Tucson, Arizona.

Curtis, Susan. Reminiscence. Arizona Historical Society, Tucson, Arizona.

Cutting, A. Howard. Journal. 1863. Henry E. Huntington Library, San Marino, California.

Daingerfield, William P. Letters. 1850–53. Bancroft Library, University of California, Berkeley.

Daniel, Pearl. Autobiography. Montana Historical Society, Helena, Montana.

Davidson, Sallie Davenport. Reminiscence. Montana Historical Society, Helena, Montana.

Davies, Anne Jones. Diary. 1882–88. Kansas State Historical Society, Topeka, Kansas.

Davis, Charles. Letters. 1850–56. Beinecke Library, Yale University, New Haven, Connecticut.

Davison, Emma Jane. Reminiscence. Idaho Historical Society, Boise, Idaho.

Day, Emeline. Journal. [1850s]. Bancroft Library, University of California, Berkeley.

DeBaud Charles. "Seventy-one Years of Experience of My Life." Reminiscence. Arizona Historical Society, Tucson, Arizona.

Delano, Ephraim. Letters. 1850–53. Beinecke Library, Yale University, New Haven, Connecticut.

Denison, Rilla Jarvis. Reminiscence. Kansas State Historical Society, Topeka, Kansas.

DeWolf, David. Diary and Letters. 1849–50. Henry E. Huntington Library, San Marino, California.

Dobbs, T. W. Reminiscence. Elijah W. Dobbs Collection. Arizona Historical Society, Tucson, Arizona.

Doble, John. Diary and Letters. 1851–65. Bancroft Library, University of California, Berkeley.

Dolman, William H. Reminiscence. Henry E. Huntington Library, San Marino, California.

Dorsey, Edith J. Letters. Arizona Historical Society, Tucson, Arizona.

Dougherty, Mary Hilger. Reminiscence. Montana Historical Society. Helena, Montana.

Dowell, Benjamin Franklin. Journal. 1851. Fred Lockley Collection. Henry E. Huntington Library, San Marino, California.

Drachman Family. Reminiscences. Arizona Historical Society, Tucson, Arizona.

Draper, Charles H. Reminiscence. Montana Historical Society, Helena, Montana.

Dresser Family. Letters. 1852–53. Bancroft Library, University of California, Berkeley.

Drew, Sadye W. Reminiscence. Montana Historical Society, Helena, Montana.

Duncan, Sarah Day. "Recollections of a Pioneer Mother." Reminiscence. Arthur B. Duncan Papers. Southwest Collection, Texas Tech University, Lubbock, Texas.

Dutton, Chester. Letter. 1878. Yale Class Records, 1938. Manuscripts and Archives Division, Sterling Library, Yale University, New Haven, Connecticut.

Ebbutt, Percy G. Letter. 1941. Kansas State Historical Society, Topeka, Kansas.

Egbert, Eliza Ann McAuley. Diary. 1852. California Historical Society, San Francisco, California.

Ellis, Moses. Letters. 1850–65. Beinecke Library, Yale University, New Haven, Connecticut.

Ellmaker, Enos. Autobiography. Henry E. Huntington Library, San Marino, California.

Emigh, G. Donald. Letters and Reminiscence. Idaho Historical Society, Boise, Idaho.

Everett, Melissa. Reminiscence. Carl Coke Rister Papers. Southwest Collection, Texas Tech University, Lubbock, Texas.

Farrell, George. Reminiscence. Montana Historical Society, Helena, Montana.

Faulkner, Harry. Collection. Western History Collection, Denver Public Library, Denver, Colorado.

Ferris, Mrs. Eddy F. Letters. 1874–78. Special Collections, Montana State University Library.

Finley, William. Journal. 1845. Beinecke Library, Yale University, New Haven, Connecticut.

Fish, Joseph. Autobiography. Arizona Historical Society, Tucson, Arizona.

Fish, Juliette G. and Emeline L. Walker. "Crossing the Plains in 1862." Reminiscence. Henry E. Huntington Library, San Marino, California.

Fisk Family. Letters. Montana Historical Society, Helena, Montana.

Flanagan, May G. Reminiscence. Montana Historical Society, Helena, Montana.

Fletcher, Ellen. Letters. 1867. Montana Historical Society, Helena, Montana.

Forman, Frank. Reminiscence. Kansas State Historical Society, Topeka, Kansas.

Fosdick, Lucy H. "Across the Plains in '61." Reminiscence. Beinecke Library, Yale University, New Haven, Connecticut.

Foster, Isaac. Journal. 1849. Henry E. Huntington Library, San Marino, California.

Foster, Roxanna C. "The Foster Family. California Pioneers of 1849." Diary and Reminiscence. Beiencke Library, Yale University, New Haven, Connecticut.

Fowler, Stella T. Reminiscence. Montana Historical Society, Helena, Montana.

Francis, Samuel D. Diary. 1852–62. Beinecke Library, Yale University, New Haven, Connecticut.

Franklin, George Washington. Diary. 1885–1935. Kansas State Historical Society, Topeka, Kansas.

Fraser, Duncan. Letters. 1864. Montana Historical Society, Helena, Montana.

French, Barsina Rogers. Journal. 1867. Henry E. Huntington Library, San Marino, California.

French, C. Adelia. Reminiscence. Montana Historical Society, Helena, Montana.

Frost, Clara. Reminiscence. Kansas State Historical Society, Topeka, Kansas.

Gabbey, Robert S. Reminiscence. Montana Historical Society, Helena, Montana.

Galloway, James H. and Emily Galloway. Diaries. 1862–65. Bancroft Library, University of California, Berkeley.

Gay, Bill. Reminiscence. Montana Historical Society, Helena, Montana.

George, Mrs. J. Raymond. Reminiscence. Southwest Collection, Texas Tech University, Lubbock, Texas.

Girdley, George. Letters. 1851. Bancroft Library, University of California, Berkeley.

Gorgas, Solomon. Letters and Diary. 1850–51. Henry E. Huntington Library, San Marino, California.

Goss, Milo. Letters. Bancroft Library, University of California, Berkeley.

Gove Family. Letters. 1849–59. Beinecke Library. Yale University, New Haven, Connecticut.

Graham, Calvin H. Diary. 1853. Kansas State Historical Society, Topeka, Kansas.

Griswold, Harriet Booth. Diary. 1859. California Historical Society, San Francisco, California.

Hall, George H. Letters. 1849–50. Beinecke Library, Yale University, New Haven, Connecticut.

Hampton, William. Diary. 1852. Bancroft Library, University of California, Berkeley.

Handsaker, Samuel. Diary. 1853. Henry E. Huntington Library, San Marino, California.

Hanna, Esther Belle. Journal. 1852. Henry E. Huntington Library, San Marino, California.

Hardin, Eliza. Reminiscence. Montana Historical Society, Helena, Montana.

Hartt, Rollin L. Letters. 1896. Montana Historical Society, Helena, Montana.

Haskell, Ursula B. Letter. 1848. Beinecke Library, Yale University, New Haven, Connecticut.

Haskell, William H. Diary. 1864. Montana Historical Society, Helena, Montana.

Hatfield, Edna P. G. Collection. Western History Collection, University of Oklahoma Library, Norman, Oklahoma.

Hathaway, Mrs. W.H. Reminiscence. Arizona Historical Society, Tucson, Arizona.

Hattich, William and Rose Hattich. Personal Papers and Teacher Examination. Arizona Historical Society, Tucson, Arizona.

Hauser, S. T. Letters. 1862. Ayer Collection. Newberry Library, Chicago, Illinois.

Hedges Family. Letters. Montana Historical Society, Helena, Montana.

Hembree, Mary. "Pioneer Days in Kansas." Reminiscence. Kansas State Historical Society, Topeka, Kansas.

Herndon, Sarah. Diary. 1866. Montana Historical Society, Helena, Montana.

Herrera, Rachael Mix. Reminiscence. Arizona Historical Society, Tucson, Arizona.

Herriet, H. Letter. 1851. Beinecke Library, Yale University, New Haven, Connecticut.

Hilger, David. Letters and Reminiscences. Montana Historical Society, Helena, Montana.

Hill, John B. "Gold: A Story of the Plains in 1850." Reminiscence. Ayer Collection. Newberry Library, Chicago, Illinois.

Hillman, John Wesley. Reminiscence. Henry E. Huntington Library, San Marino, California.

Hinman, C. S. Letters. 1861. Western History Collection, Denver Public Library, Denver, Colorado.

Hively, Sarah. Journal. 1863. Western History Collection, Denver Public Library, Denver, Colorado.

Hixon, Jasper Morris. Diary. 1849. California Historical Society, San Francisco, California.

Hockderffer, George. Autobiography. Kansas State Historical Society, Topeka, Kansas.

Hockett, W. A. "Experiences of W. A. Hockett on the Oregon Trail." Reminiscence. Kansas State Historical Society, Topeka, Kansas.

Hoffman, Henry B. and E. E. Letter. 1872. Montana Historical Society, Helena, Montana.

Holden, Maggie Lee Bullion. Reminiscence. Southwest Collection, Texas Tech University, Lubbock, Texas.

Holden, William C. Interview and Reminiscence. Southwest Collection, Texas Tech University, Lubbock, Texas.

Holliday-Pendleton Family. Letters. 1852. Special Collections, University of North Carolina Library, Chapel Hill, North Carolina.

Holmes, Olivia. Diary. 1872. Kansas State Historical Society, Topeka, Kansas.

Hoover, Vincent A. Diary. 1849. Henry E. Huntington Library, San Marino, California.

Howells, Sue. Reminiscence. Montana Historical Society, Helena, Montana.

Hughes, Frank D. Reminiscence. Montana Historical Society, Helena, Montana.

Hulin, Lester. Journal. 1847. Henry E. Huntington Library, San Marino, California.

Jennings, Mary E. C. Reminiscence. John W. Kennedy Collection. Arizona Historical Society, Tucson, Arizona.

Johnson, Mrs. Frank B. Autobiography. Southwest Collection, Texas Tech University, Lubbock, Texas.

Johnson, H. W. Reminiscence. Kansas State Historical Society, Topeka, Kansas.

Johnson, John L. Journal. 1851. Beinecke Library, Yale University, New Haven, Connecticut.

Johnson, Joseph H. Diary. 1849. Henry E. Huntington Library, San Marino, California.

Johnson, Mattie Riggs. Reminiscence. Arizona Historical Society, Tucson, Arizona.

[Jones], Ada Millington. Journal. 1862. Bancroft Library, University of California, Berkeley.

Jones, Charles. Reminiscence. Jessie K. Snell Collection. Kansas Historical Society, Topeka, Kansas.

Jones, John. Letters. 1864. Montana Historical Society, Helena, Montana.

Jones, John N. Diary. 1850. Kansas State Historical Society, Topeka, Kansas.

Jorgenson, Jorgen. Autobiography. Montana Historical Society, Helena, Montana.

Kane, Mary Gardner. Reminiscence. Arizona Historical Society, Tucson, Arizona.

Kellogg, Clarence W. "Early Day Life in California Mining Camps." Reminiscence. Bancroft Library, University of California, Berkeley.

Kelly, Mary L. F. Reminiscence. Montana Historical Society, Helena, Montana.

Kendrick, Benjamin Franklin. Letters. 1849–50. Beinecke Library, Yale University, New Haven, Connecticut.

Keys, Tennessee. Letters and Diary. 1856, 1862. Eugene C. Barker Library, University of Texas at Austin.

Kirby, Georgiana Bruce. Diary. 1852–53. California Historical Society, San Francisco, California.

Kirkaldie, F. L. Letters. 1867. Special Collections, Montana State University Library, Bozeman, Montana.

Kirkpatrick, Alma C. Reminiscence. Montana Historical Society, Helena, Montana.

Kirkwood, Mrs. John. Reminiscence. Fred Lockley Collection. Henry E. Huntington Library, San Marino, California.

Kline, Perry. Reminiscence. State Historical Society of Colorado, Denver, Colorado.

Kowlton, Eleanor. Reminiscence. California Historical Society, San Francisco, California.

Kreipie, Louise M. Reminiscence. Kansas State Historical Society, Topeka, Kansas.

Larson, Mons. Reminiscence. Arizona Historical Society, Tucson, Arizona.

LaSelle, Stanislaus. Diary. 1849. Henry E. Huntington Library, San Marino, California.

LaSueur, J. W. Autobiography. Arizona Historical Society, Tucson, Arizona.

Lathrop, George D. and Columbia Lathrop. Diaries. 1856. Kansas State Historical Society, Topeka, Kansas.

Laubach, William H. Reminiscence. Montana Historical Society, Helena, Montana.

Lewis and Clark County, Montana. Reports of Superintendant of Schools. Montana Historical Society, Helena, Montana.

Lewis, Robert A. Reminiscence. Arizona Historical Society, Tucson, Arizona.

Liles, Wright L. Reminiscence. Montana Historical Society, Helena, Montana.

Long, Christian L. Diary. 1859. Kansas State Historical Society, Topeka, Kansas.

Longworth, Basil N. "Memorandum of Thoughts, Reflections." Reminiscence in Diary Form. Henry E. Huntington Library, San Marino, California.

Lord, Bertie. Reminiscence. Montana Historical Society, Helena, Montana.

Lord, Dr. Israel. Journal. 1849. Henry E. Huntington Library, San Marino, California.

Loring, Madison. Collection. Arizona Historical Society, Tucson, Arizona.

Lyman, Esther B. and Joseph Lyman. Journal and Letter. 1853. Henry E. Huntington Library, San Marino, California.

M., S. Letters. 1883. Beinecke Library, Yale University, New Haven, Connecticut.

Madison County, Montana. School District Records. Montana Historical Society, Helena, Montana.

Maloon, Mary Eliza W. Diary. 1864. California Historical Society, San Francisco, California.

Mann, Henry Rice. Diary. 1849. California Historical Society, San Francisco, California.

Mansur Family. Letters. 1852–74. Beinecke Library, Yale University, New Haven, Connecticut.

Marshall, Margaret F. Lancaster. Reminiscence. Kansas State Historical Society, Topeka, Kansas.

Martin, Mrs. D. C. "Memories of Strawberry School." Reminiscence. Arizona Historical Society, Tucson, Arizona.

Martin, Oello Ingraham. "Father Came West." Reminiscence. Kansas State Historical Society, Topeka, Kansas.

Martin, Sarah E. Reminiscence. Arizona Historical Society, Tucson, Arizona.

Maynard, David Swinson. Diary. 1850. Henry E. Huntington Library, San Marino, California.

McCarty, F. M. Autobiography. Montana Historical Society, Helena, Montana.

McCowen, George. Diary. 1853. Henry E. Huntington Library, San Marino, California.

McGuire, Jennie T. Reminiscence. Jessie K. Snell Collection. Kansas State Historical Society, Topeka, Kansas.

McKee, Vallie. "Passing of the West." Reminiscence. Kansas State Historical Society, Topeka, Kansas.

McPhail, Elizabeth. Letters and Reminiscences. Arizona Historical Society, Tucson, Arizona.

Merriman, D. O. Reminiscence. Montana Historical Society, Helena, Montana.

Meyers, Irene A. Reminiscence. Henry E. Huntington Library, San Marino, California.

Miller, J. Edward. Reminiscence. California Historical Society, San Francisco, California.

Miller, Lillian M. "I Remember Montana." Reminiscence. Montana Historical Society, Helena, Montana.

Mills, Zella Hunter. Reminiscence. Kansas State Historical Society, Topeka, Kansas.

Minto, Martha Ann Morrison. "Female Pioneering in Oregon." Reminiscence. Bancroft Library, University of California, Berkeley.

Mitchell Family. Letters. 1858–87. Henry E. Huntington Library, San Marino, California.

Moffitt, Mabel W. Reminiscence. Arizona Historical Society, Tucson, Arizona.

Monroe, Bessie K. Reminiscence. Montana Historical Society, Helena, Montana.

Montgomery, William. Diary. 1850. Henry E. Huntington Library, San Marino, California.

Mooar, Lydia Louise. Reminiscence and Interview. Mooar Family Collection. Southwest Collection, Texas Tech University, Lubbock, Texas.

Moore, Anna Shannon. Reminiscence. Fred Lockley Collection. Henry E. Huntington Library, San Marino, California.

Moore, Frances E. "Memories of a Pioneer in Kansas." Reminiscence. Kansas State Historical Society, Topeka, Kansas.

Moore, H. Miles. Journal. 1852–80. Beinecke Library, Yale University, New Haven, Connecticut.

Mountjoy, Wiley and Ella. Letters and Reminiscences. Montana Historical Society, Helena, Montana.

Murphy, May E. "Our Pioneer Mother." Reminiscence. Kansas State Historical Society, Topeka, Kansas.

Myers, Irene Atterbury. Reminiscence. Fred Lockley Collection. Henry E. Huntington Library, San Marino, California.

Newcomb, Samuel P. and Susan Newcomb. Diaries. 1865–71. Southwest Collection, Texas Tech University, Lubbock, Texas.

Newcomb, Silas. Journal. 1850. Henry E. Huntington Library, San Marino, California.

Nixon, O. A. Journal. 1854–55. Kansas State Historical Society, Topeka, Kansas.

Norton Family. Diaries. Kansas State Historical Society, Topeka, Kansas.

Nutting, L. A. "The Nuttings." Reminiscence. Montana Historical Society, Helena, Montana.

O'Neal, Evelina M. Reminiscence. Montana Historical Society, Helena, Montana.

Organ, Mrs. E.E. "Early Pioneering in Kansas." Reminiscence. Kansas State Historical Society, Topeka, Kansas.

Organizational Journal of an Emigrant Train. 1845. Henry E. Huntington Library, San Marino, California.

Osborne County District School 37. Daily Teacher's Register. 1876–97. Kansas State Historical Society, Topeka, Kansas.

Owen, East S. Journal. 1852. Beinecke Library, Yale University, New Haven, Connecticut.

Owen, James. "Journal of a Route to Pikes Peak." 1860. Newberry Library, Chicago, Illinois.

Owen, Richard. Diary. 1864. Montana Historical Society, Helena, Montana.

Packard, Georgiana. Reminiscence. Kansas State Historical Society, Topeka, Kansas.

Palmer, Carolyn H. "Reminiscences of Early Days in Boise." Idaho Historical Society, Boise, Idaho.

Parke, Charles R. Diary. 1849–50. Henry E. Huntington Library, San Marino, California.

Parker, George D. Letters. 1838–41. Beinecke Library, Yale University, New Haven, Connecticut.

Parker, William Tell. Diary. 1850. Henry E. Huntington Library, San Marino, California.

Parrish, Susan Thompson L. "Following the Pot of Gold" and "Westward in 1850." Reminiscences. Henry E. Huntington Library, San Marino, California.

Patch, J. B. Letter. 1866. Montana Historical Society, Helena, Montana.

Peabody, Endicott. Journal. 1882. Arizona Historical Society, Tucson, Arizona.

Pearce, Joe. "Line Rider." Reminiscence. Arizona Historical Society, Tucson, Arizona.

Pelot, James M. Letter. 1960. Kansas State Historical Society, Topeka, Kansas.

Pengra, Charlotte Emily S. Diary. 1853. Henry E. Huntington Library, San Marino, California.

Perkins, Elisha Douglas. Diary. 1849. Henry E. Huntington Library, San Marino, California.

Perigo, Lynn. Collection. Western History Collections. University of Colorado Library, Boulder, Colorado.

Philo, ———. Letters. 1850. Beinecke Library, Yale University, New Haven, Connecticut.

Pinkerton, Ralla Banta. "Pioneer Days in Beaver Creek Community." Reminiscence. R. J. Bradley Collection. Southwest Collection, Texas Tech University, Lubbock, Texas.

Pomeroy, Irene. Letter. 1848. Beinecke Library, Yale University, New Haven, Connecticut.

Pond, Ananias Rogers. Journal. 1849. Henry E. Huntington Library, San Marino, California.

Posey, Walter. Reminiscence and Interview. Southwest Collection, Texas Tech University, Lubbock, Texas.

Powers, Mary L. Rockwood. "The Overland Route." Reminiscence in Diary Form. Beinecke Library, Yale University, New Haven, Connecticut.

Pownall Family. Letters and Journal. 1849. Henry E. Huntington Library, San Marino, California.

Preston, Leander A. Diary. 1860–61. Ayer Collection. Newberry Library, Chicago, Illinois.

Pringle, Catherine Sager. Reminiscence. Henry E. Huntington Library, San Marino, California.

Reed, Joseph M. Letters. 1863. Kansas Collection, Spencer Library, University of Kansas, Lawrence, Kansas.

Reynolds, Anna W. Reminiscence. Southwest Collection, Texas Tech University, Lubbock, Texas.

Richmond, Theodore. Letters. 1864. Special Collection, University of North Carolina Library, Chapel Hill, North Carolina.

Riell, Robert B. "An Introduction to Globe Arizona." Reminiscence. Arizona Historical Society, Tucson, Arizona.

Riordan Family. Letters and Diary. 1881. Southwest Collection, Texas Tech University, Lubbock, Texas.

Robbins, Carrie Strong K. Journal. 1887. Kansas State Historical Society, Topeka, Kansas.

Robinson, Edward M. Letters. 1852–55. Beinecke Library, Yale University, New Haven, Connecticut.

Root, George A. Reminiscence. State Historical Society of Colorado, Denver, Colorado.

Rowe, Charles. Diary. 1852–55, 1861–64. Henry E. Huntington Library, San Marino, California.

Rowe, William. Reminiscence. Henry E. Huntington Library, San Marino, California.

Rudd, Eliza Catherine. Reminiscence. Arizona Historical Society, Tucson, Arizona.

Russell, Fannie Forbes. Reminiscences. Montana Historical Society, Helena, Montana.

Russell, Leonora Allen. Reminiscence. Arizona Historical Society, Tucson, Arizona.

Sadler, Warren. Reminiscence. Bancroft Library, University of California, Berkeley.

Sanders, Harriet P. Reminiscence. Montana Historical Society, Helena, Montana.

Sanders, Thomas D. Reminiscence. Western History Collections, Denver Public Library, Denver, Colorado.

Sawyer, Mrs. Francis H. Journal. 1852. Ayer Collection. Newberry Library, Chicago, Illinois.

Sawyer, George. Reminiscence. Montana Historical Society, Helena, Montana.

Seymour, Bennett. Reminiscence. State Historical Society of Colorado, Denver, Colorado.

Sisk, Lizzie Moore. Reminiscence. Idaho Historical Society, Boise, Idaho.

Slaughter, Benjamin Franklin. Journal. 1871. Beinecke Library, Yale University, New Haven, Connecticut.

Smith, Alvin Thompson. Letters. 1840–52. Beinecke Library, Yale University, New Haven, Connecticut.

Smith, Dr. John. Diary. 1853. Henry E. Huntington Library, San Marino, California.

Smith, Mrs. John H. Reminiscence. California Historical Society, San Francisco, California.

Smith, Lucy May Eastman. Reminiscence. California Historical Society, San Francisco, California.

Smith, Myrtel. Reminiscence. Kansas State Historical Society, Topeka, Kansas.

Smith, Mrs. W. W. Reminiscence and Interview. Southwest Collection, Texas Tech University, Lubbock, Texas.

Smith, Walter T. Letters. 1878. Western History Collections, Denver Public Library, Denver, Colorado.

Snell, Jessie K. Collection. Kansas State Historical Society, Topeka, Kansas.

Snow, Fanny. Reminiscence. Montana Historical Society, Helena, Montana.

Stafford, Frederic. Letters. 1857. Special Collections, University of North Carolina Library, Chapel Hill, North Carolina.

Stanton, George. Reminiscence. Montana Historical Society, Helena, Montana.

Steiner, Robert E. "Children in Alder Gulch." Reminiscence. Special Collections, Montana State University Library, Bozeman, Montana.

Stewart, Agnes. Diary. 1853. Henry E. Huntington Library, San Marino, California.

Stewart, Elizabeth. Letter. 1856 [?]. Henry E. Huntington Library, San Marino, California.

Stewart, Helen Marnie. Diary. 1853. Lane County Historical Society, Eugene, Oregon.

Stocking, Lucy. Diary. 1872. Montana Historical Society, Helena, Montana.

Stone, Frank L. Collection. Special Collections, Montana State University Library, Bozeman, Montana.

Stote, Florence M. Reminiscence. Kansas State Historical Society, Topeka, Kansas.

Stubbs, Mrs. C. F. Letters. Southwest Collection, Texas Tech University, Lubbock, Texas.

Sullivan, W. W. "Crossing the Plains in '62." Reminiscence. Beinecke Library, Yale University, New Haven, Connecticut.

Summers, Sue H. Reminiscence. Arizona Historical Society, Tucson, Arizona.

Thomas, Augusta Dodge. "Prairie Children." Reminiscence. Kansas State Historical Society, Topeka, Kansas.

Thomas, Homer. Letter. 1864. Montana Historical Society, Helena, Montana.

Thompson, H. C. "Across the Continent on Foot in 1859." Reminiscence. Henry E. Huntington Library, San Marino, California.

Thoroughman, Robert P. Reminiscence. Special Collections. Montana State University Library, Bozeman, Montana.

Tipton, Aurelia R. Diary. 1878. Montana Historical Society, Helena, Montana.

Tompkins, Dr. Edward A. Reminiscence. Henry E. Huntington Library, San Marino, California.

Tuttle, Daniel. Letters. Montana Historical Society, Helena, Montana.

Underwood, George. Letters. 1850–51. Beinecke Library, Yale University, New Haven, Connecticut.

Van Court, Mrs. E. A. Reminiscence. Beinecke Library, Yale University, New Haven, Connecticut.

Varney, Jothana. Letters. 1851. California Historical Society, San Francisco, California.

Veale, Lula Black. Reminiscence. Southwest Collection, Texas Tech University, Lubbock, Texas.

Walker Family. Letters. 1872. Beinecke Library, Yale University, New Haven, Connecticut.

Walters, Louisa. Letters. 1864. Idaho Historical Society, Boise, Idaho.

Warner, Mary Eliza. Diary. 1864. Bancroft Library, University of California, Berkeley.

Washburn, Catherine Amanda S. Journal. 1853. Henry E. Huntington Library, San Marino, California.

Waugh, Frank Albert. "Pioneering in Kansas." Reminiscence. Kansas State Historical Society, Topeka, Kansas.

Werden, Frances. Diary. 1866. Montana Historical Society, Helena, Montana.

Westover, C. Letter. 1852. Beinecke Library, Yale University, New Haven, Connecticut.

Wheeler, Mrs. K. Myrtle Smith. "Tales of Pioneer Lives." Reminiscence. Kansas State Historical Society, Topeka, Kansas.

White, Daniel. Diary. 1854–59. Henry E. Huntington Library, San Marino, California.

Wildman, Augustus and Thomas Wildman. Letters. 1859–66. Beinecke Library, Yale University, New Haven, Connecticut.

Wilkins, James F. Diary. 1849. Henry E. Huntington Library, San Marino, California.

Wilkinson, J. A. Diary. 1859. Henry E. Huntington Library, San Marino, Calfifornia.

Wilkinson, J. A. "Journal Across the Plains." Reminiscence. Newberry Library, Chicago, Illinois.

Wilkinson, Raleigh L. Reminiscence. Montana Historical Society, Helena, Montana.

Williams, Carrie. Journal. 1858–62. Beinecke Library, Yale University, New Haven, Connecticut.

Willis, Cedenia B. Reminiscence. Arizona Historical Society, Tucson, Arizona.

Wilson, John S. Journal. 1859–60. Beinecke Library, Yale University, New Haven, Connecticut.

Wilson, John. Letters. 1860. Newberry Library, Chicago, Illinois.

Wilson, Robert Milton. Diary. 1850–51. California Historical Society, San Francisco, California.

Wiltbank, Effie May. Reminiscence. Arizona Historical Society, Tucson, Arizona.

Wisner, Mrs. Sarah A. and A. W. Wisner. "A Trip Across the Plains in 1866." Journal. Ayer Collection. Newberry Library, Chicago, Illinois.

Wolcott, Lucian Mclenathan. Journal. 1850–51. Henry E. Huntington Library, San Marino, California.

Wood, Charles M. Reminiscence. Arizona Historical Society, Tucson, Arizona.

Wood, Joseph W. Diary. 1849. Henry E. Huntington Library, San Marino, California.

Wood, Wallace A. Reminiscence. Kansas State Historical Society, Topeka, Kansas.

Woodson, Rebecca H.N. Reminiscence. Bancroft Library, University of California, Berkeley.

Wootten, Martha. Reminiscence. California Historical Society, San Francisco, California.

Word, Samuel. Diary. 1863. Montana Historical Society, Helena, Montana.

Wright, Harriet S. Reminiscence. Charles M. Wright Collection. Arizona Historical Society, Tucson, Arizona.

Wyckoff, Eliza J. Reminiscence. Kansas State Historical Society, Topeka, Kansas.

Yates, G. W. W. Letters. 1904. Kansas State Historical Society, Topeka, Kansas.

Zumwalt, Soloman. Autobiography. Henry E. Huntington Library, San Marino, California.

Published Primary Sources

Abbey, James. *California. A Trip Across the Plains in the Spring of 1850.* New Albany, Ind.: Jno. R. Nunmacher, 1850.

Ackley, Mary. E. *Crossing the Plains, and Early Days in California's Golden Age.* San Francisco: Privately Printed, 1928.

Andrews, John D. *Eight Years in the Toils; Sketches From a Gambler's Life.* Cincinnati: C.J. Krehbier and Co., 1890.

Angelo, C. Aubrey. *Sketches of Travel in Oregon and Idaho.* New York: By the Author, 1866.

Applegate, Jesse. *Recollections of My Boyhood.* Roseburg, Ore.: Press of Review Publishing Co., 1914.

Athearn, Robert G., ed. "Across the Plains in 1863: The Diary of Peter Winne." *Iowa Journal of History* 49:3 (July 1951): 221–40.

Ayer, I. Winslow. *Life in the Wilds of America, and Wonders of the West in and Beyond the Bounds of Civilization.* Grand Rapids: Central Publishing Co., 1880.

Backus, Harriet Fish. *Tomboy Bride.* Boulder: Pruett Press, 1969.

Baker, Sarah Schoonmaker (Tuthill). *The Children of the Plains.* London: T. Nelson and Sons, 1861.

Ballantyne, Robert Michael. *The Golden Dream; or, Adventures in the far West.* London: J. F. Shaw and Co., 1861.

Bamford, Mary E. "Child-life Among the California Foot-hills." *Overland Monthly* 2, Second Series (July, 1883): 56–59.

Barneby, W. Henry. *Life and Labour in the Far, Far West.* London: Cassell and Company, Ltd., 1884.

Barry, Louise. *The Beginnings of the West: Annals of the Kansas Gateway to the American West, 1540–1854.* Topeka: Kansas State Historical Society, 1972.

Barry, Louise, ed. "Overland to the Goldfields of California in 1852." *Kansas Historical Journal* 11 (1942): 255–56.

Batty, Joseph. *Over the Wilds to California; or, Eight Years from Home.* Leeds: F. Parrott, 1867.

Beadle, Charles. *A Trip to the United States in 1887.* London: J.S. Virtue and Co., 1887.

Bennett, Edwin Lewis. *Boom Town Boy.* Chicago: Sage Books, 1966.

Bennett, Estelline. *Old Deadwood Days.* New York: J.H. Sears and Co., 1928.

Bennett, James. *Overland Journey to California, Journal of James Bennett.* New Harmony, Ind.: Times Printing, 1906.

Bennett, William P. *The First Baby in Camp. A Full Account of the Scenes and Adventures During the Pioneer Days of '49.* Salt Lake City: Rancher Publishing Co., 1893.

Bickham, William Denison. *From Ohio to the Rocky Mountains.* Editorial Correspondence of the Dayton (Ohio) *Journal.* Dayton: Journal Book and Job Printing House, 1879.

Bieber, Ralph P., ed. "Diary of a Journey to the Pike's Peak Gold Mines in 1859," *Mississippi Valley Historical Review* 14:3 (December, 1927): 360–78.

Bird, Isabella L. *A Lady's Life in the Rocky Mountains.* Norman: University of Oklahoma Press, 1960.

Bird, J.S. *Prairies and Pioneers*. Hays, Kan.: McWhirter-Ammons Press, 1931.

Bishop, Mrs. Julia A. "Why and How I Came to Denver." *The Trail* 5:2 (July, 1912): 21–23.

Blake, Mary E. *On the Wing. Rambling Notes of a Trip to the Pacific*. Boston: Lee and Shepard, 1883.

Bonney, Benjamin Franklin. *Across the Plains by Prairie Schooner*. Eugene Ore.: Koke-Tiffany Co., 192–?

Bowles, Samuel. *Across the Continent: A Summer's Journey to the Rocky Mountains, the Mormons, and the Pacific States with Speaker Colfax*. Springfield, Mass.: S. Bowles and Co, 1865.

Bowles, Samuel. *Our New West*. Hartford: Hartford Publishing Co., 1869.

Boynton, C. B. and T. B. Mason. *A Journey Through Kansas; with Sketches of Nebraska*. Cincinnati: Moore, Wilstoch, Keys, & Co., 1855.

Boys, Samuel Evans. *My Boyhood in the Flint Hills of Kansas, 1873–1893*. Plymouth, Ind.: By the Author, 1958.

Brooks, Elisha. *A Pioneer Mother of California*. San Francisco: Harr Wagner Publishing Co., 1922.

Brooks, Noah. *The Boy Emigrants*. New York: Scribner, Armstrong and Co., 1877.

Brown, Mabel Stoll. "Mabel Stoll Brown: Prairie Child." South Dakota Historical Society, *Collections* 39(1978): 148–223.

Browne, J. Ross. *Crusoe's Island: A Ramble in the Footsteps of Alexander Selkirk*. New York: Harper & Brothers, 1864.

Bruff, J. Goldsborough. *Gold Rush: The Journals, Drawings, and Other Papers of J. Goldsborough Bruff*. Edited by Georgia Willis Read and Ruth Gaines. New York: Columbia University Press, 1949.

Bryan, Jerry. *An Illinois Gold Hunter in the Black Hills: The Diary of Jerry Bryan*. Springfield: Illinois State Historical Society, 1960.

Bryant, Edwin. *What I Saw in California: Being the Journal of a Tour*. London: Richard Bentley, 1849.

Budlong, Caroline Gale. *Memories of Pioneer Days in Oregon and Washington Territory*. Eugene: Picture Press Printers, 1949.

Cambell, Rebembrance Hughes. *A Brief History of our Trip Across the Plaines with Ox Teams in 1853*. N.p., 1905.

Carter, Tolbert. "Pioneer Days." *Oregon Pioneer Association, Transactions* (1906): 65–103.

Clappe, Louise Amelia Knapp (Smith). *The Shirley Letters From California Mines in 1851–52*. San Francisco: T.C. Russell, 1922.

Clark, Charles M. *A Trip to Pike's Peak and Notes by the Way*. Chicago: S.P. Rounds, 1861.

Cleaveland, Agnes Morley. *No Life For A Lady*. Lincoln: University of Nebraska Press, 1977.

Colt, Mrs. Miriam Davis. *Went to Kansas: Being a Thrilling Account of an Ill-fated Expedition to That Fairy Land and Its Sad Results*. Watertown: L. Ingalls and Co., 1862.

Conner, Daniel Ellis. *A Confederate in the Colorado Gold Fields*. Norman: University of Oklahoma Press, 1970.

Cooke, Lucy Rutledge. *Covered Wagon Days: Crossing the Plains in 1852.* Modesto, Cal.: Privately Printed, 1923.

Corey, Paul. "Bachelor Bess: My Sister." South Dakota Historical Society, *Collections,* 37 (1975): 1–101.

Coy, Mrs. John G. "Crossing the Plains in 1862." *The Trail* 3:6 (November, 1910): 5–7, 22–23.

Crampton, Frank A. *Deep Enough: A Working Stiff in the Western Mines.* Norman: University of Oklahoma Press, 1982.

Cummins, Sarah J. *Autobiography and Reminiscences of Sarah J. Cummins.* LaGrande, Ore.: La Grande Printing Co., 1914.

Dale, Edward Everett. *The Cross Timbers: Memories of a North Texas Boyhood.* Austin & London: University of Texas Press, 1966.

Darley, George Marshall. *Pioneering in the San Juan; Personal Reminiscences of Work Done in Southwestern Colorado During the "Great San Juan Excitement."* Chicago: Fleming H. Revell Co., 1899.

Davis, Carlyle Channing. *Older Times in Colorado.* Los Angeles: Phillips Publishing Co., 1916.

Deady, Mrs. Matthew P. "Crossing the Plains to Oregon in 1846." *Oregon Pioneer Association, Transactions* (1928): 57–64.

Dean, Frank. "Pioneering in Nebraska, 1872–1879." *Nebraska History* 36 (June, 1955): 105–21.

Delano, Alonzo. *A Live Woman in the Mines: Or, Pike County Ahead! A Local Play in Two Acts. By "Old Block."* New York: S. French, c1857.

Delano, Alonzo. *Life on the Plains and Among the Diggings.* Auburn and Buffalo: Milner, Orton and Mulligan, 1854.

Devinney, V. *The Story of a Pioneer. An Historical Sketch in which is Depicted some of the struggles and exciting incidents pertaining to the early settlement of Colorado.* Denver: Reed Publishing Co., 1904.

DeWitt, Ward G. and Florence Stark DeWitt. *Prairie Schooner Lady: The Journal of Harriet Sherill Ward, 1853.* Los Angeles: Westernlore Press, 1959.

Dickenson, Luella. *Reminiscences of a Trip Across the Plains in 1846 and Early Days in California.* San Francisco: The Whitaker & Ray Company, 1904.

Dickson, Arthur Jerome, ed. *Covered Wagon Days: A Journey Across the Plains in the Sixties and Pioneer Days in the Northwest; from the Private Journals of Albert Jerome Dickson.* Cleveland: Arthur H. Clark Co., 1929.

Diede, Pauline Neher. *Homesteading on the Knife River Prairies.* Edited by Elizabeth Hampsten. Bismark: Germans from Russia Heritage Society, 1983.

Dinkel, William M. "A Pioneer of the Roaring Fork." *Colorado Magazine* 21:5 (September, 1944): 184–96.

Dunlap, Kate. *The Montana Gold Rush Diary of Kate Dunlap.* Edited by S. Lyman Tyler. Denver: Fred A. Rosenstock, Old West Publishing Co., and University of Utah Press, 1969.

Durrell, Glen R. "Homesteading in Colorado." *Colorado Magazine* 51:2 (Spring, 1974): 93–114.

Ebbutt, Percy G. *Emigrant Life in Kansas.* London: Swan Sonnenschein and Co., 1886.

320   *Bibliography*

Ehrlich, Clara Hilderman. "My Childhood on the Colorado Prairie." *Colorado Magazine* 51:2 (Spring, 1974): 115–40.

Eisele, Fannie L. "We Came to Live in Oklahoma Territory." *Chronicles of Oklahoma* 38:1 (Spring, 1960): 55–65.

Ellis, Anne. *The Life of an Ordinary Woman*. Lincoln: University of Nebraska Press, 1980.

Faeth, Mary Lillian. *Kansas in the 80s. Being Some Recollections of Life on Its Western Frontier*. New York: The Procyon Press, 1947.

Farnham, Eliza W. *Life in Prairie Land*. New York: Harper and Brothers, 1846.

Farrell, Ned E. *Colorado: The Rocky Mountain Gem, As It is in 1868*. Chicago: The Western News Co., 1868.

Fillmore, Rollin S. *Life and Experiences of a Country Doctor in Kansas*. Long Beach: Privately Printed, 1934.

Foster, Dr. Bert. *A Rocky Mountain Parson*. Upland, Cal.: 1940.

Francl, Joseph. *The Overland Journal of Joseph Francl, the First Bohemian to Cross the Plains to the California Gold Fields*. San Francisco: William P. Wreden, 1968.

Frazier, Mrs. R. *Reminiscences of Travel from 1855 to 1867. By a Lady*. San Francisco: 1868.

Frink, Margaret Ann. *Journal of the Adventures of a Party of California Gold-seekers*. Oakland: 1897.

Frizzell, Lodisa. *Across the Plains to California in 1852*. New York: New York Public Library, 1915.

Frost, Mary P. "Experience of a Pioneer." *Washington Historical Quarterly* (April, 1916): 123–25.

Fulton, Francis I. Sims. *To and Through Nebraska*. Lincoln: Journal Co., 1884.

Gallatin, E. *What Life Has Taught Me*. Denver: F. Frederic, 1900.

Garland, Hamlin. *Boy Life on the Prairie*. Boston: Allyn & Bacon, 1926.

Geer, Mrs. Elizabeth Dixon Smith. "Diary. 1847." *Oregon Pioneer Association, Transactions* (1907): 153–79.

Gibbons, James Joseph. *Notes of a Missionary Priest in the Rocky Mountains*. New York: Christian Press Association, 1898.

Giezentanner, Veda. "In Dugouts and Sod Houses." *Chronicles of Oklahoma* 39:2 (Summer, 1961): 140–49.

Goldrick, O. J. "The First School in Colorado." *Colorado Magazine* 6:2 (March, 1929): 72–74.

Goosman, Mrs. Fred. "Early Days in Nebraska." Nebraska Territorial Pioneer Association, *Reminiscences and Proceedings* Vol. 1, 21–22.

Goulder, William Armistead. *Reminiscences; Incidents in the Life of a Pioneer in Oregon and Idaho*. Boise: T. Regan, 1909.

Green, Job E. "Pioneering in Boone County." Nebraska Territorial Pioneers Association, *Reminiscences and Proceedings* Vol. 2, 36–37.

Gunn, Lewis Carstairs. *Records of a California Family*. Edited by Anna Lee Marston. San Diego: Privately Printed, 1928.

Hafen, LeRoy R. ed. *Colorado Gold Rush: Contemporary Letters and Reports, 1858–1859*. Glendale, Cal.: Arthur H. Clark Co., 1941.

Hafen, LeRoy R., ed. "Diary of Mrs. A.C. Hunt, 1859." *Colorado Magazine* 21:5 (September, 1944): 161–70.

Haines, Francis D., Jr. *A Bride on the Bozeman Trail: The Letters and Diary of Ellen Gordon Fletcher, 1866.* Medford, Ore.: Gandee Printing, 1970.

Hall, Lucille Hathaway. *Memories of Old Alturas County, Idaho.* Denver: Big Mountain Press, 1956.

Hambleton, Chalkley J. *A Gold Hunter's Experience.* Chicago: R.R. Donnelly and Sons Co., 1898.

Hanington, C. H. "Early Days of Central City." *Colorado Magazine* 19:1 (January, 1942): 3–14.

Hardy, Lady Duffus. *Through Cities and Prairie Lands. Sketches of an American Tour.* New York: R. Worthington, 1880.

Harter, George, *Crossing the Plains. An Account of the George Harter Family's Trip from Cass County, Michigan, to Marysville, California, in 1864; taken from the Diary of George Harter.* Edited by Doris Harter Chase. Sacramento, Cal.: By the Editor, 1957.

Hastings, James K. "Boyhood in the Trinidad Region." *Colorado Magazine* 30:2 (April, 1953): 104–09.

Hastings, Lansford W. *The Emigrants' Guide to Oregon and California.* Princeton: Princeton University Press, 1932.

Hawkins, C. *The Argonauts of California, Being the Reminiscences of Scenes and incidents that occurred in California in Early Mining Days.* New York: Ford, Howard and Halbert, 1890.

Hayden, Mary Jane. *Pioneer Days.* San Jose, Cal.: Murgotten's Press, 1915.

Hayes, Augustus Allen. *New Colorado and the Santa Fe Trail.* London: C. Kegan Paul & Co., 1881.

Herndon, Sarah (Raymond). *Days on the Road; Crossing the Plains in 1865.* New York: Burr Printing House, 1902.

Hill, Alice (Polk). *Tales of the Colorado Pioneers.* Denver: Pierson and Gardner, 1884.

Hill, Emma Shepard. *A Dangerous Crossing and What Happened on the Other Side.* Denver: Press of the Smith-Brooks Co., 1914.

Hills, Georgia Burns. "Memories of a Pioneer Childhood." *Colorado Magazine* 32:2 (April, 1955): 110–28.

Hixon, Adrietta Applegate. *On To Oregon! A True Story of a Young Girl's Journey Into the West.* Edited by Waldo Taylor. Weiser, Idaho: Signal-American Printers, 1947.

Hodge, Hiram C. *Arizona As It Is; or, The Coming Country.* Boston: H.O. Houghton and Co., 1877.

Horton, Emily McCowen. *Our Family, With a Glimpse of their Pioneer Life.* N.p.: 1922.

Hunt, Nancy A. *By Ox-team To California.* San Francisco: 1916.

Hutchings, James Mason. *The Miner's Ten Commandments.* San Francisco: Senn Printing, 1853.

The Illustrated Miners' Handbook and Guide to Pike's Peak. St. Louis: Parker and Huyett, 1859.

Ise, John. *Sod and Stubble: The Story of a Kansas Homestead.* Lincoln: University of Nebraska Press, 1970.

Ivens, Virginia Wilcox. *Pen Pictures of Early Western Days.* N.p.: 1905.

Jackson, Helen Hunt. *Bits of Travel at Home.* Boston: Roberts Brothers, 1887.

James, Marquis. *The Cherokee Strip: A Tale of an Oklahoma Boyhood.* New York: Viking Press, 1960.

Jenkins, Jeff. *The Northern Tier: Or Life Among the Homestead Settlers.* Topeka: Kansas Publishing House, 1880.

Jocknick, Sidney. *Early Days on the Western Slope of Colorado.* Denver: Carson-Harper Co., 1913.

Johnson, Dorothy M. "Helena's Past As Seen Through Teen-Age Eyes and Newsprint." *Montana: The Magazine of Western History* 12:1 (January, 1962): 2–14.

Johnson, Laura (Winthrop). *Eight Hundred Miles in an Ambulance.* Philadelphia: J. B. Lippincott Co., 1889.

Johnson, Theodore Taylor. *Sights in the Gold Region, and Scenes by the Way.* New York: Baker and Scribner, 1849.

Jones, Harry. *Letters from America.* London: Privately Printed, 1870.

Jones, R.L. "Folk Life in Early Texas: The Autobiography of Andrew Davis." *Southwestern Historical Quarterly* 43:2 & 3 (October, 1939 & January, 1940): 158–75, 323–41.

Keller, George. *A Trip Across the Plains, and Life in California.* Massillon, Ohio: White's Press, 1851.

Kellogg, Harriet S. *Life of Mrs. Emily J. Harwood.* Albuquerque: El Abogado Press, 1903.

Kelly, William. *An Excursion to California Over the Prairie, Rocky Mountains, and the Great Sierra Nevada.* London. Chapman and Hall, 1851.

Kenderline, Thaddeus S. *A California Tramp and Later Footprints; Or, Life on the Plains and in the Golden State Thirty Years Ago.* Philadelphia: Press of Globe Printing House, 1888.

Kent, Lewis A. *Leadville, The City.* Denver: Daily Times Printing, 1880.

Ketcham, Rebecca. "From Ithaca to Clatsop Plains: Miss Ketcham's Journal of Travel." Edited by Leo M. Kaiser and Pricilla Knuth. *Oregon Historical Quarterly* 62:3 & 4 (September & December, 1961): 237–87, 337–402.

Kidd, William H. *Glittering Gold; or, Pencillings about Pike's Peak.* St. Louis: Missouri Democrat, 1860.

Kingman, Henry. *The Travels and Adventures of Henry Kingman in Search of Colorado and California Gold, 1859–1865.* Delavan, Kan.: Privately Printed, 1917.

Knotts, Minnie Prey. "Nebraska and Its Pioneers." Nebraska Territorial Pioneer Association, *Reminiscences and Proceedings*, 1907, Vol. 1, 24–30.

Kuykendall, William Littlebury. *Frontier Days, A True Narrative of Striking Events.* N.p.: 1917.

A Lady's Ranche Life in Montana. By I.R. London: W. H. Allen & Co., 1887.

LaGuardia, Fiorello H. *The Making of An Insurgent: An Autobiography: 1882–1919.* New York: Capricorn Books, 1961.

Lambert, Julia S. "Plain Tales of the Plains." *The Trail* 8:8–11 (January, February, March, April, 1916): 1–8, 5–12, 5–13, 5–11.

Lanning, Jim and Judy Lanning. *Texas Cowboys: Memories of the Early Days.* College Station: Texas A & M University Press, 1984.

Latta, Robert Ray. *Reminiscences of Pioneer Life.* Kansas City: Hudson, 1912.

Leach, R.E., ed. "Journal of George T. Clark." *The Trail* 6:1 (June, 1913): 5–16.

Lee, Mabel Barbee. *Cripple Creek Days*. Garden City, N.Y.: Doubleday & Co., Inc. 1958.

Lewis, Marvin. *Martha and the Doctor: A Frontier Family in Central Nevada*. Edited by B. Betty Lewis. Reno: University of Nevada Press, 1977.

Lillard, Richard G., ed. "A Literate Woman in the Mines." *Mississippi Valley Historical Review* 31:1 (June, 1944): 81–98.

Lippincott, Sara Jane. *New Life in New Lands: Notes of Travel*. New York: J.B. Ford and Co., 1873.

Lockley, Fred. *Conversations With Pioneer Women*. Edited by Mike Helm. Eugene: Rainy Day Press, 1981.

Lord, Mrs. Elizabeth. *Reminiscences of Eastern Oregon*. Portland: Irwin-Hudson Co., 1903.

Ludlow, Fitz Hugh. *The Heart of the Continent: A Record of Travel Across the Plains and In Oregon*. New York: Hurd and Houghton, 1870.

Magnuson, Richard G. *Coeur d'Alene Diary: The First Ten Years of Hardrock Mining in North Idaho*. Portland: Metropolitan Press, 1968.

Majors, Mrs. A. H. "Life in North Creede in the Early Days." *Colorado Magazine* 22:6 (November, 1945): 267–70.

Matthews, Sallie Reynolds. *Interwoven: A Pioneer Chronicle*. College Station: Texas A & M University Press, 1982.

Mclhaney, Edward Washington. *Recollections of a '49er*. Kansas City, Mo: Hailman Printing Co., 1908.

Mellard, Frank. *The Dream of a Youthful Cowboy: Sixty Years of My Life in West Texas*. Marfa, TX, 1957.

Meline, James F. *Two Thousand Miles on Horseback. Santa Fe and Back. A Summer Tour Through Kansas, Nebraska, Colorado, and New Mexico*. New York: Hurd and Houghton, 1867.

Merriam, H.G., ed. *Way Out West: Recollections and Tales*. Norman: University of Oklahoma Press, 1969.

Mitchell, Frederick W. "Correspondence of Frederick W. Mitchell Relative to His Mining Enterprises in California and Idaho, 1865–66." *Pacific Northwest Quarterly* 39 (April, 1948): 133–51.

Morgan, Dale. *Overland in 1846: Diaries and Letters of the California-Oregon Trail*. Georgetown, Cal.: The Talisman Press, 1963.

Morris, Maurice O'Conner. *Rambles in the Rocky Mountains*. London: Smith, Elder, 1864.

Morrison, John D., ed. "The Letters of David F. Spain." *Colorado Magazine* 35:2 (April, 1958): 81–112.

Murray, Margaret E. Archer. "Memoir of the William Archer Family." *Annals of Iowa* 39:5 & 6 (Summer & Fall, 1968): 357–71, 470–80.

Neall, James. *A Down-eastern in the Far West: The Reminiscence of James Neall in Oregon-California, 1845–50*. Ashland: Oregon Book Society, 1977.

Nye-Starr, Kate. *A Self-sustaining Woman; or, The Experience of Seventy-two Years*. Chicago, 1888.

O'Kieffe, Charles. *Western Story: The Recollections of Charley O'Kieffe, 1884–1898*. Lincoln: University of Nebraska Press, 1960.

Olds, Sarah E. *Twenty Miles From a Match: Homesteading in Western Nevada*. Reno: University of Nevada Press, 1978.

Orr, Ellison. "Remembrances of a Pioneer Boy." *Annals of Iowa* 40:7 & 8 (Winter & Spring, 1971): 530–60, 593–630.

Owen, Benjamin Franklin. *My Trip Across the Plains. March 31, 1853–October 28, 1853*. Eugene: Lane County Pioneer-Historical Society, 1967.

Palmer, Joel. *Journal of Travels Over the Rocky Mountains, to the Mouth of the Columbia River; Made During the Years 1845 and 1846*. Cinicnnati: J.A. & U.P. Fame, 1847.

Paul, Rodman W., ed. *A Victorian Gentlewoman in the Far West: The Reminiscences of Mary Hallock Foote*. San Marino: The Huntington Library, 1972.

Pender, Mary Rose Gregge-Hopwood, Lady. *A Lady's Experiences in the Wild West in 1883*. London: G. Tucker, 1888.

Pilgrim, Thomas. *Live Boys in the Black Hills: or, The Gold Hunters*. New York: C. T. Dillingham, 1880.

Porter, Lavinia Honey. *By Ox Team to California: A Narrative of Crossing the Plains in 1860*. Oakland, Cal.: Oakland Enquirer Publishing Co., 1910.

Price, James P. *Seven Years of Prairie Life*. Hereford, England: Jakeman and Carver, 1891.

Pringle, Octavius M. "Experience of an Emigrant Boy in 1846." In *Magic River Deschutes*, N.p.: n.d.

Pritchard, Jesse L. "To Pike's Peak in Search of Gold in 1859." *The Trail* 4:4 (September, 1911): 5–16.

Ramsdell, T. M. "Reminiscences." *Oregon Pioneer Association, Transactions*. (1897).

Reed, Charles S. "Life in a Nebraska Soddy." *Nebraska History* 39:1 (March, 1958): 57–73.

Reiley, Josephine Moorman. " 'I Think I Will Like Kansas': The Letters of Flora Moorman Heston, 1885-1886." *Kansas History* 6:2 (Summer, 1983): 71–95.

Richardson, Albert D. *Our New States and Territories*. New York; Beadle and Co., 1866.

Riley, Glenda, ed. "Eighty-six Years in Iowa: The Memoir of Ada Mae Brown Brinton." *Annals of Iowa* 45:7 (Winter, 1981): 551–67.

Riley, Glenda, ed. "Family Life on the Frontier: The Diary of Kitturah Penton Belknap." *Annals of Iowa* 44:1 (Summer, 1977): 31–51.

Riley, Glenda, ed. "The Morse Family Letters: A New Home in Iowa." *Annals of Iowa* 45 (Winter, 1980): 551–67.

Riley, Glenda, ed. "Pioneer Migration: The Diary of Mary Alice Shutes." *Annals of Iowa* 43:7 & 8 (Winter & Spring, 1977): 487–514, 567–92.

Ringo, Mary. *The Journal of Mary Ringo*. Santa Ana, Cal.: Privately Printed, 1956.

Ronan, Mary. *Frontier Woman: The Story of Mary Ronan as Told to Margaret Ronan*. Edited by H. G. Merriam. Missoula: University of Montana Press, 1973.

Roosa, Alma Carlson. "Homesteading in the 1880's: The Anderson-Carlson Families of Cherry County." *Nebraska History* 58:3 (Fall, 1977): 371–94.

Ross, Jennie E. "A Child's Experiences in '49." *Overland Monthly* 63, Second Series (March, April, May, 1914): 300–05, 402–08, 505–11.

Royce, Sarah. *A Frontier Lady: Recollections of the Gold Rush and Early California*. New Haven: Yale University Press, 1932.

Sandoz, Mari. *Old Jules*. New York: Blue Ribbon Books, 1935.

Sanford, Mollie Dorsey. *Mollie: The Journal of Mollie Dorsey Sanford in Nebraska and Colorado Territories, 1857–1866*. With introduction and notes by Donald F. Danker. Lincoln: University of Nebraska Press, 1959.

Sawyer, Lorenzo. *Way Sketches; Containing Incidents of Travel Across the Plains . . . with Letters Describing Life and Conditions in the Gold Region*. New York: Edward Eberstadt, 1926.

Sharp, Joe H. "Crossing the Plains in 1852." *Oregon Pioneer Association, Transactions*. (1895).

Small, Floyd B. *Autobiography of a Pioneer. Being an Account of the Personal Experiences of the Author from 1867 to 1916*. Seattle, 1916.

Smith, John V. *Incidents and Events in the Life of John V. Smith*. Salem: Ross E. Moores and Co., 1893.

Smith, Joseph Emerson. "Personal Recollections of Early Denver." *Colorado Magazine* 20:1 (January, 1943): 5–16.

Snyder, Grace. *No Time On My Hands*. Caldwell, Idaho: Caxton Printers, 1963.

Stegner, Wallace. *Wolf Willow: A History, a Story, and a Memory of the Last Plains Frontier*. Lincoln: University of Nebraska Press, 1980.

Stewart, Elinore Pruitt. *Letters of a Woman Homesteader*. Boston: Houghton Mifflin Co., 1913.

Stewart, George R. *The Opening of the California Trail: The Story of the Stevens Party from the Reminiscences of Moses Schallenberger*. Berkeley: University of California Press, 1953.

Strahorn, Carrie Adell. *Fifteen Thousand Miles by Stage*. New York: G.P. Putnam, 1911.

Stuart, Granville. *Forty Years on the Frontier as Seen in the Journals and Reminiscences of Granville Stuart*. Cleveland: Arthur H. Clark Co., 1925.

Taft, Mrs. Walter. "Across the Plains in the Early Sixties." *The Trail* 3:2 (July, 1910): 16–17, 21–22.

Taylor, Bayard. *Colorado: A Summer Trip*. New York: G.P. Putnam and Sons, 1867.

Taylor, Marguerite Watson. *Memories of a Wagon Trip*. Weiser, Idaho: Signal-American Printers. 1954.

Teeter, Charles and Darius. "Letters from the Boise Basin, 1864–1865." *Idaho Yesterdays* 6 (Fall, 1962): 26–30.

Thane, James L., Jr., ed. *A Governor's Wife on the Mining Frontier: The Letters of Mary Edgerton From Montana, 1863–1865*. Salt Lake City: Tanner Trust Fund, 1976.

Thavis, L. William. *Pioneering in Kansas: Iowa to Kansas in an Ox Wagon: Experiences of Capt. Charles M. Sears and Family in the '50.s.* Washington: 1917.

Thompson, Francis M. *Complete Guide to the New Gold Regions of Upper Missouri, Deer Lodge, Beaver Head . . . Salmon River, Boise River, and Powder River*. St. Louis: R.P. Studley and Co., 1863.

Thomson, Origen. *Crossing the Plains. Narrative of the Scenes, Incidents and Adventures Attending the Overland Journey*. Greensburg, Ind: Orville Thomson, 1896.

Tuller, Mrs. Miriam A. "Crossing the Plains in 1845." *Oregon Pioneer Association, Transactions*. (1895): 87–90.

Van Carr, Robert. *Black Hills Ballads*. Denver: Reed Publishing Co., 1902.

Van Gundy, John C. *Reminiscences of Frontier Life on the Upper Neosho in 1855 and 1856*. Topeka, Kan.: The College Press, 1925.

Waite, Charles Burlingame. *Emigrant's Guide to the Gold and Silver Mines of Idaho, Placer and Quartz Mines of the Boise Basin, South Boise and Owyhee*. Chicago: 1865.

Waldorf, John Taylor. *A Kid on the Comstock: Reminiscences of a Virginia City Childhood*. Palo Alto, Cal.: American West Publishing Co., 1970.

Wallace, Allie B. *Frontier Life in Oklahoma*. Washington, D.C.: Public Affairs Press, 1964.

Ward, D.B. *Across the Plains in 1853*. Seattle: Ward, 1911.

Warner, Luna. "The Diary of Luna E. Warner, A Kansas Teenager of the Early 1870s." Edited by Venola Lewis Bivens. *Kansas Historical Quarterly* 35:3 & 4 (Autumn & Winter, 1969): 276–311, 411–41.

Wells, Rev. Charles Wesley. *A Frontier Life, Being a Description of My Experience on the Frontier the first Forty-two years of My Life*. Cincinnati: Jennings & Pye, 1902.

Wenger, Martin G. *Recollections of Telluride, Colorado, 1895–1920*. Mesa Verde, Colo: Gilbert R. Wenger, 1978.

Wheatley, Mary L. "Reminiscences of the Early Sixties." *The Trail* 3:8 (January, 1911): 5–11.

Whipple-Haslam, Lee. *Early Days in California: Scenes and Events of the '50s As I Remember Them*. Jamestown, Cal.: s.n., 1925.

White, Owen P. *A Frontier Mother*. New York: Minton, Balch and Co., 1929.

Wilhelm, Walt. *Last Rig To Battle Mountain*. New York: Morrow, 1970.

Witter, Mrs. Daniel. "A Pioneer Woman's Story Written For Her Children." *The Trail* 18:3 (August, 1925): 3–10.

Wixson, Helen Marsh. "In the Sunny San Juan." In Sidney Jocknick, *Early Days in the Western Slope of Colorado*. Denver: Carson-Harper Co., 1913.

Woodin, Katharine Williams Filley. *Recollections of My Childhood on the Nebraska Pioneer Prairie Camp*. Edited by Marthalene Filley McGill. Privately printed, 1975.

Secondary Sources

The Frontier and the West

Armitage, Susan and Elizabeth Jameson, eds. *The Women's West*. Norman: University of Oklahoma Press, 1987.

Athearn, Robert G. "A Brahmin in Buffaloland." *Western Historical Quarterly* 1:1 (January, 1970): 21–34.

Barns, Cass G. *The Sod House*. Lincoln: University of Nebraska Press, 1970.

Baur, John E. *Growing Up With California: A History of California's Children*. Los Angeles: Will Kramer, 1978.

Billington, Ray Allen. *America's Frontier Heritage*. New York: Holt, Rinehart and Winston, 1966.

Blackburn, George M. and Sherman L. Ricards. "A Demographic History of the West: Nueces County, Texas, 1850." *Prologue* 4:1 (Spring, 1972): 3–20.

Bowen, William. "The Oregon Frontiersman: A Demographic View." In Thomas Vaughan, ed., *The Western Shore: Oregon Country Essays Honoring the American Revolution*, 181–97. Portland: Oregon Historical Society, 1975.

Butchart, Ronald E. "Education and Culture in the Trans-Mississippi West." *Journal of American Culture* 3:2 (Summer, 1980): 351–73.

Butchart, Ronald E. "The Frontier Teacher: Arizona, 1875–1925." *Journal of the West* 16:3 (July 1977): 54–67.

Butler, Anne M. *Daughters of Joy, Sisters of Misery: Prostitutes in the American West, 1865–90*. Urbana and Chicago: University of Illinois Press, 1985.

Conlin, Joseph R. *Bacon, Beans, and Gallantines: Food and Foodways on the Western Mining Frontier*. Reno: University of Nevada Press, 1986.

Dale, Edward Everett. *Frontier Ways: Sketches of Life in the Old West*. Austin: University of Texas Press, 1959.

De Pew, Kathryn. "William A. Hammill, Early Colorado Pioneer of Georgetown." *Colorado Magazine* 32:4 (October, 1955): 266–79.

Drache, Hiram M. *The Challenge of the Prairie*. Fargo: North Dakota Institute for Regional Studies, 1970.

Dunlop, Richard. *Doctors of the American Frontier*. Garden City: Doubleday and Co., Inc. 1962.

Dutcher, Flora. "A Sod House." *The Journal of Geography* 48:9 (December, 1949): 353–62.

Eblen, Jack E. "An Analysis of Nineteenth-Century Frontier Populations." *Demography* 2 (1965): 399–413.

Everett, Dianna. "The Public School Debate in New Mexico, 1850–1891." *Arizona and the West* 26:2 (Summer, 1984): 107–34.

Fahey, John. *The Inland Empire: Unfolding Years, 1879–1929*. Seattle and London: University of Washington Press, 1986.

Fairbanks, Carol. "Lives of Girls and Women on the Canadian and American Prairies." *International Journal of Women's Studies* 2:5, 452–72.

Faragher, John Mack. *Women and Men on the Overland Trail*. New Haven: Yale University Press, 1979.

Ferrier, William Warren. *Ninety Years of Education in California, 1846–1936*. Berkeley: Sather Gate Book Shop, 1937.

Fuller, Wayne E. "Country Schoolteaching on the Sod-House Frontier." *Arizona and the West* 17:2 (Summer, 1975): 121–40.

Gower, Calvin W. "Lectures, Lyceums, and Libraries in Early Kansas, 1854–1864." *Kansas Historical Quarterly* 36:2 (Summer, 1970): 175–82.

Griswold, Robert L. *Family and Divorce in California, 1850–1890*. Albany: State University of New York Press, 1983.

Gulliford, Andrew. "Earth Architecture of the Prairie Pioneer." *Midwest Review* 7 (Spring, 1986): 1–25.

Hargreaves, Mary W. M. "Rural Education on the Northern Plains Frontier." *Journal of the West* 18:4 (October, 1979): 25–32.

Holliday, J. S. *The World Rushed In: An Eyewitness Account of a Nation Heading West*. New York: Simon and Schuster, 1981.

Jeffrey, Julie Roy. *Frontier Women: The Trans-Mississippi West, 1840–1880.* New York: Hill and Wang, 1979.

Kirker, Harold. *California's Architectural Frontier: Style and Tradition in the Nineteenth Century.* New York: Russell and Russell, 1970.

Koop, Michael and Stephen Ludwig. *German-Russian Folk Architecture in Southeastern South Dakota.* Vermillion: State Historical Preservation Center, 1984.

Lamar, Howard Roberts. *The Far Southwest, 1846–1912: A Territorial History.* New York: W. W. Norton and Co., 1970.

Lavender, David. *Westward Vision: The Story of the Oregon Trail.* New York: McGraw-Hill Book Co., 1963.

Limerick, Patricia Nelson. *The Legacy of Conquest: The Unbroken Past of the American West.* New York: W. W. Norton and Co., 1987.

Lubick, George. "Cornelius Hedges: Frontier Educator." *Montana: The Magazine of Western History* 28:2 (April, 1978): 26–35.

Lund, Theodore. *Children of the Frontier.* New York: D. Appleton and Co., 1867.

Malone, Michael P., ed. *Historians and the American West.* Lincoln: University of Nebraska Press, 1983.

Mann, Ralph. *After the Gold Rush: Society in Grass Valley and Nevada City, California, 1849–1880.* Stanford: Stanford University Press, 1982.

McQuillan, D. Aidan. "The Mobility of Immigrants and Americans: A Comparison of Farmers on the Kansas Frontier." *Agricultural History* 53:3 (July, 1979): 576–96.

Meinig, Donald W. *The Great Columbia Plain: A Historical Geography, 1805–1910.* Seattle: University of Washington Press, 1968.

Miner, Craig. *West of Wichita: Settling the High Plains of Kansas, 1865–1890.* Lawrence: University Press of Kansas, 1986.

Moynihan, Ruth Barnes. "Children and Young People on the Overland Trail." *Western Historical Quarterly* 6:3 (July, 1975): 279–94.

Muir, Leonard Erle. *Elam Bartholomew: Pioneer, Farmer, Botanist.* Stockton, Kan.: By the Author, 1981.

Munkres, Robert L. "Wives, Mothers, Daughters: Women's Life on the Road West." *Annals of Wyoming* 42:2 (October, 1970): 191–224.

Nall, Gary L. "The Farmer's Frontier in the Texas Panhandle." *Panhandle-Plains Historical Review* 45 (1972): 1–20.

Parks, Annette White. "Children's Work and Play on the Northwest Frontier." *Henry Ford Museum and Greenfield Village Herald* November 1, 1986.

Petersen, William J. "The Pioneer Cabin." *Iowa Journal of History and Politics* 36:4 (October, 1938): 387–409.

Petrik, Paula. "If She Be Content: The Development of Montana Divorce Law, 1865–1907." *Western Historical Quarterly* 18:3 (July, 1987): 261–91.

Petrik, Paula. *No Step Backward: Women and Family on the Rocky Mountain Mining Frontier, Helena, Montana, 1865–1900.* Helena: Montana Historical Society Press, 1987.

Pomeroy, Earl. "Toward A Reorientation of Western History: Continuity and Environment." *Mississippi Valley Historical Review* 41:4 (March, 1955): 579–600.

Putnam, Jackson K. "The Turner Thesis and the Westward Movement: A Reappraisal." *Western Historical Quarterly* 7:4 (October, 1976): 377–404.

Read, Georgia Willis. "Diseases, Drugs, and Doctors on the California-Oregon Trail In the Gold Rush Years." *Missouri Historical Review* 38:3 (April, 1944): 260–76.

Read, Georgia Willis. "Women and Children on the Oregon-California Trail in the Gold-Rush Years." *Missouri Historical Review* 39:1 (October, 1944): 1–23.

Ricards, Sherman L., Jr. "A Demographic History of the West: Butte County, California, 1850." *Michigan Academy of Science, Arts, and Letters* 46 (1961): 469–91.

Riley, Emmet J. *Development of the Montana State Educational Organization, 1864–1930.* Washington, D. C.: Catholic University of America, 1931.

Riley, Glenda. "The Specter of a Savage: Rumors and Alarmism on the Overland Trail." *Western Historical Quarterly* 15:4 (October, 1984): 427–44.

Schlissel, Lillian. "Frontier Families: Crisis in Ideology." In Sam B. Girgus, ed. *The American Self: Myth, Ideology and Culture,* 155–65. Albuquerque: University of New Mexico Press, 1981.

Schlissel, Lillian. *Women's Diaries of the Westward Journey.* New York: Schocken Books, 1982.

Sharp, Mildred. "Early Cabins in Iowa." *Palimpest* 2:1 (January, 1921): 16–29.

Sharp, Verna. "Montezuma and Her Neighbors." *Colorado Magazine* 33 (January, 1956): 16–41.

Silverman, Elaine. "In Their Own Words: Mothers and Daughters on the Alberta Frontier, 1890–1929." *Frontiers* 2:2, 37–44.

Smith, Duane A. "The San Juaner: A Computerized Portrait." *Colorado Magazine* 52:2 (Spring, 1975): 137–52.

Stannard, David E. *Death in America.* Philadelphia: University of Pennsylvania Press, 1975.

Stegner, Wallace. *The Gathering of Zion: The Story of the Mormon Trail.* New York: McGraw-Hill Book Co., 1964.

Stewart, George R. *The California Trail: An Epic With Many Heroes.* (New York: McGraw-Hill Book Co., 1962.

Stewart, George R. *Ordeal By Hunger: The Story of the Donner Party.* Boston: Houghton Mifflin Co., 1936.

Stratton, David H. "The Rise and Decline of Caribou." *Colorado Magazine* 30 (April, 1953): 109–18.

Trimble, William J. *The Mining Advance in the Inland Empire.* Madison: University of Wisconsin, 1914.

Turner, Frederick Jackson. *The Frontier in American History.* New York: Holt, Rinehart and Winston, 1962.

Underwood, Kathleen. "The Pace of Their Own Lives: Teacher Training and the Life Course of Western Women." *Pacific Historical Review* 55:4 (November, 1986): 513–30.

Unruh, John D. *The Plains Across: The Overland Emigrants and the Trans-Mississippi West, 1840–60* (Champaign: University of Illinois Press, 1979).

Wagoner, Jay J. *Arizona Territory, 1863–1912: A Political History.* Tucson: University of Arizona Press, 1970.

Webster, Jean. "The Myth of Pioneer Hardship on the Oregon Trail." *Reed College Bulletin* 24:3 (April, 1946): 27–46.

Welsch, Roger L. *Sod Walls: The Story of the Nebraska Sod House.* Broken Bow, Neb.: Purcells, Inc., 1968.

West, Elliott. "Five Idaho Mining Towns: A Computer Profile." *Pacific Northwest Quarterly* 73:3 (July, 1982): 108–20.

West, Elliott. "Heathens and Angels: Childhood in the Rocky Mountain Mining Towns." *Western Historical Quarterly* 14:2 (April, 1983): 145–64.

White, John I. "That Zenith of Prairie Architecture—The Soddy." *American Heritage* 24:5 (August, 1973): 33–35.

Wishart, David J. "Age and Sex Composition of the Population of the American Frontier." *Nebraska History* 54:1 (Spring, 1973): 107–19.

Young, James A. "Hay Making: The Mechanical Revolution on the Western Range." *Western Historical Quarterly* 14:3 (July, 1983): 311–26.

Children and Child Development

Anthony, Sylvia. *The Discovery of Death in Childhood and After.* London: Allen Lane, 1971.

Bauer, David H. "An Exploratory Study of Developmental Changes in Children's Fears." *Journal of Child Psychology and Psychiatry* 17 (1976): 69–74.

Bowlby, John. "Separation Anxiety." *International Journal of Psycho-Analysis* 41 (1960): 89–113.

Bremner, Robert H., ed. *Children and Youth in America: A Documentary History.* 3 Vols. Cambridge: Harvard University Press, 1971–74.

Caplan, Frank and Teresa Caplan. *The Power of Play.* New York: Anchor Books, 1973.

Cavallo, Dominick. *Muscles and Morals: Organized Playgrounds and Urban Reform, 1880–1920.* Philadelphia: University of Pennsylvania Press, 1981.

Crain, William C. *Theories of Development: Concepts and Applications.* Englewood Cliffs: Prentice-Hall, Inc., 1980.

Danziger, Kurt. "Children's Earliest Conceptions of Economic Relationships." *Journal of Social Psychology* 47 (May, 1958): 231–34.

Elkind, David. *The Child's Reality: Three Developmental Themes.* Hillsdale, N.J.: Lawrence Erlbaum Associates, 1978.

Eme, Robert and Dwight Schmidt. "The Stability of Children's Fears." *Child Development* 49 (1978): 1277–79.

Emmerick, Walter W. "Young Children's Discrimination of Parent and Child Roles." *Child Development* 30 (September, 1959): 403–19.

Engel, Mary, et al. "Orientation to Work in Children." *American Journal of Orthopsychiatry* 38 (January, 1968): 137–43.

Erikson, Erik H. *Childhood and Society.* New York: W.W. Norton and Co., 1963.

Espenshade, Thomas J. *Investing In Children: New Estimates of Parental Expenditures.* Washington, D. C.: Urban Institute Press, 1984.

Fawcett, James T., ed. *The Satisfactions and Costs of Children.* Honolulu: East-West Center, 1972.

Garmezy, Norman and Michael Rutter, eds. *Stress, Coping and Development.* New York: McGraw-Hill, 1983.

Garvey, Catherine. *Play.* Cambridge: Harvard University Press, 1977.

Goldstein, Bernard and Jack Oldham. *Children and Work: A Study of Socialization.* New Brunswick, N.J.: Transaction Books, 1979.

Goodman, Ellen. *The Culture of Childhood: Child's-Eye View of Society and Culture.* New York: Teachers's College Press, 1970.

Harris, Dale B. et al. "The Relationship of Children's Home Duties to Responsibilities." *Child Development* 25 (March, 1954): 29–33.

Hartley, Ruth E. "Children's Conceptions of Male and Female Roles." *Merrill-Palmer Quarterly* 6 (Summer-Fall, 1960): 83–91.

Hawes, Joseph M. and N. Ray Hiner, eds. *American Childhood: A Research Guide and Historical Handbook.* Westport, Conn.: Greenwood Press, 1985.

Herron, R.E. and Brian Sutton-Smith, eds. *Child's Play.* New York: John Wiley and Sons, 1971.

Johnson, Suzanne Bennett, et al. "Assessment and Treatment of Children's Fears." In Benjamin B. Lahey and Alan E. Dazdin, *Advances in Clinical Child Psychology* vol. II. New York: Plenum Press, 1979, 108–39.

Kastenbaum, Robert. "Childhood: The Kingdom Where Creatures Die." *Journal of Clinical Child Psychology* 3 (Summer, 1984): 11–14.

Kett, Joseph. *Rites of Passage: Adolescence in America: 1790 to the Present.* New York: Basic Books, 1977.

Lidz, Theodore. *The Person: His and Her Personal Development Throughout the Life Cycle.* New York: Basic Books: 1976.

Liebert, Robert M., et al. *Developmental Psychology.* Englewood Cliffs: Prentice-Hall, Inc., 1974.

Maurer, Adah. "What Children Fear." *Journal of Genetic Psychology* 106 (1965): 265–77.

McCandless, Boyd R. and Ellis D. Evans. *Children and Youth: Psychological Development.* Hinsdale, Ill.: The Dryden Press, 1973.

Millar, Susanna. *The Psychology of Play.* New York: Jason Aronson, 1974.

Mitchell, Marjorie. *The Child's Attitude Toward Death.* New York: Schocken Books, 1967.

Moore, Charlotte D., ed. *Adolescence and Stress.* Washington, D.C.: Government Printing Office, 1981.

Moskovitz, Sarah. *Love Despite Hate: Child Survivors of the Holocaust and their Adult Lives.* New York: Schocken Books, 1983.

Muller-Schwarze, Dietland. *Evolution of Play Behavior.* Stroudsburg, Penn.: Dowden, Hutchinson & Ross, Inc., 1978.

Murphy, Louise and Alice Moriarty. *Vulnerability, Coping, and Growth From Infancy to Adolescence.* New Haven: Yale University Press, 1976.

Myer, Ernst Christopher. *Infant Mortality in New York City.* New York: Rockefeller Foundation, 1921.

Nasaw, David. *Children of the City at Work and at Play.* Garden City: Anchor Press/Doubleday, 1985.

Opie, Iona and Peter. *Children's Games in Street and Playground.* Oxford: Clarendon Press, 1969.

Opie, Iona and Peter. *The Lore and Language of Schoolchildren.* Oxford: Clarendon Press, 1960.

Opie, John. "The Tentacles of Tradition," *Advancement of Science* 20 (September, 1963): 235–44.

Piaget, Jean. *The Child's Conception of the World*. New York: Harcourt, Brace, and Co., 1929.

Piaget, Jean. *Play, Dreams and Imitation in Childhood*. New York: W. W. Norton, 1951.

Rothman, David J. "Documents in Search of an Historian: Toward a History of Childhood and Youth in America." *Journal of Interdisciplinary History* 2:2 (Autumn, 1971): 367–77.

Schlossberg, N. K. and J. Goodman. "A Woman's Place: Children's Sex Stereotyping of Occupations." *Vocational Guidance Quarterly* 20 (June, 1972): 266–70.

Seagoe, May V. "Children's Play as an Indicator of Cultural and Intracultural Differences." *Journal of Educational Sociology* 35:6 (February, 1962): 278–83.

Shapiro, Sam, et al. *Infant, Perinatal, Maternal, and Childhood Mortality in the United States*. Cambridge: Harvard University Press, 1968.

Sutton-Smith, Brian. *The Folkgames of Children*. Austin: University of Texas Press, 1972.

Sutton-Smith, Brian, ed. *Play and Learning*. New York: Gardner Press, Inc., 1979.

Tarver, James D. "Costs of Rearing and Educating Farm Children." *Journal of Farm Economics* 38:1 (February, 1956): 144–53.

Wadsworth, Barry J. *Piaget's Theory of Cognitive and Affective Development*. New York and London: Longman, 1984.

Werner, Emmy. "Resilient Children." *Young Children* (November, 1984): 68–72.

Werner, Emmy E. and Ruth S. Smith. *Vulnerable But Invincible: A Longitudinal Study of Resilient Children and Youth*. New York: McGraw-Hill, 1982.

Wiggins, David K. "The Play of Slave Children in the Plantation Communities of the Old South, 1820–60." *Journal of Sport History* (Summer, 1980): 21–39.

Wishy, Bernard. *The Child and the Republic: The Dawn of Modern American Child Nurture*. Philadelphia: University of Pennsylvania Press, 1968.

Woodbury, Robert Morse. *Infant Mortality and Its Causes*. Baltimore: Williams and Wilkins Co., 1926.

Yawkey, Thomas D. and Anthony D. Pellegrini. *Child's Play: Developmental and Applied*. Hillsdale, N. J.: Lawrence Earlbaum Associates, 1984.

Zelizer, Viviana A. *Pricing the Priceless Child: The Changing Social Value of Children*. New York: Basic Books, 1985.

Other

Ames, Kenneth L. "Material Culture as Non-Verbal Communication: A Historical Case Study." *Journal of American Culture* 3:4 (Winter, 1980): 619–25.

Bailyn, Bernard. *Education in the Forming of American Society: A Reinterpretation*. Chapel Hill: University of North Carolina Press, 1960.

Berthoff, Roland. *An Unsettled People: Social Order and Disorder in American History*. New York: Harper and Row, 1971.

Bode, Carl. *The American Lyceum: Town Meeting of the Mind*. New York: Oxford University Press, 1956.

Borow, Henry, ed. *Man in a World of Work*. Boston: Houghton, Mifflin and Co., 1964.

Bronner, Simon J. *Grasping Things: Folk Material Culture and Mass Society in America.* Lexington: University Press of Kentucky, 1986.

Clark, Clifford E., Jr. "Domestic Architecture as an Index to Social History: The Romantic Revival and the Cult of Domesticity in America, 1840–1870." *Journal of Interdisciplinary History* 7:1 (Summer, 1976): 33-56.

Coffin, Margaret M. *Death in Early America.* Nashville and New York: Thomas Nelson, Inc., 1976.

Cott, Nancy. *The Bonds of True Womanhood: "Woman's Sphere" in New England, 1780–1835.* New Haven: Yale University Press, 1977.

Craven, Avery. "The 'Turner Theories' and the South." *Journal of Southern History* 5:3 (August, 1939): 290–314.

Cremin, Lawrence A. *American Education: The National Experience.* New York: Harper and Row, 1980.

Degler, Carl N. *At Odds: Women and the Family in America from the Revolution to the Present.* New York: Oxford University Press, 1980.

Farrell, James J. *Inventing the American Way of Death, 1830–1920.* Philadelphia: Temple University Press, 1980.

Finkelstein, Barbara. "Tolerating Ambiguity in Family History: A Guide to Some New Materials." *Journal of Psychohistory* 11:1 (Summer, 1983): 117–28.

Florin, John W. *Death in New England: Regional Variations in Mortality.* Chapel Hill: University of North Carolina Press, 1971.

Glassie, Henry. *Folk Housing in Middle Virginia.* Knoxville: University of Tennessee Press, 1975.

Halttunen, Karen. *Confidence Men and Painted Women: A Study of Middle-Class Culture in America, 1830–1870.* New Haven: Yale University Press, 1982.

Higgs, Robert. "Mortality in Rural America, 1870–1920: Estimates and Conjectures." *Explorations in Economic History* 10:2 (Winter, 1973): 177–96.

Hunt, Charles B. *Natural Regions of the United States and Canada.* San Francisco: W.H. Freeman, 1973.

Jackson, Charles O., ed. *Passing: The Vision of Death in America.* Westport, Conn.: Greenwood Press, 1977.

Katz, Michael B. *The Irony of Early School Reform: Educational Innovation in Mid-Nineteenth Century Massachusetts.* Cambridge: Harvard University Press, 1968.

McMurry, Sally. "Progressive Farm Families and Their Houses, 1830–1855." *Agricultural History* 58:3 (July, 1984): 330–46.

Nasaw, David. *Schooled To Order: A Social History of Public Schooling in the United States.* New York: Oxford University Press, 1980.

Rosen, George. *The Structure of American Medical Practice.* Philadelphia: University of Pennsylvania Press, 1983.

Rothman, David J. *Discovery of the Asylum: Social Order and Disorder in the New Republic.* Boston: Little, Brown and Co., 1971.

Ryan, Mary P. "The Explosion of Family History." *Reviews in American History* 10:4 (December, 1982): 181–95.

Schlereth, Thomas J., ed. *Material Culture: A Research Guide.* Lawrence: University Press of Kansas, 1985.

Sklar, Katherine K. *Catherine Beecher: A Study in American Domesticity.* New Haven: Yale University Press, 1973.

Stannard, David E. *Death in America*. Philadelphia: University of Pennsylvania Press, 1975.

Stone, Lawrence. "Family History in the 1980s." *Journal of Interdisciplinary History* 12:1 (Summer, 1981): 51–87.

Upton, Dell. "Toward a Performance Theory of Vernacular Architecture." *Folklore Forum* 12 (1979): 180–84.

Welter, Barbara. "The Cult of True Womanhood: 1820–1860." *American Quarterly* 18 (1966): 151–74.

Wright, Gwendolyn. *Building the Dream: A Social History of Housing in America*. Cambridge: MIT Press, 1983.

Wright, Gwendolyn. *Moralism and the Model Home: Domestic Architecture and Cultural Conflict in Chicago, 1873–1913*. Chicago: University of Chicago Press, 1980.

Theses and Dissertations

Baird, Frank Pierce. "History of Education in Idaho Through Territorial Days." Master's thesis, University of Washington, 1928.

Burnet, Georgellen K. " 'We Just Toughed It Out': Women Heads of Households on the Llano Estacado, 1880–1925." Master's thesis, Texas Tech University, 1982.

Huggard, Christopher J. "The Role of the Family in Settling the Cherokee Outlet." Master's thesis, University of Arkansas, 1987.

Irey, Eugene Floyd. "A Social History of Leadville, Colorado, During the Boom Days, 1877–1881." Ph.D. diss., University of Minnesota, 1951.

McGlone, Robert. "Suffer the Children: The Emergence of Modern Middle-Class Family Life, 1820–1870." Ph.D. diss., University of California, Los Angeles, 1971.

Minnick, Nelle Frances. "A Cultural History of Central City, Colorado, From 1859 to 1880, in Terms of Books and Libraries." Master's thesis, University of Chicago, 1946.

Prude, John G. "The Early Ranch Schools of the Fort Davis Area." Master's thesis, Sul Ross State Teachers College, 1942.

Smallwood, Mary Anne Norman. "Childhood on the Southern Plains Frontier." Ph.D. diss., Texas Tech University, 1975.

Thomas Gray Thompson. "The Social and Cultural History of Lake City, Colorado, 1876–1900." Master's thesis, University of Oklahoma, 1961.

Index

accidents and injuries, 213; in farming and ranching regions, 219–25; in mining areas, 220, 222, 224, 225; in the overland migration, 215–16
Ackley, Mary, 39
Adams, Charles Francis, 150
alcohol abuse, 153–54
Alexander, Mary Jane, 231
Alexander, R. T., 96–97, 98
Alexander, Violet, 202
Allen, Chestina, 135–36, 140, 170
American West: geographical subregions, 2; relationship to the frontier, 259–62. *See also* environment; frontier
Andersen, Bertha, 88, 228
Anderson, Jimmy, 166
Andrews family, Nebraska, 238
Angelo, C. Aubrey, 69
animals, domestic: care of, 86–90; horses, 105–6, 244; play with, 107; shelter for, 57
animals, wild, 32, 43, 220, 223; fears of, 34, 41, 127; snakes, 214, 219–20
Anti-Injunction Act of 1932, 120
Anti-I-Over game, 108
Applegate, Adrietta, 115
Applegate, Jesse, 29, 30; on storms, 31–32
Aram, Joseph, 170
Archer, Margaret, 137, 189
Arizona children, *31*

Athearn, Charles, 7
Ayer, Edward, 216

Barbee, Mabel, 199
Barnhart, Milton, 91
Bartholomew, Elam, 66
Bennett, Edwin, 166
Bennett, Estelline, 3
Berry, Glen, 130
Berwyn, Nebraska, Hopkins family, *21*
Billington, Ray Allen, 252
Bird, Isabella, 147, 148, 149
bison, 31, 32, 106; collecting bones of, 90, 95, 97
Black, Sarah, 198
Black family, Texas, 19–20, 186
Boatman, Mary, 30–31, 215
bone collecting for cash income, 90, 95, 97
books and libraries, 180–81
Bonney, Benjamin Franklin, 9
Bowles, Samuel, 2
Boys, Samuel, 138
Bridges, Minnie, *205*
Brock, Caesar, 23–24, 255
Brock, Helen, 88, 255
Brooks, Elisha, 32, 36, 86, 196, 217
Brophy family, Oregon, 97–98
Brown, Abner, 187
Browne, J. Ross, 53, 150
Bruff, J. Goldsborough, 102, 153

Bryan, Hardy, 72
Bryant, Dora, 105, 186
Bryant, Edwin, 215
Bushnell, James, 197
Byrne, Martha, 199

California mining counties, causes of
    children's deaths in, 222(table)
Carlson, Alma, 44
Carnow, Alice, 236
Cascade mountains, 4, 5
cash income, 89–92
Cather, Willa, 257–58
Chester County, Montana, school,
    193
child abuse, 152–53, 203–4
childbirth, 225–29
Childers, W. H., 87
childhood: concepts of, 148, 161–62,
    165–66, 239, 250–51, 253; fears for
    the quality of pioneer, 147–56
childrearing, 148–49, 156–62
children as pioneers: abandoned and
    abused, 152–53; delinquency in,
    155– 56; fears held by, 32–42, 108,
    113–14, 126, 127, 143; influence of
    the frontier on children's
    characters, 251–55; lost, 35, 223–24;
    maturation process, 121–43, 255–59;
    mortality (*see* death, child's); play
    activities, 101–17, 121, 250;
    responses to the environment (*see*
    environment, children's perceptions
    of/responses to); risks to (*see*
    accidents and injuries; death,
    child's; disease and illness); role of,
    245–48; runaway, 154–55; sex roles
    and resentments of female, 142–43;
    unique perceptions of, 26–32; work
    (*see* work, children's)
Chipman, Jim, 48
cholera, 133, 217–18, 231
Clark, Charles, 213
Clark, John, 38, 84
Clark, John Haskins, 215
Clark, Ruth, 172
Cleaveland, Agnes Morley, 88, 105,
    125, 131, 223, 258

Clifton, Edna Matthews, 73, 93,
    122–23, 138, 142, 252
climate, 4–5, 215; inadequate housing
    and, 55–56
clocks, 61
clothing care and production, 93–94,
    142–43
Collins, Martha, 91, 97, 104, 183, 201
Colorado mining counties, causes of
    children's deaths in, 222(table)
Colorow, Ute chief, 37
community and society on the
    frontier, 167–72; distinctive nature
    of, 12–20; games used to facilitate,
    109–10; musical traditions and,
    172–76; religion and, 168–72;
    response to child's death in, 235–39,
    251; role of men away from the
    family, 162–67
Conger, Thomas, 231, 236
Conron, Clara, 204
Conwell, Effie, 12
Cook, H. C., 87
Cooke, Lucy, 60
Cooper, Job A., 207
Cowan, Troy, 87
Coxey's Reserves, 100
Crampton, Frank, 81
Crane, Addison, 27
Craven, Avery, 260
Crawford, R. D., 76
Cripple Creek, Colorado, family, *9*
Crocket, Susie, 142–43, 197
Crocket family, Cherokee Outlet, 90,
    142
Crofut, Andy, 121
Cropper, Ida, 196
Crusher Saloon, Colorado, *151*
Curtis, Mary, 226
Cushing, Johnnie, 230
Custer County, Nebraska, family, *261*
Cutting, A. H., 216

Dale, Edward E., 107, 181, 259
Dalton, Lucinda, 183
dances, 174–75, *176*
Davenport, Sallie, 217
Davies, Anne, 90

Davis, Andrew, 41, 172
Davison, Emma Jane, 80
death, child's: from accidents, 40, 219– 25; burials and tombstones, 237–39; in California and Colorado mining counties, 222(table); in childbirth, 225–29; community response to, 235– 39, 251; effect of, on pioneer children, 239–42; fears of, 37–41, 213–14; from illness, 220(table), 221(table), 229–35; in mining, farming and ranching regions, 220(table); in West Kansas farming and ranch counties, 221(table). *See also* accidents and injuries; disease and illness
death, parents', 39–40, 95–98
debates as social events, 185–86
DeBaud, Charles, 154, 155
Deer Lodge Valley, Montana, 103
delinquency in children, 155–56
deserts, 4
Devil's Gate, Wyoming, 25–26
DeWolf, David, 164
diphtheria, 233–35, 238
disciplining children, 36–37, 158–60; in schools, 203–4
disease and illness, 37, 213, 241; as causes of children's deaths, 220(table), 221(table), 222(table), 229–35; on the overland migration, 133, 216–19. *See also* death, child's
Dix family, Oregon, 19
Dobbs, Bill, 87
Dobbs, Elijah, 99
Dobbs, T. W., 99–100
Dodge, Augusta, 42, 44, 93, 122, 124, 240
Dodge, Osseon, 124, 240
Donner-Reed party, 214
Dore, Si, 166
Dowdy family, Texas, 88, 98
Dowell, B. F., 187
Drachman, Mose, 97, 166, 199, 255
Draper, Charles, 184
drought and aridity, 5, 95, 122–24, 136– 37. *See also* rainfall
drownings, 215–16, 224

Duncan, Sarah, 171
Dutton, Chester, 10
Dyer family, Texas, 95
dysentery, 217, 231, 232

Ebbut, Percy, 77
Eckles family, New Mexico, 58
economic factors in pioneering, 246–47; desire to better circumstances, 7–8; resources reflected in housing, 65–69, 92. *See also* work, children's
education, *111*, 146, 179–210; community activities related to, 184–88; curriculum, values, and goals of, 200–210; expenditures and teacher salaries by state, 194(table); facilities for, *193*, 199–200, *202*, *208*; financing, 192–95, 204–6; at home, 180–84; through play, 114–17; public school attendance patterns, 189, 191(table), 192, 195–97, 206; public school availability, 188–95; regional per capita expenditure, 195 (table); religious, 171–72; teacher quality, 198–99, 206–8; teacher recruitment, 197–99; teacher salaries, 192, 194(table); traditions and values conveyed through, 209–10, 249–50
Eisele, Fannie, 76
Ellis, Anne, 35, 47–49, 58, 63, 91, 166, 181–82, 241, 242, 256
Ellis, Rachel, 47
Ellmaker, Enos, 38
England, Mary, 186
environment: children's perceptions of/responses to, 30–32, 42–45, 103, 121–23, 129, 130–32, 141; geography, climate, and resources of frontier, 2–7; pioneer's visions/expectations toward, 27–28
Erikson, Erik, on play, 104
Everett, Melissa, 8, 14, 179, 180
exploration as children's play, 101–4, 125–26

families, frontier, 148–62, *248*; clustering of, 19–20; home furnishings and mementoes of, 57–64; response to child's death, 235–39, 251; single-parent, 95–98, 153; stresses on, 148– 56; traditional values and daily life of, 19, 156–62, 163, 247–55

farming and ranching communities: accidents and children's mortality in, 219–25; adversities experienced in, 122–24; branding activities, *137*; children's work tasks in, 74, 75–79, 82–92, 95–98, 134–38, 246; foreign-born pioneers in, 13; housing in, 52, 55–57; illness and children's mortality in, 229–35; sex/age ratios in, 16–17, 18 (table); soil and climate factors affecting, 3, 5–6; threats to traditional values in, 149–50

fears of pioneer children, 32–42, 127, 143; acted out in games, 108, 113–14

Fillmore, Rollin, 227

fires, 105, 135–36

Fish, Anna, 215

Fish, Joseph, 228

Fisk, Elizabeth, 67, 69, 71, 150, 156, 157, 183, 231

Fisk, Grace, 71–72

Fisk, Robert Emmett, 71

Flanagan, May, 2

food(s): cooking fuels, 84; equipment for preparing, 53–54; hunting for game, 83–84, *85*, 104–5, 106, 128–29, *132*; vegetable gardens, *83*; wild plant, 32, 82–83, 105

Foote, Mary Hallock, 67

Fosdick, Lucy, 55, 102

Frances, Samuel, 1, 2

freighting, 128, 146

frontier, 1–21, 245–62; child's preparation for life on the, 255–59; housing (*see* housing on the frontier); influence of the, on children's characters, 251– 55, 262; physical environment, 2–7 (*see also* environment); pioneer attitudes and motivations, 7–12, 247, 248–55; as place, process, and region, 259–62; role of children on the, 245–48; society on the , 12–20 (*see also* community and society on the frontier; threats to morality and values on the, 149–56, 255–56. *See also* children as pioneers; families, frontier; pioneer(s)

Fuller, Frank, 206

Gallagher, Charles, 145–46

Galloway, Emily, 140

Galloway, James, 140

Gally, Martha, 153, 227

gambling, 150–51, 166

games, 107–14, 250; achievement, 110– 11; of adult imitation, 112; spontaneously invented, 113–14; traditional, 107–12

gardens and lawns, 64–65, *66*, 83

Gardner, Mary, 41

Garland, Hamlin, 88, 106, 131, 258, 259

Geer, Elizabeth, 215

gender on the frontier, sex ratios, 15, 18(table). *See also* sex roles

Godley family, Oregon, 19

Goldrick, Oliver J., 186–87

"Gold Seeker's Song, The," 162–63

Gray, Mary Olive, 96

Gray, William, 19

Great Basin, 3

Great Plains, 2, 13; disorientation and isolation on the, 33, 42, *43*

Greeley, Horace, xxi, xxii

Greer, Elizabeth, 54

Hadley, Lydia, 234

Hall, Helen, 230

Hamill family, Colorado, 67, *68*

harvesting and threshing tasks, 78–79, 104

Hattich, Rose, 207

Hedges, Cornelius, 193, 195

Hedges, Edna, 92, 157, 175, 239

Hedges, Willie, 91, 92

herding, 125, *126*

Herndon, Sarah, 204

Heston, Flora and Sam, 226
Hilger, David, 87
Hill, Alice Polk, 208
Hill, Emma, 3, 175, 181
Hispanic population, public education and, 188–89
Hively, Sarah, 196
Hixon, Adrietta, 35
Hockderffer, George, 44
Hockett, W. A., 86, 219
Hodge, Minnie, 168
Holden, Maggie, 42
Holden, William, 123, 198
holidays, 168
home education, 180–84
Hoover, Jonathan, 218
Hoover, Vincent, 218
Hopkins family, Berwyn, Nebraska, 21
household labor, 92–94, 138–43, 226
housing on the frontier, 51–72; adaptions and growth of, 56–57; categories of, 51–54; gardens and lawns around, 64–65; individual economic resources reflected in, 65–69; interiors and furnishings, 53–54, 57–64; overcrowding and inadequacy of, 54–56; wagon as, *59*. *See also* traditions and values
Howard, L. S., 244
Hughes, Frank, 2
hunger, 123–24, 214
Hunter, Zella, 20
hunting for wild game, 83–84, *85*, 90, 104–5, 106, 128–29, *132*
Hutchins, Louis, 244
Hyde, Aaron J., 187

Idaho school, *202*
Indians, 145, 211; fear of, 35–36, 37, 41, 126–27, 133–34
industrialization, 6–7
Irvine, Ella, 195–96
Ivin, Virginia, 226

Jackson, Helen Hunt, 233
James, Marquis, 106, 165, 166

Jefferson County, Montana, Bluebird Mine, *16*
Jennings, Mary, 130
Joab, A. E., 199
Johnson, Luther, 225
Jones, Dollie, 123
Jones, Hub, 143
Jordan, Albert, 230

Kansas: causes of children's deaths in western, 221(table); dugout house interior, *62*; dugout school, *187*
Kellogg, Clarence, 161
Kerfoot family, 134
Kirkpatrick, Alma, 184
Kline, Perry, 36
Knowlton, Eleanor, 11
Kreipie, Louise, 42–43

La Guardia, Fiorello, 119–20
land. *See* environment; frontier
LaSeur, J. W., 182
Lewis, Earl, 128
Life of an Ordinary Woman, The (Ellis), 48–49
literary societies, 184–85
Livingston, Montana, Pine Creek School, *111*
locust plagues, 122
lode mining, 79–82
Ludlow, Fitzhugh, 3, 181
Lyman, Esther, 94
Lyman, Joseph, 94, 214
Lyman, Luther, 94

McCarty, F. M., 9, 80
McCowen, George, 172
McCullough family, Texas, 96, 98
McDonald, Joseph, 97, 98, 128
McWhorter, Owen, 44–45, 243–44, 255
malarial fevers, 229–30
Martin, Lena, 20
Martin, Oello, 42
Martin, Sarah, 237
Martin family, North Dakota, 124
Matthews, Edna. *See* Clifton, Edna Matthews

Matthews family, Texas, 20
measles, 217
Meeker, Exra, 218
Meline, James, xxii
men as pioneers: bachelor housing, 60–61; relationship to children, 162–67; sex ratios, 15, 18(table); single adult, 15, 162
metal resources, 6
Miller, Dora, 14
Miller, Henry, 23
Miller, Lillian, 65, 131, 211–12
Miller, Louie, 211, 212
Miller, Lucy, 23
Millington, Ada, 36
mining towns and camps: children's deaths caused by accidents and illness in, 220(table), 222(table), 224, 225, 229, 231; children's work tasks in, 74, 79–82, 90–92, 95–98, 127–28, 129–30; foreign-born pioneers in, 13; housing in, 52–53, 57, 66–67; pioneer resources in, 10; rarity of children in, 15, *16*, 165; sex/age ratios in, 15, 18(table); threats to traditional values in, 150–52, 153
Minto, Martha, 209
mobility on the frontier, 8–9, 14–15; games used to create belonging despite, 109–10; pressures on family life due to, 152–53
Moore, Frances, 41, 239, 255
Moore, Lizzie, 151
moral issues affecting children, 149–56, 255–56; education and, 200, 203
Morley, Agnes. *See* Cleaveland, Agnes Morley
Morrill Act, 195
Moses, John, 154, 155
mountain fever, 219
Mountain Lion, The (Stafford), 257
mountains, 2, 3, 4
Murphy, Richard, 87
musical heritage, 172–76; dances, 174–75, *176*; instruments, 63–64
My Antonia (Cather), 257–58

Nebraska: church gathering, *170*; family, *21*; farm, *261*; ranch house interior, *64*
Neher family, North Dakota, 124
Neighbors, Albert, 11
Newcomb, Samuel, 139, 169
Newcomb, Susan, 55, 139–40, 158
Newland, Cliff, 125
Newman, Luella, 220
newspapers and periodicals, 182–83
Newton, Jessie, 150
No Life for a Lady (Cleaveland), 258
Norris, George, 120
Norton, Curt, 125, 136, 140
Norton, Elizabeth, 140
Norton, John, 104, 122, 125, 136, 149, 255
Norton family, Kansas, 89, 90, 136–37, 168

O'Kieffe, Charley, 58, 84, 130, 173, 197
O'Kieffe family, Nebraska, 83
Old Jules (Sandoz), 152, 178, 257
Oliver, Charles, 55
O'Neil, Elizabeth, 11
orphans, 39
Orr, Ellison, 131
outdoor work, 124–32; vs. household labor, 140, 141
overland migration: adults' perception of, 26–28; children's perception of, 28–32; children's work tasks in, 73–74; deaths occurring during, 38–40; fears accompanying, 33–41; risks and dangers of, 214–19; survival work skills required in, 94–95, 133–34; wagon shelter used in, *59*
ox-bouncing play, 101, 113
Owen, East S., 1, 2, 218

Palmer, Carolyn, 103, 224
Parke, Charles, 34
Patton, C. F., 123
Peabody, Endicott, 237
Pearce, Joe, 126–27
Perry, Meda, 93

physicians, 227–28
pioneer(s): accidents and injuries of
    (*see* accidents and injuries);
    attitudes and motivations of, 7–12,
    247–55; disease and illness of (*see*
    disease and illness); fears of, 32–42;
    foreign-born, 13; perceptions and
    expectations of, 25–32; sex and age
    ratios, 15, 18(table). *See also* children
    as pioneers; men as pioneers;
    women as pioneers
Pinkerton, Ralla Banta, 43–44, 125,
    127
placer mining, 79, 80
play, children's, 101–17, 121, 250;
    educational, 114–17; exploration as,
    101–4, 125–26; games, formal and
    spontaneous, 107–14; transforming
    work into, 104–7
pneumonia, 230–31
poisoning accidents, 224–25
Pomeroy, Earl, 249
Posey, Walter, 43, 55, 95
Powe, Marvin, 125–26
pregnancy and childbirth, 225–29
Price, James, 209
Pringle, Catherine, 29
Pringle, Octavius, 94–95
Proctor family, Kansas, 235
production work tasks, children's,
    75–82
prostitution, 128, 151–52
Prude, John, *205*
Pugh family, Oklahoma, 20
Putnam, Jackson, 262

Railsback family, Kansas, 235
rainfall, 5–6, 56. *See also* drought and
    aridity
ranching. *See* farming and ranching
    communities
Rauck, Linnaeus, 76
Reed, Albert, 58
Reed, Virginia, 214
religion, 7; children's play and,
    113–14; community social life and,
    168–72

resources of pioneers, 10
Reynolds family, Texas, 20
Richards family, Colorado, 238
Richardson, Albert, 52–53
Rigelehuth, Katherine, 160–61
Riley, James Whitcomb, 183
Riordan, Jerry, 186
rivers and streams, 2, 3–4, 215–16
Roark, Tommy, 224
Robbins, Carrie, 58
Rocky Mountains, 3
Rogers, Barsina, 31
Ronan, Mary, 45, 80, 91, 103, 121
Roosa family, Nebraska, 66
Rose, Mamie, 96
Royce, Sarah, 59, 63, 150
Rudd, William, 8
runaway children, 154–55

Sadler, Warren, 152–53
Sager, Matilda, 245
Sager family, Oregon, 39, 245
Sanders, James, 91
Sanders, Thomas, 8, 12, 31
Sandoz, Jules, 152, 173, 177–78
Sandoz, Mari, 152, 177–78, 257
scarlet fever, 217
Schuyler family, Oregon, 19
separation anxiety in children, 34–41
sex and age ratios on the frontier,
    15–17, 18(table), 19
sex roles, 257–59; children's care of
    farm stock, 88; children's play and,
    115–17; household labor and,
    138–43, 226; resentments of female
    children toward labor divisions,
    142–43
Seymour, Bennett, 90–91, 183
Shepard, Emma, 37
Sierra Nevada mountains, 4, 5, 214
Silliman, Benjamin, 205
single-parent families, 95–98, 153
smallpox, 217, 232
Smith, J. J., 234
Smith, Samuel, 96
Smith, Walter, 81, 129–30
Smyer, Luna, 55

snakes, 214, 219–20
Snyder, Grace, 42
soil quality, 3
Sonoran Desert, 4
spelling matches, 184
Stafford, Jean, 257
Stegner, Wallace, 260
Stewart, Elinore, 63
Stockbridge, Jack, 91, 154, 155, 183
storms, frontier, 5, 31–32, 33–34
Stuart, Granville, 229
subscription schools, 186–88
subsistence work tasks, children's,
    82–92
"Sucker Bar Song," 15–16
Summers, Sue, 56
survival skills and work, 94–98
Sykes family, Turkey Tanks, Arizona,
    54

Taylor, Bayard, 106
teachers, 146; family ties of, 20;
    quality of, 198–99, 206–8; recruitment
    of, 197–98; salaries, 192, 194(table);
    subscription, 186–88
Teachman, Edward, 89
Teller, Henry Moore, 65
Thoroughman, Robert, 36
Todd, Mary Ellen, 133, 142
Tomme, Matilda, 139
traditions and values: education and,
    209–10, 249–50; fears for the
    corruption of children and a
    breakdown in, 147–56; transmission
    of, in community and social life,
    167–76; transmission of, through
    housing and homelife, 57–69,
    148–49, 156–62, 247–55
transportation on the frontier, 10;
    effect on home furnishings, 65–66
Travis, Lee, 91
Turkey Tanks, Arizona, Sykes family,
    54
Turner, Frederick Jackson, 248–49
typhus, 217

Van Court family, California, 14

Van Renssalaer family, Oregon, 19
vegetation: descriptions of native,
    130–32; as a food source, 32, 82–83,
    105; precipitation and, 5–6
Victor, Colorado, load mining, *81*
violence and child abuse, 152, 203–4
Vrooman, Ada, 198

Waldorf, John, 122, 154, 155, 165–66
Wallace, Allie, 102–3, 138, 142, 239
Wallicek, Ben, 159, 160
Walters, Louisa, 95
Ward, D. B., 94
Ward, Frances, 25
Ward, Harriet, 25, 26
Ward, Willie, 134
Warner, Louie, 128–29
Warner, Luna, 84, 106, 128, 130–31,
    135, 181, 239
Warner, William, 215
water, drinking: quality of, 32, 216,
    231; tasks of acquiring daily, 84, 86,
    89
Waugh, Frank, 13, 123–24, 132, 172,
    184
Wenger, Martin, 91
Werden, Francis, 130
Western Story (O'Kieffe), 130
Whipple–Haslam, Lee, xvii, 262
White, Daniel, 197
Whitman, Marcus and Narcissa, 39
Whittier, John Greenleaf, 209
Wilkenson, Raleigh, 197
Wilkes, Bob, 23
Williams, Carrie, 140
Williams, Katherine, 122
wind on the plains, 44
women as pioneers: attitudes
    toward the role of the home, 58;
    child rearing tasks, 156–58;
    disproportionate sacrifices made
    by, 10–12; economic elite, 71–72;
    pregnancy and childbirth, 225–29;
    sex ratios, 15, 18(table). *See also* sex
    roles
Wood, Effie, 41
Wood, Wallace, 12, 124–25

work, children's, 73–98, 124–43, 245; accidents related to, 225; cash income, 89–92; economic settings of, 73–75, 246–47; household labor, 92–94, 138–43; maturation through, 121–24; outdoor, 124–32, 140, 141; production tasks, 75–82; subsistence tasks, 82–92; survival skills and adaptability required in, 94–98, 133–38; transformed into play, 104–7

Young, Henry, 155